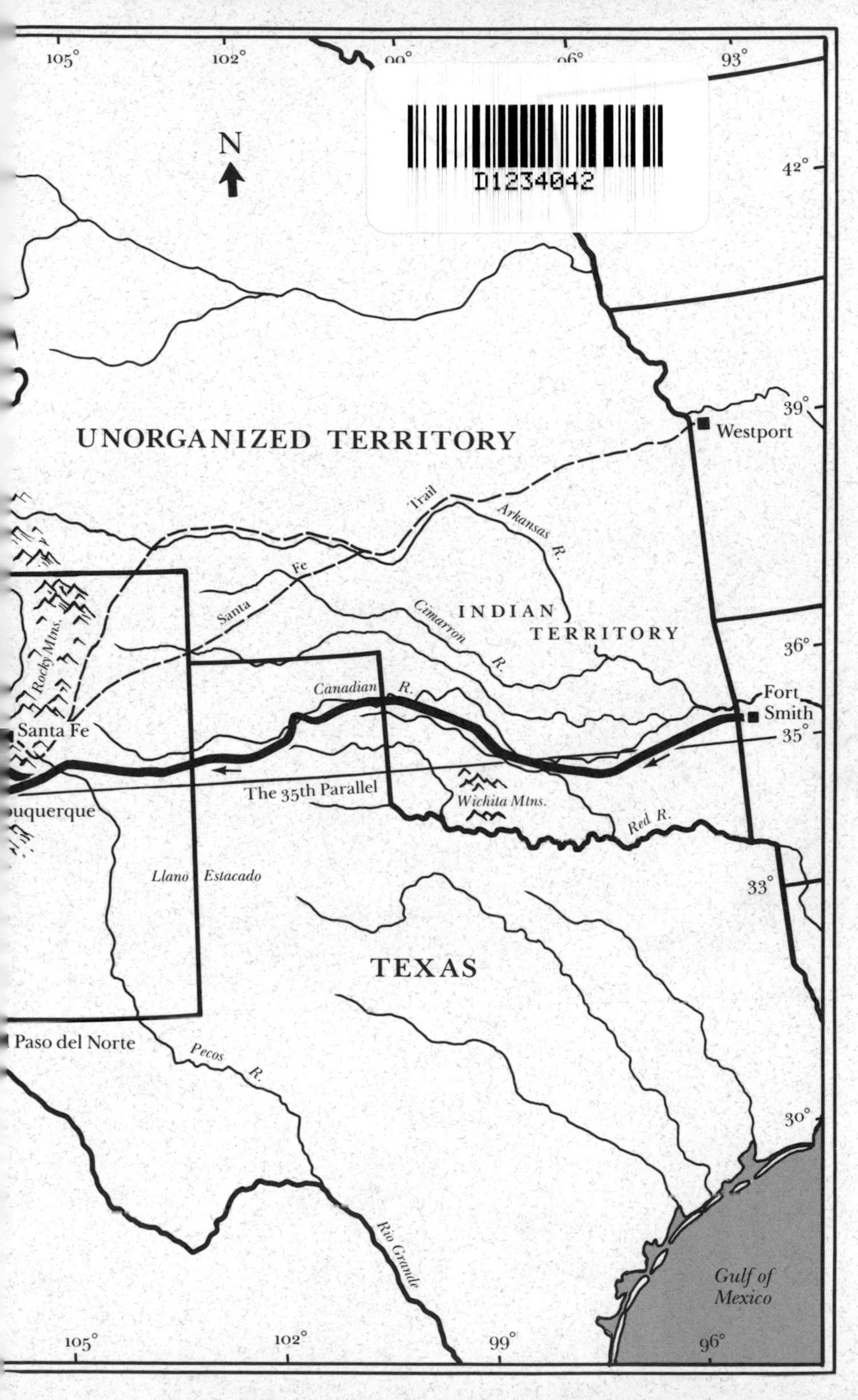
105°
102°
93°
N
42°
39°
Westport
UNORGANIZED TERRITORY
Trail
Arkansas R.
Santa
Fe
Cimarron R.
INDIAN
TERRITORY
Rocky Mtns.
36°
Canadian R.
Fort
Smith
Santa Fe
35°
The 35th Parallel
Wichita Mtns.
uquerque
Red R.
Llano Estacado
33°
TEXAS
Paso del Norte
Pecos R.
30°
Rio Grande
Gulf of
Mexico
105°
102°
99°
96°

Through Indian Country to California

Through Indian Country to California

JOHN P. SHERBURNE'S DIARY OF THE WHIPPLE EXPEDITION, 1853-1854

Edited by Mary McDougall Gordon

STANFORD UNIVERSITY PRESS
Stanford, California 1988

Stanford University Press
Stanford, California

Printed in the United States of America

CIP data are at the end of the book

Published with the assistance of the
Edgar M. Kahn Memorial Fund

The ornament used on the chapter openings is a Plains prickly pear (*Opuntia polyacantha* var. *polyacantha*), and is reproduced from Lyman Benson, *The Cacti of the United States and Canada* (Stanford University Press, 1982), p. 387.

For Alexandra and Daniel, Eve and Todd,
and for
Elena Klein

Preface

The publication of John Pitts Sherburne's diary is the result of the interest of Elena Klein of Redwood City, California. The widow of Sherburne William Klein, the great-grandson of John Pitts Sherburne, she carefully preserved a collection of Sherburne's diaries, army commissions, and memorabilia that had been passed down through the family, notably Sherburne's diary of the Whipple expedition from Fort Smith, Arkansas, to Los Angeles, California, during 1853 and 1854. In 1984 Mrs. Klein sent this diary to Stanford University Press, and the Press, for whom I had edited an overland diary in 1983, asked me to undertake the editing of it.

The original diary was written in pencil and filled two notebooks. John Sherburne, probably after he arrived in California in 1854, copied the entire diary into one large notebook, in ink. It is this copy, missing its cover and inscribed with the name of his father, John Nathaniel Sherburne of Portsmouth, New Hampshire, that is reproduced here.

Only one of the two notebooks containing the original diary has been preserved. Inscribed "Journal No. 2," it contains daily entries from September 7, 1853, to March 23, 1854. It also includes some poems, information on the West, and part of a diary John Sherburne kept when traveling overland in 1856 and 1857 from El Monte, California, to Fort Lancaster in Texas. The pencil sketch Sherburne made of himself dancing with a señorita in New Mexico, reproduced in this volume, is also from "Journal No. 2."

I have let John Sherburne's diary stand much as it is, including spelling errors, in order to preserve its textual integrity. In a few instances, and without notice to the reader, I have added or deleted punctuation in the interest of clarity. In excerpts from records left by other members of the expedition, omissions are indicated by ellipsis points. I have avoided lengthy additions to the footnotes by including in this volume an appendix with biographical information on persons mentioned in John Sherburne's diary. Additional explanations about editorial method are provided when necessary in the footnotes.

With great pleasure I acknowledge the assistance of those who made this book possible. My greatest debt, of course, is to Elena Klein, who preserved the Sherburne diary and other papers, and placed them on loan at the Orradre Library, Santa Clara University, during the course of my research. Elena has been an enthusiastic and helpful supporter of this endeavor. I am especially grateful to Professor Andrew Wallace of Northern Arizona University, who carefully read this edition in manuscript and provided me with helpful suggestions and information, particularly about the Arizona terrain, and to Dean David H. Miller of Cameron University in Oklahoma, who also read the manuscript, gave me useful advice, and provided me with prints of some lithographs by Balduin Möllhausen and a photograph of the artist. Matt Meier and Gerald McKevitt, colleagues at Santa Clara University, read parts of the manuscript and made helpful suggestions. I also appreciate the support of the Dean, Joseph Subbiendo, for this endeavor.

As always, I am indebted to several institutions and a number of librarians. I thank the Bancroft Library of the University of California at Berkeley, the Oklahoma Historical Society, and the University of Arizona Library for permission to quote from the Stanley diary, the Whipple papers, and the Tidball diary, respectively. I thank Fred Isaacs, Leanna Goodwater, and especially Alice Whistler of the Orradre Library at Santa Clara; the staff of the Bancroft Library; Robert Nespor and Kay Zahrai of the Oklahoma Historical Society; Roger Myers of the University of Arizona Library; and Ed Cass and Alan Aimone of the Archives, U.S. Military Academy at West Point. To Linda Campbell, Mary Jackson, and Kathleen Ludlum of Santa Clara University I owe special thanks for placing my manuscript on the computer. I also thank David Jackson for reproducing faded photographs and lithographs for use in this volume.

William Carver, senior editor at Stanford University Press, initiated the publication of the Sherburne diary and has remained supportive and helpful. I am particularly indebted to Peter Kahn, who has been a knowledgeable, sensitive, and warm and witty copy editor. I deeply appreciate his meticulous work.

M.McD.G.

Saratoga, California

Contents

Maps and Illustrations xiii

EDITOR'S INTRODUCTION 3

THROUGH INDIAN COUNTRY TO CALIFORNIA

Fort Smith, Arkansas, to Old Camp Arbuckle 35
Old Camp Arbuckle to Shady Creek 60
Shady Creek to Albuquerque 92
Albuquerque to Leroux's Spring 122
Leroux's Spring to the Colorado River 156
The Colorado River to Los Angeles 183

EDITOR'S AFTERWORD 217

Biographical Appendix 247 *Bibliography* 267 *Index* 277

Maps and Illustrations

MAPS

Fort Smith, Arkansas, to Old Camp Arbuckle 38
Old Camp Arbuckle to Shady Creek 62
Shady Creek to Albuquerque 94
Albuquerque to Leroux's Spring 124
Leroux's Spring to the Colorado River 158
The Colorado River to Los Angeles 186

ILLUSTRATIONS

Lieutenant Amiel Weeks Whipple 9
The Warner House in Portsmouth, New Hampshire 12
H. Balduin Möllhausen 26
Fort Smith from the north bank of the Arkansas River 37
A Choctaw youth 41
Two Choctaw women 45
A page from John Sherburne's diary 46
The Delaware Indian chief Black Beaver 55
Two Waco Indians 66
A camp of the Kiowas 86
A deserted Comanche summer camp 91
The "Egyptian Pyramid" 100
John Sherburne dancing with a señorita 104
The valley of La Cuesta, New Mexico 107
The Santo Domingo Pueblo 113
The Zuñi Pueblo 130
A Zuñi war chief and a warrior 131

Two Navajo horsemen 135
San Francisco Mountain 148
Two Indians identified as "Tontos" 170
A "cactus forest" showing the *Cereus giganteus* 176
The junction of Bill Williams Fork and the Colorado 182
Three Mohaves 191
A Mohave dwelling 193
The crossing of the Colorado River 195
"Indian curiosities" collected for the Smithsonian 197
Jules Marcou 228
Jennie Smith Sherburne 236
John Pitts Sherburne 242

Editor's Introduction

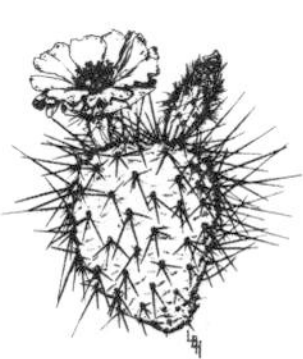

Editor's Introduction

This volume contains the text of a diary written by John Pitts Sherburne of Portsmouth, New Hampshire. Sherburne was a youthful member of one of the United States Pacific Railroad surveys authorized by Congress in 1853. In the diary he recorded his experiences from the day the wagon train left Fort Smith, Arkansas, on July 15, 1853, until two days after his arrival in Los Angeles on March 21, 1854. The commander of the expedition was Lieutenant Amiel Weeks Whipple, an officer in the Corps of Topographical Engineers. In order to understand the broad purposes of the expedition and the circumstances behind John Sherburne's appointment as one of its members, some background information is in order.

On February 4, 1853, Lieutenant Amiel Whipple received orders from his commanding officer, Colonel John J. Abert, to report to the Washington, D.C., headquarters of the Corps of Topographical Engineers. Attached since 1849 to the survey of the boundary between the United States and Mexico, Whipple at the time was completing his duties in Texas. On March 30 he boarded a Mississippi River steamboat at New Orleans, and on April 15 he arrived in Washington. Eight days later the Secretary of War, Jefferson Davis, officially notified him of his new appointment.[1]

Davis acted upon instructions from the Thirty-second Congress. In 1844 Asa Whitney, a New York merchant and railroad

[1] Whipple, Diary, Jan. 14, Feb. 4, Mar. 23, 30, Apr. 15, 23, 1853, Whipple Papers.

promoter, had presented to Congress, without success, the first serious proposal for a transcontinental railroad. But with the settlement of the Oregon boundary, the acquisition of vast territory from Mexico, and the discovery of gold in California, a once visionary project assumed a new importance. By 1852 the issue of the proper location for a railroad to the Pacific had become one of intense national interest and angry congressional debate. Since construction of more than one railroad seemed unlikely, competition among a variety of economic, political, local, and sectional interests, and dispute over who should build the railroad—the federal government, the states, or private enterprise—blocked any hopes for congressional action. In an attempt to move the project forward by substituting "the impartial judgment of science for the passions of the politicos and the promoters," a group of politicians added an amendment to an army appropriations bill. The amendment proposed that Congress authorize the Secretary of War, in cooperation with the Corps of Topographical Engineers, to institute surveys of the principal routes in order to judge their relative merits. The bill passed on March 3, 1853, and provided the Secretary with an appropriation of $150,000. Jefferson Davis immediately established an Office of Pacific Railroad Explorations and Surveys, placing in charge an old and trusted friend, Major William H. Emory of the Corps of Topographical Engineers.[2]

The Secretary of War was well aware that critics suspected him, not without good reason, of favoring a southern railroad along the 32d parallel. Nor did those critics regard the Corps of Topographical Engineers as an impartial agency, since both Abert and Emory had expressed publicly their approval of the southernmost route for a future railroad. Davis therefore acted shrewdly in his choice of expedition routes and commanders. He ordered three major surveys of routes enjoying considerable

[2]Quotation from Goetzmann, *Army Exploration*, p. 262; see also pp. 262–66. Asa Whitney's proposal, inspired by desire for trade with the Orient, stimulated other proposals from different sectional interests and nationalistic hunger for regions controlled by Mexico and Great Britain. For a good discussion of public interest in a Pacific railroad and the congressional debates on the subject, see Russel, *Improvement of Communication*, pp. 10–16, and Chaps. 7 and 8 *passim*. See also Schubert, *Vanguard of Expansion*, p. 95; Albright, *Official Explorations*, pp. 37–43.

support from different political factions. One would operate between the 47th and 49th parallels under the leadership of Isaac I. Stevens. Another, led by Captain John W. Gunnison, would move between the 38th and 39th parallels. The third, Lieutenant Amiel Whipple's command, would explore the south-central route along the 35th parallel. In addition to these full-scale surveys, a fourth expedition, led by Lieutenant Robert S. Williamson, was given the less extensive but vital charge of exploring passes through the California ranges that connected with the routes along the 32d and 35th parallels. Originally Davis planned no survey at all of the 32d parallel route through Texas and along the Gila River, apparently confident that existing information demonstrated the advantages of that well-traveled trail. But in the face of increasing criticism from other sectional interests that the 32d parallel route was a poor choice because of its inadequate water and timber and the constant threat of Indian attacks, Davis yielded to Southern pressure. In November 1853 he ordered two additional surveys along sections of the southernmost route. One survey leader was Captain John Pope, the other Lieutenant John G. Parke.[3]

Initially the Secretary of War chose only Northerners to command the expeditions; the sole Southerner was one of the later appointments, Captain Pope of Kentucky. Davis made only one political appointment, that of Isaac Stevens. A West Point graduate and former army officer recently chosen as governor of Washington Territory, Stevens was a popular choice among Northern interests. The other commanders, also graduates of the United States Military Academy at West Point, were all officers in the elite Corps of Topographical Engineers.

Founded in 1831 as an independent military unit of the War Department, the Topographical Engineers became a full-fledged

[3]The Stevens party was to move from St. Paul, Minnesota Territory, through the valleys of the Missouri and Columbia rivers to a terminus at modern Seattle. Gunnison's survey was to leave from Fort Leavenworth in Kansas Territory, cross the Rockies near the 39th parallel, move west to Great Salt Lake, and search for a pass through the mountains north to Fort Bridger on the Oregon Trail. Pope received orders to explore a part of the 32d parallel route from Dona Ana on the Rio Grande to Preston on the Red River in Texas, Parke to explore from the Pima villages on the lower Gila River to Dona Ana via Tucson in New Mexico Territory. See Goetzmann, *Army Exploration*, pp. 275–76. Accents are omitted for Spanish geographical names in this volume.

Corps in 1838 and by 1853 had evolved into a highly complex body, small in numbers but large in stature. Most of the Corps' officers were top graduates of their classes at West Point, soundly trained in engineering and the basic sciences. Though they engaged in public works projects entrusted to the War Department, their major activity had become the exploration and development of the West. Since the days of Lewis and Clark science had played a part in exploration, but the rapid expansion of the country in the 1840's produced an urgent need for more accurate information about the new frontier. In the Topographical Engineers the federal government had a cadre of men trained to lead explorations, make surveys, and create maps based on scientific data recorded with sophisticated instruments. Moreover, the Corps had forged strong links with an emerging scientific community. A new generation of professional scientists, men such as Alexander Bache of the United States Coast Survey, the botanists Asa Gray of Harvard and John Torrey of Columbia, and James Hall, the state paleontologist of New York, recommended the civilian scientists who served with army explorations. Through the Smithsonian Institution, founded in 1846 and directed by Joseph Henry and his assistant, Spencer F. Baird, experts provided the Corps with advice and technical assistance, and in turn processed the data, specimens, and artifacts collected on army expeditions. Thus at a time when an administration theoretically wedded to limited government withheld direct generous support to science, army explorations provided opportunities for scientific apprenticeships and the advancement of knowledge. Study of the data and collections further aided scientists' careers and helped turn the Smithsonian into a national museum.

Nor did such an association fail to benefit the Corps of Topographical Engineers. Under the leadership of Colonel Abert, once an assistant to the scholarly Ferdinand Hassler, former superintendent of the Coast Survey, officers traveled to Europe for study and corresponded with scientists at home and abroad. They read papers before learned societies like the American Association for the Advancement of Science and used facilities at the Coast Survey and the Harvard Observatory to test their instruments. Some of them became enthusiastic botanical collectors; others served as amateur ethnologists under the tutelage of men at the Smithsonian. A majority were only junior officers, since promotion in the peacetime army was slow, but they acted with the assurance and confidence of highly trained professionals, and they regarded themselves as bona fide members of the growing scientific community.

Though the Corps and scientific circles had worked together on a number of army explorations, the authorization in 1853 of so many expeditions at one time opened up a magnificent opportunity to compile a "great scientific inventory" of the exotic West. Major William H. Emory's appointment as head of the new Office of Pacific Railroad Explorations and Surveys virtually assured the execution of an ambitious program to aid both government and science. Emory was the epitome of the soldier-scientist. A close friend of many of the leading scientists of the day, he had written a scholarly report on the Southwest following his assignment as topographer to General Kearny's Army of the West in 1846, created a map that became a model for American cartography, and examined ancient ruins in the region, speculating upon the origins of the Indian people. Moreover, his wife was the sister of Alexander Bache, the great-grandson of Benjamin Franklin and a man at the very center of scientific activity and political life. With all these interlocking interests and connections, it is hardly surprising that 106 scientifically trained men were assigned to the Pacific Railroad surveys, and that the Smithsonian Institution worked closely with the Office of Pacific Railroad Explorations and Surveys. "Not since Napoleon had taken his company of savants into Egypt," writes the historian William H. Goetzmann, "had the world seen such an assemblage of scientists and technicians marshaled under one banner."[4] For

[4]Quotations from Goetzmann, *Army Exploration*, pp. 275, 305; see also Chaps. 1 and 6 of this superb study of the Corps of Topographical Engineers which, however, contains a number of factual errors, especially in citations and the bibliography. Other useful books for an understanding of the links between the Corps and the scientific community are Daniels, *American Science*, Chap. 2 and Appendix 1; Dupree, *Science in the Federal Government*, Chap. 4, esp. pp. 70, 79–80, 83–84, 92–95; Goetzmann, *Exploration and Empire*, Chaps. 7 and 8; Stanton, *The Great United States Exploring Expedition*, Chap. 3; and Wallace, *The Great Reconnaissance*, in which the author describes the Corps as a military brain trust (p. 5). Col. Abert, its head, also helped to found the National Institution for the Promotion of Science and the Smithsonian Institution. For Major Emory, see

each commander of an expedition, his responsibilities went far beyond leading a reconnaissance along a potential route for a transcontinental railroad.

Lieutenant Amiel Weeks Whipple, the leader of the 35th parallel expedition, had years of experience in the field. Born in Massachusetts in 1817, he entered West Point after one year at Amherst College and in 1841 graduated fifth in a class of 41 cadets. Following assignment to the Corps of Topographical Engineers, Whipple acted as a surveyor for public works projects in Maryland and New Hampshire and for a military reconnaissance in Louisiana. From 1844 to 1849 he served with the United States survey of the northeastern boundary with Canada, then moved immediately to the United States and Mexico Boundary Commission as its assistant astronomer. He later became the Commission's chief astronomer and took over the duties of the chief surveyor as well during the latter's long absence through sickness. One historian has written that Whipple was "the reliable wheelhorse" of a commission in which wastefulness, political intrigue, and petty jealousies assumed almost comic proportions.[5] Recognized as an able and conscientious officer, Whipple in 1851 received a promotion to first lieutenant. In both boundary surveys he had worked under Major Emory, and that association undoubtedly influenced the decision to appoint him as a commander of one of the major railroad surveys.

On May 14, 1853, Lieutenant Whipple received his detailed instructions from the Secretary of War. Appropriate branches of the army were to provide personnel (including a military escort), provisions, equipment, medical supplies, and arms and ammunition; military posts along the way would furnish additional

DAB, and Goetzmann, *Army Exploration*, pp. 127–42; for Bache, see Daniels, *American Science*, and *DAB*. Some of the officers mentioned in this volume (e.g. Captain Gunnison and Captain Pope) held brevet rank, that is, higher nominal rank without increase of pay. Since officers were addressed by their brevet rank, I am following that custom here, without acknowledgment of their brevet status.

[5] Quotation from Wallace, *The Great Reconnaissance*, p. 5. Information on Amiel Weeks Whipple has been obtained from the Whipple Papers; Stoddard, "Amiel Weeks Whipple," pp. 226–27, and "Charles William Whipple"; Foreman, ed., *A Pathfinder*, Introduction; Bartlett, *Personal Narrative*, I, pp. 117, 202–4, and II, pp. 356, 397, 541–43, 547; and the *DAB*. See also the Biographical Appendix to this volume.

Lieutenant Amiel Weeks Whipple, commander of the Pacific Railroad survey along the 35th parallel. Courtesy Oklahoma Historical Society.

aid if necessary. Though the expedition actually was a topographical reconnaissance rather than a precise survey, Whipple was to report on all matters affecting the construction of a railroad. He was to provide exact data on elevations and grades of mountain passes, meteorological and astronomical observations, and reports on the availability of water and timber as well as the nature of mineral resources, rocks, and soil. Construction of a map and a railroad profile, and reports about plant and animal life, white settlement, the products of the region, and the character of the Indian tribes, also were required. Unlike many army explorations, the expedition would set out as a wagon rather than a pack train, since any potential railroad route should be practicable for wagons. In addition to a "scientific corps" of men knowledgeable about engineering, geology, cartography, astronomy, meteorology, botany, zoology, and ethnology, Whipple therefore needed a small army of herders, teamsters, packers, soldiers, and guides.[6]

In choosing members of his scientific corps, Whipple relied upon his experience in working with civilian engineers and technicians and upon the recommendations of the Smithsonian Institution. A scholarly man especially interested in astronomy, he had worked with Professor William Bond at the Harvard Observatory and knew a number of the scientists at the Smithsonian. During his long sojourn in the Southwest he regularly had sent magnetic observations and Indian artifacts to Joseph Henry. While surveying in 1849 along the Gila River, Whipple had developed an interest in the Quechan Indians of the region. He collected a vocabulary for Smithsonian ethnologists and, as one of the boundary commissioners wrote, lived for months "on terms of intimacy and friendship" with the Quechans, commonly known as Yumans.[7] Whipple's official report, published in 1851, was remarkable for its careful, respectful observations of those little-known Indians, soon to suffer "reduction" by the United States Army when they actively resisted the incursion of goldseekers into their territory. Because of Whipple's new interest in Indian culture, he appointed himself as the ethnologist for the railroad expedition. He consulted with Smithsonian experts and acquired the first volume of a history of Indian tribes by Henry Schoolcraft, regarded as the foremost authority on ethnology, a science then only in its infancy. In addition Whipple successfully appealed to George Manypenny, chief of the Office of Indian Affairs, for extra funds to buy presents for Indians in order to ease his task of acquiring information. Whipple was

[6] *Reports of Explorations and Surveys*, III, pt. 1, pp. 1–2; Whipple, Diary, May 14, 1853; Whipple to Col. J. J. Abert, May 4, 1853, Whipple Papers.

[7] Bartlett, *Personal Narrative*, II, p. 173. For Whipple's friendship with a number of well-known scientists and his reliance upon officials at the Smithsonian Institution, see Whipple, Diary, Apr. 27–June 1, 1853; Joseph Henry to Whipple, July 9, 1851; Whipple to Joseph Henry, Feb. 12, 1851, Jan. 18, 1852; to Spencer F. Baird, June 3, 1853, Nov. 2, 1854; to L. C. Blodgett, June 7, 1853; to W. C. Bond, Feb. 5, 1851, Nov. 2, 1854; to Jefferson Davis, Sept. 29, 1854, all in the Whipple Papers. For Whipple's growing interest in Indian cultures, see Edwards, ed., *The Whipple Report* [1849], pp. 50, 63, 73; Whipple, Diary, Oct. 19, 1849, Feb. 18, 1852. His observations on the Quechan Indians are valued today by anthropologists and historians; see Forbes, *Warriors of the Colorado*, pp. 305–8; Scharf, "Amiel Weeks Whipple," p. 30.

conscious, he wrote to Manypenny, of the importance of "lifting the veil which yet covers to a great extent the past & present history of this singular people," who were melting away before "the westward march of the Anglo-Saxon race."[8]

By the middle of May Lieutenant Whipple and Smithsonian officials had completed their selection of the members of the scientific corps. In one instance, however, the upright commander made a personal choice based upon family loyalty. He appointed his brother-in-law, John Sherburne, as a junior member of the scientific corps.

Born in 1831, John Pitts Sherburne was the son of Colonel John Nathaniel Sherburne and his wife, the former Eveline Blunt, of Portsmouth, New Hampshire. John (known as Pitts in the family circle) belonged to one of the state's oldest and most prominent families. For generations Sherburnes had been landowners, shipowners and sea captains, surveyors, merchants, and government officials. They had intermarried with other leading New England families, attended Harvard, and sailed to Europe and the West Indies on trading ventures. Among John Sherburne's ancestors were the governors Thomas Dudley of Massachusetts, Theophilus Eaton of Connecticut, and Benning Wentworth of New Hampshire. His mother was the granddaughter of Captain John Blunt, who guided George Washington across the Delaware River before the Battle of Trenton. His father had commanded a regiment during the War of 1812 and later served in the New Hampshire legislature. Colonel Sherburne became Collector of Customs at Portsmouth in 1841, and shortly afterward received the appointment of Navy Agent of the Port.

[8]Whipple to George Manypenny, June 10, 1853; see also Whipple to Lieut. J. C. Ives, May 28, 1853, both in the Whipple Papers. Part of Whipple's copy of the first volume of Schoolcraft's treatise, published in 1851, is in the Whipple Papers. Henry Rowe Schoolcraft, originally trained as a geologist, published the six volumes of his *Information . . . of the Indian Tribes of the United States* between 1851 and 1857 (the title varied with different editions); see Daniels, *American Science*, Appendix 1, p. 222. The Smithsonian provided Whipple with standard forms of comparative vocabularies (used since the days of Lewis and Clark) to aid him in questioning Indians from the different linguistic groups; copies are in the Whipple Papers.

A drawing of the Warner House in Portsmouth, New Hampshire, where John Sherburne grew up. Built about 1713, the house is now a historical landmark. Courtesy Elena Klein.

Young Sherburne grew up in an extended family consisting at first of his parents, two grandmothers, two brothers, and three sisters. Their brick house, built in Georgian style in the early eighteenth century and known as the Warner House, was one of the loveliest in Portsmouth. Copley portraits of richly garbed ancestors graced the walls, and the family treasured letters and documents from dignitaries ranging from George III to John Hancock. Reputedly Benjamin Franklin himself had supervised the placement of the lightning rod on the Warner House in 1762, and General Lafayette in 1825 had spilled wine on the parlor carpet when visiting the family.[9]

[9] Notes on genealogy of the Sherburne and Whipple families, in Whipple's hand; Whipple to Harper Brothers (on the Sherburne family), Dec. 19, 1859, Whipple Papers; Wendell, "History in Houses"; Aubin, *A Warner House Biography*; New Hampshire *Census*, 1840; and brochures on the Warner House, built around 1816, in the possession of Elena Klein. Although known as "Pitts" among the family, Sherburne signed his name "John P." and was known as John to others. One of John Sherburne's brothers, Charles, died as a young man.

In 1843, when John Sherburne was twelve years of age, his nineteen-year-old sister Eleanor, called Ellen or Nell, married Amiel Weeks Whipple, who in 1842 had begun a hydrographic survey of Portsmouth harbor. After their marriage the Whipples lived in the spacious Warner House and made it their permanent home. Four children were born there, and Whipple, who spent all his army leave in Portsmouth, became closer to the Sherburnes than to his own family in Massachusetts. The son of a former innkeeper in Concord and a descendant of the church elder William Brewster of Plymouth Colony, Whipple regarded the Sherburne lineage as far more distinguished than his own. A deeply religious man, Whipple even converted to the Sherburnes' Episcopal church, a defection always kept secret from his mother, a staunch defender of the Elder Brewster's Puritan faith.[10]

John Sherburne therefore knew the lieutenant very well indeed, though an age difference of fourteen years obviously prevented a close relationship. In his diary Sherburne always writes deferentially of his commander as "Mr. W." or "Mr. Whipple," and no hint of kinship emerges. In his own diary and in his official journal, the lieutenant in turn referred to Sherburne in the same formal terms he used in writing of all members of his staff, only slipping a few times in his diary when he called him "Pitts." It seems that great pains were taken to conceal the relationship. None of the other members of the expedition who left records of the western journey apparently was aware of the family connection, and from Sherburne's diary it is clear that he received no preferential treatment.

Lieutenant Whipple most likely was under considerable pressure from the Sherburne family to appoint his brother-in-law to a post with the expedition. In 1853 young John Sherburne was at home at Portsmouth, presumably in disgrace. He had entered West Point as a cadet in July 1849 but was dismissed on January 31, 1853, because of "deficiency" in chemistry. His

[10]Stoddard, "Amiel Weeks Whipple," pp. 226–27, and "Charles William Whipple," pp. 11–15. For Whipple's distance from his family and his religious conversion, see Emeline Harwell (Whipple's sister) to Ellen Whipple, May 17, 1863; Whipple to Harper Brothers, Dec. 19, 1859, Whipple Papers. A son, one of twin boys, died as an infant.

record until then had been respectable if hardly brilliant. At the end of his first year his ranking was 42 in a class of 74. By the time of the semiannual examinations in December 1851, his place remained in the middle of a class reduced by then to 55 cadets. In conduct he accumulated 71 demerits one year, but on the whole he was a well-behaved cadet. In the final examinations of his third year, however, Sherburne failed in chemistry. Given another chance in the first term of his fourth year, he failed once more. Writing to the superintendent, Colonel Robert E. Lee, on January 18, 1853, Sherburne pleaded extenuating circumstances, explaining that during the previous term he had been in the hospital for several weeks and on "sick report" for some time after that and "could scarcely pay any attention to the course." In a poll of ten of the faculty, only the professors of engineering, artillery, and drawing (in which Sherburne ranked fourteenth in his class) voted to retain him. But he was permitted to resign, and West Point issued him a certificate of resignation testifying to his proficiency in the subjects passed during his three and one-half years at the military academy. That permission to resign, however, carried with it the stipulation that he could never return.[11]

In defense of a possible charge of nepotism, Lieutenant Whipple could have argued that Sherburne, then twenty-one years old, was well qualified for a junior position with the scientific corps, having completed over three years at an institution noted for its rigorous training in science and engineering. To the footloose youth such a position obviously was a heaven-sent opportunity. On May 17, 1853, John Sherburne received official notification of his appointment as "a meteorological observer and computer."[12] At the same time, Whipple sent letters of appointment to the other members of the scientific corps. These

[11] Letters of appointment of John P. Sherburne as a cadet in the U.S.M.A., Feb. 7–Mar. 5, 1849, National Archives; Merit and Conduct Rolls, U.S.M.A., June 15, 1850–Jan. 31, 1853; Staff Records, U.S.M.A., 1851–54 (vol. 5), all in Archives, U.S. Military Academy, West Point; certificate of resignation of John P. Sherburne, U.S.M.A., Jan. 31, 1853, in possession of Elena Klein. See also Whipple, Diary, June 3, 4, 1853, Whipple Papers.

[12] Sherburne, Diary, May 17, 1853; Whipple to J. Pitts Sherburne, May 17, 1853, Whipple Papers. For education at West Point, see Goetzmann, *Army Exploration*, pp. 11–16; Forman, *West Point*, pp. 50–56, 81–88.

scientists and technicians initially numbered fourteen, and all became familiar names in Sherburne's diary. Only two were army officers. Lieutenant Whipple held the titles of chief engineer, surveyor, and astronomer. His second-in-command, assigned by the Office of Pacific Railroad Explorations and Surveys, was an inexperienced topographical engineer, Lieutenant Joseph Christmas Ives, the chief assistant astronomer. The youthful Ives, born in New York, attended Yale College before graduating from West Point in 1852. At the time of his appointment he was attached to the headquarters of the Corps of Topographical Engineers.[13]

The senior members of the civilian scientific corps were Dr. John M. Bigelow, Albert H. Campbell, Dr. C. B. R. Kennerly, H. Balduin Möllhausen, and Jules Marcou. The Smithsonian Institution chose all but Albert Campbell, and Whipple personally knew only John Bigelow. The expedition's surgeon and botanist, Dr. Bigelow of Ohio, had served with Whipple on the Mexican Boundary Commission, where he collected botanical specimens for the Smithsonian "with zeal and enthusiasm." Albert Campbell, a Virginian and a graduate of Brown University, was appointed the principal assistant engineer and surveyor. A civil engineer, Campbell may have been recommended by his mentor Jefferson Davis. The physician and zoologist Dr. Caleb Kennerly, another Virginian, had "collaborated" with the Smithsonian for years and was a protégé of its assistant secretary, Spencer F. Baird. Prussian-born Balduin Möllhausen came warmly recommended to the Smithsonian as a skilled artist by Alexander von Humboldt, the great geographer-scientist, and Baron Leo Gerolt, the Prussian ambassador to Washington. The Smithsonian commissioned Möllhausen, a self-taught naturalist, to aid also in the collection of zoological specimens. The geologist and mining engineer, Jules Marcou, was the most distinguished member of the group. A native of France and a graduate of its noted École Polytechnique, Marcou had taught mineralogy at

[13]Though John Sherburne's father seemingly was comfortably off, the youth was sent on the expedition without money. Lieut. Whipple immediately had to advance him money, a practice he continued along the route. See Whipple, Diary, June 4, 1853; Whipple correspondence, Apr. 27–May 30, 1853, Whipple Papers; Cullum, *Biographical Register*. For additional material on Lieut. Ives see the Biographical Appendix to this volume.

the Sorbonne and first arrived in the United States in 1847 on a mission for the Jardin des Plantes in Paris. He became a protégé of Professor Louis Agassiz at Harvard, published extensively, and married into the prominent Belknap family of Boston.

All these senior men, with the exception of Dr. Bigelow, received salaries of $1200 per annum, a comfortable sum at the time. The middle-aged doctor was the highest paid with a salary of $1500, perhaps because of seniority in age and long experience in Western exploration under government auspices. Möllhausen was the only other member with field experience in the West. Arriving in the United States for the first time in 1849, he had lived the roving life of a hunter until 1851, when he joined Paul Wilhelm, Duke of Württemberg, on an adventurous scientific expedition to the Rocky Mountains. He had subsequently returned to Europe, but arrived back in the United States in May of 1853, eager to join one of the railroad expeditions.[14]

The remaining six men who made up the scientific corps were the junior assistants in the various "departments," as Whipple called them. He appointed Hugh Campbell of Texas, George G. Garner of Maryland, and Thomas J. Parke of Pennsylvania as assistant astronomers, and William White of Pennsylvania as a meteorological assistant. The assistant surveyors were N. Henry Hutton and Walter Jones, both from Washington and most likely recommended by Albert Campbell. Among this group Hugh Campbell received the highest salary, $900; George Garner (to serve also as Whipple's clerk), William White, and Henry

[14] Whipple correspondence, Apr. 27–May 30, 1853, Whipple Papers. On Bigelow see Meisel, *A Bibliography of American Natural History*, III, pp. 194–95, 200, 207; and Atkinson, ed., *Physicians and Surgeons*; the quotation is from Bartlett, *Personal Narrative*, II, p. 549. For Kennerly see Meisel, II, p. 99, and Smithsonian Institution, *Annual Report*, 1861. See Taft, *Artists and Illustrators*, p. 266, for Albert Campbell. For Möllhausen see his *Diary*, Prefaces by author and Alexander von Humboldt; Taft, *Artists and Illustrators*, Chap. 2; Barba, *Balduin Möllhausen*; Miller, "Balduin Möllhausen." For Marcou see Merrill, *The First One Hundred Years of American Geology*, p. 276, and Appendix, pp. 678–80; *DAB*; and *Concise Dictionary of Scientific Biography*. With regard to salaries, some comparisons may be helpful. The average salary for a male schoolteacher at the time (in Massachusetts) was roughly $300 a year, and a bank cashier earned well below $1000. The New York *Daily Tribune* estimated in 1851 that an adequate income for an urban family was approximately $800. See Unger, *These United States*, I, p. 257. For additional material on both senior and junior members of the scientific corps, see the Biographical Appendix to this volume.

Hutton were paid $800. Walter Jones, Thomas Parke, and John Sherburne received the lowest salary, $600. Hugh Campbell, Garner, and White had served as Whipple's valued assistants on the Mexican Boundary Commission. The others were making their first western journey.[15]

The Secretary of War instructed Whipple to move westward along the Canadian River through Indian Territory, cross the valley of the Pecos River, and reach the Rio Grande at Albuquerque in New Mexico Territory. The region was well-known to Indians, Mexicans, traders, and, more recently, members of army expeditions. The route, actually from Fort Smith to Santa Fe, had been explored rapidly in 1849 by Captain Randolph Marcy and Lieutenant James Simpson, Marcy's topographical engineer. Congress published their reports and Simpson provided an excellent map. The Marcy route, along the south bank of the Canadian River through present-day Oklahoma and the Texas Panhandle to Santa Fe, had been followed by many goldseekers who then moved north to join the Old Spanish Trail to Los Angeles or south to travel along the Gila Trail to San Diego. A parallel route following the north bank of the Canadian River was also popular with goldseekers. It had been pioneered in 1839 by the Santa Fe trader Josiah Gregg, who in 1844 published a description of the region in an acclaimed book, *Commerce of the Prairies*. Whipple included Gregg's book and Marcy's and Simpson's reports in his baggage. It seemed that the well-traveled route to Albuquerque posed few problems, although it passed through lands inhabited by the dreaded Indians of the southern plains, the Comanche and the Kiowa.[16]

West of the Indian Pueblo of Zuñi, beyond the Rio Grande,

[15] Whipple correspondence, Apr. 27–May 30, 1853, Whipple Papers. For Whipple's long association with Hugh Campbell, Garner, and White on the Mexican Boundary Commission, see Whipple, Diary, Oct. 28, 1850, Jan. 9, 1851, Jan. 16, 17, Feb. 5, 7, 1853, Whipple Papers; Bartlett, *Personal Narrative*, II, Appendix D, p. 601, Appendix F, p. 605.

[16] *Reports of Explorations and Surveys*, III, pt. 1, pp. 1–2; Whipple to Col. J. J. Abert, May 4, 1853, Whipple Papers; Marcy, "Report"; Simpson, "Report and Map"; Gregg, *Commerce of the Prairies*. Whipple also obtained copies of the published reports of Lieut. J. W. Abert, who in 1845 had explored the country along the Canadian River in Indian Territory, and Lieut. J. H. Simpson, who after reaching Santa Fe in 1849 had explored the Navajo country west of the Rio Grande; see Whipple, Diary, Oct. 3, Nov. 13, 1853, Whipple Papers.

knowledge of the country was much sketchier. Jefferson Davis instructed Whipple to determine the most practicable passes through the Sierra Madre and the mountains west of the country of the Zuñi and Moqui (Hopi) Indians in order to reach the Colorado River near the 35th parallel. After crossing the Colorado, he was to move west to San Pedro, the port of Los Angeles.

Anglo-Americans had little exact information on the mountainous country of present-day northern Arizona or the Native Americans who for centuries had roamed or settled there. Even the Spaniards, great invaders and explorers though they were, had failed to conquer the region, marked for years on U.S. Army maps as unexplored territory. The most recent Anglo-American knowledge had been furnished by Captain Lorenzo Sitgreaves, a topographical engineer who in 1851 led a packtrain from Zuñi to the Colorado, then followed the river south to Fort Yuma, established in 1850 at the confluence of the Colorado and Gila rivers near the Mexican border. It was a journey plagued by poor mules, inadequate provisions, and harassment by Indians. The Office of Pacific Railroad Explorations and Surveys provided Whipple with the Sitgreaves map, the first ever available for the region, but the lieutenant did not receive an advance copy of Captain Sitgreave's brief and gloomy report, published during the summer of 1853. Whipple knew that part of the Sitgreaves route had moved north of the 35th parallel. But he did not know that the expedition's instruments had been damaged by hard travel, rendering suspect the accuracy of the map, or that the map contained serious errors in some locations of important landmarks.[17]

[17] Whipple mentions the Sitgreaves report in his official journal, though not in his diary, and it is clear that he saw the report only after he returned to Washington in 1854 to prepare his journal and other reports for Congress. See particularly the entry of Mar. 9, 1854, in Whipple's official itinerary or journal, *Reports of Explorations and Surveys*, III, pt. 1, pp. 1–136. See also Wallace, "Across Arizona to the Big Colorado," p. 363, n. 90, a fine article on the Sitgreaves expedition in which Wallace uses unpublished records of other members of the expedition to flesh out Sitgreaves's account. West of the Rio Grande, trails to the pueblos of the Zuñi and Moqui Indians had been well explored in the sixteenth century by Spanish officials and missionaries, and territory bordering the 35th parallel west to the Colorado River was crossed by the explorers Antonio de Espejo (1583) and Juan de Oñate (1604); Espejo drew a sketchy map of the region. In 1777 Padre Francisco Garcés traveled from the Colorado River east to

Aware that the most difficult and dangerous part of the journey was the exploration west of the Rio Grande, Whipple immediately dispatched Lieutenant Ives, Dr. Kennerly, and Hugh Campbell to San Antonio, Texas. He instructed Ives to proceed from there under military escort to Albuquerque via Magoffinsville, near El Paso, where he was to collect valuable scientific instruments borrowed from the United States and Mexico Boundary Commission. Lest the trio idle away the hours on their journey, Whipple ordered them to conduct scientific observations and collect specimens of plant life as well as Indian artifacts and vocabularies. Upon arrival in Albuquerque, presumably well in advance of the main party, Ives was to survey the area, choose a suitable railroad crossing of the Rio Grande, and endeavor to obtain the services of Antoine Leroux, who lived in nearby Taos. A noted guide and trapper, Leroux in 1851 had accompanied the Sitgreaves expedition. Whipple knew the guide, since he had joined the Boundary Commission after his arrival at Fort Yuma with Captain Sitgreaves. From Washington the lieutenant wrote in advance to Leroux, urging him to serve as the expedition's guide west of the Rio Grande.[18]

Immediately following his appointment Whipple plunged into other preparations for the journey, including the requisition of supplies from branches of the government. The Office of Pacific Railroad Explorations and Surveys assigned him two additional army officers, Lieutenant David S. Stanley to serve as quartermaster and Lieutenant John M. Jones to command the military escort. A classmate of Lieutenant Ives at West Point and, like Ives, an "acquaintance" of John Sherburne, Stanley was then

---

the Moqui villages, somewhat north of the 35th parallel. Hunters and trappers like Pauline Weaver and Kit Carson also knew parts of the region. See Bancroft, *History of Arizona and New Mexico*, pp. 346–48, 395, 406–7, 482; Dozier, "Rio Grande Pueblos," pp. 122–34. Though there were serious errors in the Sitgreaves map, it generally was accurate. For information on the Sitgreaves map, I am indebted to Professor Andrew Wallace.

[18] Whipple to Lieut. J. C. Ives, May 28, 1853, Whipple Papers. Properly called El Paso del Norte, El Paso (now Ciudad Juarez) was in Mexico. The American settlement of Franklin, across the river, later became El Paso, Texas. For Whipple's prior acquaintance with Leroux, see Whipple, Diary, May 30, 31, 1852; Whipple to Antoine Leroux, Oct. 13, 1853, Whipple Papers. For Leroux, see the Biographical Appendix to this volume.

an officer in a regiment of dragoons stationed at St. Louis. He left immediately for Cincinnati, where Whipple instructed him to purchase army rations. Lieutenant Jones, in the same class as Whipple at West Point, was attached to the Seventh Infantry at Fort Gibson, northwest of Fort Smith in Indian Territory. With 30 soldiers mounted on mules, he would join the company near the time of departure. To his regret Whipple discovered that Isaac Stevens and Captain John Gunnison, the first of the commanders to set out on their surveys, had requisitioned most of the available scientific instruments. He spent much of his time arranging to order, buy, or borrow the delicate equipment necessary for the collection of accurate data. By the end of May, however, Whipple was able to instruct most of the members of the scientific corps to depart immediately for Fort Smith and await his arrival. Provided with $40,000 for expenses, Whipple estimated that by the time he set out along the trail the sum of $5560 would remain as a contingency fund.[19]

John Sherburne wrote the first entry in his diary on May 17, 1853, the day he received official notification of his appointment. Following instructions from Lieutenant Whipple, he left Portsmouth on June 1, stopping off in Boston to collect scientific instruments for delivery to Whipple in New York. Two days later he joined his brother-in-law in Philadelphia, where they collected additional instruments and bought red blankets, mirrors, artificial flowers, tobacco, and pipes as gifts for Indians. Proceeding to Cincinnati by rail, the two men left behind the other

[19] Whipple correspondence, Apr. 27–June 11, 1853, Whipple Papers; see especially Whipple to Col. J. J. Abert, May 4, 1853; to Chief of Ordnance, May 14, 1853; to Sec. of Interior, May 19, 1853; to Surgeon-Gen., May 24, 1853; to Lieut. D. S. Stanley, May 30, 1853; circulars to members of scientific corps, excepting Messrs. Sherburne and White, May 28, 30, 1853. See also Sherburne, Diary, June 7, 1853. For Stanley and Jones see Cullum, *Biographical Register*; *DAB*; Stanley, *Personal Memoirs*; and the Biographical Appendix to this volume. Grant Foreman, the editor of Whipple's official journal (published under the title *A Pathfinder in the Southwest*), and William Goetzmann, who cites Foreman, state that Whipple was poorly equipped with instruments; at the time he edited Whipple's journal, Foreman had no access to the Whipple Papers. But by the time he departed, Whipple had obtained a good supply that was augmented with sophisticated instruments delivered by Lieut. Ives in Albuquerque. See the Afterword, p. 217, for information on the usefulness of Whipple's maps and scientific observations because of these instruments.

meteorological assistant, William White, whose home was in Philadelphia. Whipple assigned to White the task of arranging for the transportation of supplies and equipment, including wagons and tents, obtained from the Quartermaster General's department. Arriving in Cincinnati on June 7, Sherburne and Whipple joined Lieutenant Stanley and Albert Campbell. After Whipple had purchased more red blankets and yards of yellow cotton print for Indians, and tested some of the instruments, the small party left Cincinnati on June 15, "floated" down the Ohio and Mississippi, then ascended the Arkansas River as far as Little Rock. Stopping there for a few days, Whipple placed an advertisement in the local newspaper and, John Sherburne noted, received "numerous callers for all situations from *gentlemen* to 'cooks and bottlewashers.'" Whipple hired some herders and teamsters, and one servant for $25 a month, and he also added another "gentleman" to the scientific corps, an assistant surveyor named Abner Gaines of Roseville, Arkansas. Leaving Little Rock on June 29, the party arrived three days later at Fort Smith, situated on the western boundary of the state at the junction of the Arkansas and Poteau rivers. Whipple and his party were met at the boat by Lieutenant Jones and the remaining members of the scientific corps.[20]

Although the Secretary of War had instructed Whipple to assemble at some spot on the Mississippi River, by May 30 the commander reached the conclusion that Fort Smith was the logical place for departure. Located near the 35th parallel, it was both a military post and a fair-sized town able to furnish the additional laborers and supplies needed for the expedition. Upon his arrival Whipple began the final preparations. He put his staff to work surveying the Poteau River for a suitable railroad crossing, testing the instruments, training rodmen and chainbearers for the surveying party, conducting scientific observations, and ex-

[20] Sherburne, Diary, May 17–July 2, 1853, quotation from entry of June 28; Whipple, Diary, May 17–June 29, 1853, Whipple Papers. Möllhausen wrote that, according to instructions, he proceeded to Napoleon, Ark., where on June 12 he met with other members of the scientific corps. Under revised instructions from Whipple the party then left on June 15 for Fort Smith. See Möllhausen, *Diary*, I, pp. 6–9; Whipple, circulars to staff, May 28, 30, 1853, Whipple Papers; Waller, "Dr. John Milton Bigelow," p. 328.

ploring a nearby mountain. He hired teamsters, herders, cooks, and servants, bought 240 mules and a huge flock of sheep for the commissary, and completed financial statements and reports for Major Emory and Colonel Abert. Having instructed Lieutenant Stanley to establish a camp near the fort, on July 5 he began moving the men into "Camp Wilson." By that time all the members of the scientific corps affected western attire crowned by the broad-brimmed white hats that signified their special status.[21]

Once in camp Whipple organized the corps into messes in proper military fashion and with due attention to seniority. He presided over the company from his own tent, attended by a cook and José, his Mexican orderly during the U.S. and Mexican Boundary Survey, who had agreed to accompany him to California. He placed Dr. Bigelow and Mr. Marcou in another, where they shared a cook and servants with Mr. Möllhausen. Probably because of his sketching equipment, Möllhausen received a separate tent, which he turned into his "studio." These three civilians became known as "the scientific gentlemen." Below them in the pecking order, the remaining seven men shared three tents, cooks, and servants. The only deviation in this hierarchical pattern was the inclusion of Albert Campbell among the junior members. The demotion may have been at Campbell's own request, since he had gravitated toward the company of his fellow surveyors and the lively assistants like Sherburne. This group became known as "the young gentlemen." Yet all the members of the scientific corps were young with the exception of Dr. Bigelow, then forty-nine years old; Whipple himself was only thirty-five. Marcou was twenty-nine, Möllhausen twenty-eight,

[21] Sherburne, Diary, June 2–July 14, 1853; Whipple to Col. J. J. Abert, July 23, 1853; Whipple, Diary, May 30–July 14, 1853, Whipple Papers; Möllhausen, *Diary*, I, pp. 11–27. The laborers moved into Camp Wilson with Lieut. Stanley on July 5, Sherburne and the surveying party followed on July 6, and on July 12 Lieut. Whipple with the senior members of the scientific corps made the transfer from the comfortable hotel in the town. The white hats worn by the scientific corps may have been a convention, since they were worn also by the civilians with the United States and Mexico Boundary Commission; see Bartlett, *Personal Narrative*, I, p. 20. Whipple did not survey across the state of Arkansas, but he and senior members of his corps technically followed Jefferson Davis's instructions by commencing their observations at Napoleon, situated at the junction of the Mississippi and Arkansas rivers. Whipple noted that surveys of the region would be carried out by the state of Arkansas as part of its plans to build state railroads. See *Reports of Explorations and Surveys*, III, Chap. 2, p. 3.

and Campbell twenty-six. Sherburne at twenty-one most likely was the youngest. Such was the youth of the company that Möllhausen unfailingly described John Bigelow as "the gray-beard" or the "the aged doctor."[22]

Although anxious to begin the journey, Whipple had received no word of the imminent arrival of William White with the supplies, wagons, and tents. On July 11, however, the mail brought a letter from White informing him that, because of difficulties with river transportation, he had only reached Louisville, Kentucky. Whipple therefore resolved to move forward without further delay. He borrowed wagons and tents from the quartermaster at the fort and instructed Lieutenant Stanley and the military escort to remain at Fort Smith until White's arrival.[23] With a skeleton expedition he began the crossing of the Poteau River on July 15, 1853. In this volume the text of Sherburne's diary begins on that day.

John Sherburne's diary is not the only personal record of the westward journey. The expedition was a government exploration, and Whipple's daily journal, based upon a diary he kept of the trip, is included in the twelve massive volumes of the *Reports of Explorations and Surveys* along potential routes for a railroad to the Pacific, published by Congress between 1855 and 1860. In 1941 the historian Grant Foreman edited and published Whipple's official daily journal in *A Pathfinder in the Southwest.* Whipple's diary of the trip is among his collected papers; a portion written during the passage across present-day Oklahoma, and a series of articles based upon parts of the diary, also have been published. Balduin Möllhausen produced a two-volume narrative of the trip in 1857; an English translation, *Diary of a Journey from Mississippi to the Coasts of the Pacific*, appeared in Lon-

[22] Möllhausen, *Diary*, I, pp. 34, 63, 159; Stanley, Diary, Aug. 7, 27, 1853; Sherburne, Diary, June 8, 10, 1853; Whipple, Diary, July 2, 1853, Whipple Papers. For José see Whipple, Diary, Mar. 17–19, 1853. John Sherburne celebrated his 22d birthday in August 1853. When William White finally arrived, he joined "the young gentlemen" and shared a tent with Sherburne.

[23] William White had arrived in Cincinnati on June 14 with the supplies before Whipple and his party left for Fort Smith, but he again remained behind to arrange for the ongoing transportation of the goods on another steamboat. See Whipple, Diary, June 14, July 11–15, 1853, Whipple Papers

don during the following year. Lieutenant David Stanley kept a diary intermittently between July 1853 and April 1854, and one portion, written as the expedition crossed Oklahoma and the Texas Panhandle, has been published. In his *Personal Memoirs*, appearing posthumously in 1917, Stanley included a brief description of his experiences with the expedition. Lieutenant John C. Tidball, who joined the expedition on December 12, 1853, as commander of an additional escort of soldiers, made terse entries in a diary from January 3 to February 22, 1854, when the expedition finally reached the Colorado River.[24] All these records, combined with John Sherburne's diary, provide a comprehensive picture of a memorable overland journey. In order to embellish some of Sherburne's entries or to illustrate contrasting reactions to events of the trip, appropriate excerpts from these other accounts are inserted in the text of Sherburne's diary.

Lieutenant Whipple's diary, official journal, and other reports are invaluable records. His diary, though disjointed and written with almost endearing errors in spelling and punctuation, reveals more of Whipple's personal reactions and his quiet yet commanding personality. The official journal is a polished version, with personal commentary severely edited. Both these records necessarily contain quantities of scientific data, highly technical information on engineering problems and scientific instruments, and details on the logistics of leading a many-faceted expedition. Whipple's preliminary report to Congress, presented in 1854, followed a conventional pattern common to those sub-

[24] The final report of the Whipple expedition can be found in vols. III and IV of the *Reports of Explorations and Surveys*; vol. IV contains the zoological reports and illustrations. Volumes VIII, IX, and X contain the general zoological reports by Smithsonian scientists that include analysis (vol. X) of the Whipple collection. For the published portion of Whipple's diary kept on the journey across what is now Oklahoma, see Wright and Shirk, eds., "The Journal of Lieutenant A. W. Whipple." For the articles based on parts of Whipple's diary, see Conrad, "The Whipple Expedition on the Great Plains"; "Whipple at Zuni"; and "The Whipple Expedition in Arizona, 1853–1854." The English translation of Möllhausen's *Diary* was reprinted in the United States in 1969, and a brief section of the book, describing the journey across present-day Oklahoma, has been edited by Wright and Shirk as "Artist Möllhausen in Oklahoma, 1853." Lona Shawver has edited Stanley's diary for the trip across Oklahoma and the Texas Panhandle in "Stanley Explores Oklahoma"; see also Stanley, *Personal Memoirs*. Lieut. John C. Tidball's diary is deposited in Special Collections, University of Arizona Library.

mitted by other commanders of the railroad surveys. Written for the most part in pedestrian prose, these reports when published attracted the attention of an irreverent topographical engineer named George Horatio Derby. Writing under the pseudonyms of "Squibob" or "John Phoenix," Lieutenant Derby by then had acquired a national reputation as a wit (Mark Twain was one of his admirers). After the publication of the preliminary reports on the Pacific Railroad surveys in 1855, Derby wrote a burlesque of the commanders' reports in a California magazine. As John Phoenix, "Chief Astronomer and Engineer," he described a reconnaissance, with eight scientists and 184 laborers, from the heart of San Francisco to the Mission Dolores (a distance of two miles) "with a view to ascertaining the practicability of connecting these points with a railroad." Derby included farcical details about the simplest matters and satirized the scientific pedantry that frequently marked the genuine reports. As John Phoenix he reported solemnly, for example, that all watches were set by Greenwich Mean Time ("the meanest time there is"), and he determined a distance by the solution of a mean of 1,867,434,926,465 triangles. Although that solution differed from "popular opinion," he wrote, it was accepted on the grounds that there was no disputing "the elucidations of science, or facts demonstrated by mathematical process, however incredible they may appear *per se*." In one passage that may have caused Lieutenant Whipple some private agitation, Derby wrote that the expedition included John Phoenix's four brothers and three cousins.[25] Lieutenant Derby ignored of course the value of the commanders' reports. But his satire struck unerringly at their verbosity and earnestness, even though most of the authors self-consciously sought to emulate the lyrical quality of the popular exploring journals written by John C. Frémont. An examination

[25] See "Official Report of Professor John Phoenix, A.M." in Phoenix [Derby], *Phoenixiana*, pp. 13–31; see also Stewart, *John Phoenix, Esq.*, Chap. 10. Derby's burlesque of the Pacific Railroad reports was published in the *Pioneer*, a journal founded in San Francisco in 1854, as well as in *Phoenixiana*, a collection of his satirical sketches published in 1856. Derby read the preliminary rather than the final reports of the surveys, and perhaps had read Bartlett's *Personal Narrative*, first published in 1854. Bartlett was the civilian U.S. commissioner of the United States and Mexico Boundary Commission from 1850 to 1853, and it was well known that his staff consisted of a brother and relatives of Bartlett's friends and sponsors.

H. Balduin Möllhausen, the Whipple expedition's Prussian artist, photographed in his western attire in 1854. Courtesy David Miller.

of any of these reports, including Lieutenant Amiel Whipple's, requires a good deal of fortitude on the part of the reader.

Balduin Möllhausen's *Diary* provides the entertaining descriptions of events and the personal anecdotes largely missing in Whipple's journal. But it is not a daily account, as the title suggests. Möllhausen published his book after reading the expedition's official reports and devouring available literature on the

American West. Writing for European readers to whom the region was even more exotic than to Americans settled in the East, he saw his mission as that of educator as well as travel writer. References to such matters as flora, fauna, Western heroes, Mexican settlements, or Indians furnished occasions for lengthy digressions, semiphilosophical musings, or romantic rhetoric. Moreover, it was Möllhausen's first book (the first of many), and he included reminiscences about his exploits with Duke Paul Wilhelm in 1851 that reinforced his posture as Western authority and intrepid adventurer. In fact the first volume contains almost as much about his earlier experiences as it does about the Whipple expedition. Möllhausen was casual about dates, proper names, and the sequence of events, because the diary he kept on the journey formed only a basis for his future epic on the American West. Nor was he well served by his translator, whose affection for phrases like "lofty umbrageous trees" and "a mantle of rich verdure" accentuated a prose already florid in style. Despite the lively color the jovial Prussian injected into descriptions of highlights of the trip, the reader must persevere to extrapolate a coherent chronicle of the Whipple expedition.

Lieutenant David Stanley had been eager to make his first journey across the plains, but as a member of an elite mounted regiment he failed to appreciate his role of quartermaster. From the beginning Stanley grumbled about the weary grind of supervising the teamsters and herders and carrying out his duties as commissary. Though only five years older than John Sherburne, his personality already exhibited the rigidity that made him many enemies in later life, and he rarely participated in the camaraderie of camp life. Notwithstanding occasional flights of eloquence and acerb comments that provide a counterpoint to the observations of others, Stanley's entries in his diary generally are brief and uninformative. Lieutenant John Tidball's diary, kept only for about seven weeks as the expedition struggled across present-day northern Arizona, is useful chiefly because of the entries that express his irritation with the youthful "dandies" of the scientific corps.

In many ways John Sherburne's diary provides the liveliest sense of the moment as the expedition wended its way toward the Pacific. Unlike his brother-in-law, he was free from the responsibility of composing a detailed, professional report for government and scientific circles. Unlike Möllhausen he did not keep a diary with the intent of using it as the basis for a larger epic about the West. And unlike Stanley his interest did not flag; he relished the adventure with boyish enthusiasm. Sherburne was not a confirmed diary-keeper or a gifted writer. Like many other travelers he resolved to write a diary because he knew he was entering a special time of his life. He intended it for the eyes of a family more than ordinarily interested in the expedition, and he tried to preserve for them, and for himself, the realities of his daily existence.

Thomas Mallon has written that diaries cannot keep themselves free of the personalities of their keepers.[26] There are no family records that tell us what kind of a young man John Sherburne was when growing up in Portsmouth and maturing at West Point. But from notes in the back of his diary and from the entries made between the day he left home and the time of his departure from Fort Smith, there are glimpses of the personality that emerges in his diary during the course of the journey.

Despite an upbringing in grander surroundings than most, and exposure to the punctilio of a military academy, Sherburne was happy with simple pleasures, adaptable, and considerably less class-conscious than the army officers and the senior members of the scientific corps. Though not scholarly and reflective like his brother-in-law, he prepared for the journey by studying Marcy's and Simpson's reports of their trip to Santa Fe in 1849, buying a Spanish grammar, and filling back pages of his diary with information that might prove useful. During the days spent at Fort Smith, where the inhabitants in joyful anticipation of a railroad showered attention on the members of the expedition, Sherburne thoroughly enjoyed himself. He indulged a hearty appetite and a taste for strong drink, and danced or rolled games of "tenpins" until the early hours of many a morning. He also found time for another hobby. Sherburne wrote execrable poetry, including lyrics to popular tunes, a dreadful sample of which he gives us in the pages of his diary.[27] There are indica-

[26] Mallon, *A Book of One's Own*, p. 46.

[27] Sherburne, Diary, May 17–July 14, 1853; a sample of his lyrics to a popular tune are reproduced on pp. 141–42 of this volume. Möllhausen described at

tions, too, of the equable temperament and the sense of humor, callow though it was, that are demonstrated in his diary during the long months of travel.

Although John Sherburne wrote with a regrettable circumspection dictated by the knowledge that others might read his diary, he nevertheless seems remarkably free of the inhibitions traditionally associated with a genteel New England upbringing. His brother-in-law more nearly fitted the stereotype of a decorous Victorian gentleman, unchanged by years of roughing it in the Southwest. Whipple was then and would remain a man much admired and respected. The only criticism of him that can be found is contained in the diary of a singularly contentious young officer, Lieutenant Cave Couts, who served in 1849 as Whipple's commander of escort along the Gila River. Whipple, wrote Couts, was a Washington City dandy, "modest as a young maiden" and embarrassed by the bawdy talk around the campfires.[28] Despite Sherburne's discretion and the absence of "bawdy talk," there are broad hints from the beginning of a temperament far lustier than that of his brother-in-law. In a charming sketch Sherburne drew of himself dancing with a señorita at a fandango in New Mexico, he conveys a physical image of robust sexuality.

Once the journey began Sherburne demonstrated that he was a keen observer, a trait he attributed to "Yankee" curiosity, and a faithful and accurate recorder of daily life. There are days when his entries reflect the monotony of the landscape or the routine of tasks with the slow-moving surveying party. But the daily chronicle of the humdrum as well as the exciting, and the spontaneous reactions to people and events far removed from Sherburne's earlier experience, contribute to the appeal of this "private fingering" of a western journey.[29]

---

some length the "railroad fever" that gripped Fort Smith, the enthusiastic welcome given to members of the expedition, and the enjoyment of the "delights" of hospitality by "our young and jovial troop." See *Diary*, I, p. 13.

[28] Quoted in Wallace, *The Great Reconnaissance*, p. 42, from Couts's journal; see also Scharf, "Amiel Weeks Whipple," pp. 22–23. Examples of Lieut. Couts's enlarged ego, pettishness, and desire to irritate Whipple are given in a restrained fashion by Whipple in the diary kept during his survey of the Gila River in 1849; see, for example, the entries between Oct. 24 and Oct. 27, 1849, Whipple Papers.

[29] Mallon, *A Book of One's Own*, p. xiii.

Another claim upon our interest is the diary's record of a journey that contributes to a broader understanding of the overland experience. There is a vast and colorful literature on the overland trails through South Pass, and those trails have in fact come to symbolize the path to the West. Though more than 18,000 settlers crossed the plains to California, Oregon, and Utah between 1840 and 1849, it was the discovery of gold that set in motion that epic migration, with wagons following one another in "an unending stream" across the plains. Even in 1853, at the tail end of the gold rush, over 35,000 emigrants set out for the West through South Pass.[30] Accounts of the interaction among members of wagon trains and between the travelers and the Native Americans they encountered along the way form an integral part of the history of that migration. In a recent impressive study of the overland experience before the Civil War, John Unruh's *The Plains Across*, the documentation is derived almost solely from records and monographs about the emigrants who traveled through South Pass. John Sherburne's diary provides us with an account of a journey along another overland trail, across a landscape that to this day remains less well-known than the familiar contours of the more popular routes through South Pass.

In some ways Sherburne's journey was like one taken along the California or Oregon trails before the gold rush. The members of the Whipple expedition never met an emigrant wagon train during the entire course of their trip. Though the trail across the plains to the Rio Grande had been well traveled in 1849 by goldseekers, most of their wagon tracks by 1853 were obliterated and the trail so poorly marked that, despite Lieutenant Simpson's map, Whipple was forced to engage Indian guides. Beyond the Rio Grande, in the mountains, deserts, and valleys of present-day Arizona, the expedition was truly on a pathfinding mission, blazing a trail that in the main moved well south of the one traced in 1851 by Captain Sitgreaves. Though the Indians were always a largely invisible presence, a sense of the solitude of a great uncharted space filters through the pages of John Sherburne's diary.

[30] For emigration figures, see Unruh, *The Plains Across*, p. 119, Table 1. The "unending stream" quotation is from the diary of a forty-niner, William G. Johnston, *Experiences of a Forty-Niner* (Pittsburgh, 1892), p. 79.

The Whipple expedition, at least consciously, did not transport goldseekers and settlers, and its men did not interact with other members of wagon trains. It was a western exploration, an important instrument of the nationalistic aim to develop the continent and fulfill the nation's "manifest" destiny. The expedition accurately mapped a little-known region for the first time, advanced knowledge of the sciences and the trans-Mississippi West, and pioneered a path for a future wagon road and railroad that opened up a new territory for white settlement. Its fateful mission would change forever the lives of those long settled on the southwestern land. Sherburne's diary provides us with an accurate daily account of that significant journey. Moreover, through his eyes we gain a rare picture of everyday life and social intercourse among the men thrown together for their long journey to the West. It was a journey characterized by remarkable harmony and discipline.

The diary has still another claim upon our interest. It gives an ingenuous yet fascinating account of what James Axtell has called "the American encounter."[31] Despite long periods of isolation from others of their kind, members of the scientific corps came into closer contact with people of other cultures than the emigrants who traveled west through South Pass before the Civil War. Along the way John Sherburne and his companions encountered New Mexicans of Spanish and Indian descent, living either in secluded homogeneous settlements or in the more pluralistic society of Albuquerque, whose culture had been transplanted well before the Pilgrims landed at Plymouth Rock. They met natives of the land in all their variety: settled or rather resettled Indians like the Choctaws and the Creeks; "wild" tribes like the Kiowa and the Mohave, feared alike by Anglos, Hispanics, and other Indians; *Comancheros*, the roaming traders of the plains; and Pueblo Indians who had lived for centuries in their distinctive communities. Members of the expedition, like John Sherburne, carried with them preconceived notions or prejudices about these people who had never known the "blessings" of Anglo-American "civilization." Their responses to that cultural contact add to our knowledge about Anglo-American

[31] See Axtell, *The European and the Indian*, Chaps. 9 and 10.

attitudes toward those they never recognized as fellow North Americans. Their observations frequently tell us more about Anglo-American naïveté and ethnocentricity than about the long-established people whom they perceived as aliens. Yet their responses are sometimes unpredictable. In the reactions of Sherburne and other recorders we find expressions of appreciation for some aspects of life as lived by others that provide us with glimpses of the varied and subtle cultures that coexisted on the continent.

In the case of cultural contact with Native Americans there is another dimension that emerges in John Sherburne's diary. In one sense the Indians' presence shaped the organization of the wagon train. Their anticipated behavior influenced Lieutenant Whipple's choices of equipment and supplies, personnel, routes taken, and rules of camp life. But in the actual encounters Indians rarely remained passive objects of scientific observation or strategic planning. We see them responding to the arrival of the Whipple expedition in ways that were rational and justifiable in the context of their own ambitions and experience. They extended aid or hospitality that were vital factors in the accomplishment of the expedition's mission. They acted, however, for their own reasons of trade, diplomacy, or self-protection rather than out of fear, resignation, or a simple desire for friendship. They emerge in John Sherburne's diary as important agents in the making of American history.[32]

In summary, then, the diary is a valuable contribution to a broader understanding of Western exploration, of the overland experience, and of the American encounter. In *A Book of One's Own*, Thomas Mallon writes that "diaries aren't just books that were written; they're books that happened."[33] We now can relive, through his own book, John Sherburne's experiences as the Whipple expedition struggled along a southwestern trail to California.

[32] I am much indebted to the insights on ethnohistory in Ronda, *Lewis and Clark Among the Indians*, a beautifully written, thoughtful book. See also the Introduction to Phillips, *Chiefs and Challengers*, esp. p. 1; Forbes, "The Indian in the West," pp. 206–15; and Axtell, *The European and the Indian*, Chap. 1.

[33] Mallon, *A Book of One's Own*, p. xviii.

Through Indian Country to California

"All America lies at the end of the wilderness road, and our past is not a dead past, but still lives in us."

T. K. Whipple

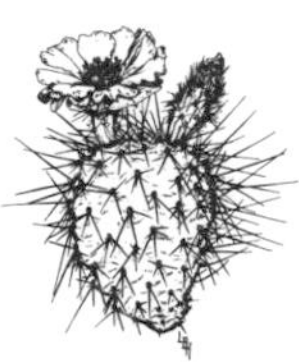

Fort Smith, Arkansas, to Old Camp Arbuckle

July 15–August 21, 1853

Lieutenant A. W. Whipple and a skeleton expedition leave Fort Smith on July 15, 1853, as we know, with wagons borrowed from the quartermaster at the military barracks. The party crosses the Poteau River and sets out across Indian Territory in what is now eastern Oklahoma. On July 24 Whipple's supply train, military escort, and a herd of cattle, sheep, and mules finally join the company at the Choctaw agency in Skullyville, about fifteen miles from Fort Smith. The wagon train, containing some seventy men in all, will follow the trail broken in 1849 by Captain R. B. Marcy. Beyond Skullyville the route passes through farmlands cultivated by Choctaw, Chickasaw, Shawnee, and Creek Indians, all members of tribes resettled in Indian Territory. Traveling along the south side of the Canadian River, the company on August 17 reaches a Delaware Indian settlement at an abandoned army post known as Old Camp Arbuckle. There it rests for four days while Lieutenant Whipple seeks a guide across the prairie.

During this time the wagon train travels slowly, hampered by a muddy trail, difficult creek crossings, and the tedious work of plotting a profile for a future railroad. Although this is considered an easy leg of the journey, the expedition travels only 198 miles in 38 days. It is aided by a succession of Indian guides, required because Lieutenant Whipple frequently is unable to find the signs of Marcy's earlier trail. Members of the expedition are impressed by the Indians of this region chiefly because they have adopted some of the ways of the "civilized" world of white people.

John Sherburne's diary during this first leg of the journey reflects his inexperience and his introduction to the work of a surveying party. His high spirits and interest in his new surroundings survive the frustrations of the slow journey, and his carelessness in immediately breaking two of the precious barometers troubles him not at all.

July 15. Struck tents and started on the route leaving escort to come with stores, etc. We are finally on our way across the prairies & every one seemed glad to start. I cannot leave Fort Smith without regret, for I've made many pleasant acquaintances who probably I shall never meet again. Farewell, kind friends. Your hospitality & kindness has bound me with a tie which years will not sever. May prosperity attend you *all.* Crossed the oporto[1] between 11 & 12, found the mud very deep & had some difficulty in drawing teams. The scenery is magnificent. Immense cotton-wood & undergrowth of cane-brake. Country remarkably level. Started for Camp 5 p.m., but got caught in a severe thunder shower. Wet & muddy; arrived at Camp after dark. No tents pitched. Went back to Ringg's House & slept all night on floor, with wet clothes. A rattlesnake killed by one of the party today—measured 4 ft. 9 in. in length, with 7 rattles & button. Mr. Whipple's Caratella got "mired" & broke down, obliged to leave it till morning & walk.[2] Made 3½ miles today.

July 16. Left Camp 6 a.m., surveyed 2¾ miles of route. Found road tortuous & muddy. A great abundance of timber, consisting of Cotton wood & sometimes a stray oak. Undergrowth of cane-brake. Campbell performed evolutions over his mules head,

[1] The Poteau River joins the Arkansas River from the west, immediately above Fort Smith. Sherburne must have heard the name and spelled it phonetically.

[2] *Carretella* (not caratella) is the Spanish word for a small, two-wheeled cart not much bigger than a wheelbarrow; Lieutenant Whipple spelled the word "carretela." Sketches of the mule-drawn carts, however, shows that they resembled the longer two-wheeled carts known in Spanish as *carretas.* Whipple bought two in Fort Smith, one for himself and one to carry the delicate scientific instruments and the surveying equipment. "Ringg's House," where Sherburne slept, was a farmhouse occupied by George Ring, a white man formerly from Kentucky who had married a Choctaw woman and "in her behalf possesses a large estate." No non-Indian could acquire land in the Choctaw Nation without the agent's permission. See Whipple, Diary, July 14, 15, 1853, Whipple Papers; and Whipple's official daily journal, July 15, 1853, in *Reports of Explorations and Surveys,* III; henceforth cited as Whipple, *Report.*

Balduin Möllhausen's drawing of Fort Smith from the north bank of the Arkansas River. Note the military barracks to the right. Courtesy Oklahoma Historical Society.

seating himself in a mud hole—much to the annoyance of himself & *pants*,—but to the amusement of all others.

July 17. Sunday. Remained in Camp No. 1. Read Bar [barometer]—every hour during day. Bill Rogers, cousin,[3] & Lieut. Stanley came from City [Fort Smith] to see us, brought the very acceptable present of a bottle of Brandy & Whisky, with sundry messages from the fair sex.

July 18. Turned out 4½ [4:30 a.m.], left Camp 6¾ [6:45], reached point of survey 7.45 [a.m.]. Nothing alarming or amusing occurred today, excepting my being unfortunate enough to smash Bar. No. 781—

July 19. Moved Camp about 5 miles farther West, to Choctaw Agency, Camp No. 2. Run the [survey] line to that place. Smashed Bar. 780. Camped about 2 p.m. Had invitation to dine at Agents. Recd. news from City that White had arrived from Napoleon [Arkansas] with freight.[4] Much rejoicing.

[3]Bill Rogers and his cousin, referred to by Whipple as the "Messrs Rogers," most likely were relatives of Capt. John Rogers, a prominent citizen of Fort Smith who owned the hotel where members of the scientific corps stayed upon first arriving in the town. Lieut. Stanley as quartermaster had remained behind with Lieut. Jones and the military escort to await the arrival of William White with the equipment and supplies. See Whipple, Diary, July 2, 17, 1853, Whipple Papers, and *Report*, July 22, 1853; Möllhausen, *Diary*, I, p. 13.

[4]Lieut. Whipple received word from the quartermaster at Fort Smith that on July 18 William White had arrived with the stores. The agent who invited Sherburne to dine was Douglas H. Cooper, the recently appointed agent to the Choctaw Indians who was stationed in Skullyville, a mile or so east of present-day Spiro, Oklahoma. See Whipple, Diary, July 11, 16, 18, 19, 25, 1853, Whipple Papers.

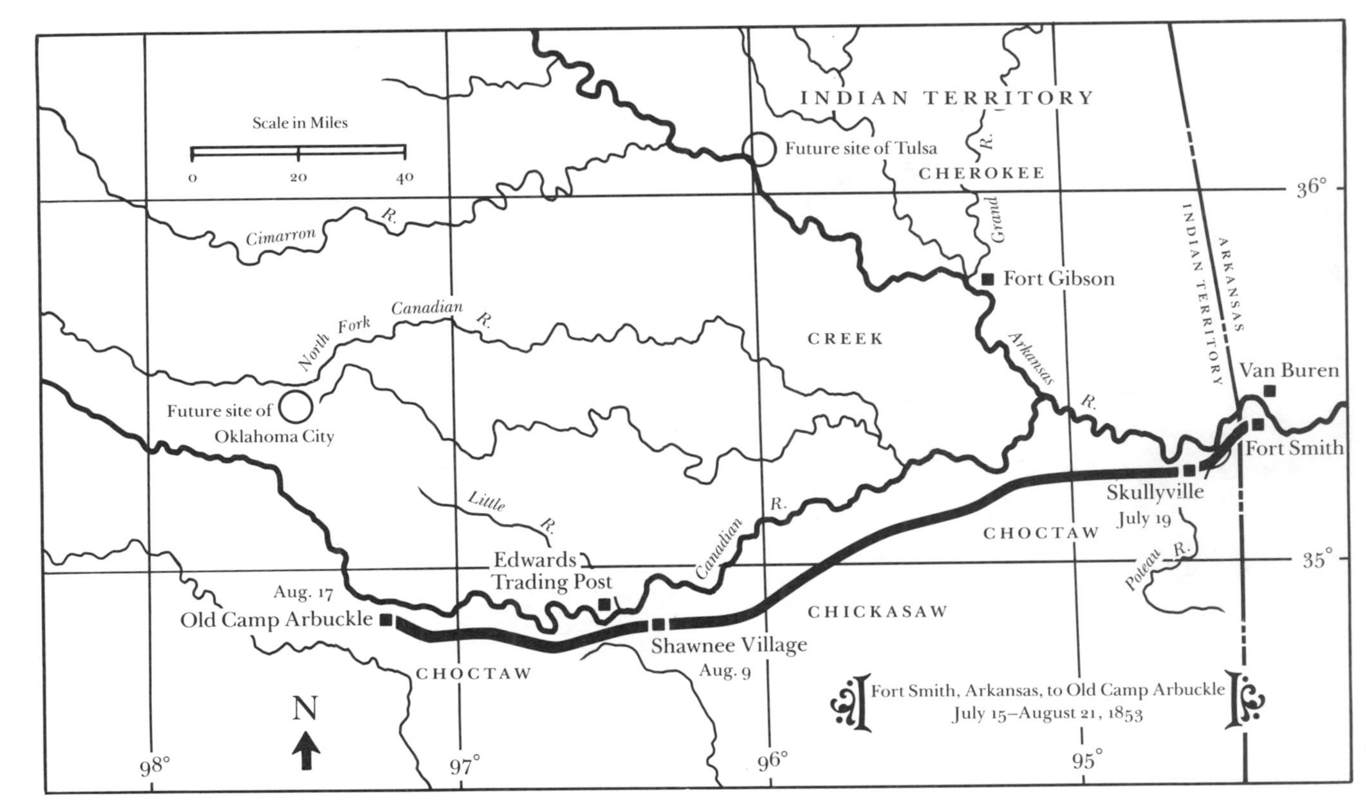

Fort Smith, Arkansas, to Old Camp Arbuckle
July 15–August 21, 1853

Whipple, *Report*: "Six miles from Ring's plantation we reached Scullyville, the seat of the Choctaw agency. The village consists of about thirty houses, most of which are stores, where the Indian may supply himself with articles of use or ornament."

Möllhausen, *Diary*, I, p. 32: "The town itself consists of a kind of broad street, formed of log-houses and gardens, and does not differ much in appearance from many other thriving villages; Indians, Negroes, and Europeans are seen moving about—domestic animals of all sorts enliven the farmyards, gardens, and streets; the sound of the threshing machine is heard, and the regular fall of the smith's hammer upon the anvil, and in general there is an appearance of lively industry about the place."[5]

July 20. Mr. Whipple & José went to City to see White & make arrangements for the remainder of the party, wagons, etc. to join us.

July 21. Quite sick all day. Mr. Whipple did not return. Made progress of 7 miles on the line.

July 22. Quite unwell. Took an emetic, 3 blue pills, 3 seidlits & 45 grs. quinine. Mr. W. returned from City.

July 23. Much better, tho' weak. Party started on reconnaissance to shorten road, returned before dinner with "barked shins" & scratched faces for their *pains*. Gaines took a flying leap over his mules head, striking his *stern* against a tree, thereby not only rending pretty severely the fundamental part of his pants, but removing a portion of his hide beneath said aperture, causing a deep injury to his feelings. Recd. news that a portion of our wagons, etc., were encamped at the place we last left (Camp No. 1, Ringgs). Garner quite sick, gone to Hotel [Skullyville] to sleep. Did not move camp today, on account of sickness of several of the party. Harnessed up at sunrise for a start but order countermanded.

July 24. Decided to remain here till remainder of party joins us, they reached us at 11 a.m., with the exception of two wagons which were left in the mud of the "Arkansas Bottom." Stanley & White remain with them. Camp presented quite a lively & interesting appearance, full of Soldiers, Teamsters, etc.

Went to church this morning, with remainder of party & was

[5]Since Möllhausen's *Diary* was not a daily account, a citation for any excerpt from it gives the volume and page number. Each excerpt from other records is for the same day as Sherburne's preceding entry, unless otherwise noted.

well paid for doing so. During the sermon, the preacher mentioned our party & "hoped the surveyors who started their extensive surveys through our Continent, would not neglect religion, etc."[6] Although in a place where there should be solemnity, yet many things occurred to cause a smile. Services were performed in the school-house, near Camp. The congregation consisted of about 50, one-third of the males & two-thirds of the females were Indians. During the service a young "papoose" "tuned his pipes." The mother, taking the child & a pitcher of water from the floor, coolly left the house & shortly after returned without her charge. The congregation made themselves "at home." Some eating, some chewing tobacco, & some walking out & in the door. The services commenced with singing, which I was unfortunate to lose [miss]. The preacher stated that he had a bad cold & would thank some one present, if they would strike up the tune. So after giving out the Hymn, one of the party struck up an old air, in which he was joined by those present. The singing was described as decidedly "original" & beyond comparison.

A few remarks I must not forget which occurred in the sermon. The following was a portion. "Parents can love their children too much, wives can love their husbands too much, husbands can love their wives too much (but 'tis not very probable, for my father, who was a Baptist preacher used to say, he never heard of or believed there was a man who loved his wife *too much*. They are not apt to do it), but you cannot love your God too much."

A strong scent of Indians filled the room & "perambulated" round the "circumbulating" space for some distance. The Indians of this place, with a few exceptions, are a dirty looking set, nearly devoid of beauty.

White and Stanley arrived. Much amusement in camp tonight,

[6]The preacher was the Rev. Cyrus Byington, a New Englander who had been a Presbyterian missionary to the Choctaws in Mississippi and accompanied them when the tribe was removed to Indian Territory. He compiled a Choctaw-English dictionary and translated the Bible into Choctaw. Whipple obtained from him a Choctaw vocabulary. The lieutenant wrote that young Choctaw males dressed "fancifully," and they used paint to beautify their faces. See Whipple, *Report*, July 25, 1853, and *Reports of Explorations and Surveys*, III, Part III ("Indian Tribes"), pp. 24–25, 63–64. See also Foreman, ed., *A Pathfinder*, p. 35, n. 15; Baird, *The Choctaw People*, pp. 43–44.

A lithograph of Möllhausen's field sketch of a Choctaw youth. Lieutenant Whipple wrote that the dress of young males was "fanciful," and their faces were decorated with red or blue paint. *Reports of Explorations and Surveys,* vol. III.

marking Camp-stools, each endeavoring to have his marked, emblematic of his occupation, & so as to secure it for himself. The following were the marks. Dr. Bigelow (Dr. & Botanist), an enormous cactus—Mr. Marcou (Geologist), hammer & anvil—Mölhausen (Topog[r] & Naturalist), Scull & cross-bones—Campbell (Surveyor), a camel and Pyramid—Parke (Astronomer), chronometer—Garner (do [ditto]), sextant—Jones & Gaines (Rodmen), flags—Myself, Bar. & mountain.

Camp flooded with Indians, in paint & dress, to have their pictures taken [drawn].

Möllhausen, *Diary*, I, p. 34: "Although the Indian population is of course accustomed to intercourse with whites, the appearance of our expedition, with its military escort, attracted a great deal of attention. . . . It happened, also, that a council of Choctaw chiefs was being held at the same time, so that it was no wonder if people flocked to the spot from far and near, and that the town assumed its gayest aspect. . . . Our camp was a great point of attraction, and as I had set up a kind of studio in my tent, many of the Indians came crowding that way, evidently speculating on the chance of having their portraits taken in their splendid full dress."

July 25. Remaining two wagons arrived. Went in evening to hear a Choctaw Chief make a speech in Choctaw. It was a strange language, tho' not unmusical. After him several others made *excellent* remarks.[7]

Whipple, Diary, Aug. 4, 1853: "The Chief with quiet dignity addressed [the audience]. In silvery tones and with well modulated cadence, persuasive in manner and without apparent effort he held the crowds in mute and undisturbed attention. Their dress was as various as there are degrees between the civilized & the Barbarian. From the breechcloth the simple shirt the pants, you saw the gay hunting shirt, the calico frock the high crowned hats with silver bands, beaded moccasins, wampum belts. And there too sat a few of the tribe dressed in their daily attire and listening to their Choctaw Chief—men who but for the swarthy complexion of their skin might sit in Broadway unnoticed. With beaver hat vest of satin & coat & pants of black broadcloth they seemed perfectly at their ease."

July 26. Camp No. 3. Moved Camp to-day about 8 miles. Had to get several extra wagons, the freight is so large. Endeavored to assist one of the men in catching his mule, which got loose & when caught would not allow him to mount. After a while I mounted, when the mule commenced a series of plunging & kicking. I kept on very well as long as he kept in a vertical position, but suddenly jumping [to] one side he left me in the air—thro' which I descended rapidly to the ground, but without personal damage. White & self commenced sketch of road with

[7] The Choctaw Nation was divided into four districts, with an independent chief at the head of each. The chief who gave the first speech was Cornelius McCurtain of Skullyville. Since all speeches were delivered in Choctaw, Sherburne's comment about the "excellent" remarks is impressionistic. Whipple reported that "we, unfortunately, not understanding Choctaw, soon grew weary, and returned to camp." With the addition of the military escort, teamsters, and herders, the expedition numbered about 70 men. Möllhausen wrote that about 70 soldiers made up the escort, but Whipple requested and received 30 soldiers from Fort Gibson. See Whipple, *Report*, July 25, 1853; Whipple to Quartermaster General,

compass & Bar., worked till dark & then started for Camp. It being farther than we anticipated, night overtook us. It was so dark, we were obliged to walk before the Car[a] [carretela] to show the driver the road. All the *firearms* we had with us was a scythe, swath & bowie knife. A short distance from Camp, met a couple of men with lanterns, sent in search of us. Arrived safely in Camp.

Stanley, Diary: "Survey still behind—discouraging—extremely expensive."

July 27. Camp No. 4. Struck Camp this morning & moved 5 miles. Went out with White in Caratella to continue our Top. [topographical] sketch of road. Got as far as Camp No. 3 at 3 o'clk & returned to Camp No. 4. Saw a deer today but out of shooting distance. Not being able to find a tent to pitch, slept in Car[a]— The Teamsters had a great deal of trouble in catching mules that got loose in evening— Recd. letters from home by express—

July 28. Did not move Camp today. Went out with Campbell & party with Bar. Dismounted to fire at a couple of deer, when my mule broke loose & could not be caught untill back to Camp. I walked about 2 miles where the Teamster brought him, shortly I joined the party. Missed our way back to Camp & were an hour in finding it again. Parke & self went out in the woods "foraging" & brought back a fine "porker."

July 29. Camp No. 5. Struck tents & moved 5 miles. White and self [worked on] Top. road between camps. Met a Cherokee half-breed with two horses—from his expression concluded he had stolen one of them. Enjoyed roast pig for breakfast, left before the owner (if there was one) had time to discover his loss. Saw a considerable number of partridges on the Road. Jones, W., of Washington, desires, with the advice of the Dr., to return home as his health will not permit him to go on, therefore handed in his resignation. Any quantity of letters written [to go] by him. Took advantage of the chance and wrote some of my friends of

---

May 24, 1853, Whipple Papers; Wright and Shirk, eds., "The Journal of Lieutenant A. W. Whipple," p. 253, n. 34; Möllhausen, *Diary*, I, p. 15.

Ft. Smith, Little Rock & Van Buren. Lost a mule in the evening—he broke his halter & left the party [for parts?] unknown. Dr. killed a large rattle-snake—

July 30. Camp No. 6— Moved camp 6 miles, found very poor & muddy water. Jones left this morning very downhearted. I took his place for the day as "rodman." Got on a wild mule—(the same one that threw me before), which ran off with me, pitching my rod one way & me another. Run me against a tree & bruised my left arm— Run the line about 6 miles.

July 31. Camp No. 7— Struck tents 6½ a.m. & moved camp 10 miles to "Sans Bois" creek. Run the line to this place. Stopped at an Indian lodge, bought honey, butter, a doz. hens & some Turkeys. About a dozen Indians came into Camp, mounted on their ponies. Passed a large extent of prairie to all appearances lately burned. Saw smoke in the distance probably arising from the same fire.

Whipple, Diary, Aug. 4: "From the Choctaw Agency we passed many comfortable farm houses and saw many of these peaceful quiet Indians. Few could talk English. Everywhere in the wildest forest we rode singly & unarmed as *fearless* of violence from natives as we would be in New England."

August 1. Camp No. 8— Struck tents 8½ & moved 7½ miles to another branch of the Sans Bois. Water poor & muddy. Rifles, pistols & ammunition issued today. Met considerable quantity of Indians on the route, surprised some of them by allowing them to look thro' the telescope. An Indian came into camp dressed in nothing but a shirt & sack coat, a handkerchief tied round his head. Engaged an Indian guide for part of the route. Stopped at an Indian lodge & bought them out. Saw today the *prettiest Indian girl* that I have yet seen on the route. Run the line into Camp about 5 p.m., through thick woods for 5 miles. The Indians made considerable hooting & yelling round Camp in the evening but nothing is to be feared from them as they have not a "stealing or fighting character" in this part of the country. Passed quite a large number of Indian lodges on the route. One of the men was thrown from his mule today & dragged considerable distance—he was only scared & not hurt. The Indians instead of endeavoring to stop the animal, took to their heels, per-

Balduin Möllhausen's field sketch of two Choctaw women. Courtesy Oklahoma Historical Society.

haps thinking it the Railroad which they'd "heern tell on." Had a number of Indians following us during the day, looking on with wonder & amazement. Plenty of burnt prairie today.

Stanley, Diary: "Bad humor all day. Oh, that God may forgive me the wickedness I have and am constantly guilty of on this expedition, owing to the constant crosses and consequent fits of bad temper I fall into."

August 2. Camp No. 9— Struck tents $5\frac{1}{2}$ a.m. & moved about 8 miles. It rained quite furiously a couple of hours after we started & the portion of us running the line got soaked to the skin. We dried, however, before arriving at Camp, which was 5 p.m. Passed thro' woody country most of the way, & over one very bad & rocky hill. The country so far, is well adapted for a Railroad, being very level, with a great abundance of "Post-oak," "Red-oak," "Black-jack" and "Cotton-wood."

Saw a number of Indians, bought a large supply of honey, butter & chickens. A large rattle-snake killed near Camp, six feet long with thirteen rattles & a button. Passed more burnt prairie.

A page from John Sherburne's diary. Courtesy Elena Klein.

Stanley, Diary: "Bad humor, as usual, owing to young gentlemen putting their tents according to their own inclinations."

August 3. Lay in Camp all day to make profile of route, etc.

August 4. Camp No. 10. Struck tents 6 a.m. and moved 17½ miles. Run the line to Camp 6 p.m. Crossed a large extent of prairie & some fine wood-land. Two wagons broke down today after leaving Camp, one being the wagon containing our mess-chest & eatibles. Rather hard work to get enough to satisfy the cravings of hunger. The wagons did not arrive during the night.

Stanley, Diary: "Found our careless men had lost four of our young mules. Hard work anticipated tomorrow. Prayed to God to preserve me from the wickedness one is so much liable to commit from the state of humor produced by such trying journeys."

August 5. Camp No. 11— Struck tents 7 a.m. & made a march of 2½ miles. The remaining wagons joined us before leaving Camp. Kept ahead of train & run to the Camp ground an hour before it arrived. It was delayed by bad hills & ravines. A number of wolves were howling round Camp during the night, & one seen in the vicinity of the Tents.

August 6. Camp No. 12— Struck tents 7 a.m. & moved 13 miles to "Cold [Coal] Creek." One of the wagons overturned shortly after leaving Camp 11. No damage otherwise than breaking the bows of the wagon & spilling the baggage, consisting of pork & flour.

Started to run the line from Camp 11 to 12, left the road to run round a hill & on account of the road changing its direction, did not meet it again—run 10½ miles without finding it & were obliged to leave a Station flag & retrace our steps to the road. Arrived at camp at dusk. Had a severe Thunder storm in the evening. Met a U.S. train going from Ft. Arbuckle to Ft. Smith for supplies, under command of Lieut. Douglass of the Infty, an old acquaintance of mine.[8]

August 7. Camp 13— Struck tents early in the morning & moved camp 5 miles. Went back to point where we stopped yesterday. Changed direction of route & returned to road. Run into Camp 6½ p.m. Passed through fine prairie & wooded land.

August 8. Camp 14— Struck tents 6 a.m. & run 9½ miles, thro' hilly & rocky Country. Crossed one of the hills known in Simpson's map as "rocky hill." It well deserves its name & appears to be an entire mass of rocks thrown together. Crossed "Prospect hill" where a magnificent sight presented itself, comprising beautiful hills & prairies as far as the eye could reach. The woods had an artificial appearance & were lined on the edges of the prairie, resembling an immense painting. Arrived at Camp 5½ p.m.

August 9. Camp 15. Struck tents 6 a.m. & moved 9 miles. Crossed several high & rocky hills, more difficult than those of yesterday, one being from 400 to 500 ft. in height. Crossed several very deep gulleys, or dry beds of streams, one of which the banks were very steep. So much so that they were obliged to harness the mules on behind pulling up hill & also to fasten the

[8]Lieut. Henry Douglass of the 7th Infantry graduated from West Point in 1848; see Cullum, *Biographical Register.* See also Stanley, Diary, Aug. 6, 1853. On August 5 the expedition crossed Gaines Creek, then the eastern boundary of the Chickasaw district in the Choctaw Nation. The wagon train now has reached the site of present-day McAlester, Oklahoma.

wagons each side by ropes, to the trees, letting them down in this way. We passed in the Caratella, after the wagons. Took out the mules & let it down with ropes. Took out the bucket containing the Instruments in order to avoid breaking them. One mule kicked it over breaking the glass of the Aneroid Bar^{r}. but doing no serious damage.[9] Were obliged to carry the Instruments most of the way by hand on account of the roughness of the road. Arrived in Camp 4 p.m. One of the wagons broke down, smashing one tent pole, thus leaving us without a tent for the night. I slept camp fashion, on the ground in the open air. Passed through Shawnee village. Saw quite a number of Indians who furnished us with milk & melons.

Whipple, *Report*: "Following the western slope of the hills, we found a trail which led us through thick woodlands, until, having crossed the valley of the stream, we entered the Shawnee village. A large peach orchard, whose trees were loaded with fruit, first met our view. Houses, surrounded by gardens, orchards, and fields of grain, were scattered along the banks of a clear rivulet. Upon reaching the road we found the advanced party of the survey; they were waiting for the train, and refreshing themselves with melons at a comfortable looking farm-house. The Indian men were robust and intelligent; and the women, dressed in neat calico frocks, with silver ear-rings, and brooches of Shawnee manufacture, were by far the best looking of their race that we have ever seen. Some of the young girls were almost white, with regular and pretty features."

August 10. Camp 16— A mule got away last night but was found a short distance from camp this morning. We were visited last night by a number of very good looking Indian Squaws & Indians. They brought Irish & Sweet potatoes, milk & peaches. They remained in Camp till after dark. There was one Indian boy among them who was quite handsome & who I took quite a fancy for. He could speak a little English and was a Chickasaw. When he was about leaving he turned to me and said, "Goodbye." "I'm going." "I shall see you no more." He then held his hand for my pipe which I was smoking at the time, saying, "Let me smoke." I passed it to him & after a half-dozen puffs he re-

[9] See Whipple, *Report*, Aug. 9, 1853. An aneroid barometer measures the pressure of air by its action on the elastic lid of a box exhausted of air, rather than by the height of a column of mercury or other fluid that it sustains.

turned it, mounted his pony, & left me. Smoking is a sign of friendships.

The train started this morning as we left on the line. About twenty paces from Camp, in a bad gully, one of the wagons broke down. They were obliged to put all the baggage in the remaining wagons, which were already overloaded.

It was the intention to go fifteen miles today, but on account of the extreme difficulty of the road, they were able only to make 8 miles. We run the line $3\frac{1}{3}$ miles past Camp, so as to have a good start for tomorrow. Saw today a novel way of drying clothes. A member of the party (Campbell) having washed his clothes before leaving camp, had remaining a pair of drawers, undried. In the course of the morning I saw a person coming across the prairie, whom at first I took for an Indian. On a nearer approach it proved to be Campbell, with his wet drawers buttoned around his throat, the legs streaming out behind, presenting a singular appearance.

Quite an interesting circumstance occurred this morning which turned a joke on me. By some mistake I put the crupper on my mule with the strap of the Canteen beneath it. In the course of the morning we stopped at a small creek for water. I pulled the canteen partly off to fill it & in my hurry forgot to replace it. After riding a short distance I was assailed with bursts of laughter from several of the party. I, of course, stopped to enjoy the fun, but found it at my own expense. My Canteen had slipped down so as to hang on the mules tail & dangled against his legs. The mules tail was sticking out parallel to his back which kept the canteen in its position & made both a ridiculous and amusing picture. The Dr. seemed to enjoy it highly.

Crossed a considerable quantity of prairie land & timber. Came to several small ponds, filled with fish. Möllhausen succeeded in catching 1 doz., which graced our board the next morning.

A couple of young fellows came out today from Ft. Smith & brought the mail. I was much disappointed in not receiving a letter, but got a quantity of papers, among them was the Ports. [Portsmouth, New Hampshire] Journal containing the list of party for the survey. One of the young fellows wanted to go with us but could not—he offered to go without salary. There was quite a lively time in camp last night. A number of Indians & squaws came to visit us & in the evening the Teamsters amused them by a dance, one of the number playing on the violin. Several quite pretty Indian girls in camp during afternoon. Had a difficult time with the Caratella while running the line. We went down a deep gully, very stony & the mules were unable to pull out again. Were obliged to take them out to prevent upsetting. By the aid of ropes and poles were enabled to get out of the scrape in about ¾ of an hour.

August 11. Camp 17— Started just before train & left them far behind. The camp was moved but 9½ m. to wait (so said rumor) for an Indian guide— Run the line 5½ m. beyond camp & returned 5 p.m.— Did not see a living soul on the whole route, untill returning, when within ½ mile of Camp met several Indians going to Camp with bags of peaches.

August 12. Lay in Camp today. Sent the wagon-master after Chism, the Indian guide at Little River.[10] He did not return during day.

I learn that the creek where the amusing Canteen incident occurred, is to be called "Canteen Creek" in honor of the circumstance. Ball cartridges were issued today & everyone seems to be trying his skill firing at mark. We are now about 125 miles from Ft. Smith—50 or 60 miles more and we will be in the heart of the wild Indian country. Then we will have to look out for squalls, squaws & squallus [children]. Powder for breakfast, bullets for dinner & Indians for supper.

August 13. Still at Camp & waiting return of wagon-master with guide. Last night saw the prairie on fire in the distance apparently a couple of miles. Several meteors observed about

[10] "Chism" was Jesse Chisholm, the noted part-Cherokee trader, guide, and Comanche interpreter whose name was commemorated in the Chisholm Trail. He married the daughter of a Creek Indian woman and James Edwards, a white man who owned a well-known trading post on Little River, which joined the Canadian River on its north bank. The expedition is traveling along the south bank of the Canadian River, designated on present-day maps as the South Canadian. In his *Report* under the date Aug. 10 Whipple mentioned that he obtained a Shawnee Indian vocabulary from a guide. For Chisholm and other significant figures mentioned in Sherburne's diary, see the Biographical Appendix to this volume.

9 p.m. last evening & evening before. They were mostly of great brilliancy, crossing the Heavens from N. to S. & leaving behind them a trail of considerable length. Wagon-master returned in evening without guide. Mr. Whipple concluded to go back to-morrow with Campbell and join us in a couple of days. We will leave this place tomorrow.

August 14. Camp 18— Turned out 4 o'clk, breakfast at 5 & left camp 6 a.m. As we left Camp they were striking tents & hitching teams. It was not certain when we left how far the days march would be. Mr. W., Campbell, Dr. and José left this morning for Shawnee village to be absent several days. They intend making a reconnaissance of the country, to see if the rocky hills can be avoided. About 6 miles from Camp saw 6 [?] Indians, 2 in prairie & 2 in bushes. They were mounted on ponies & had rifles. It looked rather suspicious although 'tis said they are friendly. Yesterday there were numerous sketches of the Canteen incident—entitled "Improved way for cooling water by Jno. P. Sherburne." Some of them were highly amusing. There was an exciting scene occurred in the train which I missed by being in advance. A wild mule mounted by a soldier started off full run causing a stampede of six wagons. They run about 300 yds. when the leading wagon brought up against a tree, stopping those in rear. Run the line today 20 m. from old camp (17). Started back 3 p.m. & found ourselves 11¾ miles ahead of train. They marched by 8½ m. & encamped on 2nd branch of "Boggy" so called.

Whipple, Diary: "Having gone back 7 miles to Shawnee Town after much questioning I learned that one Indian, named Johnson, knew something of the country in question. When found . . . for 3 dolls. per day he was willing to guide us. . . . Johnson appears to be a fair specimen of the Shawnee Indians. He possesses a little shop in which he sells coffee, sugar, saddles etc. He has several fields of good corn, squashes etc. He has a magnificent peach orchard, trees breaking under the burden of fruit."

August 15. Camp 19— Started this morning before train—arrived at one point for continuing operations at 10 [a.m.]. Continued till 11½, then concluded to wait for train. Waited till 12¾ when a couple of Soldiers came up at a gallop, telling us we were on the wrong road. Then "there was the devil to pay." We had however taken notice of a road passing to the right, which I had followed a couple of miles, thinking perhaps I should learn the route, or meet some Indians and enquire where it led. In this I was disappointed & finally cut over into old road. Finding our mistake, took a sight to the right across prairie & struck the road about a mile distant. Continued along road with train & encamped 15 miles from old camp. We continued the line & run a mile past Camp. The road at commencement was bad in several places. In one instance they were obliged to cut away the bank so as to enable them to proceed with the wagons. After leaving the main trail, the road again continued bad. Saw prairie burning in every direction. The scenery of the day was beautiful, rolling prairie & woodland.

Mr. Whipple & party returned from Shawnee village tonight. They were disappointed in Chism, but obtained an Indian named Johnson to go as far as old Camp Arbuckle where we hope to find Beaver as a guide.[11] They were misled on their return by one trail & travelled several miles further in consequence. They saw a large wolf but were not able to catch him—supposed to be a "sheep-wolf." Mr. Warren, the man who supplies us with corn, went bathing this evening, leaving his pants containing pocketbook, bedding & several other articles a short distance from shore. On his return he found the Indians had stolen his pants, pocketbook & bedding, leaving watch & several other articles in saddle bags. The amount of money in pocketbook was $125, mostly in gold. He expects to get it from the Seminole agent, as the thieves were Seminoles & the agent will take it from their

[11] Beaver was Black Beaver, a Delaware Indian chief and the most celebrated Indian guide and interpreter of the region. He had been the guide for the 1849 Marcy expedition to Santa Fe. Black Beaver settled at Old Camp Arbuckle with members of his tribe after the post was abandoned by the army in 1851. Near present-day Byars, Oklahoma, the settlement also was known as Beaversville or Beaverstown. Johnson, the Shawnee guide, was not the first Indian guide used by Whipple. A Choctaw guided the expedition from July 31 to Aug. 5, and another Shawnee from Aug. 6 to 8. Shawnees from Texas and other southern locations established settlements in this region in 1839 and later were joined by Kansas Shawnees. Whipple, who considered the Shawnee men and women handsome people, noted that Shawnee men, like many Delawares, invariably wore moustaches. See Whipple, *Report*, Aug. 15, 16, 1853, and *Reports of Explorations and Surveys*, III, Part III ("Indian Tribes"), pp. 25–26; Foreman, ed., *Marcy and the Goldseekers*, p. 166; Foreman, ed., *Adventure on Red River*, p. viii.

annuity.[12] We passed the Indians on the road & from their description, they will undoubtedly be discovered. There were three Indians, a squaw & several *dogs*. A number of the thieving scoundrels came to Camp tonight to sell chickens, corn, etc. I thought tonight I would like for some of my home-friends to see me as I stooped over the creek & washed a few articles of clothing—with pistol and bowie knife in belt, 2 month's beard on my face, pants tucked into boots, & calico shirt. I scarcely think they would recognise me.

Lost our viameter last night, in the road—found it again this morning.[13] It is my luck to find everything I lose, excepting my *character*. My knife I lost & found—penknife, pistol, handkerchiefs, pipe, & several other things I've lost & found. I hope this will last the trip through, tho' if I should lose my "scalp" 'twould be rather difficult to find it again.

August 16. Camp 20— Struck tents early this morning. Had a very hard days march, over rough road & through a great quantity of timber—one wagon broke an axletree from overloading—they were obliged to take out a portion of the load, lock the wheel & drag it the remainder of the way. Passed over a very sandy creek, with high banks, called "Topopha" [Tukpafka, now Sandy] Creek. The mules had "their hands full" to pull the wagons across. The land had the appearance of being washed up by the waves of the ocean. It resembled a sea-shore & quite carried me back to old times & Rye Beach [New Hampshire].

I forgot to mention a very amusing circumstance which occurred at Shawnee Village the night the [Whipple] party stopped there. Campbell slept in a low bed in the house. About the middle of the night he was aroused by a goat, trying to butt him out of bed & it was with some difficulty he could rid himself of the unwelcome visiter. In the morning they [the party] were aroused by the united voices of cows, sheep, mules, dogs, pigs,

[12] The Seminole Agency was nearby, across the Canadian River. Warren was Abel Warren, an experienced trader to the Comanches and long associated with Jesse Chisholm and Black Beaver. He sold corn, harness, mules, and horses to Whipple. See Whipple, Diary, July 26, Aug. 3, 1853, Whipple Papers; Foreman, ed., *Marcy and the Goldseekers*, p. 166.

[13] Frequently called odometers, the viameters were attached to the wheels of one of the *carretellas* and one of the wagons; they measured mileage by recording the revolutions of the wheels.

goats, horses, and cats singing a chorus to the sun. The pots & kettles were hung on a pole in the middle of the Lodge & over them the fowls roosted during the night. They were all void of appetite at breakfast in the morning.

This morning a sick soldier was sent to Ft. Arbuckle as unable to proceed with us.[14] The Dr. thought he would not live if he went along. A sergeant was sent with him. The wolves were howling [around] Camp all last night.

During the day our cook shot a Turkey & the guide a fawn, the first one shot by the party, although a great many have been badly frightened.

Made a march today of 14 miles, in spite of roads & rocks. Got the line into Camp about same time as wagons & run a mile ahead. Hutton & 'self thought we would ride ahead & see the country. We returned in about an hour & instead of finding ourselves in Camp where we expected, we were at the edge of the woods & the Camp nowhere in sight. We had by some mistake taken the wrong road. Still there were the marks of the Caratella, they too had taken the wrong road. Following their trail, we brought up in Camp. We resolved to "keep dark" and laugh at them for their carelessness. They were however as sharp as ourselves & did not mention it. The next morning we had quite a laugh at the expense of all parties concerned.

On our arrival at Camp, we found Dr. in great tribulation, as he had laid down his knapsack while hunting for botanical specimens & on his return to the place, found it gone. It contained all his notes since leaving Ft. Smith. He thinks an Indian stole it. Saw the remains of an Indian Camp with crosspoles & moccasins hanging from them.

August 17. Camp 21— This morning, the Dr. offered a bottle of whisky to anyone who would find his notes, for he thought they might have been misplaced. A bottle of whisky soon found its applicants, a search commenced & one fellow brought them

[14] Fort Arbuckle was about 30 miles southwest of Old Camp Arbuckle, on the Washita River, near present-day Davis, Oklahoma. The fort had been established in 1851 by Capt. R. B. Marcy after army authorities decided its location was more suitable than the temporary post of Camp Arbuckle, built the year before by Marcy. See Hollon, *Beyond the Cross Timbers*, p. 109.

A lithograph of a crude field sketch of Black Beaver by Möllhausen. A Delaware Indian chief and noted guide, Black Beaver declined to lead the Whipple expedition across Comanche and Kiowa territory to Albuquerque. Hastily drawn as it was, the sketch nevertheless captures what the artist described as a clever face that bore "a melancholy expression of sickness and sorrow." *Reports of Explorations and Surveys,* vol. III.

in, winning the prize. The Dr. insists that some one changed it to play a joke upon him as he was not in the place where 'twas found.

Today we made a march of twelve miles to Beaver's, the celebrated Indian guide, who was out with [Capt.] Marcy. The road was good for travelling all the way, but very parched & dry. In some places there were cracks two inches wide & the depth visible to five or six feet.

We camped near Beavers house & endeavored to obtain him for a guide, but being in bad health he would not go anyhow. He is quite a fine looking Indian. In the afternoon sent for Chism & Bushman in hopes to obtain one of them as far as New Mexico, where we can obtain guides.[15] Found at Beaver's an abundance of melons. The party supplied themselves with pipes, leggins & moccasins of buckskin.

August 18. Did not move Camp today as Mr. Whipple wished to obtain a guide and also repair all damages. Nothing of *great* importance happened during the day. Just before dinner, Chism & Bushman both arrived, but would give no decided answer, whether they would go or not—they would say in the morning. Hicks, the wagon-master, taken very sick last night. White & self gave up our tent & slept out. The night before we could not find our bedding as it had been misplaced & so we slept on the tent fly without anything to serve as a cover. Towards morning I woke up with cold feet & in fact cold all over. I saw White moving around in the dark & in answer to my inquiry of "What he was doing," he said, "My feet are cold & I'm putting on my boots"—following his example, I put on mine, after which we slept comfortably till daylight.

Wrote home in evening by a soldier on his way from Ft. Smith to Ft. Gibson.[16] This undoubtedly the last opportunity of writing before reaching Albuquerque. Quite a number of Choctaw, Chickasaw & Seminole Indians in Camp today.

August 19. Wolves howling round camp but none came in sight. They (not the wolves) have concluded to remain in camp today to make arrangements, if possible, for Indian guides.

P.M.—we have remained here, but without any satisfaction. All the guides have backed out & say they wont go, as they'll have to return across the prairie alone & through enemies. It is said the Commander of escort, Lieut. Jones, will not take his troops without a guide. In that case we all hope Mr. Whipple will go anyhow & trust to luck. There's no danger but we will find our way. The only trouble is for water & on account of the Indians. Today the escort was "turned out" & had an "Inspection of Arms"—also they had ball cartridges issued to them. The inspection is to be daily for the future, so as to be ready in case of

[15] Another famous Delaware guide, John Bushman, had accompanied Capt. R. B. Marcy on an expedition to the Red River in 1852.

[16] Fort Gibson, northwest of Fort Smith in the Cherokee Nation (now Oklahoma), was built in 1824 on the Grand River near its confluence with the Arkansas. It was an important supply depot.

emergency. This seems to contradict the rumor afloat concerning Lieut. Jones' unwillingness to proceed. We had a shooting match today, distance 120 yds. I did not stand any show at all, only coming out third best. Wrote home by Mr. Warren for the last time.[17] I did not send by the soldier as I expected, but had a more favorable opportunity.

August 20. Still in Camp today, with a little more hope of obtaining a guide. Several have been in Camp during day, but I believe have come to no decided conclusion. We have been decidedly unlucky at this Camp. Yesterday bought eight cattle @ $120 & put them in Black Beavers yard for the night. They were bought of Chism. During the night they broke loose & since have not been heard from. Several of the men have gone in search of them. This morning as the mules were out with the herders, by carelessness about 50 of them got away & were not missed for some hours after. Men were sent in all directions & have succeeded in bringing back all but three or four. I doubt if they are found. A Mexican boy came into Camp today. He was stolen from Paris [Parras], Mexico, when quite young, by the Comanches and finally bought from them by Chism. He now lives with him as his son. He is treated as such & Chism says he resembles a lost son of his own. He is a very interesting boy & appears happy. Can talk Spanish quite well & English. Says he recollects his father & mother. If Chism goes with us he will take the boy along with him. There are quite a number of Mexicans here purchased in the same manner. The Indians are Delawares in this region, with a few Seminoles & scattering [of] Choctaws & Comanches, tho' the latter but seldom seen.[18] This is the last

[17] Abel Warren was returning to Fort Smith. In addition to mail, Warren carried with him specimens for the Smithsonian Institution. Whipple issued pistols and rifles to the scientific corps and the teamsters and herders at Camp Arbuckle. See Whipple, Diary, Aug. 19, Sept. 3, 1853, Whipple Papers.

[18] Old Camp Arbuckle was near settlements of Kickapoo, Seminole, Choctaw, Chickasaw, and Creek Indians. The Comanches, a Shoshonean people, were seldom seen so far east, but they were much feared by the Indians resettled in Indian Territory. The presence of the resettled Indians and their hunting forays into territory beyond the barrier of the Cross Timbers were resented by nomadic Indians of the southern plains like the Comanches and Kiowas, who relied on the buffalo for their livelihood. At Old Camp Arbuckle Whipple collected Delaware, Shawnee, and Comanche vocabularies from Jesse Chisholm and Black Beaver, both fluent in many languages. See Whipple, *Report*, Aug. 19, 1853; *Re-*

Camp where we can have our animals out during the night with safety. The weather since our stay here has been remarkably warm. The Ther. has been today 104°—yesterday 100.°4—& one other day 114°—tho' the latter in a place not entirely free from the sun.

Whipple, Diary: "When I saw Chisholm I asked him if he had made up his mind not to go with us? He replied that he had made up his mind not to go with us. I was provoked. We had tried flattery & kind treatment we had invited him to our table and treated him like a gentleman. We had offered money & provisions more wages than any of these guides had ever before received and they all—every one—decline going with us. Their excuse was fear of Indians on their return. I told Chisholm that it was nonsence. . . . I told him that I was annoyed & offended that men as intelligent as I had supposed him should show so much apathy in the operations we are engaged upon. That they should refuse—even when offered high wages—to aid in explorations for a railroad which would be vastly more beneficial for their country than a mine of gold. . . . I was surprised at their stupidity & offended at their indifference."

August 21. The eight cattle lost night before last were found yesterday evening & brought back. They were about 8 miles from Camp. They were put in the same place again & later in the evening, while the Teamsters were endeavoring to put in some more, two of the wild ones broke out again & left. They were chased till one o'clock by three Teamsters, mounted, but finally made their escape.

The little Mexican boy is hired to go with us as Interpreter with the Comanches. There are a large number of whites with the Comanches, as slaves, mostly Americans—also some Mexicans—among them several young girls of 15 to 18 yrs. of age. Why is this allowed when it can be prevented? Lay in Camp again today. Sent out in search of the lost cattle & mules.

Today being Sunday & the work not being absolutely necessary, it was suspended. I believe 'tis decided to leave Camp tomorrow. We go without any guide excepting the Mexican boy. We anticipate much suffering for want of water.

Gaines, acting rodman, has concluded on account of ill health

---

ports of Explorations and Surveys, III, Part III ("Indian Tribes"); Hollon, *Beyond the Cross Timbers*, p. 100; Wallace and Hoebel, *The Comanches*, Chap. I.

to give up the trip. Many of us think he's tired of it & perhaps does not like the idea of meeting the Indians on the prairies. He is to go tonight for Ft. Arbuckle with Beaver provided he can make arrangements.

Whipple, *Report*: "Chisholm possesses several Mexican captives purchased from the Comanches. Their names are, Vincente, son of a man called Demensio, from Parras, and formerly of Tinaja; Mazimo, Guadalupe, Cidro Canales, and Mariana Transito. Besides these are two young women whose names are forgotten. Vincente was a long time with his captors, and speaks the Comanche language perfectly. He is a bright, active, intelligent lad, and Chisholm is very fond of him; but on account of our need for an interpreter, he has kindly given him permission to join our party."[19]

Möllhausen, *Diary*, I, pp. 95, 97: "Vincenti, or in better Spanish, *Vincente*, was a handsome well grown Mexican boy, but with a very artful expression of countenance. . . . It was evidently necessary that the incorrigible little villain should be closely watched; for . . . it appeared perfectly possible that should he see occasion he would betray the whole party of white travellers to the Indians."

[19] Whipple agreed to pay Vincente $25 a month and to provide for his passage home from Albuquerque to the Edwards trading post at Little River. According to Whipple, Chisholm bought the youth from the Comanches for $200 in goods and intended to raise him as his own son. Comanche raids into Texas and the northern provinces of Mexico had been common for years, and large numbers of women and children were carried away as captives. Despite the U.S. promise in the Treaty of Guadalupe-Hidalgo (1848) to protect Mexicans from these raids, they had continued; Indian agents at the time could do little more than urge the chiefs to cooperate. The United States also agreed to return captives, but the Army was reluctant to assume this responsibility. See Whipple, Diary, Aug. 19, 21, 23, 1853, Whipple Papers; Hagan, *United States–Comanche Relations*, pp. 9–16; Richardson, *The Comanche Barrier*, pp. 193–210; Wallace, *The Great Reconnaissance*, p. 94. According to the viameter, the expedition has traveled approximately 198 miles on this leg of the journey.

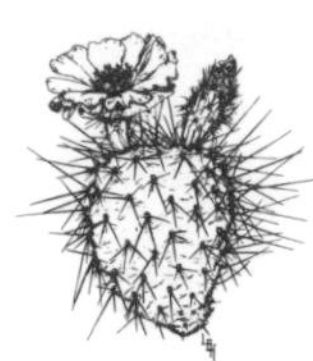

Old Camp Arbuckle to Shady Creek

August 22–September 14, 1853

On August 22 the expedition leaves the Delaware Indian settlement to set out across the prairie. The scientific corps now is reduced to ten members, since two of the assistant surveyors have resigned because of sickness. Expecting to meet the dreaded Comanches, every man on the wagon train is armed. Members of the expedition know from experience that there will be few signs of the Marcy trail, and in any meetings with the Indians of the southern plains they must rely upon a Mexican boy, a former captive of the Comanches, who now accompanies them as their interpreter.

The wagon train continues to follow a route south of the Canadian. It crosses the beautiful valley of the Washita River and passes landmarks like Rock Mary, named in 1849 by the Marcy expedition. The wagon train on September 6 reaches the Antelope Hills, at the 100th meridian that denotes the western boundary of Indian Territory, and passes into the Texas Panhandle. On September 14 camp is made at a lovely spot, unimaginatively named Shady Creek in 1849 by Lieutenant James Simpson. It is situated on the edge of the Llano Estacado, *or Staked Plain, a barren plateau first crossed by white men in 1541 under Coronado, the Spanish conquistador, and long a bailiwick of the Comanches.*

Along the way the expedition experiences prairie fires, the bad water of a gypsum region, and a tempestuous "norther." The wagon train is guided for a time by helpful Kichai and Waco Indians. Members of the expedition meet fleetingly with two elderly Comanche warriors and parley with a party of Kiowas, nomadic allies of the Comanches and, like them, fierce protectors of their territory.

John Sherburne faces this leg of the journey with a certain amount of apprehension intermixed with excitement at the thought of possible skirmishes with Comanches. But he is curious about the legendary "wild tribes" of the southern plains and vividly describes the Kiowas and their camp. The other diarists, including Lieutenant Whipple, are unanimous in their condemnation of these "savages," so unlike the agreeable agricultural Indians they met on the first stage of their western journey.

August 22. Camp 22. Turned out this morning at 4½ [4:30], took breakfast before sunrise & started on without any guide, excepting the little Mexican boy, who knew nothing of the route. We found a good deal of difficulty at times in tracing the trail as the grass had nearly obliterated it in some places. After trouble succeeded in tracing it. We made the longest & hardest march today of any day since starting. The ground was dry & parched & the hot sun was striking directly on our heads. Very little timber was seen on the route excepting at a distance. Part of the route was over burned prairie. Made a march of 20 miles & arrived in Camp at 4 o'clk in afternoon. In surveying the route, we kept just ahead of the train & arrived into Camp with it. On our way we saw a fine Buck but had no chance to get a shot at it. One of the party gave chase after a prairie wolf, but without effect. Several prairie chickens [grouse] were also seen. Just before arriving at our Camping place a fire broke out in the prairie ahead of us—on our left—so the wind would blow it directly across the path & prevent our progress. It was started by the Indians, supposed to be Kioways.[1] We saw two of them on the top of a prairie

[1]The Indians were not Kiowas but Kichais, probably from a settlement of those farmers and hunters on the opposite side of the Canadian River, near present-day Lexington, Oklahoma. The Kichai, Whipple wrote, were neither numerous nor warlike and formed "a sort of connecting-link between the wild Indians and the semi-civilized." Whipple was concerned that this prairie fire, and subsequent fires, were set deliberately to impede the wagon train's progress. But he also was aware that Indians set fires in order to prepare fresh grass for buffalo herds. Contrary to popular thought, Indians actively controlled their environment. See Whipple, Diary, Aug. 22, 26, Sept. 2, 1853, Whipple Papers. See also Möllhausen, *Diary*, I, p. 108; Davidson and Lytle, *After the Fact*, I, Chap. 5, for Indians as shapers of their environment.

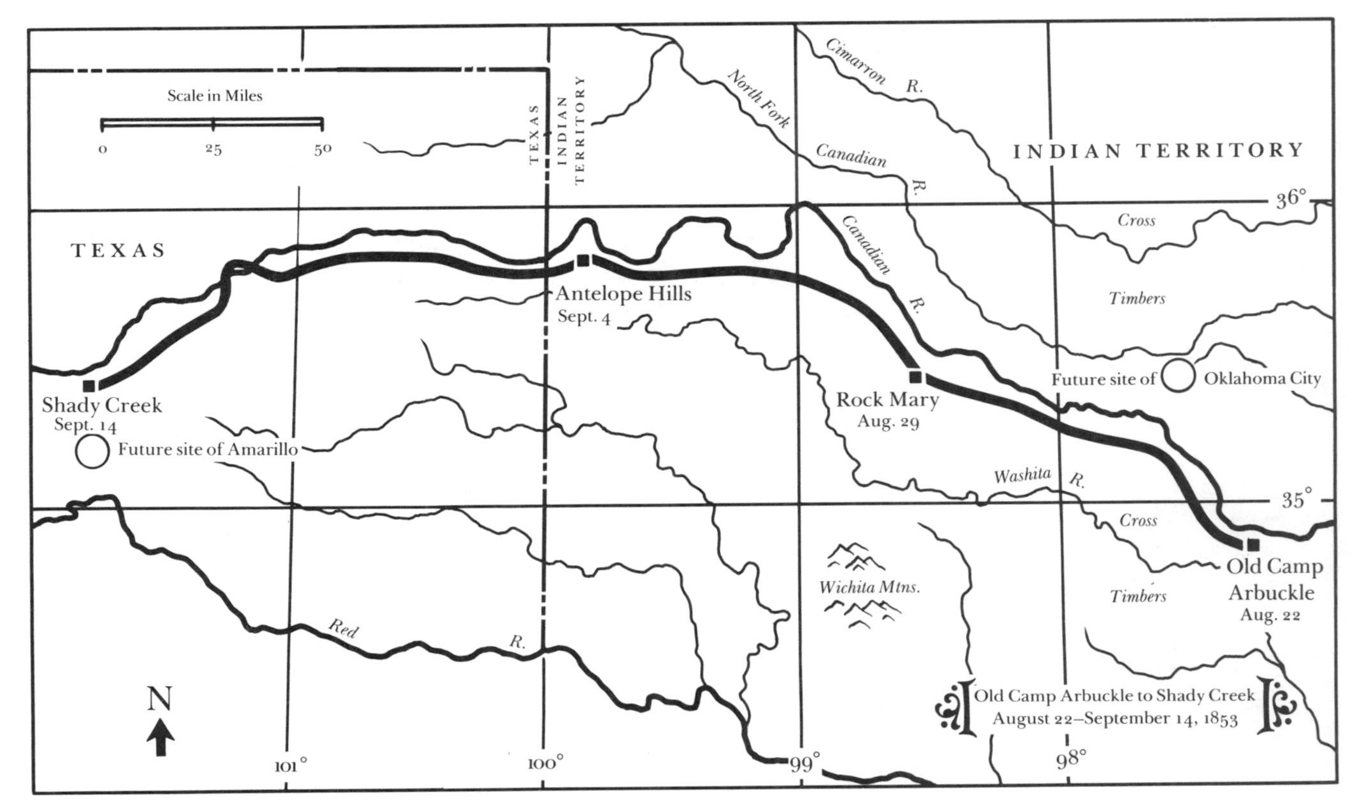

Old Camp Arbuckle to Shady Creek
August 22–September 14, 1853
INDIAN TERRITORY
TEXAS
TEXAS
INDIAN
TERRITORY
Scale in Miles
0
25
50
Cimarron R.
North Fork
Canadian R.
Canadian R.
Washita R.
Red R.
Cross
Timbers
Cross
Timbers
Wichita Mtns.
Future site of Oklahoma City
Future site of Amarillo
Shady Creek
Sept. 14
Antelope Hills
Sept. 4
Rock Mary
Aug. 29
Old Camp
Arbuckle
Aug. 22
36°
35°
101°
100°
99°
98°
N

ridge in the distance. Luckily for us, our days march was nearly over, & we found water, tho' poor, before we reached the fire. After camping, pitching tents, attending to animals & the necessaries of Camp life, we lit our pipes & lay down, to wait for that highly desired thing—"*Supper*"—But we were not destined to rest long. In a few minutes we heard the cry of "The Prairie is on fire." In another moment some one shouted, "Turn out, every man with a blanket." Then there was a general rush of Surveyors, Computers, Teamsters, Herdsmen, Cooks, Servants, etc. to the scene of conflict. Some with blankets & others with branches. It caught from a camp fire & luckily for us the wind blew the flames from the tents & wagons. The dried grass was so plentiful that the fire run back & it was with difficulty it could be stopped on the side towards Camp. However, it was finally done & the other side running into a ravine, the progress of the flames was soon arrested. Late in the evening we found that the fire started by the Indians was backing over the ridge a short distance from Camp in spite of the wind & would in a short time be down upon us. The only prevention was to start a fire to meet it. Near Camp was a line where the dried grass met the green. This was decided on as the starting point. After arming the men with wet blankets & thick branches, the fire was started. It was then about dark. In half an hour the prairie was on fire for miles & for the first time I saw for myself that which I've long desired to see—a *prairie on fire*. I can truly say I was not disappointed. The flames rolled up for 6 or 8 ft., perhaps more—10 ft., & the heavy columns of smoke for 50 ft. It was a magnificent sight. It burned for hours & long after we turned in, a dry tree would burst out in flames, illuminating everything around. The full moon rose over the scene & increased its splendor. It reminded me of that *old familiar piece of poetry:* "*The moon rose with her battlestained eye*," etc. It was a very amusing sight to see the fellows rush into the fire. They seemed in a moment to forget their 20 miles march & became quite excited. The Indians begin to trouble us soon. We anticipate much trouble from them before getting through, as they know of our coming for many miles ahead. Myriads of grasshoppers & other insects were in flight before the flames & a wolf was seen running full speed, with his tongue hanging from his mouth. We passed today close by the ridge separating the Canadian River from the prairie. In some places the ground was red, resembling powdered brick & very compact.

The herders returned this morning with the lost "beef," but no news of the mules—so we left them behind. Last night several meteors were seen as well as the night previous. Also a comet in the West, 12° N., Elevation 15°, with quite a long train. Mr. Whipple observed on it in the evening, 'tis supposed to be the one long expected by astronomers.[2] Gaines left us this morning as we started from Camp. He goes for Ft. Arbuckle, another of the party gone & another less for the Indians to scalp.

I noticed today some small birds called cow birds, so tame as to light on the backs of the animals. They were of a lead color & remained in camp most of the time.

Möllhausen, *Diary*, I, p. 106: "The Black Beaver gave us the benefit of his escort for the first day, and brought us to a spot where, on close examination, the tracks of old wagon wheels were discovered. It was the path by which, years before this, some Delawares had led Captain Marcy. 'Only go straight on along this road,' said the Beaver, as he left us, 'and you will come to the Rio Grande.' Nobody but an Indian, certainly, would have thought of calling it a road, where the eye could distinguish nothing of the kind."

August 23. Camp 23. Started rather early this morning—prairie burning all around in the distance. Travelled 11 miles & camped again. Today the birds lit on the backs of the mules & were so tame they could be struck down with a whip. I saw it done by one of the Teamsters.

Gave chase after a prairie wolf this morning but my mule was too slow & I was not able to get a shot. Also saw several prairie chickens & three fine deer. Most of our route over burnt prairie, the remains of the fire yesterday. Saw this morning a beautiful "mirage" making a perfect picture of a sheet of sparkling water—perfect enough to deceive those who were as little acquainted with it as myself. Our Mexican boy was thrown from his mule

[2] According to Möllhausen, who incorrectly noted that the comet was seen first on August 18, it was the comet observed by a noted German astronomer at Göttingen on June 10, 1853. In the southern hemisphere it was observed at the Cape of Good Hope early in January 1854. Möllhausen received this information from Alexander von Humboldt. Whipple, an avid astronomer, observed the comet closely until August 31. See Möllhausen, *Diary*, I, Notes, p. 345.

today, but not injured. The mule started at something in the bushes & as the saddle turned the boy went off with it. Before the frightened animal was caught, both stirrups were broken, saddle thrown off & broken in several pieces. "After gathering up the fragments," proceeded on. Fresh tracks of Indians seen in several places. In one place they crossed a sand hill & the dust had not settled where they stopped. There was a clump of bushes a short distance & it was quite evident they had crossed a few minutes before & were in the bushes.

Two Indians came into camp this evening about 4 o'clock. They told our Interpreter (Vincente) they were Keechis [Kichais] & were going to Wishitaw town. They had on buckskin leggins and a blue cloth wrapper round the waist. No covering on the upper part of the body. One had his hair braided behind—the front part hanging on his shoulders. His ears were pierced in about a dozen places & had pegs of wood placed in to keep the holes open. They had no rifles, but bows and arrows. After getting from them all the information possible, they were asked if they were hungry & signifying they were, they were carried to the table & done justice to what was placed before them. Shortly after they left Camp & we saw no more of them. They asked for tobacco, upon leaving, which was given them.

This evening had an oyster supper, quite an affair for the prairies. It was the cancelling of an old election bet between two members of the party. The bet took place before the last Presidential Election & in Mexico.[3]

The country still a vast prairie with a few scattering trees. The soil still having the reddish hue. Near Camp was a tree presenting such a peculiar appearance that it attracted the attention of everyone. The bark had peeled off leaving the wood perfectly white, & it looked precisely as though it had been whitewashed. The tree was Cotton wood. Camped on a branch of Walnut Creek.

[3]Stanley, Diary, Aug. 23, 1853, wrote that Lieut. Whipple gave the supper, using canned oysters, to settle a bet made with another member of the party (either Dr. Bigelow, George Garner, or William White, all of whom had served with him on the Mexican Boundary Commission in 1852). Whipple apparently had supported the Whig candidate, Gen. Winfield Scott, who was defeated by the Democrat Franklin Pierce.

A lithograph of Möllhausen's sketch of two Waco Indians who visited the expedition's camp on August 23, 1853. Lieutenant Whipple later complained that the artist failed to capture the "wild look" of the pair, though at the time he made no comment upon their appearance except to write that one of them looked sick. *Reports of Explorations and Surveys,* vol. III.

Whipple, Diary: "This evening two Ki-chais came into this camp. . . . They were feasted & smoked & then they confessed they were not Ki-chais but Huecos [Wacos]. . . . I called Vincente to talk with them. They could speak neither Spanish, English nor Comanche. But this did not disconcert my linguist. With a few grunts and hoots interlarded among signs with the hands and contorsions of every limb of the body, he carried on a most rapid & interesting conversation. It struck us all as being one of the most amusing sights we have ever witnessed. The words were of the Caddo language and the signs were those of the universal Indian race. Questions & answers were made with more rapidity in these signs than they could be uttered in any language. These mute symbols seem like the wings of thought soaring above the impediment of words."[4]

Möllhausen, *Diary*, I, pp. 114–35: "The newcomers belonged to the tribe of Wakos. . . . They were two tall, slender young men, their limbs almost girlishly delicate. . . . A light woollen blanket was wound round their hips, leaving the upper part of the body entirely bare; they wore leggings and mocassins of soft leather, and a quiver made of rich fur, and filled with poisoned arrows, was slung carelessly to their copper-colored shoulders; their youthful Indian faces were set in a frame of coal black hair, and were not without an expression of subtlety and cunning; red and blue lines were drawn, in Indian artistic style, round their eyes and over their prominent cheek-bones, and their scalp locks were fashionably dressed with coloured feathers."

August 24. Camp 24. Struck tents early this morning & followed the trail of yesterday, which we left, to Camp. We were guided by an Indian who came into Camp before we left, he said he was a Keechi. About 1½ miles from camp came to deep ravine which appeared impossible to cross with wagons. Some of the party crossed on mules & reported several ravines on the other side, worse & more impracticable. The Teamsters were then at work cutting through. The Indian had disappeared after endeavoring to entice some of the party to his village, which he said was a little distance ahead.

We were joined by another Indian [a Kichai] who while hunting fell in with us. He said the Indian who had just left us had *lied*, that we had left Marcy's trail before reaching the last camp (23) & taken the wrong trail.[5] An inducement being offered him,

[4]See Gregg, *Commerce of the Prairies*, p. 418, who wrote that the "language of signs" had become the medium of communication among the different bands and tribes and had been brought to perfection by the Plains Indians. The Waco Indians belonged to a small tribe of hunters and farmers who lived close to a village of Wichita Indians (Sherburne's "Wishitaw town"), near present-day Rush Springs, Oklahoma. Members of the two tribes frequently intermarried, and both belonged to the Caddoan linguistic family. Whipple collected a short list of their vocabulary, and Möllhausen sketched the two men. Whipple thought the sketch failed to capture the "wild look" of the pair. See Whipple, Diary, Aug. 23, 1853, Whipple Papers; *Reports of Explorations and Surveys*, III, Part III ("Indian Tribes"), p. 27; Foreman, ed., *Adventure on Red River*, p. 126.

[5]The first Indian was in fact another Waco; see the entry for August 26, below. The second Indian was a Kichai and Whipple collected from him another vocabulary. The wagon train now is traveling along the edge of the Cross Tim-

he consented to show us the road. We then turned back & in a heavy rain retraced our steps. The rain ceased after giving us a decided wetting. We passed by Camp 23 & after retracing our steps two miles beyond it, turned to the left, which shortly brought us to the proper road. After finding this we had several bad ravines to cross, in one of which was a fine stream of running water. About 4 o'clock, came to a stream 10 ft. wide & 5 ft. deep & no possible way of crossing without throwing a bridge across. As it was late & very little possibility of getting across before dark, camp was pitched but 7½ miles from the last. Little gained after a hard days work. Camped on Pecan [Walnut] Creek, so called on account of the quantity of nuts growing upon it.

The Teamsters were set at work constructing a crossing. The Indian said he would remain & go on with us tomorrow. The country was similar to that crossed yesterday. We came on several wild Turkeys, prairie chickens & one deer, but they were all *shy*. They keep off the prairie as much as possible as 'tis nearly all burned. The sheep gave out today & they were obliged to kill several, to prevent their dying a natural death. The cattle stand it quite well & as yet show no sign of fatigue. The comet was visible this evening as soon as dark. It appeared with increased brilliancy & with its train increased to about 7°. It was observed during the evening & presented a very interesting appearance through the telescope. Our Indian who had been with us during the day left in evening, promising to return in morning & travel one more day with us.

Stanley, Diary: "We were guided [later] today by a Keechio, a most rascally looking fellow."

August 25. Camp 25. Shortly after striking Camp this morning we came to a bad ravine, which they were obliged to fill up. The ravine which stopped us yesterday was crossed by the bridge which the Teamsters had constructed. We managed quite easily to keep the trail of Marcy as it became more distinct in the

---

bers, a belt of scrub extending north from the Brazos River in Texas and across Oklahoma into southern Kansas. Varying in width from five to thirty miles, the Cross Timbers formed a natural barrier between the prairie and the arid plains beyond. See Whipple, *Report*, Aug. 24, 26, 1853; Gregg, *Commerce of the Prairies*, pp. 360–61.

low ground. The country was more covered with timber than any we had crossed for some days. Last evening as one of the guard was "walking post" he saw an Indian making off with one of the mules. The Indian instantly disappeared & was nowhere to be found. The general alarm was given, we all picketted our saddle animals close to the tents, so as to hear them if they were moved. This however was unnecessary as we were not troubled any more. We are now obliged to sleep with our revolvers under our pillows.

Last night was the first that we were troubled by the Musquitoes, since leaving Ft. Smith. We camped in low ground & they came in myriads. All the sleeping in Camp, put together, would not make a good *nap*. We all lay till about 12 & finding we could not sleep, turned out & smoked for an hour or so to drive away the unwelcome guests but without effect. After that I wrapped myself in a blanket & nearly suffocated. It was a worse time than was described in the old song, where "They bite through boots & all." Everyone was stirring at daylight, & congratulating each other on their nights rest. Our Indian returned this morning, he said he slept in the timber on the hill where there were no musquitoes, thus showing his sagacity over ourselves. Ahead of us, the prairie was burning brightly all night, apparently a mile or two distant. I noticed along the route a great many flowers that are cultivated in the States. There were "Verbenas," "Fleur de Luis," "Marygolds" & various others of richer colors than those of the States. Passed the "Natural Mounds" spoken of by Marcy, but saw no curiosity in them, they were merely risings of dirt & stone.[6]

On our route came on a deserted Indian Camp by the side of a stream. A Buck-skin was hanging on a tree near by, cinders and remains of fire lying round. We crossed again the running stream of water today.

One of our "Beef" died on the route today, disease said to be the "Mullan."[7] We all regretted her not having been killed last

[6]These were not the singularly shaped Natural Mounds named and described in 1849 by Lieut. James Simpson, which the expedition reached only on August 29. Möllhausen described these landmarks as formations of red sandstone eight to ten feet high and resembling gigantic urns or vases. See *Diary*, I, pp. 154–55.

[7]Sherburne surely means "murrain" (frequently called anthrax or Texas fever), a disease that attacks domestic animals, especially cattle.

night as we were in need of a supply of *fresh meat*. Just as we were leaving camp this morning a negro hailed in sight & shortly after came into Camp. He proved to be from Little River with our mail, which was forwarded to that place by Capt. Montgomery [quartermaster at Fort Smith]. He was hailed with great rejoicing by all hands, but unfortunately for me I had no letters. There were however several papers (Boston Journals) which were highly acceptable on the prairie 250 miles from Ft. Smith. He left after delivering & taking a "lunch."

I saw this morning an original manner of washing one's face and hands. The Indian who was with us performed that ablution in the following manner. Taking a mouth full of water, he spirted it on his hands & after rubbing them together several times, placed the palms of both hands on his forehead, drawing them perpendicularly down to the chin. This he repeated several times. After washing in this manner, as much as his nature would admit of, he wiped both face and hands with his hair. Then being satisfied, lit his pipe and "squatted" for a smoke.

Travelled but 12½ miles today & stopped at Camp 25. As one of the Teamsters was unhitching team, a mule kicked him severely in the breast. It was some minutes before he could speak. The whole print of the animals feet were on his breast. Saw today several deer & some other game.

August 26. Camp 26. Just before starting from Camp an Indian belonging to the "Huico" [Waco] tribe came into Camp. He belonged to the same tribe as the one who lied to us & came to give us the good opinion of his tribe. He said the Huico Chief was coming into Camp to see us & had already started for Camp. We could not wait his pleasure & left without being able to see him. The Indian left but joined us again before many miles were over. He kept us on the right road.

After travelling a couple of miles, we came upon burning prairie in front of the train. It was travelling a "2-40 gait" towards us.[8] The train was turned off in a spot of green grass. We set fire to another place and 'twas with difficulty we could prevent its reaching the train. Finally got a place burned through and passed

[8]This gait was a fast trot. The record for a trotting mile at the time was two minutes and forty seconds. See Matthews, *A Dictionary of Americanisms*.

at a gallop. Immediately after getting through, the flames closed behind us, sending up clouds of flame and smoke. Several deer and four mustang seen on the route at a distance. The mustang followed us all day. We came to the Emigrant Trail leading into Marcy's and which Marcy speaks of in his map.

Part of the day was rainy & cool. After getting into Camp there was quite a storm, accompanied with thunder & lightening. Made 12½ miles.

Stanley, Diary: "Left camp this morning accompanied by a most villainous looking Wacoh as a guide."

August 27. Camp 27. Last night was the coldest we have had. Ther. this morning 57°, & everyone was rigged out in flannel & overcoats. It continued very cold & showery during day. Our Indian left us this morning as his horse was sick & he could go no farther. On the route met with the remains of an ox team. The wheels & portions of team & ox bones were lying round in a space of 50 ft. Saw today several mustang, turkeys, prairie chickens, & 13 deer, among the lot only one Turkey was killed, tho' numerous shots were fired. Route covered with yellow crocus & daisy. Made 15½ miles. Several late Indian Camps were seen & near this Camp an Indian hut was found, constructed of sticks bent in a bow form & bark placed as thatching or roofing.

Just after arriving at Camp, Campbell took his mule to water in the neighboring creek. The bank was very steep & of soft clay, bearing the resemblance of stone. He tread on the edge when his feet slipped & he slid down the whole length of the bank, about 12 ft., running his feet & legs into the water. Quite a laugh was raised at his expense.

August 28. Camp 28. Very little of interest occurred along the route today. Quite a quantity of small game was seen from which two turkeys & a rabbit were procured. About 9½ [9:30 a.m.] came in sight of the Canadian, apparently about ½ a mile on our right. Saw it only once during day. Came on a deserted Indian Camp similar to the one of yesterday, belonging to the "Kickapoo" tribe. An old Indian horse was also met with nearly dead & vultures flying over him waiting for their prey. He was nearly dead & appeared the *perfect image of despair.* It would have been a good deed had someone put a rifle ball through his head &

ended his misery, as well as completing the joy of his enemies the "Buzzards."

One of the soldiers went asleep today while riding a mule. I noticed him rolling to & fro & finally his mule stopped short in the road. The fellow remained still, with his head down & appeared perfectly unconscious of what was going on around him. It was not till the Caratella struck his leg, that he seemed conscious of the real state of things. Opening his eyes he looked wild for a few moments, then foolish, & started ahead. I have often heard of sleeping in strange places & in strange manners, but never before on the back of a mule, exposed to the rays of a hot mid-days sun. Travelled 14 miles today.

I have received a very different idea of the prairies, from what I had formed. Instead of a long level barren space, I find it so far a series of waves, as it were, or ridges, rising & falling alternately. There have been but very few views where neither shrub or tree could be seen. The soil is a red marl, in many cases sand-stone. Flowers abound, among which the Cactus is by no means the least. You find of it a variety of species, some with oblong & some with spherical leaves.

August 29. Camp 29. Today we made a march of 19½ miles & during the whole days march we saw not a drop of water excepting what was brought from the last Camp. Several objects of interest were seen along the road, the most interesting of which was Rock Mary so called by Marcy. We passed, with it on our left, several others of nearly the same height on the other side of road. Rock Mary was a circular pile of rock—red sand-stone, 160 ft. in height & with the sides making an angle of 45°. Many of the party ascended to the top, where they found a quantity of names, probably belonging to some of Marcy's party, as the dates corresponded to the time of his passing the place.[9] They said the

[9]Rock Mary was the most striking of the Natural Mounds, situated near present-day Hydro, Oklahoma. Young officers with the 1849 Marcy expedition named it after Mary Conway, a "belle of the prairie" traveling with an emigrant train escorted by Capt. Marcy. Lieut. Simpson estimated the height of the rock as only 60 feet, and wrote that in form it was like a pound cake, well puffed up. Whipple remarked that the mounds varied in height from 75 to 100 feet. The wagon train now is leaving the Cross Timbers. See Simpson, "Report," p. 7; *Reports of Explorations and Surveys*, III ("Extracts from Preliminary Report"), p. 11; Hollon, *Beyond the Cross Timbers*, p. 64.

view from the top was magnificent. As far as the eye could reach was rolling prairie, interspersed with scattering trees. Beneath them rolled on the train (not cars) & party, the bright bayonets of the escort & fire arms of the party glistening in the sun added to the interest and beauty of the scene. I regret having lost it.

As we neared Rock Mary, two deer started from a clump of bushes & after running parallel to the train for some distance crossed the road ahead of us & bounded away.

At this camp the elevation was much higher than any point before attained on the route. It was on the rolls of the prairie, beside a fine stream of water & where there were a large quantity of Turkeys.

The Comet appeared tonight with increased brilliancy, the trail was from 16° to 18° in length. It set very rapidly. One of the Teamsters—an old man—was kicked tonight by a mule. He made considerable fuss about it, but recovered very rapidly when the Dr. spoke of bleeding him. Before the Dr. returned with his Instruments, the old man had taken a *chew of tobacco & left.*

August 30. Camp 30. Just before leaving Camp this morning I was shown by Vincente the manner the Comanches make fire. He took two small round sticks, making a hole in one & pointing one end of the other. Placing the pointed end into the hole, he gave to the stick a rapid circular motion by rubbing it between his hands, causing sufficient friction between the portions of wood in contact to char it & cause it partially to ignite. It furnishes a useful manner for lighting pipes when matches are scarce, tho' *rather* hard on the hands. The route today was not very interesting until late in the afternoon.

We travelled 16½ miles. Several deer were seen crossing the track in advance of us. The first Buffalo was seen today, by the Dr. I did not get a sight of it. One of the party professed to have seen a Rocky Mountain goat, but the story was not generally credited by the party. It was supposed to be a deer. Half a dozen antelope seen today.

In the afternoon we came to the first gypsum hill [near present-day Arapaho, Oklahoma]. On the sides of the hill were numerous openings & on riding over the top it sounded hollow, showing it to be one vast cavern inside. One of the apertures, larger than the rest, was entered as far as practicable by a member of the party. At the opening was a vaulted arch, about 6 ft. in height. Passing through an aperture in the sand, there was a vaulted cavern of about 8 ft. in height & to all appearances this arrangement of caverns proceeded for some distance before reaching the large one. It could be entered no further on account of the smallness of the entrance, which was a disappointment to the scientific, curious, & adventurous. Two meteors, one of which was very brilliant, were seen this evening. Also the Comet which had decreased in brilliancy & was evidently rapidly leaving the earth. Left Marcy's trail this morning.

Möllhausen, *Diary*, I, p. 163: "The journey through this gypsum region lasted five days: towards the end of the time the want of good water was much felt, and every one had to quench his thirst with a bitter draught. Unfortunately it was found not only that the thirst became more troublesome than ever, but a general feeling of indisposition prevailed throughout the party, and the food, which seemed also affected by a disagreeable flavor, became quite distasteful to us. Under these circumstances it will not seem surprising that much of our accustomed good humour and cheerfulness disappeared, and that we jogged along, with as much patience as we could, but in a very dull mood."

Stanley, Diary, Aug. 31st to Sept. 4th: "During this time, owing to sickness . . . no daily record of occurrences has been kept. Gypsum abounds extensively through this entire region and the water is made very nauseous by the great amounts of salts it holds in solution."

August 31. Camp 31. Quite a quantity of Indian signs were met with on the route today. Signal fires were seen, one in front of us & apparently a great distance in advance. As we encamped in the evening, a bright fire was visible in the Eastward, apparently burning prairie. We also had evidence of an Indian Camp. Many Indians were doubtless round camp during the night but we saw nothing of them. Occasionally we heard the hooting of an owl, sometimes near, sometimes in the distance. Supposed by some to be Indian signals. The route was a continuation of rolling prairie, interspersed with numerous water courses, some of which were difficult to pass. The water was strongly impregnated with sulphate of magnesia & very brackish. Great difficulty was found in crossing one of the streams; the train was delayed several hours. Ten mules could with difficulty draw the teams up the steep bank. In the evening we camped quite late, after making a march of 12½ miles, on a running stream [Comet Creek], about 15 ft. in width & in some places several ft. deep.

A tree was met with on the route, on which were engraved a U.S. Coat of Arms & a ship at Sea, also the inscription, "Pat Kearny," "July 7th, 1849" (or 1851 could not be discerned which) "Liberty." Supposed to be one of Marcy's party of 1849.[10] Passed one stream full of large green turtle, fish called *gar*, buffalo & cat fish. On the banks were partridges & wild ducks. Two bears & several deer were seen today. The bears were fired at & one of them struck, but they escaped without chance for another shot. Prairie wolves, also, were seen. Shortly after arriving in Camp a herder killed ten rattlesnakes, two old & eight young ones. The former about 6 ft. in length. As we were leaving Camp this morning, one of our mess shot an immense turkey, which served as two meals for eleven men.

September 1. Camp 32. This morning we had rather a late start, as we were encamped on a stream which 'twas necessary [to] bridge before crossing. The route was quite good. Made 15½ miles & camped 3½ p.m.

Just as the train came up a deer started from the thicket & struck into the open prairie. About a dozen of us started after it & had a splendid chase of a couple of miles on our mules before bringing it down. We all fired on a full gallop & when the deer fell he had six balls in him. The chase was very exciting & much enjoyed on my part.

As we left Camp this morning the escort Corporal undertook to have a fit. He fell under one of the wagons, which passed over his foot. The wagon alone weighs 1500 lbs., saying nothing of the baggage. Strange to say, it only bruised his leg & foot, not breaking a bone. He was put into a wagon & the train proceeded. This morning saw a herd of nine antelope. Fired at them several times but missed, they *would not* get within shot.

September 2. Camp 33. Today we were delayed by numerous streams, which [we] were obliged to prepare before crossing. Made a March of 14 miles. Water very brackish, containing great

[10] Pat Kearny was not with the Marcy expedition, which reached its destination of Santa Fe on June 28, 1849. On this day Whipple expressed admiration for the richness of the valleys of the Washita and Canadian rivers, which he considered eminently suitable for a railroad route; see his *Report*, Aug. 31, 1853.

quantities of Sulphate of Magnesia. It is a regular "shothecary pop"[11] & make no mistake. On the bank of one of the streams saw a carcass of a Buffalo which to all appearances had fallen over the bank & died.

Prairie burning round us all night & we feared it would be down on Camp but the wind prevented it. It presented a beautiful appearance in the evening. A line of fire was visible as far as the eye could reach. Today in places the prairie grass reached even to the top of my head, while riding along.

The Comet has disappeared & is no longer visible, which much disappoints the astronomers of the party (?).

I learned today from our Mexican boy, a simple method of curing the ring-worm. "Scratch it till red and rub on gunpowder until it smarts, or rub it with the top of the bark of a green walnut."

We passed today over a small hill which appeared composed mostly of oyster shells. It is probable hundreds of miles from any oyster beds of the present-day.

September 3. Camp 34. This morning just after starting from Camp, we got into the prairie fire. It was burning both sides of us & we were obliged to run the gauntlet between them. Had our longest days march of 21 miles. Passed the point where Marcy's trail takes the Emigrant trail.[12] We followed this trail towards the Canadian & camped at 6 p.m. on a small creek of brackish water.

Saw the Canadian on the right about ½ mile & the "Antelope hills" so called, about 14 miles ahead of us. The character of the country changed as we approached the Canadian. From the rolling prairie, came small mounds & ravines, making for us a very difficult road. On the route saw a quantity of Buffalo bones & chase was given a *live* Buffalo but without effect. The Buffalo was now all farther north grazing. Any quantity of deer & other game seen during the day, among other things, a herd of Ante-

[11] "Shothecary" may refer to a soda or pop bought in an apothecary's shop, hence the "rhyme." Druggists or apothecaries sold sodas at this time. From camps 30 to 33, the expedition passed through the fertile Washita Valley.

[12] According to Whipple, Camp 34 was the end of the emigrant "cut-off" taken by Marcy for a few miles. The camp (Marcy's Camp 40) was near present-day Strong City, Oklahoma. See Whipple, *Report*, Sept. 3, 1853.

lope & a black bear. We passed out of the Gypsum country today but the water still continues brackish, excepting deposits of rain water.

At 6 p.m. we arrived at Camp. Our usual hour for breakfast is 6 a.m. & for dinner 8 p.m., a stretch of 14 hours between meals & rather too long for a person of my appetite. Were it not for a lunch I take along there might be a case of "found starved." The prairie grass was very high today reaching in some places 6 in. above my head. It is the intention to lay by tomorrow to rest animals & allow the party to do their washing. The latter is very desirable as several weeks have elapsed since we've laid by. They hope to entice some Indians into Camp, give them presents, etc.

Most of the party object to stopping here, as the water is bad & we have encamped in a little basin, surrounded by hills so the breeze cannot reach us. It will be exceedingly warm. As yet we have seen no Indians at all of the Comanche tribe. No doubt they are all around us & following us, as we occasionally see fresh signs of them.

I expect our first visit from them will be in the night in search of mules.

September 4. Camp 35. This morning everything was arranged for remaining in Camp, but the water was so brackish & salt as to render it unfit both for washing and drinking. Soap would decompose & become useless. Mr. Whipple was persuaded to go on until we found good water. Starting about 8 a.m. we proceeded along the Canadian "bottom" for 12½ miles, then striking in to high land, found a fine spring of water, with a pond by the side of it from 10 to 12 ft. deep. We pitched tents & formed "corral" on table land close by, about 3 p.m.

In the night, about 3 o'clk, a loud noise was heard in the vicinity of Camp, which sounded like human voices. I was asleep & did not hear it. Those of the party hearing it went out with their revolvers & *came back* again without any satisfaction. It was supposed to be Indians or deer and was heard by the sentinals. Just before starting from Camp, 3 deer came down to drink, as they saw us they stopped a minute and then bounded away. Saw on the route any quantity of Buffalo carcasses, supposed to have been destroyed by the wolves. A herd of animals was seen in the distance, supposed to be Buffalo.

September 5. Lay by today & there was a general turn out for washing. Everyone appeared busily engaged & shortly after sunrise the ground, tent-cords, tents & every place, were covered with clothes drying in the sun. The pond of water was a ley[lye]-pot, with soap-suds in any quantity floating on the surface & looking like a vast washing-tub. The bank was lined with men washing, presenting a *picturesque* appearance. Our Camp today is by far the best we have yet had. Situated on a high table land with a view for miles on every side & where the refreshing prairie-breeze could sweep over us. The evening was fine. The distant sky in the South & West was illuminated by the prairie fires. The full moon had risen over the Camp & every-thing was clothed in the splendor of a moonlight evening. This was soon brought to a close. About 10 p.m. a few "Nimbus" clouds appeared in the North, old Boreas [north wind] opened on us & it was with difficulty we could keep our tents from coming down on our heads. The rain also favored us with a little shower. This lasted a short time, but until morning the air was quite cold.

During the heat of the day, the Ther. was 101 degrees, very warm. The day passed without a sign of an Indian in Camp. On a distant hill appeared to be an Indian standing by the side of his horse, but as the object remained stationary for several hours it cannot be supposed that it was a human being. We want them in Camp but they appear afraid of us. Tomorrow we leave.

September 6. Camp 36. Just after starting from Camp this morning (for our Caratella came before the train) we came to a sandy creek with rather steep bank, tho' low. I waited on the opposite side for the Caratella to cross. It started & as one front wheel struck the sand, down it sunk. The Caratella remained poised for a few minutes on two wheels, then gradually going over, it fell directly across a puddle, spilling White, Driver, & contents into said puddle. At first I scarcely dared smile, but as White raised his head above the bars, still standing in the water, the scene was so ridiculous that I could not restrain myself from bursting in a loud laugh. We examined the Caratella & found nothing broken but the Whiffle-tree. Then came the Instruments, for we had all the Chronometers, 3 Barometers, several Thermometers, and other kind of *obs"ometers"*. We found only one Bar^{r}. broken though we expected to find them all. The sextant & artificial horizon box were wet, but this was soon remedied. The Dr. & servant came along just then as if sent providentially. After enjoying a hearty laugh at our mishap, we raised the Caratella & put things in order before the arrival of the train.

The Dr. in the meantime found several new Botanical specimens & no doubt felt grateful to us for capsizing & leading him to the place. Every thing being in readiness, we again started on the route. I went ahead & took the station on the top of the next hill, about 1½ miles distant, so as to allow the Surveyor to continue & not delay the train for us. After reaching the station I waited a long time for White to come. Getting tired I dismounted, seated myself on the ground & using my mules forelegs to lean against, I went to work bringing up my Journal which had got far behind. I waited an hour. The train was two miles on the one side & Caratella not visible on the other. The thought struck me that something must have happened so, mounting, I turned back to satisfy myself as to the cause. I had gone about ¾ of a mile when I saw an Indian crossing the road in front of me. He stopped, looked around, then recrossing the road, again disappeared. On riding to the spot, no one was visible. I began to fear that White was in trouble, but my fears were soon dispelled when little farther on I heard him coming.

The cause of the delay was the loss of the viameter from the wheel. The sand on it prevented the spring from holding it. Having passed ½ mile before missing it caused the great delay. His pistol was wet & unfit for use. He had my rifle & I a "six-shooter," but there was no necessity for them as no Indians were seen. Mr. Whipple being very anxious about us, had waited several miles farther on, at Antelope Hills.[13]

Plenty of game today, five Buffalo were seen and fired at, one deer killed & 5 Turkeys. Antelope & prairie dogs were also seen. Made today 17¾ miles & camped on Canadian with very bad

[13] The Antelope Hills are near the intersection of the Canadian River and the 100th meridian, which at the time denoted the western boundary of Indian Territory. On this day the wagon train leaves present-day Oklahoma and crosses into the Texas Panhandle. The expedition, which had been moving north and west, now is heading directly west. It camped about 3½ miles west of the present Texas-Oklahoma line, and will follow Josiah Gregg's route of 1840; the Marcy route in 1849 moved well away from the Canadian River. At Camp 42 on Sept. 12 the wagon train returns to the Marcy route.

water. On the opposite side is a high bank of white sand ½ mile long & about 20 ft. in height. On the route found quite a vineyard with an abundance of small blue grapes, very sweet & nice.

September 7. Camp 37. One of the most exciting scenes occurred on the route today that we've yet had. We had travelled some hours on the route. The Dr., as usual, had strayed away from the train to the bank of the Canadian to Botanize. Very little was thought of him until we heard seven shots in rapid succession, then a cessation & six more. We knew 'twas a "six-shooter" & rifle, by the report. Lieut. Jones, commander of escort, rode in that direction & as he rose to the brow of a small hill, he saw, as he thought, two horsemen, to all appearances Indians riding at a furious rate about a mile distant & where the Dr. was supposed to be. He rode back, took six mounted escort & started at full gallop. Several of us, unable to withstand the excitement, started also. The party numbered twelve. We kept on a mile, expecting every moment to see Comanches. All were in the highest state of excitement. Dr. no where to be seen. We still kept on at a gallop, each urging his animal to the utmost with sticks & spurs. Away we went over hill & dale, until we came to the Bank of the Canadian. There the mystery was at once solved. In the middle of the Canadian & standing on a sand-bar was a large Buffalo. He was wounded & José (Mr. W's servant) approaching him. Another was seen lumbering off in the distance. We swam our animals into the river & reached the sand-bar. The Buffalo was already wounded with six pistol balls & stood at bay. A rifle ball from one of the party [Lieut. Stanley] struck him in the side. Standing motionless a few moments he fell with his death wound & was dispatched in a short time.

He was a noble fellow. After depriving him of his tongue, we left him a prey for the wolves & panthers, being so far from the train we could take none of the meat. Riding back, we met the Dr. who had fired several shots at a rattle snake. This accounted for all the shooting we had heard. We rode back to the train where we arrived in a couple of hours, found them all waiting anxiously for the news. They were soon satisfied & the train proceeded again.

Two of the party who were later returning than the rest met two Comanches & brought them to the train. After going along with us for some time they left us, saying their Camp was about 2 miles distant & they would bring the rest of their party.

They disappeared & have not since been seen. They came probably to learn the strength of the party & their chances of stealing animals. In answer to the inquiry "Are there many Comanches here?" They said, holding up their hands, "Mucho, mucho, m-u-cho Comanche," at the same time pointing all around. A pipe was offered them. Taking a puff, they blew it at the sun & muttered something, then at the ground with a few more words.

We expected a call from them during the night but were disappointed. Today made a march of 16¼ miles along the bank of Canadian. The soil was very sandy & very difficult for the animals to pull through. Arrived at the Camp [near present-day Canadian, Texas] quite late in the evening. Several of the party went hunting on our arrival. One of them saw a panther. It was howling round Camp all night & sounded like a child crying. Another one of the party shot a Turkey about dark & in his haste to get it jumped into a water hole up to his armpits. He hauled himself out as soon as possible leaving the Turkey to its fate & returned to Camp. The night was quite cold. Ther. 53° which made us pull up the blankets before morning.

During the day passed a prairie-dog haunt. The ground was filled with holes but none of them could be seen. Thermometer this morning at sunrise 53°.4— 3p.m. 83°.2.

Whipple, *Report*: "The relief party, scouring the prairies, found a wounded buffalo, which one of them kindly pierced with a rifle ball and put out of its misery. It was the first killed upon the trip, and consequently a glorious achievement. A short distance beyond they came across a small party of well-mounted Comanches, whom they brought in prisoners. The Indians appeared wary, cautious, and watchful. Having told us that upon the other side of the Canadian there were large numbers of their tribe, they suddenly forgot all their Spanish, and by signs desired us to know that they could not understand a word we said to them. Indians think it undignified to speak other than their native tongue. Hence, all great chiefs have interpreters. We sought for Vincente, but, as usual when wanted, he was chasing buffalo or deer over the prairies. That is his passion. The Indians declined our invitation to camp. Before allowing them to depart we gave them a pipe and tobacco to smoke. They performed the operation in a singular manner. The first two puffs, with much ceremony and muttering between, were sent towards the sun. The next, in similar manner, was blown down to the ground. When the artist had taken their portraits, they were allowed to go."

Möllhausen, *Diary*, I, p. 182: "The visitors were two gloomy-looking, elderly warriors mounted on magnificent horses, which obeyed in the most graceful manner the slightest touch of the rein fastened to their lower jaw, and seemed to form one body with their riders, who rode without saddles. A blue blanket formed the only clothing of these savages, and they held their bows and arrows in readiness for immediate use, while the wildness of their appearance was much increased by the very long hair that fell round and partially covered their bronze faces."

September 8. Camp 38—Ther. sunrise 55°.9— 3 p.m. 84°— On Canadian. Made a march today of 18¼ miles through sandy soil. After arriving at Camp we found several specimens of agate and Jasper, some quite fine. Crossed today "Dry River." The particular peculiarity of this river is that during the night there is running water & during the day it is dry. The sand is of such a peculiar quality that as soon as the sun strikes it the water rapidly disappears. Numerous prairie dogs were seen today looking from their holes but none could be shot.

Any quantity of grapes were found on the route. At a place a quarter of a mile from Camp there is an immense vineyard, for the space of a few square yards there must have been half a dozen bushels. Several bushels were brought into Camp & the Cooks set to work making pies, etc. Opposite Camp is a range of high hills looking like an immense rampart. It extends as far as the eye can reach on both sides & puts one in mind of the Chinese Wall. We were troubled today by myriads of Buffalo gnats. They got in ones ears, eyes, nose, & in every possible place to render themselves disagreeable. They were very small & scarcely discernable. Game today has been rather scarce. Nothing of any consequence has been seen. The creek just crossed & where the grapes were found has been called "Grape Creek"—

September 9. Camp 39— Ther. sunrise 56°.5— 4 p.m. 84°.2— on Canadian.

Today there has been a series of interesting incidents from the time of leaving Camp in the morning untill our encampment again in the evening.

About an hour after starting came upon an old Comanche Camp, which had been deserted in the Spring for Buffalo hunting & was all ready for their reception again on their return before winter.

There were three "Corral" yards with the cross-poles lying all ready for use. There were also poles standing for their tents to be stretched upon. It was evident it had not been occupied for some months. A little farther we came on the remains of an extensive Camp. To all appearances occupied within two days. It extended for a long distance & calculated to have contained several hundred. There were signs of a large number of horses. Some of the bushes & vines were not entirely dead & the ground was cut up with the feet of their animals.

About one o'clock several of those who headed the train, as they reached the summit of the hill, gave the cry of "Comanches," "a Comanche Camp ahead." As we rose the hill, the Camp was visible in a small grove, at the foot of the next rise. Their horses were also seen & everything gave evidence of a large Indian Camp. We halted, every one examined his revolver & rifle to see that they were in shooting order. Our Interpreter, Vincente, was sent ahead with a white handkerchief, a sign of friendship. We all followed him slowly, knowing we would either be received as friends or be obliged to fight. Shortly we saw our Interpreter returning with an Indian, the Indian holding the signal of friendship in his hand. He was a Chief. He first met the Dr. whom he welcomed by putting both arms round his neck & embracing him. The next he welcomed was Lieut. Jones & in the same manner. The remainder were only honored with a shake of the hand. After him came six or seven other Indians who shook hands with us & *appeared exceedingly* glad to see us. They proved to be Kioways.[14] After the usual necessary performance of grunting was over, they led the way to their Camp. It was composed of near a dozen huts. Mostly of cloth but several also of skins. In all

[14] The Kiowa, allies of the Comanche since 1790, were similar nomadic people dependent upon the buffalo for their livelihood and fierce in protecting their territory. Like Comanches they were notorious among Anglo-Americans and Mexicans for their raids along the Santa Fe Trail, on New Mexican villages, and into Texas and Mexico. The expedition's camp is beside a stream flowing into the south bank of the Canadian, which Whipple mistakenly identified as Valley River, the name given by Lieut. Simpson in 1849 to another creek twenty miles westward. The correct name was Indian Creek. See Simpson, "Report," p. 11; Archambeau, ed., "Lieutenant A. W. Whipple's Railroad Reconnaissance," p. 77.

there were about twenty Indians, as many squaws, numerous "squallus." They had about five hundred horses which made us think at first their Camp was much larger. As they were anxious for us to encamp near them, we encamped about a quarter mile distant on the same stream. After entering their camp we saw several Mexicans who proved to be traders from Santa Fe.[15] They were much rejoiced at our arrival for they had about exhausted their stock of goods & feared robbery & perhaps murder from the Indians. They immediately decided to return with us the next morning. After we had got into Camp we learned there were three Mexican prisoners with the Indians & we understood they desired to return with us. Two of them were men & the other a girl about 18 yrs. of age. A council was held with the Indians & they appeared very friendly until it was proposed to buy these captives. Then they were quite indignant & most of them left the Camp, saying it was not the part of friends to try & take their Captives. After they had gone, the matter was discussed, whether they should be taken by force or left prisoners. No decision could be arrived at. It was known very well if they were taken by force it would raise the Kioway and Comanche tribes against us, so as to nearly if not entirely stop the Survey. It was finally concluded to go & see if they wished to return & to see if they were well treated & happy. It was found in conversing with them that they had been in Captivity for seven years. The two men had no desire to go back. The girl was the wife of a chief & had a child several years old.[16] She wished to return yet

[15] Commonly called *Comancheros*, a term coined or popularized by Josiah Gregg in *Commerce of the Prairies* (1844), New Mexican and Pueblo Indian traders had moved across the plains since the late eighteenth century to barter bread, flour, and corn meal for the horses, mules, buffalo robes, and meat supplied by the Comanches and Kiowas. August and September were the chief trading months. Kiowas, unlike Comanches, had a bad reputation with the traders. By 1860 the *Comancheros* had become notorious because of their traffic in guns and whiskey. See Kenner, *History of New Mexican–Plains Indian Relations*, especially Chaps. 4 and 8, for a fine study of this trade.

[16] One of the Mexican males had been captured five years before; the woman, wife of the old chief, had been a captive for seven years. One man, Andres Nuñares, told Whipple that he had no desire to leave since he was well treated and owned considerable property in mules and horses. He gave Whipple a Kiowa vocabulary. Particularly interesting because the Kiowa language bore little resemblance to other Indian languages (except for a puzzling similarity to the language of the Taos Pueblo in New Mexico), this vocabulary was the first

she appeared quite happy & quite probable was as contented as she would have been in Mexico. She was quite good looking, but not *pretty*. It was resolved not to interfere with them but leave them to their fate.

I went down to their camp just before dark for the purpose of satisfying myself as to their mode of living & in fact, like a Yankee, to pry into everything. The Indians were anything but an inviting looking set, tho' several of them were quite passable.

I noticed among the squaws, very small feet and in some quite regular features. Their tents were formed of several poles tied together at the top, the bottom spreading on the ground. They were from 10 to 12 ft. in height. Hanging in one part of the camp was an immense & splendid head-dress, formed with different colored feathers so long that it must have trailed on the ground. In another place was hung a scalp—probable that of an Indian Chief of some other tribe. On my approach towards it, I was warned back by the cries & signs of the Indians, who were not willing that I should even look at it. One of the squaws appeared very much pleased with my knife & pistol. Drawing the knife from the scabbard, she examined it very closely, then signifying that 'twas good, restored it to its place. Then seeing the butt of the pistol shining, she drew it partly out, but on discovering what it was pushed it in again, covering it with the nap of the holster & signifying for me not to use it. Presents were made them, among which was a "Beef"—after firing a couple of arrows into it, they drove it to their camp and dispatched it. They [the Kiowa warriors] were ornamented in every possible shape. Several of them had large circular silver ornaments, hanging from their head nearly to the ground, growing smaller as they went down, the top one being several inches in diameter & the smaller a half an inch. One had a silver cross hanging from his neck.[17] In the evening we heard them singing in a wild strain, occasionally laughing and shouting. Made 11½ miles today.

---

studied by ethnologists at the Smithsonian Institution. See Whipple, Diary, Sept. 8, 1853, Whipple Papers; *Reports of Explorations and Surveys*, III, Part III ("Indian Tribes"), p. 80; Kenner, *History of New Mexican–Plains Indian Relations*, pp. 214–15.

[17] Whipple speculated that the cross was probably a trophy from a raid on some Mexican church. But crosses, usually bought by Plains Indians at the Taos

A lithograph of Möllhausen's drawing of the camp where the Kiowas were surprised by the Whipple expedition on September 9, 1853. Note the "immense and splendid head-dress" that so impressed John Sherburne. Courtesy David Miller.

Stanley, Diary: "Our party was put on the qui vive about ten o'clock upon our coming upon a very large, newly formed Indian trail and still more so by our seeing shortly afterward a herd of Indian ponies. Mr. Whipple and our Mexican to the advance and after going about a mile, or thereabouts, we came in sight of their lodges. . . . We had completely surprised them—and such a commotion! The children, women and dogs broke for the woods, the warriors for their horses and one old chief came out in the innocent garb of nature, to learn our intentions. Having shown him the white flag he came up and embraced us. The Doctor,

---

Pueblo fair, had been traded among Indians for high prices since the seventeenth century. They were seen as emblems of military rank and usually worn by chiefs. Whipple wrote that some of his men tried to buy the fine ornaments but there was nothing in the train to vie with their magnificence and tempt the Kiowas to exchange their property. See Whipple, *Report*, Sept. 9, 1853; *The American Heritage Book of Indians*, p. 379; Kenner, *History of New Mexican–Plains Indian Relations*, p. 14.

who I pointed out as a Medicine Man, came in for an extra hug from this stalwart chief. . . . We visited the camp in the evening and I was most completely disgusted with their domestic life—and felt as though I never had more reason for thanking God that I was born civilized."

Whipple, *Report*: "We pitched camp on a slight eminence overlooking the village, and could not but admire their selection of ground. Valley River [Indian Creek] and the Canadian are at this point fringed with timber, and the wide meadows are covered with a thick carpet of grass. Scarcely were the tents pitched when the Kai-o-was began to assemble for the counsel. A wilder-looking set can scarcely be imagined. Cunning, duplicity, and treachery, seemed stamped upon every lineament of their features."

September 10. Camp 40. Ther. sunrise 56.°9— 3 p.m. 89°.

This morning before leaving Camp we had all the Indians, squaws & pappooses of the country in to see us. One old fellow had on a military coat buttoned up to the chin, no pants, a blanket being wound round the waist & dragging on the ground.[18] They brought some of their horses for sale, the price being $20, but as no trust can be put in them, no one thought it advisable to purchase. The Mexican traders came up with their pack mules & donkeys, numbering about twenty. As the Country ahead of us for several miles was composed of numerous sand hills which 'twas thought doubtful whether we could cross or not, took the advice of the Mexicans & crossed the Canadian. Travelled several miles on the other side & recrossed. Considerable trouble was found in crossing on account of the quicksand. Two of the wagons "stalled" & with some trouble were got out again. The water where we crossed was about 3½ ft. deep. The Dr. when he crossed got into the quicksand. His mule sunk to his belly—then rolled over, tumbling the Dr. into the mud & water to the amusement of the bystanders & "lookers on." We travelled 16 miles

[18] Whipple noted the "fine blue blankets" worn by the Kiowas. One of the chiefs told him that the Indian agent of the region had given them to his people. Blue blankets were given to Apaches, Comanches, and Kiowas to celebrate the Fort Atkinson (Kansas) Treaty of July 27, 1853. Under the Treaty, signed only three weeks before, the Indians received annuities in goods in return for agreeing to the establishment of military posts and some rights of way through their territory. The Indian chiefs also agreed, under protest, to return their Mexican captives, but Indian agents could do little more than fruitlessly urge the chiefs to cooperate with this clause. See Whipple, *Report*, Sept. 8, 1853; Hagan, *United States–Comanche Relations*, pp. 15–16.

taking into consideration the crossing & the recrossing of the river. In a direct line was about 12 miles. Country very barren—soil sandy.

Quite an amusing incident occurred after arriving at Camp. Mr. Marcou, our Geologist, went into the Mexicans Camp & endeavoring to speak Spanish by a construction from French he asked them, as he thought, to come into Camp—but by a mispronunciation of words, they understood it as an invitation to supper. Shortly after, a couple of the greasy Mexicans[19] came down & took supper in his mess—much to the annoyance of the Scientific gentlemen but amusement of everyone else.

Stanley, Diary: "We awakened this morning by the most annoying, to me, of voices—an old Indian chief of the Kioways, who, not satisfied with the presents Mr. Whipple had given them yesterday, was back to beg for more."

Whipple, Diary: "This morning the Indian chief was in my tent and gave an excuse for the Mexicans [captives] not able to go with us. He brought his sunny boy for a present & soon came his [Mexican] mother. Both were soon sent back and sadly did I see them depart. I asked Mr. Jones what he thought of taking them by force and he very properly replied that it was not our mission. . . . We will undoubtedly find captives with every party on our route. If we attempt to rescue them we can do it but at the peril of the duty assigned us. It is hoped that the government will send a special detachment to treat with the Indians and take by force or otherwise the many captive Americans as well as Mexicans now slaves of Comanches and Kioways. . . . One of the Mexican traders reported that the Indians had robbed him of several articles. The chief was directed to see them restored. He went to the village as if to obey; and almost instantaneously their skins were packed, the lodge-poles tied to the sides of horses, and the whole party mounted, ready for a start. Secure in the fleetness of their horses, with their captives guarded, they quietly awaited our departure."[20]

[19]The term "greasy" to describe Mexicans had become a household word among Anglo-Americans and antedated the Mexican War. Most Anglos accepted the belief that Mexicans rarely washed and lived in conditions of filth. For an excellent study of the hardening of attitudes toward Mexicans and their culture, particularly after the Mexican War, see Robinson, *Mexico and the Hispanic Southwest in American Literature*, especially pp. 38–39. See also Noggle, "Anglo Observers of the Southwest Borderlands," p. 122.

[20]The situation between members of the expedition and the Kiowas became tense only after the subject of the Mexican captives was broached; Möllhausen agreed with Stanley that the Kiowa camp was surprised by the appearance of the

September 11. Camp 41. Ther. sunrise 56°.4— 3 p.m. 92°.9. This morning we started in good season & before night made 20 miles. Country & soil same as yesterday. While travelling, a fine deer ran through the train & so quickly that no one thought of firing at him but let him escape unscathed. A large grey wolf was also seen as we approached our Camping ground. The Mexicans camped a short distance from us. We purchased Buffalo robes from them today—which added much to the comfort of our beds during the cold nights. Passed today an Indian grave—over it was a rude, circular frame constituted of boughs—over the grave was a pile of stones about a foot in height.

About 2 p.m. noticed the prairie burning behind us. Supposed it to be the Kioways following as they struck their tents in the morning after we left & came up the river, tho' on different sides. It proved however to have been the traders to draw the Indians for trade.

Shortly before arriving at Camp in the evening two Indians were seen on a hill about a couple of miles distant.

September 12. Camp 42. Ther. Sunrise 60°.3— 3 p.m. 90°.9. This morning as we were leaving Camp, three men came in, apparently Indians, clothed in buckskins. We supposed them to be Comanches, but they proved to be New Mexican traders just from Mexico. They were in search of Indians but could find none. Their pack mules were left some miles behind & they returned to them. In the evening our march ended at their Camp which was 19 miles from our old Camp & where there was excellent water & plenty of it. They numbered, together, with the five from the Kioways, about 12 or 15. So we had quite a large Camp. They look precisely as the wild Indians (that is to me), putting aside their buckskin leggins. Had I met them in the prairies should have taken them for such. Our march was over very

---

wagon train. The Kiowas were not a war party: they were returning from a meeting with the Indian agent (Major Thomas Fitzpatrick) at Fort Atkinson, Kansas; there were only twenty warriors; they carried with them their lodges; and women and children were part of the group. David Conrad's conclusion that the Whipple expedition "left the Kiowas much as they had been found—in a tense situation of impending battle," seems overstated. See Conrad, "The Whipple Expedition on the Great Plains," p. 58; Whipple, *Report*, Sept. 9, 1853; Möllhausen, *Diary*, I, p. 212; Wallace and Hoebel, *The Comanches*, p. 300

mountainous Country. We left the Canadian & took to the high prairie. Some ascents were very steep. Ascended about 450 ft. during the day & have still to ascend.

The New Mexicans have been frightened out of their notion of visiting the Kioways & intend going North for the Comanches.

The mules nearly gave out today as the travelling was very hard for them, the first portion being sandy—the latter mountainous & stony.

Whipple, *Report*: "Seeing several Indians in the Mexican camp, we sent to inquire who they were. They returned with the messengers, to speak for themselves. They were Pueblo Indians from Santo Domingo [New Mexico], with flour and bread, to barter with the Kái-ò-wàs and Comanches for buffalo robes and horses. They were mounted on mules, wrapped in serapes, or Mexican blankets, and wore head-dresses, beads, and other Indian ornaments. There were six or eight of their party scattered over the prairie in search of Comanches. Thus far they have been unsuccessful, the majority of the wild tribes not having returned from their northern hunting tour."

September 13. Ther. sunrise 63°.1— 12 [noon] 89°.3— Today we were obliged to lay by on account of the mules. As usual, the day was mostly taken up in washing and cleaning firearms.

My days work consisted chiefly in washing, cleaning pistol and rifle—making buckskin pants & smoking pipe. The Camp is beautifully situated being on a hill with the full benefit of the prairie breeze & a fine prairie view in every direction. This is the highest place yet reached.

September 14. Camp 43. Ther. Sunrise 53°.7— 3 p.m. 93°.7— On Shady creek— On the route today crossed a slight eminence on the top of which was erected a rude wooden cross formed by two branches. It was supposed to be the grave of some Californian or Mexican who was murdered by the Indians. The Mexican Traders still continue with us today also two of the others whom we met on the 12th. The remainder have gone to the Comanches. Quite a number of deer were seen—at one time five or six were seen running in different directions. Made 20 miles today. At our Camping ground has been a recent Comanche Camp & within a week. There are about 50 huts standing, constructed of boughs, showing the Camp to have been very large. They

A lithograph of Möllhausen's drawing of the deserted Comanche summer camp on the banks of Shady Creek, where the expedition made a campground. The artist wrote that the huts, made of boughs, were so low that they could be entered only in a crouching position. *Reports of Explorations and Surveys,* vol. III.

must have had an immense number of horses as the ground in every direction is cut up & the grass eaten close.

After pitching tents & arranging matters I went over & examined their tents [huts] & found there a small bow & a piece of fossil wood, the latter evidently used to rub with as 'twas much worn—also found a small stone hammer or hatchet.[21]

[21] Möllhausen (*Diary*, I, p. 226) wrote that members of the expedition and New Mexican traders engaged in "a grand fandango" one evening, but since no other diarist mentions such an occasion it probably was a figment of his imagination. The wagon train has moved well away from the Canadian River, and now proceeds southwest. The expedition has traveled approximately 335 miles on this leg of the journey.

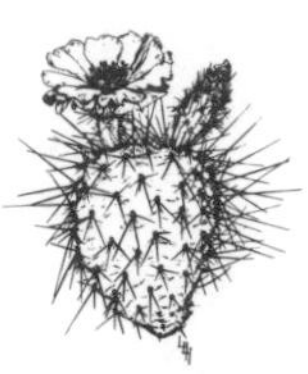

Shady Creek to Albuquerque

September 15–November 7, 1853

On September 15 the Whipple expedition leaves its camp on Shady Creek and moves westward along the south bank of the Canadian River. After crossing part of the barren plateau known as the Llano Estacado *in one day's march of nearly 28 miles, on September 19 it passes from Texas into New Mexico Territory. The expedition then follows a broad, beautiful valley known to New Mexicans as* Plaza Larga. *On September 24 the wagon train leaves the Canadian River, which veers to the north, and moves west toward the first New Mexican settlement of Anton Chico, situated on the Pecos River. There Lieutenant Whipple divides the expedition in order to explore two possible routes for a railroad. The main party under Albert Campbell, with the wagons and the military escort, travels on a direct route west to the Rio del Norte or upper Rio Grande and Albuquerque. Lieutenant Whipple leads a "trotting train" that includes John Sherburne northwest toward Galisteo, some 22 miles south of Santa Fe, and from the Santo Domingo Pueblo continues south along the Rio Grande. On October 5 the two parties reunite in Albuquerque.*

On this leg of the journey members of the expedition meet other bands of Mexican and Pueblo Indian Comancheros, who regularly travel across the southern plains to trade with Comanches and Kiowas. They attend lively fandangos at Anton Chico, and the men with the trotting train experience some excitement at the more isolated settlement of La Cuesta, where initially they are mistaken for raiding Comanches. At Santo Domingo on the Rio Grande they visit with hospitable Pueblo Indians, and they pass a succession of New Mexican and Indian villages before arriving at Albuquerque.

Because Lieutenant Ives reached the frontier town one day after the expedition instead of weeks before as Lieutenant Whipple had planned, preparations for the forthcoming journey take longer than expected and cause the commander no little anxiety. For more than four weeks members of the expedition remain in Albuquerque. During that time John Sherburne does not keep his diary regularly and tells us little about the work that occupied the members of the scientific corps during the daylight hours. We learn, however, that young Sherburne thoroughly enjoys the nocturnal life of a town that retains much of its Mexican past, and his roving eye finds some of the local señoritas "quite beautiful."

September 15. Camp 44. Ther. sunrise 54°.5— 3 p.m. 96°.7. This morning the Mexicans started at day-break about 2 hours sooner than ourselves. At 1 p.m. we passed them as they were lying by to rest their animals. After Camping they passed us at 5 p.m. & were soon out of sight. Quite probable they will not see us again untill our arrival at [New] Mexico, where they will carry the first news of our approach.

Travelled 20 miles today—passed two fine streams, one supposed to be Red [Bank] creek. Encamped on "Beautiful view creek." I scarcely know from what it derived its name. More timber passed than usual— Soil sand & clay. Near us are the remains of an Indian Camp—recently deserted. The brilliancy of the moon was noticed by every one, in the evening. Could easily read by the light of it.

Quite a curiosity was discovered just before leaving Camp this morning. In a grove of trees near the Indian Camp was discovered a mound of earth raised about 6 in. from the ground. The top level about 6 in. in width & 6½ in. in length. The top was strewed with herbs & the whole covered with an oblong frame of boughs interwoven. At each end & a few feet distant was a mound—small & circular—enclosed, as it were, in a circular trench. On the top of one was found a brass bracelet & several small strings of beads of different colors.[1] At a short distance another similar to this was found but without the beads. In a third

[1] This mound may have been a grave. Josiah Gregg, *Commerce of the Prairies*, p. 439, wrote that Comanches buried their dead with most of their jewelry. Lieut. Whipple collected the artifacts for dispatch to the Smithsonian Institution. See *Reports of Explorations and Surveys*, III, Part III ("Indian Tribes"), pp. 52–53.

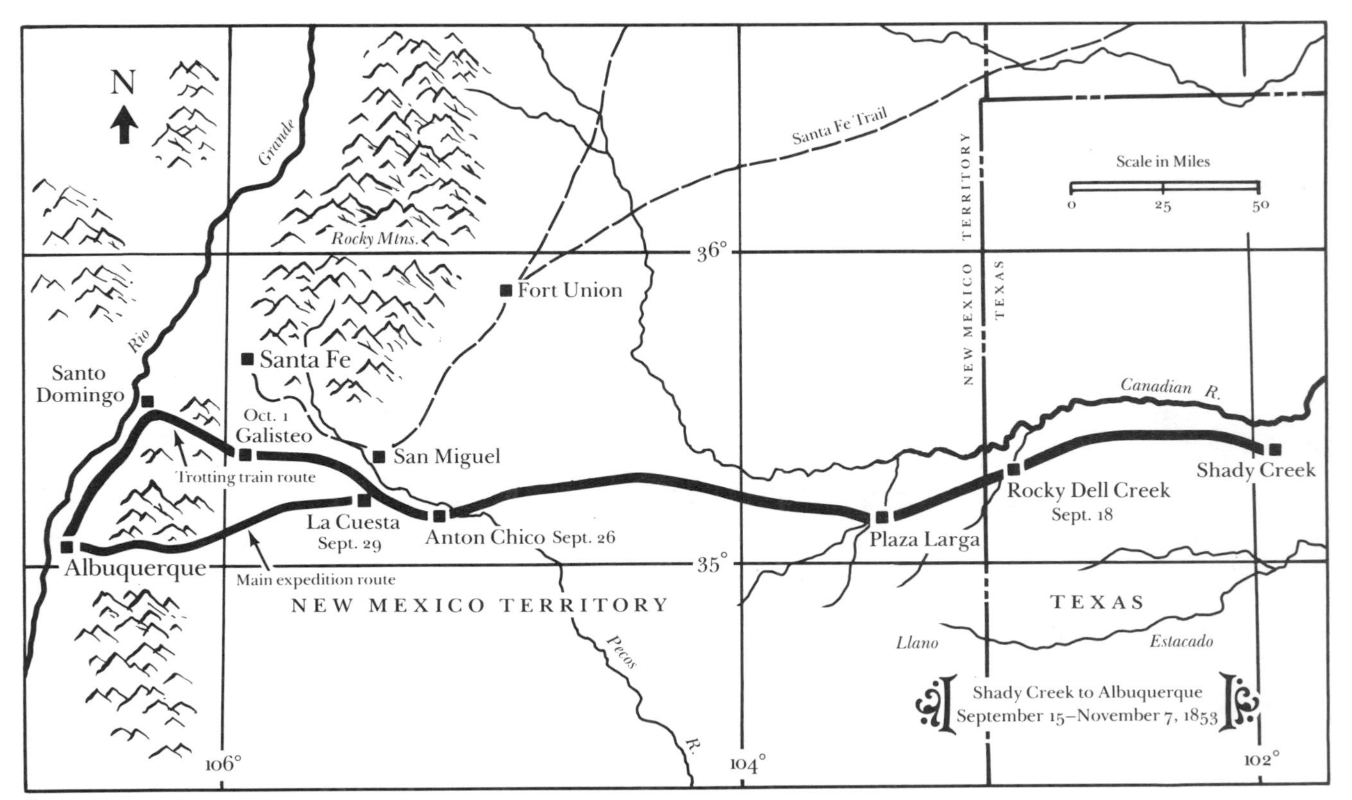

Shady Creek to Albuquerque
September 15–November 7, 1853

place was a small mound, circular, enclosed in an equilateral triangle. The whole triangle was raised from the ground. At the foot or base of this were four sticks lying on the ground & near four circular holes. These sticks were about 6 ft. in length, were evidently stuck in these holes & parrallel to the base of the triangle. No one knew the meaning of these particular signs. Some supposed it to be an offering, others to be the grave or graves of warrior or warriors. The latter I think, is the most probable case.

September 16. Camp 45. Ther. Sunrise 66°.2— 3 p.m. 94°.7. Near Encampment Creek. It was extremely difficult travelling today. A very heavy wind blew directly in our faces & so strong at times, as to take away our breath & cause it to "back" it. We started from Camp this morning a short time after sunrise & travelled till 4 p.m. making 20½ miles. The general character of the Country changed greatly today. From the rolling prairie & sunken valley, we went into the rocky & sandy dell. Natural mounds or peaks running out in all directions. Some circular at the base & running up 50 or 60 ft., then terminating in a kind of dome or cupola. We passed through a field of immense cactii—some 5½ & 6 ft. in height. The leaf of the same form as a braided chain watch.[2]

Found two streams of good water. Soil changed from sandy to a hard earth or clay. The mules & cattle gave out today & there was difficulty in getting them along. One cow they were obliged to shoot as she could not go farther. Quite a quantity of deer & antelope were seen, also an elk but not within shooting distance. It is the intention to make a long march tomorrow as wood & water are scarce. The last "feed" of corn was issued to the animals to night to serve them for the trip.

September 17. Camp 46. Ther. Sunrise 61°.5— 3 p.m. 89°. This morning we were turned out at 4½ & after taking a cup of coffee, struck tents, harnessed up & were well on the route before the sun had risen. At 8¾ arrived at "Encampment Creek," 8½ miles from Camp 46 [45], where the animals were watered, grazed &

[2]This cactus may be the *Opuntia arborescens*. Dr. Bigelow noted that it was first observed 200 miles east of the Pecos River and it grew no higher than five to eight feet. He described the cactus as "singular and rather pretty." A botanical drawing shows that its conformation did resemble a braid. See *Reports of Explorations and Surveys*, IV ("Botanical Character"), p. 3 and Plate XVIII.

we took our breakfast. After resting several hours we again started about 11¾, the mules having a fresh start. We knew wood & water was about twenty miles distant. We travelled until dark & the mules were really broken down. Still our next Encampment ground was 4 miles distant. The sun was down & there was a deep cañon before us. As the night came on the animals seemed to take fresh life & started off at a much brisker pace. When we arrived at the edge of the cañon & we could not *begin* to see down into it—down we went & after "perambulating" round 'mid rocks, gulleys & ruts for an hour or so, arrived safely to the top on the other side. We got out just as the moon was rising over the hills behind us, to show us the difficulty through which we had passed. It was remarkable that we should arrive at the cañon the only time during the day or night when it 'twas really very dark—at that space between the setting of the sun & rising of the moon.

After passing this cañon & in fact while in it we saw the flashes of distant fire arms which we knew belonged to the members of the party who were ahead in search of a good camping ground & were signals for us. We returned them—continued on.

Shortly after one of them came to meet us & led us to the spot chosen. It was about 8½ [p.m.]—at a distance from Encampment Creek of over 19 miles & from our last Camp of very nearly 28 miles (27m., 4552 ft.), making our longest days march by about 7 miles. Shortly after leaving Encampment Creek we saw on a prairie slope ahead of us, a large party of Indians. To all appearances 60 or 70 & we supposed them to be Comanches. As we kept on we saw three of them approaching with their bows & arrows. They proved to be Pueblo Indians from N. Mexico to trade with Indians. Their party separated, about 20 with their mules passing us, the others passing round the ridge so as not to be seen by us. At short intervals they were seen looking over at us. Their object in not meeting was unknown.

The first ridge after leaving Camp this morning, brought us on the "Llano Estacado" or "Staked plain."[3] Our whole march

[3]This high, barren plain stretched from western Texas to southeastern New Mexico. The *Llano Estacado* apparently either received its name because early Spanish explorers marked a trail along it with stakes, or because its bluffs resembled stockades. Sherburne is following Lieut. Simpson's "Report" of Marcy's

during the day was on it—as far as the eye could reach was a level table land without sign of bush or shrub. With the exception of a cañon every 5 or 6 miles the plain was uninterrupted. We travelled only on the edge of it. It extends on the S & W for an immense distance. The "mirage" today was exceedingly fine. In some places it bore a resemblance to a sheet of water & in other of burning prairie. The illusion was so perfect as to make one actually believe himself in "fire & water." A very large number of antelope were seen today—a dozen or twenty were round the train all [along] the route, sometimes shooting across the road ahead of us & sometimes behind. Several shots were fired at them but without effect. We have still continued rising for the last five days & are now about 4000 ft. above the level of the sea.

September 18. Camp 46. Ther. Sunrise 56°.5— 3 p.m. 80°.5. "Rocky Dell Creek" [Aqua Piedra]. The mules were so much used up this morning that we lay by. As 'twas Sunday not much work was done & we had plenty of time to mend, wash, etc. Near the brink of the water is a large sand stone which was found to be covered with Hieroglyphics, animals & reptiles of all descriptions. Some were cut in the rock & some painted red & black. A portion of them were very old & could scarcely be recognized. Others quite recent & fresh. This Stone stood at the foot of a high vertical cliff which overhung the water. Near the Stone & buried in the sand were found four Indian arrows, one with a copper head & the rest iron. These symbols were evidently cut by Indians from ages past to the present time. A sketch of rock & contents was taken by our Draughtsman.[4] In the evening after it had become quite dark & before the rising of the moon one of the herders gave the alarm of Indians. Every one seized his arms & rushed out. Lights extinguished & every necessary precaution taken.

1849 expedition. All the names he uses for landmarks are those given by Simpson. The Smithsonian geologist, W. P. Blake, admired a sketch of the *Llano* by Möllhausen because of its topographical accuracy. See *Reports of Explorations and Surveys*, III, Part IV, p. 23.

[4] Lieut. Whipple thought the inscriptions "worthy of more notice" than that given by Lieut. James Simpson in 1849 and asked Möllhausen to sketch the "most prominent." Simpson described the drawings and carvings as rude, clumsy, and "of a puerile character." Möllhausen agreed that they were "childish attempts." See Whipple, Diary, Sept. 18, 1853, Whipple Papers, Möllhausen, *Diary*, I, p. 264; Simpson, "Report," p. 12.

In less than a minute the escort were in line & ready for a "general muss." Taking the way of the signal I found one Indian surrounded. He proved to be a Pueblo with a party of nine from Santa Fe.[5] Fearing we would think them Comanches & charge their camp during the night, this one came to let us know who they were. He could speak English quite well. We had pretty good evidence of the rapidity with which our camp could be put in fighting trim. The Teamsters were evidently disappointed in not having a row.

September 19. Camp 47. Ther. Sunrise 54°.6— 3 p.m. 62°.1. Travelled 21¼ miles & encamped on a stream of good water. Also passed several good water streams on route. Country still continuing rolling prairie. Soil sandy. No interesting, amusing or ridiculous scene occurred on the day's march. Any quantity of game today.

September 20. Camp 48. Ther. sunrise 56°— 3 p.m. 70°.5. Last night we had a very heavy storm—rain, thunder & lightning in abundance. The thunder very heavy. Four tents out of six blew down but for a wonder I was one of the lucky ones. All the tents were pitched again in the rain. One of them blew down a second time & the occupants were taken into the neighboring tents, "wet, famished and hungry." Campbell came into my tent—looking like a drowned rat. The storm delayed the train till 9 a.m. as every thing was drenched & breakfast was late in consequence of the difficulty in the Culinary Department. An unusual quantity of antelope seen today—50 or 60 must have crossed the road near us.

September 21. Camp 49. Ther. sunrise 50°— 3 p.m. 75°.5. Passed several old Indian Camps today. Made 19¾ miles [through Plaza Larga] & halted on "Tucumcari Creek," also passed Tucumcari Mountains. Last night was the coldest we have yet had. Ther. at sunrise 50°. As we arrived at Camp met a Mexican. His party were behind with pack-mules & goods. He appears one of

[5]This Indian and his companions, Comancheros from New Mexican Pueblos, told Whipple that Pueblo Indians had painted and carved the inscriptions; the spot had been a camp on a favorite buffalo hunting ground. Whipple collected a short list of the Indians' vocabulary. This is the last night spent in Texas. On the following day the expedition crosses into New Mexico Territory. See *Reports of Explorations and Surveys*, III, Part III ("Indian Tribes"), p. 90.

the most civilized yet seen. Passed "Fossil Creek" today but no *fossils* obtained. Five or six prairie dogs were shot on the route.

Whipple, Diary: "A man coming from the hills ahead proved to be another Mexican bound for Comanche land for trade. He says there are 15 of his party with bread flour tobacco etc. desirous to meet Comanches and [Kiowas] on the return from their hunt of buffalo. I had no previous idea of the extent of this Indian trade. . . . The Mexican says that formerly they [Comanches] ranged thus far. But now the rancheros of New Mexico fearlessly graze their sheep in immense flocks that whiten the valley & hills. . . . How plainly does this fact tell the tale of the Comanches, that they are passing away!"[6]

September 22. Camp 50. Ther. sunrise 53°.5— 3 p.m. 83°.1. Shortly after leaving Camp this morning we met a party of Mexicans & Pueblos encamped with their mules & goods. After passing them we met quite a large number belonging to the same party. It was the largest party yet seen by us. About 2 miles on the route passed a high, circular peak called "Egyptian Pyramid." A party of us ascended it. We were an hour going up as it was very steep. By the barometer the height was about 500 ft. On the sides & summit were found a large quantity of oyster shells. The summit was near 5000 ft. above the level of the sea.

The hill was Geologized by Mr. Marcou, Botanized by the Dr., animalized & sketch-ized by Möllhausen, Topographized by Campbell & Barometer-ized by myself. We reached Camp about 2 hours after the train & at dark. On different parts of the hill & even on the summit we found natural reservoirs filled with clear cool water.

After leaving the hill passed through an immense field of cactii in which there were large herds of antelope, numbering each about 150. Some attracted by us came quite near. The rolling prairie still continues interspersed with large hills & mountains. Soil sandy & red marl. Our water at Camp tonight was un-

[6] Although Whipple clearly recognized the threat to the Plains Indians from the spread of "civilization," the Comanches fought for their survival until 1875. For additional comments by Whipple on the plight of these Indians, despite his dislike for them, see *Reports of Explorations and Surveys*, III, Part III ("Indian Tribes"), p. 7. See also Wallace and Hoebel, *The Comanches* (Chaps. I and II; Hagen, *United States–Comanche Relations*, Chap. 5. For the expansion of the sheep frontier at this time, see Kenner, *History of New Mexican–Plains Indian Relations*, p. 116.

The "Egyptian Pyramid," officially named Pyramid Mount, which was climbed and studied by members of the scientific corps on September 22, 1853. This fine Möllhausen lithograph was admired by Smithsonian geologists for its topographical accuracy. Courtesy Oklahoma Historical Society.

usually bad. It was bright yellow with marl & clay & very thick. The bread made from it was of a chocolate color. Coffee looked like soap suds & thick enough to be eaten with a spoon. Arrived at Camp before the remainder of the small party, but they soon joined us. Made a little over 22 miles. Passed more timber than usual.

Stanley, Diary: "Rode ahead of the train in the evening and from a highpoint two miles west of our encampment got my first glimpse of the Rocky Mountains. How the destiny of man exceeds and puts to fault all calculations and expectations. Little did I suppose when I read the fascinating stories of Lewis and Clark and indulged in dreamy reveries over my own fancies that one day I too should tread the sublime wilds of these far off mountains. Our camp was made on a small lagoon of the most disgusting water we have yet been forced to use. It was semi-fluid only, owing to the great amount of red mud mixed in it. Our coffee was intolerable and bread mixed with this water had the appearance of being made of red lead."

September 23. Camp 51. Ther. sunrise 52°— 12 [noon] 83°. Made 18½ miles. Country same as yesterday. Considerable timber consisting of cedar & some scattering pines. A large abundance of water found. One antelope killed on the route & several others badly frightened. After arriving at Camp several of us endeavored to dig out a prairie dog for a specimen. After digging a long time found it useless. Then filled the hole with water, but without success. The animal still persisted in "keeping house" in spite of our endeavors. In some portion of route today hilly on both sides of road rising with nearly perpendicular sides.

September 24. Camp 52. Ther. sunrise 43°.3— 3 p.m. 80°.5. Made 14½ miles & camped on "*Hoorah Creek*."[7] It was the intention to proceed 15 miles farther to Gallinas River, but the cattle & mules were not in the state to allow it. A broken down mule was shot this morning as unable to walk.

Two antelope were killed today & I wounded one but was unable to recover it as I was out of ammunition & separated from the party. Plenty of water on the route today. Soil sand, clay, & red marl. Prairie interspersed with beautiful wooded hills.

Passed along the edge of "Llano Estacado" but kept [to] the valley below it.

September 25. Ther. sunrise 41°.2— 3 p.m. 79°. Lay by today, on "Hoorah Creek" about 4 miles from the Pachas [Pecos] & 31 from Anton Chico, the nearest settlement. On one side of Camp & to the Eastward, is a large flat table rock, the top projecting & the whole resting on a slender foundation. It resembles a large umbrella. Beneath it the ground, which is of hard clay & sand stone, is worn smooth on account of its being used by Mexicans as a sleeping apartment. Each end is protected from the wind by rude walls of stone. On the west side of Camp & about ½ mile distant, is a high hill the sides of which are covered with "Corrals" built of stone, used by Mexican herders to corral their

[7]Lieut. Simpson named the creek "Hurrah" because, as the first affluent of the Pecos River, it heralded the beginning of the final stage of the journey to Santa Fe in 1849. The Canadian River now turns to the north and the expedition continues west on the 35th parallel toward the Pecos River. See Foreman, ed., *Marcy and the Goldseekers*, p. 221.

sheep at night. This is the place where Capt. Marcy first speaks of meeting herds of sheep. It is out of the range of Indians tho' sometimes visited by roving bands for pillage. Some think this cannot be the place as the sheep spoken of are not to be seen. We have heard from Anton Chico & learn they have an abundance of butter, eggs, milk, cheese, melons, grapes, etc. including all the luxuries of civilized life. We long to reach the land of "chicken fixins" and "flour doins." It is the intention to make an early start & reach there tomorrow night. The Lord willing, wind & weather permitting, if not tomorrow, the next day, *anyhow.*

We had fine excitement today, chasing antelope. One of the Escort went to the river Pachas, 4 miles distant, & then wounding an antelope, chased him to Camp. Every one started in pursuit & had a fine chase of about a mile on foot. Then the antelope fell from exhaustion. As we drew near him, he started up & received his death wound, tho' running about 100 yds after receiving it.

Vincente wounded one this afternoon with his pistol. He had no more ammunition, nor even a knife, so he had recourse to the original manner of Lariatting him & tying him to a stone. He came to camp for assistance & the deer was found in the place specified. A portion of him graced our board.

Dr. went to the Pachas about 11½ this morning botanizing, expecting to return about the middle of the afternoon. Sunset came & no Dr. At dark he had not arrived & we felt exceedingly anxious. A signal fire was built on a neighboring cliff & pistols discharged to lead him to Camp in case he was lost. Finally a small party started in search & met him a short distance from Camp, saying in his peculiar manner, "D-m it, d-m it, I always make a fuss when there's no need of it."

September 26. Camp 53. Ther. sunrise 46°.3— 3 p.m. 79°. This morning turned out at 3 o'clock, took breakfast by candlelight & started at day break for Gallinas River, thence to Anton Chico. Reached the river 11 o'clk, 15 miles, & found it filled with water. Kept on untill we arrived at a spring of water 23¾ miles from Camp 53 [52]. As all the animals were very much fatigued, concluded to go no farther. Mr. Whipple, Mr. Marcou & José went to town leaving us to follow in the morning.

Three antelope killed today. Met several Mexican herders with immense flocks of goats, sheep & cows.

September 27. Camp 54. Ther. sunrise 59°— 3 p.m. 77°.6. Started early this morning & reached Anton Chico in less than three hours, it being 5¾ miles. Had I entered the town without expecting to see any settlement I should have thought myself in a large brick kiln.[8] The houses exactly resembled piles of unfinished bricks, the smoke still issuing thro' the top. They were built of "adobes," that is of oblong and rectangular pieces of clay. Square holes cut for windows but no glass. Some of the more aristocratic having wooden shutters inside, one story high & flat roofs. The inhabitants were rather dark, tho' *some* of the *senoritas* were pretty. I visited many of the houses & found the inhabitants hospitable and polite. The exterior of the house is brown, the color of dirt, the interior white-washed, with hard clayey floors. Benches holding their beds were arranged along the walls.

They were clothed very poorly & the little children entirely destitute of clothing. They appeared very happy & one would have thought them void of care. They were living mid crowds of eggs, milk, butter, etc. Also all kinds of vegetables, including whiskey, which they furnished in abundance. In the evening they made a fandango for us. Of course we all attended & no one was sorry for doing so.

The senoritas were dressed finely, with dresses of silk & muslin, many with white dresses. Several I noticed with very pretty feet, enclosed in "Americano" gaiters of cloth & patent leather. These were probable brought from Santa Fe by their [word illegible]. The dancing was very graceful, especially waltzing. They moved without a particle of exertion & seemed to take fresh life at every step. When the dance was over, the senoritas took one side of the room & the "hombres" the other. Very little

[8] Möllhausen, like Sherburne and Stanley, also compared the houses to brick kilns; this was a common observation. Anton Chico, the first Mexican settlement on the route, is situated on the west bank of the Pecos. Möllhausen estimated its population at 300 and Whipple at 500, the number given in 1849 by Marcy. See Möllhausen, *Diary*, I, pp. 309, 411; Stanley, Diary, Sept. 27, 1853; Whipple, *Report*, Sept. 26, 1853; Noggle, "Anglo Observers of the Southwest Borderlands," p. 116.

John Sherburne's sketch of himself dancing with a señorita at a fandango in Anton Chico, the New Mexican settlement reached by the expedition on September 27, 1853. Sherburne drew this sketch in pencil in the back of his original diary. Courtesy Elena Klein.

or no conversation was carried on between the sexes, which was much more agreeable for me as I was an "ignoramus," as far as regards the Spanish language. The fandango room was a long whitewashed apartment, the floor of hard clay, sprinkled to avoid dust. The music consisted of fiddle & guitar, every few seconds the musicians joining in with a song & at the top of their voices, all the verses being extemporaneous. Nearly every one smoked, the senoritas smoking cigarettos [*cigarrillos*], the men some cigarettos & some pipes. No smoking was done by those dancing.[9] Several dogs were running round the room occasion-

[9] Only Sherburne and Stanley wrote about the first fandango. Sherburne's appreciation of the women and the fandango was echoed in many contemporary Anglo-American accounts. Products in the main of middle- and upper-class Victorian society, where women wore hoopskirts and corsets and behaved with strict decorum, male reporters reacted enthusiastically to the more relaxed Hispanic society. Most commented on the short skirts, the smoking that would have branded Anglo women as prostitutes, and the graceful, sensual dancing. Sherburne's repeated mention of "small female feet" (see also September 9 and

ally fighting, receiving a kick from some one. A large sheep was by no means the least amusing thing to be seen. He would chew tobacco in large quantities & butt everyone that looked hard at him. Many peculiarities I noticed which I could not trust on paper. The Mexicans & Americans are not on very good terms here. For fear of a row the "alcalde" prohibited any Mexican from carrying pistols or knives in the room. He also requested us to conform to the same order. So we wore our pistols until we reached the room & left them in the house of an American [Mr. Kitchen] living near by.[10] Many took their knives in with them. The evening passed off quietly. All the men here go armed like a gang of desperadoes—with pistols in belt & knife in sheath. Rows & murders are not uncommon—he who comes out safe is the best fellow.

Stanley, Diary: "Marched into Anton Chico to-day and found much to our disappointment that no corn could be procured for our half-famished mules. We encamped near this little town, which at a distance resembles a large brick kiln. . . . We met at this place an American and an Englishman, traders, settled down in this miserable little town, but seemingly enjoying a very happy life. Mr. K. [Kitchen] was found a quite hospitable fellow, but full of bravado and boasting. We had a fandango given us at night and here for the first time, I had the opportunity of seeing the Spanish dance in the true Spanish style."

September 28. Ther. sunrise 57°— 3 p.m. 65°.3. It was the intention to divide the party today—one starting in the morning, taking the direct route for Albuquerque—the other starting this p.m. & taking the more Northern route, through the principal towns on the Rio Grande & elsewhere.[11]

October 3) reflected either "displacement" of sexual interest to female attributes less shocking to Victorian sensibilities or fascination with limbs hidden from view by the long skirts worn by young Anglo women of his circle. Only a few Anglo-American writers were scandalized by the Mexican women's dress and behavior. This admiration of the women was in marked contrast to an almost universal disparagement of the men, particularly those considered of a lower class. See Stanley, Diary, Sept. 27, 1853; Robinson, *Mexico and the Hispanic Southwest in American Literature*, pp. 23–24, 42–45; Lecompte, "The Independent Women of Hispanic New Mexico," pp. 17–18; Weber, *The Mexican Frontier*, p. 220.

[10] Identified by name by Whipple, the American trader had married a New Mexican woman. Whipple referred to Kitchen's house as a mansion. The alcalde, whose position was inherited from Spanish government, served as a combination mayor and magistrate. See Whipple, *Report*, Sept. 26, 1853.

[11] Lieut. Whipple planned to explore two trails to Albuquerque. He placed his

The latter party to consist of Mr. Whipple, Mr. Marcou, Mr. Mölhausen, Dr. Bigelow and myself—also 2 wagons & Teamsters, 1 caratella & driver, Dr.'s servant, José & Vincente. Four of the escort to accompany us. The whole party consisting of 15. During the day there was heavy rain accompanied by thunder & lightning. The mules were across the river & could not be driven over as the river had risen rapidly & was rushing with great rapidity, so much so as to render it dangerous for any one to attempt a crossing. By this we were prevented from starting today. Towards night the river fell sufficiently to allow a fording for the animals.

Tonight the alcalde gave us a fandango, more select than that of last night & much better attended. More beauty was visible than last evening. The remainder of the performance much the same as last evening, even the sheep & dogs were present. The Alcalde (or mayor) superintended affairs.

Möllhausen, *Diary*, I, p. 313: "We all set to work directly to rummage up the most elegant ball costume that circumstances permitted; needles and thread were seen in brisk motion in all quarters, and chasms and openings in our well-worn garments, originating either in accident or in severe service on our long journey, disappeared as if by magic. An artificial black was, for the first time in many days, superinduced upon our *chaussure* [shoe]; and the most gorgeous shirt collars and fronts were manufactured out of stiff drawing paper. We were a comical-looking group, nevertheless, when we set off in the evening to the festive scene, being summoned thereto by the church bells, which are obliged to accommodate themselves to the double duty of calling people to Divine Service and to the fandangos. . . . The dancing began. . . . The bright-eyed Senoritas were indefatigable, the degenerate descendants of the Spaniards looked with evident complacency at their own nimble limbs, and the wildest excitement gleamed from the bearded visages of the Americans."

September 29. Camp 55. Ther. Sunrise 49°.5— 3 p.m. 71°.9. The whole train started this morning in good season but we left them behind as we started in a trot for La Cuesta, intending to

---

surveyor, A. H. Campbell, in charge of the main party, which traveled on a more direct route west to Albuquerque. His "trotting train" followed part of the 1849 Marcy trail north by way of Galisteo, then left that trail at Santo Domingo to move south along the Rio Grande to Albuquerque. Whipple made no mention of the fandangos in his official *Report*.

Möllhausen's drawing of the lovely valley of La Cuesta, reached by Lieutenant Whipple's "trotting train" on September 29, 1853. Inhabitants of the isolated New Mexican settlement at first mistook the party for a band of dreaded Comanches. Courtesy Oklahoma Historical Society.

return & camp with them tonight, as Cuesta was only 15 miles from Anton Chico & about 6 from the road taken by the train. Unfortunately for us, we passed the turn off road & had to retrace our steps for some miles. We did not arrive at La Cuesta till 5 p.m. & concluded to go into camp. We could not approach this place with wagons as it was situated in a valley 600 ft. deep & approached only by steep hills. It is said to be the most beautifully situated town in N. Mexico. As we went down the hill on foot, leading the animals to water, the children caught sight of us & set up the cry of "Comanches." This they ceased as we drew near the town. We found them not as hospitable as at Anton Chico. There was no American living in the place & they looked upon them with an "evil eye," tho' not daring to do them any injury which they thought would be found out. The town was much larger & prettier than Anton Chico, but built of the same material.

In the evening Mr. Whipple went into the town to get corn &

"fodder" for the animals. As he had already some difficulty with one of the Mexicans he took a man with him & a couple of revolvers. It was very dark & we were all sitting round the camp fire smoking. Suddenly a shot was heard—then another. We all jumped & grabbed the first weapon we could find. I was lucky enough to get two revolvers. Taking two soldiers we all started down the hill, leaving two soldiers & an old man (who by the way was once a Baptist or a Methodist preacher)[12] to tie up the mules & guard Camp. We lost the road on the start, but I struck for the town the nearest way followed by the two soldiers. We ran down places which in the day time we would have considered impracticable & dangerous, but we kept on. Several times I heard the rattling of guns on the rocks as the soldiers tumbled head over heels. When I reached the bottom of the hill, only one soldier was with me. His gun was cocked, primed, & bayonetted. Repeated & numerous shots were heard as we run down the hill, mingled with yells & shrieks of women. The shots sounded precisely as revolvers fired in haste. As we entered the town we met José who luckily had found the road & reached the town before us, but without any arms. He burst into the first house & they told him no one had been there from Camp. This we knew to be false, so we headed for the only light visible. Just before arriving there & within a few rods of the house, we met Mr. Whipple & a Mexican with a load of "fodder." The firing & noise we heard came from a large fandango which was then in full blast—whether they were fighting or not I do not know. We turned back & had to retrace our road among the rocks. We met the rest of the party at the bottom of the hill & about half way up met the other two soldiers & old man, who unable to repress their "risible" faculties had tied up the mules & come along to join the "general muss." We arrived back to camp pretty well tired out & with an excellent appetite for our suppers.

[12] Both Whipple and Möllhausen mentioned this man. Whipple employed him as a driver in Skullyville on July 26 and used the man's wagon to store extra goods. Apparently he had traveled from St. Louis with dry goods for sale, intending to proceed on from Skullyville to Texas. Möllhausen, who wrote that the preacher was known to all as "the Old Man," traveled with him on the steamer from San Pedro to San Francisco in 1854. The preacher then was dressed in a black suit and "showing" himself as "a gentleman." See Whipple, *Report*, July 26, 1853; Möllhausen, *Diary*, II, pp. 316–17.

There is no doubt but there was rascality intended for 'twas evident from various circumstances that they had an understanding between themselves. Instead of conducting them [Whipple and herder] through the front door by which they entered & which was the nearest way, they led them through a narrow passage between the wall & "acequia" (ditch filled with water) a place scarcely wide enough for them to walk. While they were near the middle of it, one at the end calls out, "Where are they?" The answer was, "Here." Just at that time we arrived with our force & a little boy runs up & cried out, "They have come after them." Several other incidents render it pretty certain they were up to some kind of deviltry. However everything passed over & we had quite a laugh over the adventure. A few of the Mexicans we saw afterward appeared sorry or mortified that such a thing had occurred & one said anything he had was at our service.

Met large flocks (or rather herds) of sheep & goats today. Soil sandy. Large quantity of timber, principally pine.

Whipple, *Report*: "As we entered the valley a loud clamor was heard from the nearest rancheros, and we found that the villagers had taken us for a band of Comanches; for this solitary spot is seldom disturbed from without except by those unwelcome visitors. When their apprehensions were quieted and they found us to be Americans, they displayed a singular mixture of rudeness and civility, for they saw us as few in number and unarmed. They insisted upon our accompanying them to a ball in the village, but at the same time were heard talking to each other of the 'Gringos.' . . . At length they carried their impertinence to such a pitch that a demonstration was made by our party which showed the villagers that we had the will to chastise any further displays of it. They immediately apologized, and afterwards treated us with respect."[13]

September 30. Camp 56. Ther. sunrise 50°.6— 12 p.m. 56°.9. Rose very early this morning, before daybreak. Took breakfast

[13] Lieut. Whipple on an earlier trip in the afternoon with Mr. Marcou was unarmed. He returned in the evening with one of the herders and both carried arms. Sherburne's account agrees with Möllhausen's and with Whipple's longer description in his diary. Though Whipple (who spoke some Spanish) remarked in his diary that he thought highly of Mexican friends made during his years with the Boundary Commission, he was referring to well-educated, cosmopolitan Mexicans. In his attitude toward the villagers of Mexican and Indian descent he exhibited the cultural superiority and condescension toward a recently conquered people that were common among Anglo-Americans of the time. See Whipple,

& ready to start before the sun was up. The Mexicans however had the start of us for they came with pack-mules laden with eggs, chickens, peaches, apples, & onions. We travelled very rapidly, arrived about 9 a.m. at the place where the remainder of party camped last night a distance of 9 miles from La Cuesta. It was raining but their Camp fires were still blazing. We caught up with the train about 3 p.m. & travelled in company till about 4 when we camped at the Laguna (lake) on the prairie. Before we had time to pitch our tents, a thunder storm came upon us. At the same time with the thunder and lightning, came hail & sleet. It was very cold after the storm which lasted near an hour. We noticed a hill on our left quite white with snow. The night was the most disagreeable we've had. Travelled today 26 miles. Saw a drove of sheep bound for Albuquerque numbering 8000. They tread down the grass level with the ground on both sides of the road. Plenty of timber & water on route.

Whipple, *Report*: "The mules have had plenty to eat during the night, we were enabled to leave camp at daybreak. Many Mexicans visited us even at that early hour, and were remarkably polite and communicative, not having forgotten the lesson we gave them."

October 1. Camp 57. Ther. sunrise 41°.5— 3 p.m. 57°.8. Before starting from Camp saw the Rocky Mountains quite plainly in view all along the route. We left early, the train going straight on, while we turned off at the left & arrived in Galisteo about sunset. Distance 24 miles. Here we found the Mexicans dressed in true Mexican style, the men wearing loose pants & broad-brimmed hats, the fairer sex a loose dress & veil thrown over their heads. I saw several carrying crocks of water on their heads.

Plenty of timber on route. Soil sandy & clayey, very boggy, the wheels occasionally sinking to their hubs in the mire. Went in town about dark with Mr. Whipple to obtain "fodder" for the animals—although it took us till near nine o'clk did not succeed in finding any. *How far did we look for it? La Eco dice "como lejos?"*[14]

Diary, Sept. 29, 1853, Whipple Papers; Möllhausen, *Diary*, I, pp. 319–20; Noggle, "Anglo Observers of the Southwest Borderlands," pp. 113–24.

[14] The Spanish loosely translates as "The echo says 'how far?'" Though Sherburne carried with him a Spanish grammar, he knew little Spanish at this time. He seemingly looked up the appropriate words in a dictionary, but the sentence is grammatically incorrect. The Spanish should read *"El eco dice '¿Cuán lejos?'"*

We were much surprised by a call from two Americans—Major Waitman & Judge Baird who were from Albuquerque & were to spend the night at Galisteo. They told us Lieut. Ives had not arrived & no news of him. We expected they were there six weeks ago.[15] They told us a mail left Santa Fe in a few days & no other for two weeks. Took advantage of the opportunity & wrote home.

Möllhausen, *Diary*, I, p. 323: "Lying on the slope of a gently rising ground, Galisteo is prettily situated, and makes, from a distance, an agreeable impression, which, however, vanishes as soon as you enter its dirty streets showing signs everywhere of extreme poverty, and find yourself regarded by everyone you meet with mistrustful glances. Most of the male population, with their bearded faces and dirty blanket-wrappers, looked like banditti; and there was an impudent and profligate expression on the faces of the women, who greeted us besides with looks of mocking defiance."

October 2. Camp 58. Ther. sunrise 29.°5— 12 [noon] 69.° Last night the coldest night yet passed. Ice was found on the edges of the creeks & gulleys. Started this morning for San Domingo, on the Rio del Norte. After going 15½ miles & finding San Domingo was still 21 miles distant concluded to go into Camp, so made an early camp near several ranchos.

Found some excellent grapes I think the most delicious flavored I have ever eaten. Near Camp were hills of volcanic description. This morning sent José to Santa Fe with dispatches & letters.

October 3. Camp 59. Sunrise Ther. 32°— 3 p.m. 78.°7. Started quite early this morning & in a short time came to a town the name of which I could not distinguish, but it sounded like "see-a-nigger."[16] Not seeing any persons *unusually black*, concluded I must be mistaken. Passed through five or six small towns & arrived at San Domingo before dark, after a march of about 25 or 27 miles. The exact distance could not be determined as the

[15] The two men, Richard H. Weightman of Albuquerque and Spruce M. Baird of nearby Pajarito, were close friends and allies in New Mexican territorial politics; Baird is incorrectly identified as Spence Baird in Foreman, ed., *A Pathfinder*. This was the first information Whipple had received of Ives, his chief assistant, whom he had expected to reach Albuquerque well before the main expedition. For Weightman and Baird see the Biographical Appendix to this volume.

[16] The town was Cienaga (sometimes known as Cienguilla), about 15 miles south of Santa Fe. In the front of his diary, under "Errata," Sherburne noted the correct name.

viameter fell off & the count lost. Passed through a cañon about five miles in length. Ridge on both sides rising perpendicularly about 2500 or 3000 ft. & covered with rocks of volcanic description. The bottom of the cañon was traversed by a stream of fresh water, on the banks of which were volcanic rocks & large masses of scoria or lava.

San Domingo is a Pueblo Indian place. We visited most of the houses & found them very glad to see us. They entertained us with fresh "tortillas" & water melons.

The females are remarkable for their small feet & hands, also beautiful white teeth. Soil today, very sandy.

Möllhausen, *Diary*, I, pp. 332, 336–37: "This was Santo Domingo, an ancient settlement of the Pueblo Indians. . . . As the houses are built close to one another, there are formed upper, as well as lower, streets, which lead past the doors of the dwellings on the second and third stories, and establish an immediate connection between them. There are no doors on the ground-floor; but the ascent from the street is by ladders, which can be drawn up when the security of the inhabitants is supposed to require it. An opening in the flat roof of the first story gives access to the interior, while other ladders lead from the platforms of the lower stories to the second and third. . . .

"The Pueblo church . . . evidently owes its origin to Catholic missionaries. [Inside] there was a kind of altar; and the walls were of smooth clay, on which hung some old Spanish pictures,—the sole decoration, with the exception of some rude Indian paintings, among which we remarked the figure of a man on horseback riding over a troop of men: a *Conquestador*, therefore, and evidently an allusion to the Spanish conquest. The Catholic and Aztec religions were evidently blended in these representations; the Holy Virgin is often found in company with an Indian figure denominated Montezuma."[17]

Whipple, Diary: "This pueblo is a strong contrast to Mexican towns, exhibiting vastly more architectural taste, more unity of design in the adaptation of the ornamental to the useful. The contrast . . . between

[17] The Spanish introduced Catholicism to the Pueblo Indians in the sixteenth century. In 1680 all the Pueblo Indians united in rebellion against Spanish rule, and Santo Domingo was at the center of the revolt. They were reconquered in 1692 and the Pueblo Indians maintained their churches and called themselves Catholic. Many travelers noted the "harmonious practice" of a blend of two religions. But, as Edward H. Spicer observes, the Pueblo Indians "integrated fragments of the faith but not the system, and hence it is no cause for wonder that the Catholic Church regarded no Pueblo village as a Catholic community." See Spicer, *Cycles of Conquest*, p. 508; Noggle, "Anglo Observers of the Southwest Borderlands," p. 119; Dutton, *American Indians of the Southwest*, p. 56.

A lithograph of Balduin Möllhausen's drawing of the Santo Domingo Pueblo with its Catholic church and its distinctive multileveled houses whose upper stories were reached by ladders. The hospitable Pueblo Indians welcomed the Whipple party with tortillas and melons on October 3, 1853. Courtesy David Miller.

these Indians & the wild Apaches & Comanches requires a passing notice. . . . The latter have no fixed abode, they have neither habitation nor a home. To plunder is their occupation, their hand is against every man and every man's hand is against them. Not so the Pueblo Indians. Quietly & peacefully they dwell in houses, cultivate their own fields and seem to possess the blessings of civilization."[18]

October 4. Camp 60. Ther. sunrise 39°.3— 12 [noon] 89°.5. Did not make an early start this morning. Left 9½ or 10 a.m. Passed through numerous small towns on the bank of the river [Rio Grande], some of which were quite pretty. Saw several peach or-

[18]Whipple approvingly regarded the Pueblo Indians as "semicivilized," like the Indians of eastern Oklahoma. Möllhausen, who was contemptuous of New Mexican villagers, similarly approved of these Indians, finding them friendly, good-natured, and "rather prepossessing in appearance." See *Reports of Explorations and Surveys*, III, Part III ("Indian Tribes"), pp. 9–10, 12, 29; Möllhausen, *Diary*, I, pp. 333, 336–37.

chards surrounded by high adobe walls, the tops of which were covered with cactii, an effectual way of keeping out robbers. Found melons & grapes in abundance. Made 24½ miles & Camped at Bernadillo, an Indian pueblo.[19] The pueblo's houses are two stories high, built of adobes & entered in the upper stories by ladders. Passed through San Felippe [Felipe] today.

October 5. Ther. sunrise 40°.3— 3 p.m. 93°.2— Camp 61. Left Bernadillo this morning at day-break & arrived at Albuquerque early in the forenoon about 9. Found them [remainder of the party] all comfortably situated in Camp & expecting us. The town is built of adobes, no wood houses, even the Fort & Barracks are of the same material.[20] Found Lieut. Ives & party had not arrived & nothing known of them. They were passed by a mail stage 50 miles from San Antonio, Texas & by the next 150 miles. These are all the accounts of him. Considerable anxiety felt on his account.

Made nearly 12 miles this morning. Found here letters from home dated Aug. 4. Expect more by the Texas mail on the 12th.

Miscellaneous News—Scraps—Etc.

October 6. Albuquerque, New Mexico— Camp 62 [61] of the trotting train & Camp 59 of main body. Ther. sunrise 40°— 3 p.m. 84°. Work commenced today. It is the intention to lay here about 5 or 6 weeks to recruit the mules & then start for the Pacific. Are not able to obtain provisions here or clothes for the soldiers. Have got to send to Fort Union, 200 miles, for them. Wood is 15 miles distant at San Antonio, New Mexico. Lieut.

[19] Bernalillo, as it is spelled, was not an Indian Pueblo. The Pueblo where the Whipple party camped was neighboring Sandia. See Whipple, *Report*, Oct. 4, 1853.

[20] The post, established in 1845, recently had become the headquarters of the Military Department of New Mexico. There was no true fort, and buildings for offices, barracks, and so forth were rented. The main party had arrived on October 3. Whipple estimated the population of the town, including ranchos and "environs," at 2,500; Möllhausen reported that the population of the town proper was between 700 and 800. Whipple officially wrote only a brief account of the long stay in the town but made daily entries in his diary about his preparations for the forthcoming journey. Lieut. Stanley did not keep up his diary during the stay. Vincente, the young Mexican hired as interpreter at Old Camp Arbuckle, now disappears from the records of the journey. See Simmons, *Albuquerque*, pp. 149–52, 170; Möllhausen, *Diary*, II, pp. 9–10; Stanley, Diary, Oct. 3, 1853; Whipple, *Report*, Oct. 5, 1853.

Ives arrived today having been detained five weeks by sickness. Mr. [Hugh] Campbell was behind & will be here probably tomorrow. Dr. Kennely [Kennerly] remained behind to take charge of a sick officer & will be here as soon as possible.[21] One man of the party was buried in "Devils Hole" [Texas] & one eaten by the wolves. One of the mail carriers in company was shot by the Indians. They came upon an Emigrant train just as they were to be attacked by the Comanches & thereby prevented it. They saw more Indians than we did.

Two mules of their party were choked to death in the night. José arrived tonight from Santa Fe, he got there too late for our letters & brought no mail in return.

There are fandangos here every night, among the lower classes. They are monopolized by the Teamsters & soldiers. It is the intention to have an *aristocratic* one soon.

October 7. Ther. sunrise 37°.5— 5 p.m. 94°. One of the wagons from Mr. [Hugh] Campbell's train came in today, the remainder of the mules having broken down & unable to proceed. Mr. C. remained with them. Sent back sufficient mules to bring them along & expect them tomorrow as they are but 20 miles distant. Fandango tonight.

Möllhausen, *Diary*, II, pp. 18–19: "As we were, above all things, anxious to make at the various balls of Albuquerque a rather less ragamuffin appearance than we had done at Anton Chico, many a good dollar belonging to our party found its way into the shops, and was joyfully exchanged for an article of a tenth of its value. . . . When the evening bell

[21] With only a few men and two wagons, Lieut. Ives had spent weeks at Fort Inge, Texas, waiting for a military escort, essential because the route to Albuquerque was attacked regularly by Comanches and Apaches. The late arrival of this party was a blow to Whipple and necessitated a much longer stay in Albuquerque than originally planned. Despite their adventures, Ives and party delivered reports on scientific data, zoology, and botany—though no reports on the Indian tribes who plagued their journey. Whipple was so excited by the sophisticated scientific instruments collected from the United States and Mexican Boundary Commission by Ives that he wrote hundreds of words in his diary and *Report* describing them in technical terms. Among the instruments was a "Fox" dip-circle for measuring elements of magnetism and an astronomical transit. Fort Union, mentioned by Sherburne, was established in 1851 on the Santa Fe Trail east of Las Vegas in New Mexico Territory and served as a supply center. See Whipple, Diary, Oct. 6, Whipple Papers, and *Report*, Nov. 7, 1853; *Reports of Explorations and Surveys*, IV; Möllhausen, *Diary*, II, pp. 29–30; Conrad, "Explorations and Railway Survey," p. 75; Lamar, *The Far Southwest*, p. 95.

of the old church began to sound, the best dancers of the company hastened . . . with exemplary punctuality to perform their devotions to the fair and gaily-dressed Mexican ladies. We found that, though the balls were public, the company consisted of two distinct classes; the one formed by the more cultivated inhabitants of Albuquerque, which was joined by the officers of the garrison and the members of our Expedition; the other of a wild throng of very rough fellows, who in their own circle might dance, shoot, quarrel and swear to their hearts' content; and they had just as little desire to submit to the restraints of our more decorous society as we had to mingle in theirs."

October 8. Ther. sunrise 34°— 2 p.m. 90°. Mr. C. & wagons arrived today which increased our camp considerable. A fandango given us tonight by Don Salvador Armijo.[22] The room was fitted up very prettily, floors carpeted, walls hung with pictures, looking glasses & chandeliers. The "elite" of the town were present. The Senoritas were dressed "au fait" & some were quite beautiful, being of lighter complexion than many American girls—this latter remark, however, applies to a very few.

Dr. [Bigelow] & Mr. Marcou left this morning for the Mountains to explore, the former for "Cactacia," the latter for geological specimens. They took a four mule caratella & several men, intending to remain absent several days.

Möllhausen, *Diary*, II, p. 9: "Albuquerque lies about five hundred yards from the Rio Grande, and has a rather ruinous aspect. . . . The habitations are all built on flat ground, or at most only slightly raised on a bed of clay, and the interior is as rudely simple as possible, though not altogether without convenience; and among the more opulent inhabitants apartments may be seen, to which by means of whitewash a neat and pleasing appearance has been given. Boarded floors are an unknown luxury, and both rich and poor content themselves with hard stamped clay, which only the wealthy cover with straw mats and carpets."

October 9. Ther. sunrise 34°.6— 3 p.m. 83°. Nothing of importance today. Large fandango tonight (Sunday). House crowded.

October 10. Ther. sunrise 41°.5— 3 p.m. 86°.6. Two fandangos tonight. Three prisoners in the garrison broke out through the wall last night & made their escape. They were seen by a sentinal who fired at them, but without effect. 'Tis thought they have

[22] Salvador Armijo, a merchant and landowner, was a member of one of the influential New Mexican families considered socially acceptable by the officers and gentlemen of the expedition. See the Biographical Index to this volume.

gone towards Santa Fe. They were under sentence of a Court-martial & feared severe punishment.

October 11. Ther. sunrise 42.°6— 3 p.m. 88.° All anxiety for the mail today, in anxious expectation for letters. The Teamsters have taken a sudden notion of enlisting & several of them seem anxious to get away from us. They are undoubtedly influenced by others.

October 12. Ther. sunrise 50°— 3 p.m. 85.°3. Mail not yet arrived, tho' due nearly 24 hours. Three fandangos tonight, one for our benefit which we all attended.

October 13. Mail not arrived. Fandango tonight.

October 14. Ther. sunrise 39.°8— 3 p.m. 86.°7. Mail arrived from San Antonio, Texas, today but no letters from home—one from Van Buren, Ark. Entered quarters today with Garner & Parke.[23]

Whipple, Diary, Oct. 17: "Since my arrival at this place I have received much information regarding the route between Zuñi and the Rio Colorado, all of which tends to convince us that the difficulties attending the railroad exploration & survey expected to be performed by my party are far greater than anticipated in Washington. In 1851 Capt. Sitgreaves with Mr. Leroux for guide made a try across to Rio Colorado, reported most unfavorably on the route traversed. Mr. Walker, the well known mountaineer, soon followed but by a more northern route, and it was believed in Washington that his route was remarkably adapted for a location of a railroad. To my surprise, however, Mr. Thomas a gentleman who accompanied him . . . tells me that the route is altogether impracticable. Finally this very season, Mr. Aubrey, distinguished for energy and enterprise, left California for the purpose loudly proclaimed of discovering the route in question. He too was unfortunate . . . and advises us to avoid his trail.[24] The three distinguished guides of this country

[23] The campground was only a few feet above the level of the Rio Grande, and constantly wet and cold. Whipple took a room in an officer's house, Möllhausen moved to a room in the army surgeon's house, and the military escort moved into the barracks. See Möllhausen, *Diary*, II, pp. 6–7; Whipple, Diary, Oct. 11, 16, 1853, Whipple Papers.

[24] As we know, Whipple carried with him Capt. Sitgreaves's map drawn by the artist and topographer Richard Kern, but he had not read the official report of the 1851 expedition. He learned more about this trip in Albuquerque. Mr. Thomas, a trapper and mountain man who had accompanied Joseph R. Walker across present-day northern Arizona also in 1851, told Whipple that the Walker route was "terrible," with "volcanic mountains piled on mountains denying passage almost to pack mules." Thomas provided Whipple with a rough map of the route, which at times followed the Sitgreaves trail north of the 35th parallel and

therefore, each following the route of his selection, have signally failed in their object. This conclusively proves the great difficulties we must be prepared to contend with or doubtless fail likewise. One of these difficulties is the hostility of the Indians. Each of the parties referred to fought their way. . . .

"The escort which accompanied us from Ft. Smith commanded by Lieut. J. M. Jones, if the deficiency resulting from sickness and desertion may be supplied, I conceive to be sufficient [to protect] the main body of the party. But now being compelled to have reconnoitering parties continually far in advance and perhaps even obliged to resort to a permanent division of the party I feel constrained to apply for additional escort—25 mounted men to protect our operations through this department to the boundary of California."

October 18. Mail arrived from Santa Fe—but nothing for me.

October 20. Capt. Sturgis arrived with a company of dragoons.[25]

October 21. One of our Teamsters shot today in a fandango—not badly injured, only losing a portion of his ear. A row occurred in a fandango tonight & three Americans from Santa Fe cleared the room in about 5 minutes.

Whipple, *Report*, Nov. 7, 1853: "Upon our arrival here, Indian depredations and anticipated troubles upon the Mexican frontier caused considerable excitement throughout the Territory. The troops were actively employed as scouts or in preparation for serious encounters. General Garland, the commanding officer of the department, being upon a tour of observation . . . the acting commissary remaining at this

---

passed through the Moqui Indian villages. François X. Aubry (not Aubrey), a colorful trader and explorer, completed a pack trip on September 10, 1853, that New Mexican newspapers hailed as a practicable wagon route from Albuquerque to California. Aubry gave Whipple a rough map and his notes of the trip; he declined to accompany the expedition as a guide, claiming he was too afraid of the hostile Indians who had plagued his journey. Whipple wrote that Aubry's route was too far south of the 35th parallel, that it was "utterly impracticable" for wagons and that the enthusiastic newspaper accounts were "absurd." See Whipple, Diary, Oct. 9, 11, 1853, Whipple Papers; Conrad, "Explorations and Railway Survey," p. 81; Gilbert, *Westering Man*, pp. 236–43; "Diaries of François Xavier Aubry, 1853–1854," in Bieber, ed., *Exploring Southwestern Trails*, pp. 353–77. Aubry's diary of his pack trip was very vague about the route.

[25]Samuel Davis Sturgis, an 1848 graduate of West Point, was a first lieutenant in the Dragoons. Lieut. Whipple asked for a detachment of dragoons, but the commanding general could not spare them and promised instead an additional escort of infantry mounted on mules from Fort Defiance. See Cullum, *Biographical Register*; Whipple, Diary, Oct. 24, 27, 1853, Whipple Papers.

post was unwilling to take the responsibility of diminishing the supply of stores on hand, by furnishing the sustenance required for our party for the remainder of the survey. Not being able to purchase elsewhere, we were obliged to await the return of the commanding general.[26] He arrived on the 21st ultimo [October] and immediately directed every assistance to be granted us that his department could afford."

October 23. Campbell, H., came near being shot today by a ball from a musket fired carelessly by a Dragoon. The ball passed so near as to part the hair on the back of his head.

October 24. Very heavy wind today. All the tents of Camp with two exceptions were blown down. Snow all around us.

October 25 to November 7. Nothing of particular importance happened during this space of time.[27]

We had a fandango given us as often as twice a week & the night before leaving Mr. Whipple gave a large fandango in return for the politeness & attention we had received. It was acknowledged to be the best fandango of Albuquerque. It was given in true American style, with a set supper table & appeared to be enjoyed by all. It was attended by the aristocracy of Albu-

[26] Lieut. Whipple did not mention in his official report that, unable to await the return of Gen. Garland, he had borrowed money from a rich landowner and merchant, Dr. Henry Connelly (later governor of the Territory), in order to buy supplies and mules. Gen. John Garland had become the commanding officer of the Military Department in July 1853. With these additional expenses in Albuquerque, Whipple exceeded his budget. See Whipple, Diary, Oct. 9, 12, 1853, Whipple Papers; Simmons, *Albuquerque*, pp. 152, 165; Whipple to Jefferson Davis, May 18, 1854, Whipple Papers.

[27] Möllhausen wrote that the "gaieties" of Albuquerque were not allowed to retard preparations for departure. Whipple was constantly busy preparing for the journey, and Lieut. Ives was placed in charge of recording scientific observations. The Rio Grande was explored for a suitable railroad crossing, and the scientists explored the surrounding countryside. The quartermaster bought and tamed mules. Members of the scientific corps copied reports, notes, sketches, and the railroad profile, and packed specimens for dispatch to the Smithsonian Institution. On October 22 Antoine Leroux of Taos wrote to Whipple that he was too sick to accompany the expedition as a guide, so the lieutenant employed José Manuel Savedra, a Mexican who claimed he had once accompanied the Moqui Indians to the Colorado River in an expedition against the Mohave Indians; Savedra hired additional herders and teamsters in Albuquerque for Whipple. Shortly before the expedition left Albuquerque, however, Leroux agreed to serve as guide. Whipple, feeling obligated to Savedra, hired him as an additional guide for the forthcoming journey. See Whipple, Diary, Oct. 14–Nov. 7; Whipple to Antoine Leroux, Oct. 14, 1853, Whipple Papers; *Report*, Nov. 7, 1853; Möllhausen, *Diary*, II, pp. 6–7.

querque & vicinity.[28] Nearly every night was signalized by a row of some kind, perhaps somebody shot or beaten half to death. Sometimes a fight occurred in which 20 or thirty were engaged. Only two difficulties occurred in our private fandangos. One on account of a soldier who being drunk & dressed in womans clothes insisted on entering the room. Being pushed out he "flared up," pulled off his dress & bonnet, & saying "I was shot once in this room & will have revenge," he rushed into the room. As he entered he was struck three times in the arm with a knife, by the Mexican who gave the fandango. This infuriated him the more & he rushed on untill laid senseless by a blow on the temple from a stone. The blow was so severe as to throw him several feet & through a partition of cloth which separated the room from the bar & gambler's monte-bank (invariable accompaniments of a dance). As soon as he sufficiently recovered, he was taken out & sent to the Hospital. The dance continued till morning, the little row having given fresh life to it. A party of soldiers afterward came to avenge their comrade. As the door was kicked in & fire arms were about to be used, the "Officer of the day" arrived & prevented further trouble by sending all the men to their Companies. The other fuss arose from a drunken fellow firing into the ceiling & putting the Senoritas to flight.

A few days before leaving, a general melee commenced against dogs as a number of them had gone mad. Quite a quantity were killed near the Camp.

During my stay in Albuquerque saw a Catholic funeral, Military funeral, a burial & numerous other sights. On "All Souls day," the 1st of Nov. the Catholics took their offerings to the priest.[29] The church was filled with pigs, hens, chickens, eggs,

[28] Lieut. Whipple did not mention this fandango in his official report and merely noted in his diary that he gave a "grand ball." Möllhausen reported that invitations were sent out to "all the good folks of Albuquerque whom we could regard as educated and presentable." See Whipple, Diary, Nov. 7, 1853, Whipple Papers; Möllhausen, *Diary*, II, p. 20.

[29] All Souls' Day is not the 1st but the 2d of November and is known as the Day of the Dead. On that day New Mexican families brought offerings to the church to honor their dead, and the atmosphere was a festive one. For this holy day and for Mexican attitudes toward death, see Robinson, *Mexico and the Hispanic Southwest in American Literature*, pp. 274–79. The expedition has traveled approximately 310 miles on the journey from Shady Creek to Albuquerque.

onions, turnips, beans, young ones & in fact *all* the *produce* of the country. While hens were cackling in one corner, pigs were grunting in another & children rolling over piles of vegetables, squalling. Bells ringing from morning till night & for two days without cessation.

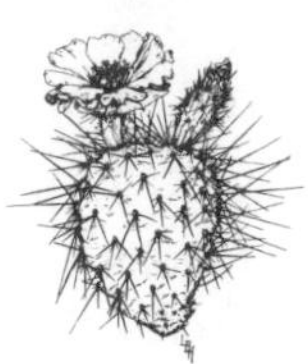

Albuquerque to Leroux's Spring

November 8–December 30, 1853

On November 8 John Sherburne leaves the hospitable town of Albuquerque. With a small party under Lieutenant Ives he moves south to survey the road to the Indian Pueblo of Isleta, chosen as the most suitable site for a railroad crossing of the Rio Grande. Lieutenant Whipple, who has secured the services of two guides, Antoine Leroux and José Manuel Savedra, leads the wagon train two days later on a more direct route to the West. On November 14 the two parties reunite near the Indian Pueblo of Laguna. The expedition follows the San Jose River, crosses the Sierra Madre, and on November 20 reaches the Indian Pueblo of Zuñi. There the expedition finds the population devastated by smallpox, but a council of Zuñi chiefs decides to provide Whipple with guides for the journey to the Little Colorado River.

Traveling west along the 35th parallel, north of the Sitgreaves trail of 1851, the wagon train crosses into present-day Arizona on November 29. It reaches the Little Colorado on December 5, and one week later is joined by an additional escort of troops from Fort Defiance, under the command of Lieutenant John C. Tidball. Lieutenant Whipple then leaves the vicinity of the Sitgreaves trail, which continues north along the Little Colorado, and turns southwest toward the southern base of San Francisco Mountain, a landmark named in the seventeenth century by Franciscan missionaries. By then the wagon train makes "quite a display" with its thirteen wagons, two carts, over one hundred men, and huge herd of mules, cattle, and sheep.

Exploring ahead of the wagon train, Lieutenant Whipple finds a trail across the rough volcanic country, and on Christmas Eve the expedition reaches the Cosnino Caves, near present-day Flagstaff, Arizona. Three days later it arrives at Leroux's (now simply Leroux) Spring, at the base of San Francisco Mountain. There the main party rests while Lieutenant Whipple once more explores ahead to determine the future route.

During this time members of the expedition embark on what to them is a journey into unknown country controlled by Indians and never before undertaken by a wagon train. They pass through Navajo territory, but those dreaded and despised Indians remain as elusive as the Comanches. They experience their first stampede, their first case of smallpox, and a memorable celebration of two cultures on Christmas Eve. But the intense cold and hard travel through the snow of the mountain region exhaust both men and animals, and by December 29 eight men are on the sick list. The expedition has taken 52 days to travel only 360 miles.

Young and robust, John Sherburne remains healthy, interested in his surroundings, and in good spirits. Weightier matters, however, absorb his brother-in-law. When the expedition arrives at Leroux's Spring, Lieutenant Whipple confesses that "the great question" of the future route sits like a night-mare upon his breast.

November 8. Camp 60. Bid farewell to Albuquerque & its hospitable inhabitants. It would not become me to mention the sighs, groans & tears of the Senoritas—that I'll leave for others with a more lively imagination. The trains separated. Lieut. Ives, Dr. Kennely, Mölhausen, Campbell H. & A., White, Parke & my self crossing the river with the intention of going to Isletta [Isleta], that being the place most practicable for a bridge across the Rio Grande. The remainder of the party to start in two days & meet us at Laguna, about two days march from here.[1] On account of a scarcity of surveyors I was relieved temporarily from the Meteorological Dept. to take survey of the road. In crossing

[1]On November 10 the main party under Lieut. Whipple will take the direct route westward. Sherburne's party, under Lieut. Ives, leaves this day to survey a longer southern loop to Isleta before moving west to join the main party at Laguna, 46 miles from Albuquerque. Whipple's railroad profile followed the southern loop from Albuquerque via Isleta to Laguna, the future route of the Atlantic and Pacific Railroad, later the Atchison, Topeka, and Santa Fe (henceforth called the Santa Fe).

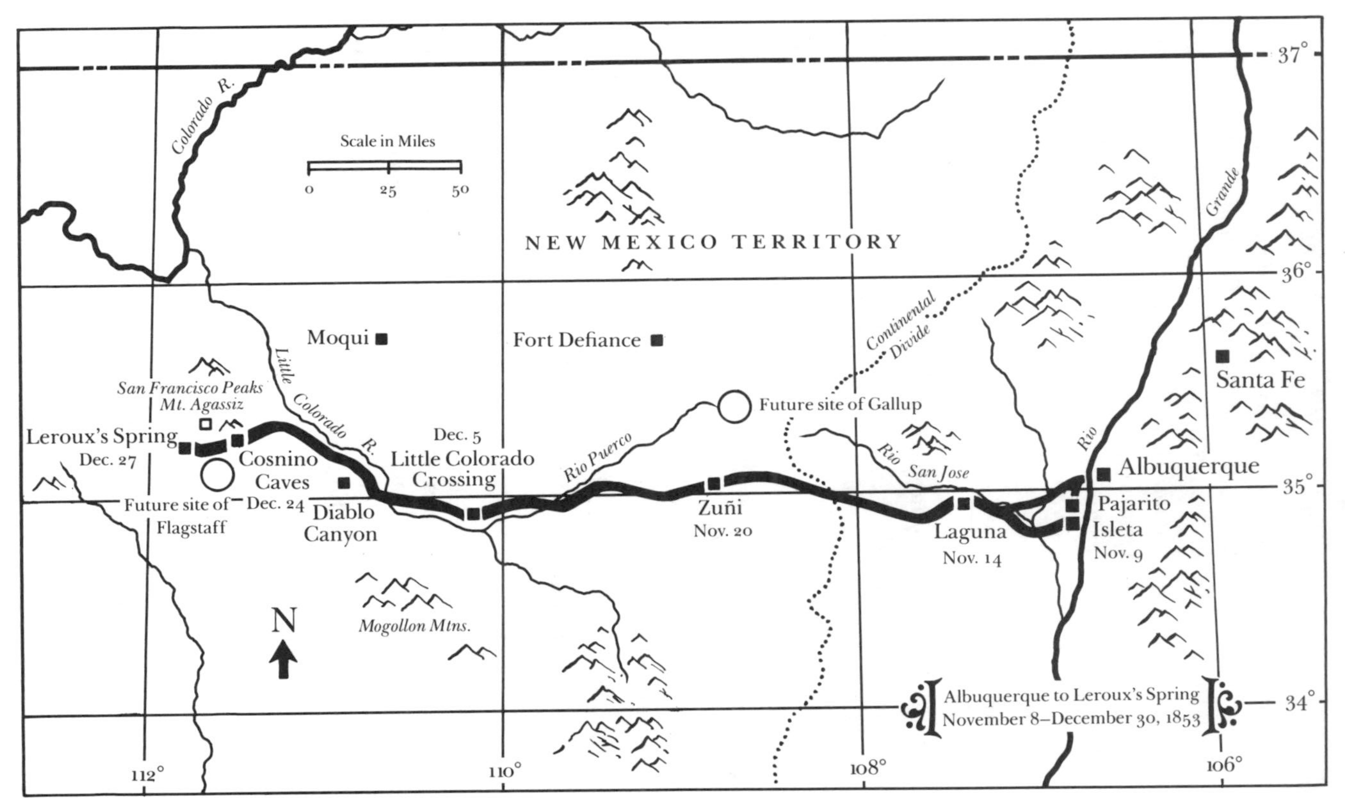

Albuquerque to Leroux's Spring
November 8–December 30, 1853
NEW MEXICO TERRITORY
Scale in Miles
0
25
50
Colorado R.
Little Colorado R.
Rio Grande
Rio Puerco
Rio San Jose
Continental Divide
Santa Fe
Albuquerque
Pajarito
Isleta
Nov. 9
Laguna
Nov. 14
Future site of Gallup
Zuñi
Nov. 20
Fort Defiance
Moqui
Dec. 5
Little Colorado Crossing
Diablo Canyon
Cosnino Caves
Dec. 24
Future site of Flagstaff
San Francisco Peaks
Mt. Agassiz
Leroux's Spring
Dec. 27
Mogollon Mtns.
N
37°
36°
35°
34°
112°
110°
108°
106°

the river, which was commenced about an hour before sundown, we stuck in the middle. The Caratella & two wagons stuck in the sand & a third wagon broke the tongue.

We recd. a reinforcement from Camp & succeeded in getting all across camping on the opposite side about 8 p.m. After taking supper, several of us recrossed the river which was about 3 ft. deep to bid a *long last* farewell to our friends generally & particularly. Returned about 12 o'clk.

November 9. Camp 61. Got wagons repaired this a.m. & started on route. Passed through several Mexican towns. Stopped at Pajarito at the earnest request of Mr. Hubbel & took dinner with him.[2] Passed through Isletta & camped near it on the bank of river. Distance 13 miles.

November 10. Camp 62. Ther. sunrise 24°.5. Took survey of crossing this morning & continued on route. Left the train & road to take a survey along the river bank. Did not reach road till dark. Struck towards Camp, but lost our way & obliged to stop at 9 o'clk to rest our mules & get warm. After building a fire & making ourselves as comfortable as possible, gave the animals an hour's grazing—started again. At 12 o'clk as we were about concluding to give up the search & lay by till morning, came onto the trail. We were then obliged to build another fire as we were chilled through, the Ther. being down to 26° or 24°. Arrived in Camp at 2 in the morning chilled through & finding Camp in anxiety (*excepting those asleep*) they having sent out in search of us with extra mules & hearing nothing. A cup of hot coffee set us right & we turned in. Made 19 miles.

November 11. Camp 63. Ther. sunrise 23°. Started early this a.m. Travelled through a Country very sandy and uneven, interspersed with volcanic peaks. Got into Camp after dark. Made 18¾ miles.

November 12. Ther. sunrise 25°. Lay in Camp to wait for the train. The Missionary of Albuquerque passed through, telling us

[2] Pajarito was a settlement six miles south of Albuquerque on the west bank of the Rio Grande. Almost certainly "Mr. Hubbel" was James Lawrence Hubbell, a former U.S. soldier married to the Hispanic heiress to a 45,000-acre Pajarito land grant. Known as "don Santiago," Hubbell will ride with the party until November 17. See Stanley, Diary, Nov. 17, 1853; Simmons, *Albuquerque*, p. 161; Whipple, Diary, Oct. 28, 1853, Whipple Papers.

that the train was about 12 miles behind in Camp & would join us tomorrow.

Near Camp on a bluff is the ruins of an old Mexican town, long since deserted.

Whipple, *Report*, November 13: "Opposite Lieutenant Ives' camp is the point of a red sandstone bluff, one hundred and fifty feet high, upon which are perched the dilapidated stone houses of Rancho Colorado. . . . The houses, as Captain Simpson describes, had been converted to sheep-folds; but how sheep could have clambered up the nearly perpendicular walls . . . none could understand."

November 13. Ther. sunrise 27°. The train arrived about 2 p.m., took dinner with us & then kept on to the town [Laguna] where we join them tomorrow.

November 14. Camp 64. Ther. sunrise 25°. Started this morning at sunrise & came in sight of the train at Laguna about 9 a.m. Gained on them untill about 12, when lost the viameter which delayed us an hour & they got into Camp at Cubero before us. Arrived there about 3½ p.m. A fandango was given us by the Alcalde. The generality of the females are lighter complexion than those of Albuquerque but cannot vie with them in beauty. Passed today through a wild but volcanic Country, soil sandy most of the way. Made 10 miles.

Möllhausen, *Diary,* II, pp. 57, 60: "Before following our waggons, [Dr. Kennerly and I] . . . went to see the town [of Laguna], and in the burial place of the Indians my friend Kennerly contrived to pocket, unobserved, a very well-preserved skull, which he triumphantly exhibited to me when we got beyond the reach of sharp Indian eyes . . . ; but if the Indians had had any idea of the robbery we had committed, we should probably not have been allowed to escape so easily. We did succeed, however, in carrying it off unobserved to the camp, and there made all possible haste to hide it in one of the waggons. . . . [At] a Mexican settlement, the town of Covero [Cubero] . . . the houses, crowded closely together, presented a melancholy picture of poverty and dirt, and such of the population as we saw about gave the impression of people who would only work just as much as was necessary to keep them in existence, and enable them to dance an occasional fandango.

November 15. Camp 65. Ther. sunrise 28°. Made 15 miles today & halted on a fine stream of water. Country mostly volcanic & very *wild.*

November 16. Camp 66. Ther. sunrise 25° Made 18 miles & halted for the first time without water. Had sufficient in the train for bread & coffee but none for the animals. Passed by a large quantity of volcanic rocks thrown together in the wildest confusion, heaped in some places forty feet high. Abundance of pine timber today. One wagon broke down which delayed the train an hour. Lieut. Jones, Campbell, H.[A.], & Leroux our guide, started this a.m. for Fort Defiance intending to join us again in about five days.[3] The train will not pass that way. I still continue the Survey on the main route.

November 17. Camp 67. Ther. sunrise 29° Started before daylight this morning with trains & without taking breakfast. White & self obliged to wait till light enough to read compass & viameter. Arrived in Camp in time for breakfast. Travelled a little over 8 miles & camped on "Cold Stream" [Agua Fria] at 10 a.m. Very little lava today. Country mostly heavily timbered with tall pines. Fire-arms & ammunition reissued today as we are on the borders of the Indian Country (Navahoes). A prospect of snow during day & slight fall in evening.

November 18. Camp 68. Ther. sunrise 17°3. Coldest morning. Travelled nearly 18 miles & camped at "Inscription Rock" so called on account of the numerous names & inscriptions upon it. The oldest name was dated 1620. Near the rock is a fine spring. On the summit is the ruin of an old Pueblo settlement, long since deserted. The rock is about 300 ft. in height & on one side perpendicular.[4]

[3] On October 24, as we know, Lieut. Whipple had requested from Gen. Garland an additional escort of 25 dragoons because of anticipated problems with Indians. The general could not spare his prized mounted troops, but promised an escort from Fort Defiance of 25 infantry, some mounted on mules. Established in 1851, Fort Defiance (in present-day Arizona) was 190 miles northwest of Albuquerque, at Cañon Bonito. Whipple dispatched his men "to hasten the escort." The guide Sherburne mentions is Antoine Leroux, the French-Canadian guide for the Sitgreaves expedition of 1851, whom Whipple was so anxious to hire even before he left Washington, D.C. See Whipple, Diary, Oct. 24, 27, Nov. 17, Whipple Papers, and *Report*, Nov. 7, 1853; Bender, *The March of Empire*, p. 38.

[4] Long a Spanish landmark known as *El Morro* because it reminded early explorers of a Moorish castle, the mesa (now a national monument) was named Inscription Rock in 1849 by Lieut. James Simpson. The oldest Spanish name apparently was carved in 1605. Whipple estimated that the Indian carvings, much fainter than the Spanish, were at least 400 years old—a conservative estimate in

Passed over the great dividing ridge [the Continental Divide along the Zuñi Mountains] this a.m. On account of the abruptness of ascent & grade was obliged to make a reconnaissance with Mr. W. Run the line through a Cañon with much less grade. Very cold all day, with occasional flits of snow.

November 19. Camp 69. Ther. sunrise 9°.7. Travelled 14¾ miles & camped at "Pescado Spring."

November 20. Camp 70. Ther. sunrise 19°. Travelled 12 miles & Camped about 5 miles from Zuñi,[5] where we are to wait for Lieut. Jones, Campbell & Leroux from Ft. Defiance.

Stanley, Diary: "At 2 p.m. came in sight of the Pueblo of Zuñi. . . . We found that the smallpox had been raging in the place and out of somewhat more than a thousand inhabitants, one hundred had died from the disease. Among the deaths was that of Chas. Overman, the agent of Capt. Ker[6] and it was with sad feelings that I entered the miserable place where this poor man had breathed his last, suffering from a horrid disease and in the midst of strangers, uncivilized and ignorant of the art of caring for the sick. . . . Passed a night of much suffering from the cold."

November 21. Camp 70. Ther. sunrise 20°. Lay in Camp today—a portion of party went to Zuñi.[7] The small-pox is raging

---

the light of later archaeological studies. The ruin on the summit was Atsinna, an Indian pueblo abandoned by the late 1300's. See Simpson, "Report of an Expedition," p. 119; Whipple, *Report*, Nov. 18, 1853; Ortiz, ed., *Handbook of North American Indians*, vol. 9, p. 469.

[5] An ancient Pueblo, Zuñi (frequently now spelled with a plain "n") lies on the banks of the Zuñi River, 40 miles south of present-day Gallup, New Mexico. There is a vast anthropological literature on this fascinating Pueblo and its culture, but the history of Zuñi before the late nineteenth century has been neglected. See Simmons in Ortiz, ed., *Handbook of North American Indians*, vol. 9, pp. 206–23, esp. p. 222, and pp. 467–513.

[6] Croghan Ker, a captain in the U.S. dragoons until 1851, was the sutler at Fort Defiance. He accompanied the expedition from Albuquerque and supplied Quartermaster Stanley with corn. Ker returned to Albuquerque on November 29, carrying mail and specimens for the Smithsonian, and the animals henceforth had to depend on winter grasses. See Stanley, Diary, Nov. 13, 28, 1853; Whipple, Diary, Nov. 11, Whipple Papers, and *Report*, Nov. 13, 29, 1853.

[7] Because of the epidemic, Sherburne and most of the other members of the expedition did not enter the Pueblo. Perhaps the medical supplies did not include sufficient smallpox vaccine to help the Indians, but their chiefs may have preferred their own remedies. Epidemics of European diseases like smallpox were so catastrophic for Indians that some scholars have proposed viewing them as a "disease frontier" rolling in advance of other frontiers. Recent scholarship

fearfully carrying off the inhabitants by dozens & everything is in confusion in the town. It is an Indian pueblo.

Möllhausen, *Diary*, II, p. 97: "Its houses are built like those of Santo Domingo, in the terraced style, with from three to seven stories, one above the other, each smaller than the one below it, so that each possesses a small fore-court or gallery; but the streets below the houses are very narrow, and sometimes entirely covered by building over. There is a Roman Catholic church in the town . . . very simple in its interior decorations, having only a few bad pictures and worse statues round the walls."

November 22. Ther. sunrise 22° Still in Camp—waiting for the party from Ft. Defiance. Also bringing up a portion of the work.

November 23. Ther. sunrise 16°5. The "Gobernador" visited us today & held council in Camp.[8] He is an aged man, about 75 or 80. He appeared sad, as he had lost two nephews by the small-pox.

Whipple, *Report*: "A small party visited the pueblo today. . . . Upon reaching the town of Zuñi, a most revolting spectacle met our view. Smallpox had been making terrible ravages among the people, and we were soon surrounded by great numbers—men, women, and children—exhibiting this loathsome disease in various stages of its progress. . . . We ascended to the house-tops, climbing ladder after ladder. . . . Here

suggests that the Indian population of the United States dwindled by more than 90 percent between the late fifteenth and the middle of the nineteenth century, chiefly because of epidemics. Such a theory, however, depends upon more accurate estimates of the early population than are available. Nevertheless, the impact of European diseases upon Indians is almost impossible to exaggerate. See Utley, *The Indian Frontier*, p. 12; Jacobs, "The Indian and the Frontier," pp. 44–48; Ortiz, ed., *Handbook of North American Indians*, vol. 9, p. 193; Dippie, *The Vanishing American*, pp. xv–xvii; Davidson and Lytle, *After the Fact*, I, chap. 5.

[8] The gobernador, the governor and "ruling spirit" of the Pueblo, introduced himself by his Spanish name of Pedro Pino, customary when dealing with whites. Zuñi's social organization was sophisticated, with a council of caciques, or chiefs, who appointed other officials such as war chiefs and peace chiefs, the latter likened by Whipple to superintendents of police. Officials, however, were regarded only as first among equals. Through conversations with Zuñi officials, Whipple (immune to smallpox) collected a vocabulary and information on the Pueblo's culture, writing at length in his diary and more briefly in his official reports. Whipple's respectful observations have been neglected by anthropologists. See Whipple, Diary, Nov. 23–26, Whipple Papers, and *Report*, Nov. 23, 26, 1853; *Reports of Explorations and Surveys*, III, Part III ("Indian Tribes"), p. 31; Driver, *Indians of North America*, p. 398. For an analysis of Whipple's observations and speculations, based chiefly on entries in his diary, see Conrad, "Whipple at Zuni," pp. 28–48.

A lithograph of Möllhausen's drawing of Zuñi Pueblo, in which he exaggerated the height of the cliffs towering behind the Pueblo in order to dramatize the setting. In this lithograph, some of the artist's detail of the Pueblo was removed. Courtesy David Miller.

A lithograph of Balduin Möllhausen's drawing of a Zuñi war chief and a warrior. The chief holds a rawhide Navajo shield, decorated with the head of Montezuma, which Lieutenant Whipple bought for the Smithsonian Institution. *Reports of Explorations and Surveys,* vol. III.

are many tamed eagles. They are caught in the cliffs when young, and become quite domesticated. The people are not willing to part with them. From the top the pueblo reminds one of an immense ant-hill, from its similar form and dense population. The number of inhabitants is estimated at 2000."

November 24. Ther. sunrise 27° Camp flooded with Indians from Zuñi, some with fresh marks of small-pox on faces and hands. The "Gobernador," his war-chief & Lieut. came today in their war dresses & had their portraits taken by Mölhausen. Jones, Campbell & Leroux arrived today from Ft. Defiance.[9]

[9] Lieut. Whipple had instructed A. H. Campbell to make a survey of the route on the way to Fort Defiance, 60 miles northwest of Zuñi. Campbell then recom-

They went there for the purpose of obtaining an increased escort of 25 men by order of Gen. Garland. The escort will meet us on our first or second days march. Sevadra (our guide No. 2) left us today to find a road for wagons & good camping places.[10] We start without a road as this is the extent of wagon travelling. The remainder of the road we have to find.

November 25. Ther. sunrise 23°.5. Camp full of pueblos—Sevadra returned today with information of a sandy road, by cutting down trees. Water four miles the other side of Zuñi. It is the intention to start tomorrow.

November 26. Camp 71. Ther. sunrise 26°.7. Struck camp about 11½ & made a march of 9 miles to the other side of Zuñi. Camped on a running stream of water.

Passed through the town of Zuñi & saw victims of the small pox at every corner. They were in every stage of the disease.

Left the road today at Zuñi & with our guides took a nearly westward course across the country. Clouds during evening & slight fall of rain.

November 27. Ther. sunrise 44°.8. Raining nearly all night. The first rain since Sept. 30. Also raining all day. Obliged to lay by & send Teamsters to cut the road through the timber, which is ahead of us & extends no one knows how far. For certainty 20 miles, as it has been explored that distance.[11]

---

mended the northwest detour as the more suitable route for a railroad. The railroad profile drawn on the route from Isleta followed this northwest detour through "Campbell's Pass" in the Sierra Madre, then ran along the valley of the Rio Puerco of the West to the point where it joined the expedition's route at the Rio Puerco crossing (Camp 75). The railroad profile became the route of the Santa Fe Railroad. Möllhausen sketched a war chief and a warrior. The chief carried a rawhide shield of Navajo manufacture that Whipple secured for the Smithsonian. See Whipple, Diary, and *Report*, both entries for Nov. 24, 1853; *Reports of Explorations and Surveys*, III, Part III ("Indian Tribes"), pp. 30, 52.

[10] As we know Lieut. Whipple employed José Manuel Savedra (not Sevadra) on October 22 in Albuquerque after receiving word that Antoine Leroux was too sick to accompany him. Retained as a second guide, Savedra received half the amount ($1200) paid to Leroux. See Whipple, Diary, Oct. 14, 22, 1853, Jan. 14, 1854, Whipple Papers, and *Report*, Nov. 7, 1853. See also the Biographical Appendix to this volume.

[11] The other diarists also believed that they were heading into country unexplored by white men. No wagon train had made the journey before, but Whipple for one knew that others such as Sitgreaves, Aubry, and Walker had crossed the region before him. Whipple, however, believed that his expedition would find a new path due west along the 35th parallel. Even though he frequently crossed or

There is a great peculiarity here in this climate. The Ther. ranging from 9° to 30° at sunrise & from 50° to 70° in the middle of the day. A delegation of several Indians from Zuñi came in Camp just before dark, with information of a good road. It appears that after we left they had a meeting to discuss whether or not 'twould be for their benefit to tell us of the proper and best road. Coming to the conclusion that 'twas best, they sent a delegation to bring the information & offered two of their men as guides.[12]

Tomorrow we retrace our steps a few miles & take a new start from Zuñi.

Whipple, *Report*: "At noon the Zuñi war chief arrived to inform us that a council upon our affairs had been held the preceding night. . . . They approved of the objects of our expedition, and determined to afford all the aid in their power. They knew of a better route to the Colorado Chiquito [Little Colorado] than that which Savedra proposed, and offered to send guides to show it to us. No recompense was asked. This illustrates a trait in Indian character—to act with deliberation, and not from impulse."

November 28. Camp 72. Ther. sunrise 23°.5. One of the Mexican packers run off last night carrying a mule. It is the intention to send a couple of Indians for him. He is the fourth or fifth packer & herder that has taken French leave. Retraced our road a couple of miles & struck off in a valley to the left of the road, found there a good passage for wagons & no trees to cut. The two Indians from Zuñi accompanied us. The place chosen was far superior to that of yesterday. The soil was sandy, in many places the wheels sunk from 8 to 12 inches—otherwise there was no trouble. Encamped in a beautiful spot surrounded by high hills, sheltering us from the wind. Plenty of wood, but no water.

---

paralleled the Sitgreaves trail between Camps 76 and 106, Whipple with his wagons frequently could not follow the routes chosen by the earlier explorers, all leaders of pack trains. See Whipple, *Report*, Nov. 29, 1853; Möllhausen, *Diary*, II, pp. 22, 94; Stanley, Diary, Nov. 26, 1853.

[12] Actually there were three guides, José Hacha, José Maria, and Juan Séptimo. The first two, both war chiefs, were father and son. The third, described by Whipple as a wealthy man, was an unofficial guide; he later became the gobernador of Zuñi. They were familiar with the territory stretching to the Little Colorado because it was a Zuñi hunting ground. See Stanley, Diary, Nov. 26, 1853; Whipple, Diary, Nov. 27, Whipple Papers, and *Report*, Nov. 28, 1853; Horgan, *Lamy of Santa Fe*, p. 305.

We stopped about 11 at a spring, watered the animals & filled the canteens & kegs. Made nearly 11 miles. Air very cold. Ther. ranging from 40° to 46°. Appearance of snow this morning, but clouds dissipated shortly after sunrise. Very heavy frost last night. 9 p.m.— Camp looks remarkably picturesque tonight. Wood is plenty & fifteen camp fires are in full blast, the flames curling up in every direction. The songs of the herders, mingled with the crackling of the cedar, the neighs of the mules & the bleating of the sheep makes one feel quite romantic. Groups are gathered round their respective fires discussing the topics of the day—occasionally making the air ring with a merry laugh. A spirit of life appears to pervade the party. On the West side of Camp are our tents. In front is the Corral with the animals stretching their heads over the ropes as though astonished at the unusual bustle. On the opposite side is the soldiers Camp, illuminated by several fires which reflect brightly on the sun-burnt features gathered round them. On the right are the Camps of our Mexican herders & packers, the sheep gathering round the fires & forming a portion of the family circle.

Descended today 60 ft.

November 29. Camp 73. Ther. sunrise 34.°5. Travelled 20 miles today over a heavy sandy road the wheels sinking half way to the hubs most of the time. Crossed a ridge where the ascent was very steep—obliged to cut away the trees & dig the road. The wagons got down without much trouble. Did not pass through much timber tho' an abundance on each side principally cedar. Water brackish. The water tonight is about a quarter of a mile from Camp & in a circular well [Jacob's Well] the diameter of the top being about 200 ft. and the descent to the water about 100 or 125 ft. The path leading down is a winding one gradually approaching the bottom. The descent being so steep as not to be approached immediately. A party of Indians amounting to about 70 were seen tonight, a mile from Camp—probably Navahoes. They encamped not far from us. The runaway Mexican was brought back last night but no signs of the mule—he denies taking it tho', but few are in doubt about it. Descended today 276 ft.

November 30. Camp 74. Ther. sunrise 30°— Descended 269 ft. Travelled 7½ miles—camped near several springs, the water bub-

A lithograph of Balduin Möllhausen's drawing of two Navajo horsemen who approached the expedition's camp on November 30, 1853, but left upon learning of a case of smallpox in the camp. Lieutenant Whipple complained that the artist gave the Navajos the features of Pueblo Indians, but the sketch is an excellent rendition of Navajo costume. *Reports of Explorations and Surveys,* vol. III.

bling thro' the sand.[13] Plenty of water but no wood in Camp. The ground in the vicinity is covered with pieces of wood, petrified into agate, flint & some a species of Jasper.

The last day of Autumn in the States. Weather here is clear & mild. Ther. ranging from 50° to 60° in the middle of the day.

Saw two antelope, the first seen since arriving at Albuquerque. Soil very sandy. Saw an Indian signal today. It consisted of a straight column of smoke. As soon as the train turned the bluff & came in sight it suddenly vanished. It was about 6 miles dis-

[13] These were the Navajo Springs, a few miles west of present-day Navajo, a station on the Santa Fe Railroad. There on Dec. 29, 1863, federal officials inaugurated the government of Arizona Territory. The wagon train had crossed into present-day Arizona on the preceding day; the landmark of Jacob's Well, noted by Sherburne, is in Arizona. See Barnes, ed., *Arizona Place Names,* pp. 13, 17.

tant. Evening— Two Navahoes appeared on a ridge about 500 yds from Camp near 7 o'clock.[14] They were mounted on their ponies & held long lances. At first they appeared afraid to approach but finally met several who went from Camp to see them. Nothing could induce them to come into Camp. They would take nothing to eat, drink or smoke, so great was their fear of catching the small-pox.

One of our Teamsters has been sick with the small-pox for a week or more. His face is covered with marks of the disease & great fear is had of [it] spreading thro' Camp. Nearly all of the party have been newly vaccinated so as to prevent it if possible.

Möllhausen, *Diary*, II, p. 115: "We were startled by the cry of 'Navahoes!' passing through the camp; but it appeared there were but two of this robber tribe, who had cautiously approached us to reconnoitre. . . . The two Indians carried on a dialogue with [the Zuñi guide] at some distance . . . they were somewhat in fear of him, as he had come out of a town where the small-pox was raging; and when they learned that we, too, had some cases in our camp, their fear increased so much that they disappeared very soon. The Indians have suffered so severely from this malady that their terror was not at all surprising, and it is very possible that we may have had our small-pox patients to thank for remaining unmolested by the Navahoe Indians during our whole journey through their hunting-grounds."

December 1. Camp 75. Ther. sunrise 24°.5. A beautiful day for the first day of Winter. Made a little over 12 miles & arrived at Camp about 4 p.m. No wood or water. Encamped on the dry bed of a stream where water was finally found by digging. Road today very sandy. No timber & very little grass.

December 2. Camp 76. Ther. sunrise 24°.5. Descended 13 ft. Made 11½ miles. Road very sandy. No wood. Water 1½ miles from Camp.

We are encamped on the bank of an "arroyo" about 2 miles wide & 200 ft. deep in the bottom of which are mounds of red & brownish earth thrown together in the wildest confusion forming a most magnificent sight. In some places the mounds will

[14] Whipple wrote that the Navajos were hunters from Cañon de Chelly, a stronghold in the heart of Navajo country north of Fort Defiance; he estimated the Navajo population at 10,000. Since the expedition met with no other Navajos, Whipple obtained a vocabulary from one of the herders who had been their prisoner for nine months. See Whipple, *Report*, Nov. 30, Dec. 7, 1853.

ascend about 30 ft. & in others 100 or more, the top pointed & the whole resembling the base of a stalagmite cave. It extends in both directions as far as the eye can reach. Passed today immense masses of petrified wood.[15] Whole trees, with very long bases lying on the ground in a complete state of petrification—the half of one tree being smoky cornelian. Anxious to take a specimen, I broke off a horizontal section having a vein of red & white cornelian. The large quantity of petrification led us to the supposition that a grove of trees had fallen & turned into that state.

On the left of Camp, about 20 miles distant is a range of mountains, snow-capped.

A large quantity of antelope seen today.

Evening— In the arroyo near Camp is a fallen grove of trees, petrified. The largest of which measured 9 ft. in diameter at the stump or base, the length was not measured as the tree was broken.

December 3. Camp 77. Ther. sunrise 26°.5. Descended 270 ft. Country very sandy. Made nearly 12 miles. In crossing a very sandy creek [Lithodendron] a great deal of trouble was had. The wagons sunk to the axle-trees & the mules to their bellies. Nearly every wagon stalled in the sand & water. Tho' the crossing was but ¾ of a mile it took two hours before the train was entirely over. Double teams were necessary for every one, one wagon tongue broke & the wagon had to be unloaded before it could be extricated. Another wagon pulled the tongue from the bolts.

Quite a quantity of petrified wood today—one tree being completely encased in a sandstone boulder. The tree was of sandstone & cornelian both red & white. No wood in Camp—water 1 mile distant & very poor.

December 4. Ther. sunrise 25°. Lay by today— Camp assumed a "Sunday like" aspect, scarcely a sound could be heard. The weather was very warm & parties might be seen lying in their shirt sleeves in some shady spot, reading their old letters.

The escort is expected daily, we expect a mail by Lieut. Tidball,

[15] The expedition is in the region of the magnificent Petrified Forest, since 1906 a national park. On December 1 the train crossed to the north bank of the Rio Puerco of the West and now is near (somewhat north of) the Sitgreaves trail The railroad profile followed the Whipple expedition's route, the later path

the commander.[16] There was a stampede among the sheep last night. The wolves run them round Camp & then over the hill on the West side of Camp. They were found about two miles distant this morning & apparently all safe.

Leroux went ahead today reconnoitering & came back towards evening reporting the Little Colorado about 10 miles distant. Water clear. Plenty of wood.

December 5. Camp 78. Ther. sunrise 19°.5. Descended 130 ft. Made 12 miles & camped on the Little Colorado. On the banks were shot a porcupine, grey owl & other animals for specimens.

Road today, sandy. Plenty of wood in Camp. Tonight the two Indians of Zuñi accompanied by a Moqui, came charging into camp. The Zuñians were sent a couple of days ago into the Moqui villages to obtain us a guide to the Rio Colorado.[17]

At Moqui village they found everyone dying with the smallpox which raged fearfully. Horses grazing without owners, corn lying loose & everything in a most dreadful state.

Every old inhabitant with two exceptions had died with the disease. Dead men lying in every house—also round the houses, on the ground & on the banks of the River. As the disease took them they would leave their houses, go a little distance & die. The children appeared to have been spared & were playing among the corpses. In the language of the Indian "The Moqui nation is extinct." This disease is raging among all the Indian tribes of this Country. We are very much alarmed for fear we will have it in Camp as the Teamster who now has it is just at the

---

of the Santa Fe Railroad through such present-day Arizona towns as Holbrook and Winslow. See Foreman, ed., *A Pathfinder*, p. 153, n. 8.

[16] John C. Tidball, an artillery officer stationed at Fort Defiance, graduated from the U.S. Military Academy in 1848. See Cullum, *Biographical Register*, and the Biographical Appendix to this volume.

[17] José Maria and Juan Séptimo had left for the Moqui villages on November 30; José Hacha remained as guide. Officially called the Hopi after 1895, the Moqui occupied seven pueblos in present-day northeastern Arizona. Even more isolated than the Zuñi Indians, the Moquis were brought into closer contact with whites, and their diseases, after the establishment of Fort Defiance in 1851. The expedition's route for the next thirty miles runs parallel to the Sitgreaves trail across the river. This camp is somewhat north of the junction of the Rio Puerco and the Little Colorado, near present-day Holbrook, Arizona. See Whipple, *Report*, Nov. 29–30, 1853; Möllhausen, *Diary*, II, p. 100; Ortiz, ed., *Handbook of North American Indians*, vol. 9, p. 525; Wallace, "Across Arizona to the Big Colorado," p. 333, n. 17.

stage when infection is most probable. The Indians informed us that a short distance from us there was an encampment of "Coyotaros"[18] & that we would pass through there tomorrow.

Whipple, *Report*: "This evening [the Zuñi Indians] came prancing into camp. . . . Their mission had been performed, but no Moqui guide could be obtained. The smallpox had swept off nearly every male adult from three pueblos. . . . They were dying by fifties per day; and the living, unable to bury the dead, had thrown them down the steep sides of the lofty mesas upon which the pueblos are built. There wolves and ravens had congregated in myriads to devour them. The decaying bodies had even infected the streams, and the Zuñians were obliged to have recourse to melons both for food and drink."

December 6. Camp 79. Ther. sunrise 19°.2. Descended 117 ft. Made 14½ miles up the river & camped on its banks. Road not as sandy as of late but filled with deep arroyos which caused much delay to the trains. Broke several wagons & obliged to unload one. The pack mules & some of the party went ahead & camped. It became dark when we were about 3 miles from them & had they not turned back we would have been obliged to Camp without them. As it was did not meet them till long after dark. Did not see the Coyotaros as expected. They are on the opposite side of the river. Our Zuñi Indians left us this morning to return home.

Another Teamster taken sick today, probably with the small pox but not certain as yet. Found a fossil tree today, measuring 7.4 ft. in diameter.

December 7. Camp 80. Ther. sunrise 12°. Descended 83 ft. Made 8½ miles. Road very bad. Several of the wagons stalled in the mud & mire & several mules gave out. Halted on bank of Little Colorado.

December 8. Camp 81. Ther. sunrise 15°. Ascended 2 ft. A little over 5 miles today. Road bad—proposed to lay by here till explorations are made. Cold all day with signs of snow. Camp on Rio.

[18] Called Coyoteros by the Spanish, these Indians formed one of the largest subgroups of Western Apaches. Athapaskan-speaking people, Coyoteros ranged from the Black River through the headwaters of the Salt River to the edge of the Mogollon Rim of present-day Arizona. They were little known to whites until Anglos began to interfere with their ranges in the 1860's. See *Reports of Explorations and Surveys*, III, Part III ("Indian Tribes"), p. 14; Spicer, *Cycles of Conquest*, p. 244.

Whipple, Diary: "From a high hill 2 miles north of camp far as the eye could reach the valley swept northward. Here then we propose to reconnoitre westward toward the southern slope of San Francisco Mountains hoping to avoid the circuitous course recommended by both guides Leroux and Savedra.[19] It is decidedly against their opinion and advice that this exploration is attempted. But it is necessary to see with our own eyes the obstacles said to render our route, directly on our parallel of 35°, impracticable."

December 9. Camp 82. Ther. sunrise 27°. Moved Camp 1½ miles today, to a camp of good water, wood & grazing, where we are to lay until the return of the reconnoitering party which starts tomorrow.

About 8 p.m. the mules took a stampede, frightened probably by the wolves. All camp turned out & rushed up the hill where they were grazing in expectation of seeing Indians. The escort headed by Lieut. Jones bringing up the rear. On our arrival at the herd they were found docile & gentle having stopped of their own accord. The herders were the most frightened. We retraced our steps back to Camp enjoying the alarm. A general disappointment prevailed. It was thought by Leroux there were Indians in the vicinity.

Whipple, *Report*: "Near by is the remnant of a ruin as extensive as any yet seen.[20] An isolated hill of sandstone is the foundation of this ancient pueblo. . . . In few places are the faces of walls visible above the debris of stones, vigas [rafters], and pottery. The colors of the latter are black, red, white, and yellow, worked into a variety of figures, but representing no animals. The indented kind, said to be very ancient, is here found in many patterns. A stone axe and several pretty arrow-heads of obsidian or cornelian were picked up from the ruins."

December 10. Ther. sunrise 33°. Prospect of snow all day—air quite chilly. This morning about 2 o'clk as the mules were turned out, they took a stampede which gave the Camp another alarm.

[19] Whipple did not mention in his official report that he declined to take his guides' advice. The Sitgreaves trail, the guides' preference, moved farther north along the Little Colorado to Grand Falls before heading northwest away from the river. See Wallace, "Across Arizona to the Big Colorado," pp. 337–38.

[20] This ruin was one of the Homolovi group (Homolovi I) of prehistoric pueblos built by ancestors of the Hopi and situated near present-day Winslow, Arizona. Whipple's official report included the first published account of Homolovi. See Ortiz, ed., *Handbook of North American Indians*, vol. 9, p. 123; Wallace, "Across Arizona to the Big Colorado," p. 336.

It was however quieted by the wagonmaster saying, "all right." At day-light it was reported that half of the mules were gone. The remainder were driven into the corral & counted showing over 80 missing & the best mules of the party. Camp was instantly alarmed & after finding from track the direction taken, dispatched Americans & Mexicans in pursuit. They came for provisions for several days, intending to keep chase till successful. About noon several of the party started, consisting of the Quarter Master, White, Hutton & Leroux. A messenger came in about two stating that nothing had yet been learned of the runaways. About 4 p.m. another came in stating they were all found at our 1st Camp on the river, a distance from here of 35 miles. Everyone gave over the chase but the Mexicans & they succeeded in finding them. They were brought back to Camp about 8 p.m. in rather a lame state having travelled 70 miles. Two gave out on the way back—one was shot & the other rubbed with gunpowder & left back till morning, hoping by that time to be sufficiently recovered to reach Camp.

The cause of the stampede is unknown. Some attribute it to wolves, but the most probable conclusion is, that they were started by two wild horses that are attached to the train. Great blame is given the American herders for not reporting the loss before morning. They probably disliked the idea of being sent for them.

The exploring party which was to start this morning were obliged to remain & will not get off before Monday the 12th, on account of the dilapidated state of the mules. Had the mules not been recovered the train would quite probable have been left here with the exception perhaps of one or two wagons. This would have put a damper on the spirits of most everyone.

Tune of "Nelly was a Lady"

Now I'm unhappy & I'm weeping
Cant sing my good old songs today
Last night while we were all a sleeping
Eighty mules got scared & run away

Chorus— Now we all were sober
When morning came,
For we feared we'd have to go
And leave behind the train.

But we all were happy
When evening came
For the mules they all came back
And we could take the train.

The Author.

Dedicated to the "U.S.P.R.S.N.M.R." party.[21]

Whipple, Diary: "Lieut. Jones' horse chose however as usual to take fright, at a coyote probably, and created an estampede [estampido] of the mulada. . . . Four of our Mexican men trustworthy & brave . . . spurred on their jaded animals in pursuit until they overtook the frightened horses that led the mulada. . . . Mexicans upon such occasions I prefer to men of any other nation. They appreciate the importance of success. Fatigue & hunger they count for nothing and life itself they would forfeit sooner than the confidence reposed in them. . . . In my estimation few Americans appreciate the merits of our new citizens acquired with the acquisition of New Mexico. Their virtues as well as their vices are peculiar but compared with the ignorant class of the population of eastern states they are vastly superior."

December 11. Ther. sunrise 43°.5. Sprinkling of rain & hail today. Mules not in proper state for the exploration party, so concluded to wait till tomorrow. The mule left back yesterday, was brought up this morning in pretty good condition. Another porcupine killed today.

December 12. Ther. sunrise 35°.8. The morning was so blustering that the exploration party thought it advisable not to start. Weather squally with occasional showers.

About 2 p.m. the escort of Lieut. Tidball hove in sight & came down to Camp. Lieut. T. brought us our mail from Ft. Defiance as we expected—of course he was joyfully welcomed. I recd. letters from home & other correspondents as well as a good supply (5) of Boston & Ports'm Journals. He brought with him 25 soldiers, 150 sheep & 53 mules. Our caval yard[22] consists of 230 mules—& altogether we have 450 sheep. Adding to these, 13 wagons & 2 caratellas makes quite a display. The number in

[21] The initials no doubt stand for "United States Pacific Railroad Survey New Mexico Route."

[22] Sherburne spells phonetically the word "cavallard" or "caviliarde," a corruption of the word "cavallade" or "caballada." It was a term used in Texas and New Mexico, meaning a herd of horses or mules.

Camp is about 130—of these 50 are soldiers—scientific party 13—Lts. Jones, Stanley & Tidball. The remainder made of up Teamsters, Cooks, servants & packers—of the latter, half are Americans & half Mexicans.[23] The escort was delayed a short time by some mules straying away during the night for several miles. Camp has assumed a lively aspect. Newspapers & letters in rapid circulation & plenty of news (to us) flying around. In the evening the new escort made the Camp resound with their merry songs.

Möllhausen, *Diary*, II, p. 129: "On the second day after the stampede there was again a stir and excitement in our camp, but this time it had an agreeable cause, namely, the arrival of Lieutenant Fitzball [Tidball] with the men under his command—five-and-twenty wild daring-looking fellows, whose physiognomies, and entire bearing, were strongly indicative of their having been long in remote, uncivilized territories. They were provided with pack mules, and also with so many for the saddle that half the men could be mounted."

December 13. Ther. sunrise 42°.2. Exploration party started this morning amounting in all to about 30. They took provisions for 10 days. The party consisted of—

Lieut. A. W. Whipple—Chief of party
Lieut. J. M. Jones—Commander of Escort
A. H. Campbell—Topographer
Wm. White, Jr.—Meteorological observer
N. H. Hutton—Surveyor
Jno. M. Bigelow—Physician & Botanist
Leroux & Sevadra—guides
12 soldiers & one Corporal. The remainder consisting of herders, packers, cooks, servants.

Of course no wagons were taken—nothing but packmules— I was left to continue the Barometric Observations tho' I would gladly have gone had I been able.

Quarter Master & Lieut. Tidball crossed the river with them to find a good place to move Camp, as the grass here is getting very poor.

[23] There was some confusion about the number of men with the expedition. Whipple thought there were about 115; Möllhausen estimated the number at 114. Although Möllhausen wrote that there were 16 wagons, Sherburne is cor-

December 14. Camp 83. Ther. sunrise 30°. Left Camp today about 9½ & travelled 4 m. 3380 ft. Camped about 2 on West bank of Little Colorado. Had great difficulty in crossing the sheep which delayed us near an hour. From 30 to 50 were thrown down the steep bank into the river before the remainder would follow. As all the Scientific party had gone exploring, I had to be Surveyor, Topographer, Barometer observer & Viameter reader.

December 15. Ther. Sunrise 24°.5. Lay in Camp to day— Another Teamster broke out with the small pox—he has been sick for several days past.

This afternoon two soldiers & a Mexican came with dispatches from Mr. Whipple, stating he had found a deep cañon where he expected to make a passage through the mountains, that he had followed it to the river about 20 miles from here.[24] He sent orders to reduce transportation as much as possible & move the Camp to that place where he would meet us & hoped to find a passage for wagons. It is proposed by the Quarter Master to throw away all boxes & barrels that can possibly be dispensed with & when we meet Mr. W. to let him decide what else shall be thrown away. It is expected that the tents will go next as they can be spared better than anything else.

Twenty-two of our pack mules have gone with the Exploring party but Lieut. Tidball has kindly offered 12 of his to supply the deficiency. These with the spare saddle mules will probably be sufficient to transport everything that the wagons cannot accommodate. Lieut. Ives relieved me to day from taking Topog'y which made my duties easier.

December 16. Camp 84. Ther. sunrise 7°.5. Last night was the coldest night yet experienced by us & the day throughout by far the coldest. The highest point of the Ther. being 40°—at 9 p.m. 11°.8. A very heavy frost fell last night. This morning the ground

---

rect. See Whipple, Diary, Dec. 12, 1853, Whipple Papers; Möllhausen, *Diary*, II, p. 30; Stanley, Diary, Nov. 10, 1853.

[24] Whipple could not cross this canyon, which in disgust he named Cañon Diablo. It is 225.5 feet in depth, and 26 miles west of Winslow, Arizona. His exploring party rode northeast along its rim, crossed it near its mouth, and then moved west toward San Francisco Mountain. Whipple, unlike Sitgreaves, named all landmarks after entering this region. Many, like Cañon Diablo, still bear his names. See Whipple, *Report*, Dec. 13–18, 1853.

had the appearance of a slight fall of snow. Left Camp this a.m. about 9½ leaving behind—*nothing*—after all the hue about transportation. Travelled along the Little Colorado 11 miles 1210 ft.—road good—very little sand, mostly clay & gravel. Quite a number of black tailed deer seen today & rabbits in abundance. The latter gave us a good breakfast this morning. Another Teamster taken sick today, feared to be small pox. Last night the Teamster already sick with that disease was delirious nearly all night. About 8 p.m. he was found walking around camp with his bed on his shoulders hunting, as he said, for camp. He was taken back to the wagon & about 11 when he was supposed to be asleep, he again started off & was found by one of the sentinals, some distance from Camp with a tin cup in his hand dipping water from the ground & drinking. He was brought back, water given him & a watch put over him for the night. This morning an attendant was given him, also a tent to sleep under. It is feared he got cold last night & as he has never been vaccinated, will go hard with him.

December 17. Camp 85. Ther. sunrise 8°. Left camp this morning made 16 miles 1812 feet. Arrived in Camp at Sunset. Road rather sandy. Arrived at the place from whence Mr. Whipple sent his dispatches, but found him gone—saw his trail.

Teamster very sick today, owing to cold taken the night he was exposed. The disease has appeared in his mouth. Fears are entertained of no recovery.

Several other Teamsters complaining. Probability of our laying here till further dispatches & orders.

December 18. Ther. sunrise 8°.5. Lay by to day—expect to hear some tidings of the exploring party by tomorrow night as they have already been absent 6 days. One week from today is Christmas & two weeks New Years. We will spend them both between this & the Colorado. Parke taken sick with rheumatism in the left knee, he has suffered a great deal today, being in severe pain. No position is comfortable for him & he is unable to move without help.

Nothing heard from Explo'g party— This evening Garner, Mölhausen & myself took two men with wood & went to the top of a hill a short distance from Camp to build a signal fire hoping it might be seen by the party & returned, but were disappointed.

A few minutes before we were to start down the hill we heard a noise like thunder coming from the direction of the caval yards, at the same time a cry of "Stampede" from the herders. We repeated the cry, which resounded through Camp & started everyone to their feet. All followed the herd. Those on foot, myself among the number, although running, were so far distanced by the mules that when we were two miles from Camp the sound of the stampede could not be heard. Those herders mounted kept with them for six miles & succeeded in bringing them back about two hours after the start. The whole number of mules stampeded was about 200—a dozen of the escort mules were tied & served for mounted men to pursue. Quite a rivalry between the Americans & Mexicans. The latter have been considered far superior in pursuing & finding runaway animals. At the last stampede the Americans were rather mortified & in fact angry at the praises bestowed on them [the Mexicans]. Tonight as if anxious for the Stampede they started at the first alarm & succeeded in keeping ahead of the Mexy's & in finding the mules. They now feel equal to their rivals.

The mules in their course took across a deep arroyo. The descent perpendicularly being about 15 ft. & the ascent on the opposite side being about 20 ft. nearly perpendicular.[25] They did not swerve from their course. I was told by those present that at the bottom of the descent they were piled about 10 deep, tho' none appeared hurt by the jump. The opposite bank which they ascended resisted the efforts of those on foot & they were obliged to take a place lower down & less steep. It was quite dark & the arroyo was partially concealed by shrubbery, so that about a dozen men fell down into it cutting their hands & otherwise bruising themselves. Had it not been sandy at the bottom, the effects would have been serious. Some are complaining of broken shins, others of sprained back & cut hands. I saw two fall, one striking on his head & with such a shock as to discharge his pistol—the other striking on his "bellie" & knocking the wind out of him. Both pretty badly scared. Cool tonight.

[25] Following Whipple's instructions to Lieut. Ives, the wagon train is now near the mouth of Cañon Diablo, at which point it is only an arroyo, as described by Sherburne. See Whipple, *Report*, Dec. 14–15, 1853; Foreman, ed., *A Pathfinder*, p. 163, n. 2; Barnes, ed., *Arizona Place Names*, p. 68; Marshall, *Santa Fe*, p. 168.

Ther. 9 p.m. 12° Teamster very sick to-day.

December 19. Camp 86. Ther. sunrise 10°.5. Left Camp this morning & moved 4 m. 2834 ft. in search of better grass. No one went ahead to find the state of the ground & we found ourselves in a place unable to proceed & no grass. Will have to go back again tomorrow, probably 2 miles. Parke better today— Teamster about the same.

December 20. Camp 87. Ther. sunrise 10° Near Camp this morning is a sand stone *rock*—on which are many curious inscriptions & the name "John A. Knight, March 12, 1851."[26] Most of the inscriptions & symbols are Indian. Moved today 3 m. 2934 ft. back on the road of yesterday & one mile from the old Camp 86. Encamped about ½ of a mile from the road of yesterday. At 3 p.m. as "our mess" were at dinner, we heard a cry of "Here they come." On going from the tent, I saw the guides Leroux & Sevadra about ½ mile from Camp & heading for it. In a short time the party headed by Mr. W. & White were seen winding round the bluff a short distance from us.[27] They rode in, all well & in fine spirits. After the necessary shaking of hands was over, was asked the question "Have you found a road?" Our minds were immediately relieved by a general answer of good road, plenty of water & grass, past the mountains. From there to the Colorado is represented by our guides as being a level mesa or table land to the Colorado, interspersed with arroyos but easily passible. In reaching the mountains we have to cross an arroyo over 100 ft. in depth [Cañon Diablo], but it can easily be bridged as 'tis in the vicinity of immense pines. They saw plenty of snow, in one case 'twas 10 or 15 inches in depth. There was a great rejoicing in camp on account of one of the party [Stanley?] being

[26]John A. Knight may have been with Joseph Walker's expedition in the spring of 1851. He was not a member of the Sitgreaves expedition, which set out in the autumn of 1851. This is the last camp on the Little Colorado. The expedition now heads southwest toward San Francisco Mountain. See Gilbert, *Westering Man*, pp. 239–40; personal communication from Professor Andrew Wallace about the membership of the Sitgreaves expedition.

[27]In Whipple's *Report*, Dec. 20, 1853, the Ives party reported that, during the stampede of Dec. 18, the men in pursuit of the mules narrowly escaped breaking their necks. Since Whipple was separated from the main party during much of this time, there is little information about the wagon train in his diary and *Report*. See Whipple, Diary, Dec. 20, 1853, Whipple Papers; Möllhausen, *Diary*, II, p. 144.

A lithograph of Möllhausen's drawing of San Francisco Mountain. In this region the expedition celebrated a memorable Christmas Eve. Courtesy Oklahoma Historical Society.

determined that the wagons should go under & trying with *all his influence* & *authority* to effect that result.

There appears now no great obstacle to prevent us taking our wagons to Calafornia [*sic*] & accomplishing that which has never been done before. I can already imagine the rejoicing of the friends of this road in that vicinity as they see a train of 12 or 15 wagons winding their way through the streets.

Christmas we hope to spend at Leroux' spring, on San Francisco Mountain, where there is an abundance of water & wood as well as grass for the animals. In one month we hope to cross the Colorado & in two months to enter Los Angeles—the distance being estimated at 400 miles.[28] The party on their return were remarkably hard looking, as the smoke from the pine wood had blackened their faces & would not yield to water. They had travelled about 25 miles since morning.

[28] Sherburne is too optimistic.

December 21. Ther. sunrise 26°.5. Lay by today to recruit. Reduced transportation by throwing away pork barrels, boxes, mess-chests, harness, wagon covers, etc. Parke better tho' feverish. Teamster about the same.

December 22. Camp 88. Ther. sunrise 27°.5. Made 11 m. 1812 ft.— Road good. No wood (excepting small bushes) or water in Camp. 9 p.m. snowing.

December 23. Camp 89. Ther. sunrise 28°. Started early this morning in the midst of a snow storm. Very cold throughout day. Ther. being at the highest 37°. We reached camp very late—about sundown, making but 13 m. 2242 ft. When we reached Camp snow was two and a half inches deep. It was very difficult travelling for the mules on account of the snow clogging the wheels and their feet. Before reaching Camp a number of them gave out and were obliged to be replaced by others. The night was intensely cold, the Ther. at 10 p.m. being down to 3°.5, the coldest yet experienced by us. We had an abundance of wood as we encamped in thick timber of pine and cedar. Also good water.

It snowed nearly all the day and we were obliged to dismount often and build fires to warm ourselves. The road (excepting snow) was good, latter part being entirely volcanic. The place passed over by the wagons was a hard ground of ashes and cinders, on each side volcanic peaks and jagged rocks of lava.[29] As we rode on to a "mesa" it represented a vast amphitheater. On every side rose conical volcanic peaks, numbering about 10 or 12. We were on a huge plain perhaps 5 or 6 miles in width. On our right was a cañon about 70 ft. deep. Lieut. Ives and Dr. Kennely taken sick today with fever & ague (so says the Dr.). Ives quite sick.

Not much game on the road today, nothing seen excepting rabbits and one fox. Dr. Bigelow who left the road saw a herd of near 1000 antelope, and others of the party saw antelope and

[29] The expedition is entering the southern edge of what now is known as the San Francisco Volcanic Field. Called Sierra San Francisco by the Spaniards in the early seventeenth century, it was first described in print by Capt. Sitgreaves. The Sitgreaves trail moved in a loop along the northern edge of the Field back south around San Francisco Mountain to the Mogollon Rim, and then west toward Bill Williams Mountain. See Wallace, "Across Arizona to the Big Colorado," pp. 335–36.

blacktailed deer. On account of the mules 'tis decided to lay by tomorrow and also next day it being both Christmas and Sunday.

December 24. Ther. sunrise $-3.^{\circ}5$ (below zero). Lay by. Our Camp is near a number of caves, called "Conino Caves."[30] I visited them today with Mr. W. They are natural, being formed by the lava running from above. They number 30 or more. Some are very large and have from one to five smaller ones in back. They were formerly inhabited by the Conino Indians, from whence they derive their name. The traces of the Indians still remain in the shape of broken pottery, etc. In one of the largest caves were several niches apparently dug out in the wall and lined with pieces of pottery. Most of them were walled inside with dirt and stones, the front partially walled with stone. Dirt has recently fallen in these caves to a large amount but still in most of them I could stand erect and when inhabited were in all probability 10 or 12 ft. in height. The whole country in this vicinity is volcanic.

Tonight is one of the most memorable nights of our trip. Tomorrow being Christmas, a double ration was issued the men and preparations made for a merry Christmas. In the evening the Mexicans obtained permission to build fires, say mass and fire four rounds of cartridges in commemoration of "buenos [buenas] noches." They commenced soon after dark by setting fire to the thick trees round camp so that at one time there were near a dozen fires going, illuminating everything around. It was a grand sight to see the noble pines 100 ft. in height in a blaze shooting the forked flame high in the air. During the conflagration of pines one read mass and at certain portions of the service guns were discharged by the others.

Just after dark, Lieut. Jones came with the compliments of his mess for us to celebrate "buenos noches" by partaking of "egg-nog." Repairing to his tent, we found an abundant supply of bottles & glasses in the center of which was a bucket of "egg-

[30] Whipple named the Cosnino (not Conino) Caves during his exploration of Dec. 19. Cosnino was the term used by Antoine Leroux for the Havasupai Indians, a small band of Yuman stock living in the vicinity. Another name for the Havasupai was Coconino; like Cosnino, it was a corruption of the Moqui name for those Indians. See Whipple, *Report*, Dec. 19, 23, 1853; Stanley, Diary, Dec. 23, 1853.

nog." The remainder of the party had already assembled. After taking a "round" or so and having a few songs 'twas proposed to send for the Mexican songsters. They came numbering three or four. After instilling in them the "proper spirit" they favored us with a theatrical play in which "The Devil" played no small part. After this was finished the two opposition singers gave us a song, extemporaneously, first one singing a verse and then the other. They sang an hour or so, without ceasing and continued until obliged to stop from "exhaustion." In the course of the song they brought in every one of the party a number of times making some very laughable and amusing rhymes. The celebration broke up about 12 with every one of the party more or less merry. Even the steady old Dr. was unable to relieve his feet of his boots and was obliged to call in his Mexy boy to pull them off.

Whipple, *Report*: "Christmas Eve has been celebrated with considerable eclat. . . . An Indian dance, by some *ci-devant* Navajo prisoners, was succeeded by songs from the teamsters, and a pastoral enacted by the Mexicans, after their usual custom at this festival. Leroux's servant, a tamed Crow Indian, and a herder, then performed a duet improvisated, in which they took the liberty of saying what they pleased of the company present—an amusement common in New Mexico and California, where this troubadour singing is much in vogue at fandangoes. . . . The plaintive tones of the singers, and the strange simplicity of the people, lead one's fancy back to the middle ages. In this state of society, so free from ambition for wealth or power, where the realities of life are in a great measure subject to the ideal, there is a tinge of romance that would well repay the researches of a literary explorer."

December 25. Ther. sunrise 3°.5. Visions of roast Turkeys, plum puddings and mince pies are rolling through my brain. I would like a slice off one of the many New England puddings today. Even if it were not of the best quality. Still I would not have it thought we were destitute of all the luxuries of life. I will give you the "Bill of fare" of our mess at dinner. "Leg of roast mutton," "Beef a la mode," "Bass," "Wild Duck," "roast squirrel," and "claret" formed part of the Bill. In one of the other messes they were so luxurious as to have "oyster soup" and "jam."[31] The day passed very pleasantly and much to the satisfaction of all.

[31] Lieut. Stanley's mess had the oyster soup. Only Sherburne and Stanley could bring themselves to write about food after the celebration the evening before.

December 26. Camp 90. Ther. sunrise −5°.5 (below zero). Travelled 12 mi. 410 ft. and camped without water, though an *abundance* of snow. It was the intention to go to San Francisco spring but the mules were pretty well tired and 'twas thought expedient to camp before reaching it. The snow increased in depth being the latter part of the day about 12 in. deep. A few bare places served to partially graze the animals. An antelope shot today by Dr. Kennely, also numerous squirrels by members of the party. The squirrels of this country are very large with long hair on the ends of the ears, stripes of red on the back and long bushy tail, tipped with white. Dr. Kennely and Lieut. Ives quite sick today.

December 27. Camp 91. Ther. sunrise 29° Travelled 12 m. 3956 ft. & halted at Leroux' spring—passed San Francisco Spring on route. Snow about 18 in. deep. Lieut. Ives broke out today with the varioloid.[32] Campbell, H. taken sick with symptoms of small pox. Several others slightly sick.

Whipple, Diary: "Where we are to go now is a great question that sits like a night-mare upon my breast. Leroux says we cannot proceed west nor southwest. North northwest to Savedra's [Sitgreaves's] route he proposes to lead us—then west & southwest to Mohave River. To that route I have several objections. It is circuitous. It is said to keep upon a dividing ridge, so as to be level for a long distance. Favorable as the latter may seem it follows of necessity that the descent to the Colorado must be sudden & precipitous so as to present an insurmountable barrier to a railroad. . . . We must therefore . . . descend Williams Fork to within striking distance of Rio Colorado. Both Leroux & Savedra say that terrible cañons & mountains render this impossible. Still we deem it proper to explore so as to satisfy ourselves by occular proof."[33]

Whipple merely noted that it was a pleasant day, and Möllhausen piously observed that it passed "in perfect quiet, in thinking over past times and distant homes." See Stanley, Diary, Dec. 25, 1853; Whipple, *Report*, Dec. 25, 1853; Möllhausen, *Diary*, II, p. 154.

[32] Varioloid is a modified form of smallpox, occurring in those who have had smallpox or been vaccinated. Whipple named Leroux's (now simply Leroux) Spring when his exploring party first reached it on December 17. At the head of what is now Fort Valley, it is about seven miles northwest of Flagstaff, Arizona, and 7,600 feet above sea level. Leroux had discovered this fine watering place in 1851; the Sitgreaves expedition had approached it from a different direction, passing around the northern end of San Francisco Mountain. The Santa Fe Railroad later followed the Whipple reconnaissance route from Camp 82 (modern Winslow) to nearby Flagstaff. See Whipple, *Report*, Dec. 17, 1853; Wallace, "Across Arizona to the Big Colorado," p. 343.

[33] Whipple, of course, wanted to avoid following the Sitgreaves trail, which

December 28. Ther. sunrise 23°.5. Lay by today to recruit animals. Much difficulty in finding grass as 'twas mostly covered with snow. Campbell, H. quite sick today. Lieut. Jones taken sick tonight.

A small exploring party consisting of Mr. Whipple, White, Leroux, Sevadra & a Mexy went out today about 6 miles & returned about 3 p.m.[34] Found rather good country for wagons.

Stanley, Diary: "Dr. K. and myself determined to try and ascend to the top of San Francisco Mountain.[35] . . . After ascending more than two-thirds of the way to the top, we were compelled, much against our inclination, to stop as the labor became insupportable. . . . With the excellent glass we had, I could see quite well an extent of country much greater than the State of Ohio. On the east we could see to the Sierra Madre. West the Colorado. South the mountains on the Gila, but if the view was magnificent it was equally disheartening to the explorer for a railroad route. The country is decidedly one of mountains and chain upon chain can be seen in every direction. Our sight was equally discouraging as to the fate of our expedition. Snow covered the ground for fully eighty miles to the west and the Doct. and I pronounced the fate of our waggons at a glance."

December 29. Ther. sunrise 36°. Men obliged to lay by today on account of sickness & no means of transportation of them. There are eight on the sick list. A cook taken last night. San Francisco Mountain [Mt. Agassiz] measured yesterday & found to be 9688

---

eventually veered to the northwest above the 35th parallel. Whipple depended on the Sitgreaves map, which showed Bill Williams Fork rising to the southwest of Bill Williams Mountain, and then flowing west into the Colorado River at the 35th parallel. But, on the basis of incorrect information from Leroux, the Sitgreaves party had mistaken an affluent of the Verde River for Bill Williams Fork. The source of the latter (the Big Sandy River) actually was 120 miles west of Leroux's Spring. From there the Big Sandy flowed to join the true Bill Williams Fork. See Wallace, "Across Arizona to the Big Colorado," p. 348; Foreman, ed., *A Pathfinder*, p. 174, n. 17; Conrad, "The Whipple Expedition in Arizona," p. 164.

[34] Whipple evidently ascended Wing Mountain, 5 miles southwest of Leroux's Spring. From this spot Whipple named a peak farther west after Capt. Sitgreaves, and another to the northwest after Major H. L. Kendrick, Sitgreaves' commander of escort. See Whipple, *Report*, Dec. 28, 1853; Barnes, *Arizona Place Names*, pp. 74, 86, 91; personal communication from Professor Andrew Wallace, Nov. 5, 1987.

[35] The San Francisco Peaks, named in the early seventeenth century by Franciscan missionaries, rim the caldera of an extinct volcano. The whole massif properly is called the San Francisco Mountain. The highest peak, Mt. Humphries, is 12,633 feet above sea level. Lt. Stanley and Dr. Kennerly probably attempted to

ft. above Camp being between 16000 & 17000 ft. above level of sea as this place is near 7000 ft. above. 'Tis thought by some to be a mistake, that it cannot be more than half so high. Quite probable will be measured again tomorrow. A party of four attempted to ascend it yesterday. Two gave out when near the bottom. The other two got about half way up & finding the snow two feet deep returned to camp pretty well exhausted.

December 30. Ther. sunrise 12°.5. Lay by again today. The sick are all better this morning & no new cases. The Teamster who was dangerously sick was able to be out yesterday. This morning an exploring party consisting of Mr. Whipple, Dr. Bigelow, Campbell, A., White, & Leroux with Lieut. Tidball & 25 escort—also Mexys, cooks, servants, packmules, etc. etc.—started on a scout. They do not intend returning to this Camp, but propose sending us directions where to proceed. They took ten days rations & expect to be ahead for that length of time finding a road & occasionally or semi-occasionally sending back dispatches. We are anxious to leave this camp as a heavy fall of snow will lay us up. It is hardly possible to distinguish a White man from a Mexy, in this country. The timber is all heavy pine, giving out while burning a very black thick smoke. This smoke is settling on everything & everybody renders the skin so black as to entirely change a persons appearance & make him anything but an American in looks. The greatest difficulty is that only partially yielding to soap & water, it gives the face the appearance of a striped pig, or a warrior painted for the war party.

Another survey of San Francisco Mountain made today. It was found to be a mistake in the base line of 1000 ft., a 50 ft. chain being used in place of 100 ft. "Que suerte! Como es possible?" The mountain is 4½ miles distant & a little over 4600 ft. in height.[36] P.m.— Teamster took cold yesterday & in consequence very sick this morning. Very cool. Ther. 9 p.m. 17°.5.

Stanley, Diary: "Everyone in camp presents the appearance of a coal

---

climb Mt. Agassiz, which rises directly above Leroux's Spring to 12,356 feet. I am indebted to Professor Andrew Wallace for advice on this region.

[36]The Spanish translates as "What luck! How is it possible?" The expedition has traveled approximately 360 miles on this leg of the journey.

heaver, or blacksmith who has neither indulged in the luxury of a wash, nor the extravagance of a clean garment for a long period. Our young gentlemen with white hats look most decidedly dirty—and all begin to wish ourselves at the end of our journey and our troubles over. Propose to move tomorrow; I fear the attempt—nous verrons."

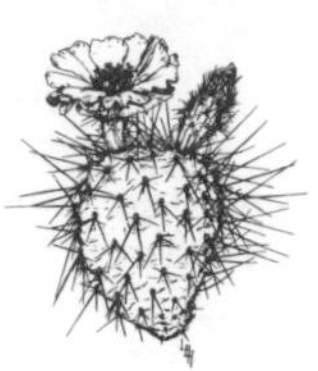

Leroux's Spring to the Colorado River

December 31, 1853–February 20, 1854

Leaving the camp at Leroux's Spring on December 31, the expedition continues moving west. Passing through the Chino Valley, which teems with wildlife, it travels close to the Sitgreaves trail of 1851. During this entire leg of the journey Lieutenant Whipple, with an exploring party, moves ahead of the wagon train. On January 3, 1854, he discovers to his dismay that the river marked on the Sitgreaves map as rising near Bill Williams Mountain and flowing west-southwest to the Colorado River, named Bill Williams Fork, turns too far south. For over one month the commander guides the wagon train west, continually searching for the elusive river. Whipple ignores the advice of his two guides, Leroux and Savedra, to follow the Sitgreaves trail, which moves northwest above the 35th parallel and away from the precious streams of water. The wagon train instead breaks a path through the Juniper Mountains and travels northwest on a curve through Cactus Pass, in what is now called the Cottonwood Range. On February 5 the expedition reaches the Big Sandy River, which flows far to the south to join the true Bill Williams Fork. Traveling west beyond the junction of these two rivers, the expedition on February 20 finally reaches the Colorado River. It has taken 52 days to travel 260 miles.

This is the most trying leg of the long journey. At first snow, sleet, and the rough, arid terrain hamper progress across the mountain ranges leading to the Big Sandy. Even when the weather improves, the trail remains difficult along the canyons of the Big Sandy and Bill Williams

Fork. Once more Lieutenant Whipple finds that the Sitgreaves map is in error. That expedition had marked the junction of the Bill Williams Fork and the Colorado at the 35th parallel. Whipple finds that the junction is closer to the 34th, and thus he must travel north along the Colorado to cross the river at the 35th parallel.

The wagon train collapses during the desert journey south then west from the junction with the Big Sandy River. Cattle are shot or left behind, the mules falter, supplies are abandoned, and the train is reduced to two wagons and one cart. By February 10 food is running out and the men are placed on half rations. The only consolation during these months of uncertainty and hardship has been the freedom from harassment by the Indian bands that had plagued the journeys of earlier pack trains crossing part of this landscape.

Though suffering from intermittent attacks of chills, fever, and "inflammatory rheumatism," John Sherburne remains cheerful, resilient, and observant. During the darkest hours of February he finds time to pick flowers by the wayside and exult in the increasing signs of spring. Arrival at the Colorado, he tells us, restores the spirits of all, and on February 20 the members of the scientific corps raise their glasses in a joyful toast to the great river.

December 31, 1853. Camp 92. Ther. sunrise 17°.5. Last day of –/53. Clear & cool.

Started from Camp this morning at 10, the invalids being well enough to travel, & made a march of 8 m. 2112 ft. Country thickly timbered with large pines, or as it was expressed in Topography of one of the party—"*deeply pined.*" Snow quite bad, in some places 2 ft. in depth. No water in Camp. Grass very little & none excepting on the neighboring hills.

Lost a mule last night by death. Whether died a natural death, or from hunger, cold & fatigue is not stated. Quite probable tired of Life. Several of the animals strayed away during the night but found again this morning.

January 1, 1854. Camp 93. Ther. sunrise 29°.5. The first day of the year –/54—a happy New Year to all. This morning at day break a soldier & two Mexy's came express from Mr. Whipple having left him last evening. They brought tidings of good road, no snow, plenty of wood & grass, but water scarce. While travel-

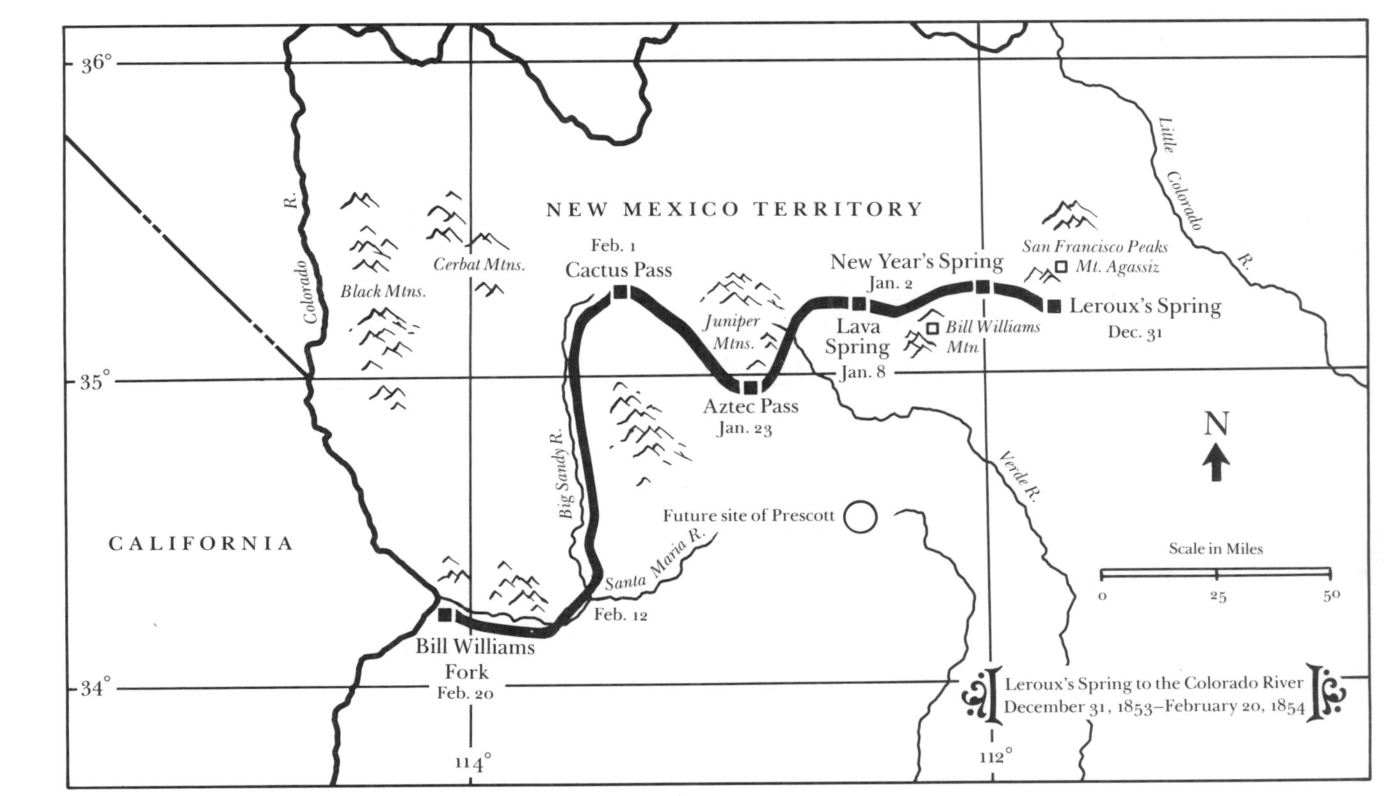

Leroux's Spring to the Colorado River
December 31, 1853–February 20, 1854

ling during the night they were attracted by camp fires & thinking it our Camp rode towards it but on near approach found it an Indian Camp & "skittered."

Travelled 6 m. 1584 ft. No water in Camp—an abundance of snow. Grass scarce— Passed an old Camp of [Whipple's] exploring party.

January 2. Camp 94. Ther. sunrise 24°. Travelled 8 m. 3792 ft. & halted at New Years Spring (so called) plenty of wood & water, but the latter so bad that we used snow in preference.[1]

Snow gradually diminished today untill our arrival at this place, where there's scarcely any. This appears to be the line of separation of snow & dry land. As far as the eye can reach is a beautiful valley, without snow.

The only white spots ahead are on the tops of hills & mountains. Travelled nearly all day along trail of exploring party. After our arrival at Camp, according to agreement, built signal fires on the hills which were kept up till late in evening, but saw no return.

An Indian was seen near Camp by two Mexy's & tho' on foot, he ran with such rapidity as to render pursuit on mules out of the question.

January 3. Ther. sunrise 20°. Lay by in hope of hearing from Mr. W. Kept signal fires nearly all day but heard nothing.

Sevadra went out this morning with 12 soldiers, in search of water for our next Camp, has not returned. Probably will not till tomorrow. We cannot move untill he comes.

January 4. Ther. sunrise—omitted. (Porque? —Porque dormiendo.)[2] Still lying by—Sevadra did not return today. His delay cannot be accounted for as he took but one days provisions for himself & two for the men. If he does not come tomorrow, some anxiety will be felt for him.

[1]Somewhere near present-day Williams, Arizona, this spring was about 23 miles west of Leroux's Spring, almost due north of Bill Williams Mountain. Lieut. Whipple named it when his exploring party visited there on the morning of New Year's Day. See Whipple, *Report*, Jan. 1, 1854; Conrad, "Explorations and Railway Survey," pp. 116–17.

[2]The Spanish translates as "Why? Because sleeping." Though Sherburne failed to record the temperature, someone else did or the records were concocted. According to the official barometric observations, the temperature at 7 a.m. was 30°.1, rising to 42°.4 by noon. See *Reports of Explorations and Surveys*, III, App. D, p. 237.

Nothing yet heard from the exploring party. This being their sixth day out. Several members of the party went Bear hunting today. They saw plenty of immense tracks but no "Barrs"— They have apparently emmigrated.

January 5. Ther. sunrise 27°.8. Sevadra & party returned this p.m. about 4 nearly starved & dead from thirst. They had scoured the Country for 20 miles in the westerly direction but found no water. Country good for wagons—one of their mules gave out & was left from three to four miles out where he will be sent for tomorrow. They saw no sign of exploring party. Most probable they have gone towards "Bill William's" mountain in the S.W.[3] We hope to hear tomorrow. Undecided whether to leave tomorrow or not, but probable we will remain here 'till we hear from the party. Several squalls of snow between 2 & 4 p.m.

January 6. Ther. sunrise 22°. Snowing this morning at Sunrise & continued 'till 11 a.m. Ground covered. Very cold during day. Ther. being at highest 28°.

About 3 p.m. the Ex'n party were seen a half mile distant coming towards Camp. Everyone was overjoyed to see them as we were tired of lying by & doing nothing. They were pretty well disgusted with the trip, as might easily be seen, tho' none would admit it. Their mules in rather a bad condition & will not be able to travel tomorrow.[4]

January 7. Ther. sunrise 11°.5. Did not move today as the

[3] Bill Williams Mountain was marked on the Sitgreaves map. It was named in 1851 by the expedition's cartographer, Richard Kern, for a friend of Leroux's, "Old Bill" Williams, another celebrated guide and mountain man who in the 1830's had lived alone along the river that also bears his name. In the spring of 1849, after surviving John C. Frémont's disastrous fourth expedition, Williams was killed by Ute Indians in the San Juan Mountains while returning from Taos, New Mexico, to recover some of the expedition's supplies; Richard Kern's brother Edward was killed with Williams. See Barnes, ed., *Arizona Place Names*; Wallace, "Across Arizona to the Big Colorado," p. 348; Lamar, ed., *The Reader's Encyclopedia of the American West*, p. 1273.

[4] Whipple's exploring party had covered over 100 miles in eight days and first had moved southwest searching for the Bill Williams Fork, marked on the Sitgreaves map. On January 3, Whipple discovered to his dismay that the supposed Bill Williams Fork turned too far south. He then moved northwest searching for a river that flowed to the west. His party crossed a valley Whipple named Val de China (now Chino Valley northwest of Prescott, Arizona) because of its rich grama grass, known to Mexicans as "de China." To Whipple's relief, he also discovered a system of streams flowing west and southwest. See Whipple, Diary, Whipple Papers, and *Report*, Dec. 30, 1853–Jan. 6, 1854.

Ex'on mules were in bad condition & were obliged to be shod. Tomorrow we will undoubtedly start. Nearly all the Camp are in good health. Six have had the small-pox & varioloid—among the latter Dr. Kennely & Lieut. Ives. Many others have been sick with fevers etc.—the first symptoms. I have been "under the weather" for several weeks past with "*Inflammatory rheumatism*" but nearly recovered. Parke nearly well. The "small-pox wagon" was washed & smoked today & will be ready tomorrow to "return to duty."

Möllhausen, *Diary*, II, pp. 169–70: "On the 7th [6th] of January, Lieutenant Whipple and his people at last returned to us. He had not found the country positively inaccessible for waggons, but his report as to the nature of the ground did not sound very favourable. The snow, he said, did not extend much beyond where we were, but when it ceased, a rough lava-covered ground succeeded, from which our mules, shod as they were, would probably have much to suffer in their hoofs. . . . During our stay at New Year's Spring, the smiths were constantly employed in examining the hoofs of the mules, and shoeing them afresh when necessary; and after the return of the reconnoitring party, the same thing had to be done for their animals."

January 8. Camp 95. Ther. (omitted). Made today 9 m. 5100 ft. Country very rocky & hilly. Plenty of wood, water & grass in Camp [Lava Spring].

January 9. Camp 96. Ther. sunrise 19°. Made 10 m. 480 ft. No water in Camp, plenty of wood. One mule of the escort shot this morning being unable to travel. Country decidedly rough. Passed down one hill, the side inclination being so great that the united efforts of six men could scarcely prevent the wagons overturning. Part of the road had to be cut, the timber (cedar) was so thick. Descended during day 400 ft.

January 10. Camp 97. Ther. sunrise 28°. Travelled 13 m. 2872 ft. Road good— Plenty of wood, water & grass in Camp.[5] Very

[5] The expedition is following the trail of Whipple's reconnaissance north of west. In the last two days it has left Cataract Creek (Lava Spring) to pass around the head of what is now Ash Fork Draw to a stream Whipple first named Lunar and then changed to Partridge because, as Möllhausen wrote, the birds were found "in masses" along its banks. In fact this whole region teemed with wildlife. Here the expedition's route runs close to the Sitgreaves trail. Camp 97 is about 4 miles northwest of modern Ash Fork, Arizona. See Whipple, Diary, Whipple Papers, and *Report*, Jan. 3, 10, 1854; Möllhausen, *Diary*, II, p. 175; Wallace, "Across Arizona to the Big Colorado," p. 340.

little cutting to do on the march. Half a dozen pioneers are always kept ahead to clear road for the wagons. Descended today 472 ft. Just before reaching camp, the road got very rocky much to the sorrow of many of us. In Mr. Whipple's mess all their cups were broken excepting one. In Lieut. Jones mess, they lost a plate & we lost two tumblers two mugs & a bowl—which makes quite an opening in our domestic furniture. Some of us will have to return to the old *tin* cups again.

A "Black Tailed Deer" killed today by one of the Escort.

January 11. Ther. sunrise 20°.5. Lay by today as no water is known ahead. Another exploring party started in search of it. It consisted of Mr. Whipple, Dr. Bigelow, Campbell, A., Mölhausen, White, Leroux, Sevadra, 10 soldiers, cooks, packers, servants, etc. They took ten days provender. If water was discovered before night, they were to raise a smoke between 4 & 4½ p.m. which was to be looked for from Camp. The signal was watched for in vain. About dark, Sevadra & brother[6] came back with intelligence that there was water all along the cañon on which we were encamped. We move tomorrow.

January 12. Camp 98. Ther. sunrise 15°.5. Travelled 3 m. 5146 ft. down the Cañon—plenty of wood, water & grass. After arriving, the wagon master & Sevadra were sent to search the country ahead to see if a Camping place for tomorrow could be found. Our Camp tonight is in the bottom of a Cañon 176 ft. deep. Vegetation has already commenced along the route—a pretty good evidence that Spring is coming. The grass looks green & the bushes are shooting out. In a few weeks the country will be delightful.

January 13. Camp 99. Ther. sunrise 20°.5. Last night about sundown a great smoke was discovered S.W. of us, supposed to be a signal fire of Ex'n party. We returned it & kept it up till dark. It is uncertain whether it was a Camp fire or not & even if it were a signal fire. What does it mean? Quien sabe? [Who knows?] It was determined to start this morning on a risk, accordingly striking tents about 8½—the train started in the direction of the fire. After following the cañon for 3 miles, the mules

[6]The guide's younger brother had joined the expedition in Albuquerque as a herder. Whipple considered him "one of our most worthy and trusty Mexicans." See Whipple, Diary, Jan. 11, 1854, Whipple Papers.

were watered & we struck out of it, taking the S.W.—the cañon running E. Road during day generally good. Made 13 m. 4230 ft. & halted in a small cañon—wood in vicinity scarce— Found their Camp fires still burning about 1½ miles above us but no water excepting in a small hole, holding about three buckets. Expect to leave tomorrow.

January 14. Ther. sunrise 42°. Last night about 11 a couple of soldiers—express—came in. They started from here yesterday morning to tell us to come on, but on account of hills & cañons passed us on the route. They found our old camp & followed our trail. Plenty of water just above their Camp, the mules are sent there today. The instruction was to watch for their signal fires & if were seen at noon to strike for them—if at sunrise or sunset to follow their trail. We will lay here today, unless their fires are seen at noon in that case will probably move *after dinner.* P.m.—no fires seen today. 'Tis not known whether any were made, as there has been a very high wind all day & heavy clouds, so as to obscure everything in the shape of smoke. A great quantity of water [Picacho Spring] found this p.m. in vicinity of Camp.

January 15. Ther. sunrise 27°.5. A heavy wind sprung up last night & carried away two tents, the others being saved by an extra supply of pins. The occupants of the fallen tents lay under them till morning as 'twas impossible to pitch them again. Lay by today— About 3 p.m. the Ex'n party returned rather "disgusti."[7] They had been W. & although finding a good road, the grade was too great for a Railroad. We are tomorrow to strike S.W. on a

[7] The correct Spanish word for disgusted is "disgustado." Whipple's exploring party had moved southwest and discovered a good camp at Picacho Spring, at the base of a mountain Whipple named Picacho (Peak), southwest of present-day Ash Fork, Arizona. Coyote Butte was the name given to Picacho by Richard Kern of the Sitgreaves expedition. It is surprising that Leroux did not inform Whipple of Kern's name for the peak. Whipple directed Lieut. Ives to bring the wagons to the spot. On Jan. 14 Leroux had conceded that the Sitgreaves map probably erred in the location of the Bill Williams Fork. Since Whipple realized that both guides were lost, and since mountain ranges seemed to block passage west, the Lieutenant decided to rejoin the wagon train and then continue exploration to the southwest. His decision, he wrote, was much to Leroux's discomfiture, since the guide had used "every artifice" to cause Whipple to follow the Sitgreaves trail to the northwest from Picacho Spring. Whipple now will explore continually in advance of the wagon train. See Whipple, Diary, Jan. 11–14, 1854, Whipple Papers; personal communication from Professor Andrew Wallace about Kern's naming of Coyote Butte.

risk. The accounts of Country are bad but there is no help for it. In fact nothing is known of the Country as neither of the guides have been over it. Indian smokes seen ahead last night—on the mountains.

January 16. Camp 100. Ther. sunrise 10°. This morning the exploring party started again S.W. increased by Lieut. Jones & 16 men. On account of the high position of our Camp & its exposure to the wind it was deemed expedient to move into a more sheltered spot. Accordingly moved 4816 ft. & camped in the bottom of a cañon where we were sheltered from the wind & where it howled 60 or 70 ft. over our heads.

January 17. Ther. sunrise 30°. Had a severe attack of fever & ague last night but this morning feel quite well again, excepting slight headache. No signals from Ex'n party.

January 18. Ther. sunrise 12°. Had another attack of fever & ague this morning more severe than the last. The chill lasted 1½ hours & fever rest of day & night. Near dark a signal fire was seen apparently 15 miles distant. It was returned & arrangements made for starting tomorrow. Commenced snowing 7½ p.m.

January 19. Camp 101. Ther. sunrise (not taken). Started this a.m. with 1½ ft. of snow on ground & in the face of a cold storm of rain & sleet.

The most disagreeable days travel since leaving Ft. Smith— Made 7 m. 3142 ft. & halted in a grove of Cedars, where we were sheltered from the wind— Snow stopped ½ hour before reaching Camp— All men chilled through. As we arrived in Camp, met a Mexy & two soldiers from the other party. They made the fire 15 miles distant from here so as not to be obliged to come all the way back. They brought the best kind of news from the Ex'n party. About 5 miles from here is a spring of water & about 15 miles is a running stream—course S.E. First rate road for wagons & the best of grass. We could not have got better news from them. We start tomorrow & make a short cut for the stream where we will in all probability meet the remainder of party as their rations give out tomorrow night.

No water in the Camp tonight. Good grass, sticking through the snow.

January 20. Camp 102. Ther. sunrise 8°.5. Coldest day yet— Ther. at highest during day being 20°.5—at 9 p.m. stood −5°

(below zero). Started this morning under direction of the guide sent back. He proposed taking a short cut & reaching the river tonight. Made a mistake in the road by taking the wrong valley & run us out of the way about 3 miles. He travelled the road before in a heavy snow storm which was the cause of losing the way. After retracing, travelled untill Sunset & reached a spring which the Ex'n party discovered [Turkey Creek], distance 9 m. 4562 ft. The road by which we were taken was very bad, being through hills—rocky & irregular. Broke one wagon tongue. Having no other & it being late unloaded wagon & left it.

January 21. Camp 103. Ther. Sunrise 0° Made an early start this morning & after a rough & rocky road struck the river. Before arriving saw a signal fire from the Ex'n party which we returned. After striking the river, which was called "Rio del Pueblo,"[8] travelled up untill met the Camp of the party—making 5m. 4358 ft.

We found them all in good health (excepting headaches, which the Dr. said they got from drinking their coffee *too weak*) & anxiously awaiting our arrival as their provisions were exhausted. They told us vague stories of living on wild ducks, turkey & the like which I dare say were true—

They had been farther ahead & at the source of this stream, a few miles above, found the head of another running S50°W. If this continues its course & good road, we will have no trouble for water. Road from here for 8 or 10 miles very rough & rocky.

January 22. Camp 104. Ther. sunrise 26° Started about 10 a.m. & made 6 m. 4286 ft.— Arrived at Camp at dark— Road very bad. Train delayed a great deal by hills, cañons & arroyos— In crossing one place, two wagons & one Caratella upset pitching out the contents—one of the wagons turned over twice before it stopped, throwing down the mules. No damage done excepting the smashing of wagon bows. When within half a mile of Camp the road got very bad & although the teams were doubled the

[8] Whipple had named this stream Pueblo Creek on January 17 because of the quantity of ancient ruins found along its banks. On his exploration Whipple followed Pueblo (now Walnut) Creek nearly due west and finally discovered a passage through a low range just beyond the creek's headwaters. Whipple's written accounts of the route are confusing because of his constant backtracking to rejoin the wagon train and retrace the trail he had explored ahead. See Whipple, Diary, Whipple Papers, and *Report*, both entries for Jan. 16–23, 1854.

mules could not draw the wagons. They were entirely given out with the hard days work. The soldiers, Teamsters & Mexy's were turned out & taking one wagon at a time, then finally pulled them all & pushed the mules into Camp with all the cheers, shrieks & uncouth noises imaginable.

Möllhausen, *Diary*, II, p. 194: "We had before us the primeval wilderness. . . . It was not, however, the grand primeval forest . . . nor the dreary deserts characteristic of this mountain chain; but low cedars, and scattered oaks and pines, growing as irregularly as if they had been flung there at random among fantastically formed rocks, and masses of rolled stones. . . . The utter deathlike stillness of the solitude, where every word spoken, and every footfall, were distinctly re-echoed, had something in it strangely oppressive. Even the animals appeared to shun the place."

January 23. Camp 105. Ther. Sunrise 26.° This morning the loads were mostly taken from the wagons by pack mules & carried to the top of a high hill over which we were obliged to pass. The wagons were unloaded at the top & from there to Camp the road was good & easy for the mules. After crossing the hill we were past the dividing ridge of the two streams & through the difficult ridges. The pass between these ridges was called "Aztec Pass"[9] & the ridges "Aztec Ridges"— We are now through one of the most difficult places. Made today 6 m. 562 ft. & halted on the stream running S.W. For a great distance ahead there appears to be a valley. Prospects brightening & the wagons *may get through after all*—

Whipple, Diary: "Beyond the country looks far from inviting. Mountain chains seem to encircle us. Many are the dark forebodings in camp. But the Kind Providence that has led us from Colorado Chiquito through several mountain ranges at a distance seemingly impenetrable will we trust guide us to the end."

[9] Aztec Pass is about 50 miles northwest of present-day Prescott, Arizona, between the Juniper and Santa Maria mountains. Whipple named the pass because of the ancient Indian ruins found at the base and summit of the range. The railroad profile, later the route of the Santa Fe Railroad, was drawn on a more direct route from New Year's Spring to Picacho Spring, then southwest and South to Aztec Pass. See Whipple, *Report*, Jan. 21, 23, 1854; Foreman, ed., *A Pathfinder*, p. 199, n. 1. For a description of the extensive ruins in the region of Pueblo (Walnut) Creek, which indicated a once flourishing Indian population, see Fewkes, "Casa Grande, Arizona," pp. 207–9.

January 24. Camp 106. Ther. sunrise 38°.9. The march today was along the stream. Road very muddy & miry, on account of the warm day melting the snow. The wagons would frequently sink half way to the hub. We marched 5 m. 4834 ft. Plenty of water, also wood & grass in Camp— It is the intention to lay by at this place [Cañon Creek] & explore ahead as there are two valleys one a little W. & the other a little S. of W.

Whipple, Diary: "[The] direction of our creek surprises and somewhat alarms us for we here confidently hoped to find a branch of Bill Williams Fork. It now seems quite probably an affluent of the Yampais.[10] To settle this question we propose tomorrow to renew our explorations."

January 25. Ther. sunrise 38° The mules stampeded three times last night but the herders made out to keep back the main body. This morning between 30 & 40 were missing but I believe have all, or nearly all, been brought back. An exploring party started this morning about 10 o'clk— It consisted of Mr. Whipple, Dr. Bigelow, Campbell, A., White, Lieut. Tidball & 16 men, besides cooks, herders, packers, etc. We may hear from them tonight & move tomorrow. No doubt there is an abundance of water, the only trouble is, a good road for the wagons. Commenced raining this p.m. about 5 o'clk which changed into snow at 8— Made a bet of a bottle of wine with Mr. Marcou that we will not reach the Colorado in two weeks from this date.

January 26. Ther. sunrise 11° Continued snowing during night but at sunrise this morning not a cloud to be seen. Quantity of snow fallen 2 in. Nothing heard as yet from the other party (10 a.m.) will probably hear some time today. Sun very hot & snow going rapidly. Ther. 10 a.m. 49°— The storm last night drove the wolves into Camp. They were howling round the tents nearly all night. The disagreeable night prevented their being

[10] By then even more confused about the route, Whipple decided that this creek finally was the Bill Williams Fork; he later named it Cañon Creek after realizing that it was not the elusive fork. Yampais Creek, marked on the Sitgreaves map as Rio Yampay (and now called Truxton Wash), moved west of north along the Sitgreaves trail, the future route of part of the Santa Fe Railroad from near present-day Ash Fork, Arizona. See Whipple, *Report*, Jan. 26, 1854; *Reports of Explorations and Surveys*, III ("Preliminary Report"), p. 16; Sitgreaves, "Report," Oct. 30, 1851; Barnes, ed., *Arizona Place Names*, p. 344; Briggs and Trudell, *Quarterdeck and Saddlehorn*, p. 212.

molested. 9 p.m.— Sevadra & brother came in from the Ex'n party about 12— They brought tidings of good road & plenty of water. We move onward tomorrow. 'Tis thought that the stream we are now upon is "Bill Williams' Fork" [still Cañon Creek]. Wolves howling round & even in Camp tonight but no one could get the chance of a shot at one of them. We expect to be at the Rio Colorado in about 8 or 10 days. The provisions give out on the 25th of next month & we have no time to waste. Owing to the loss of a bag of coffee, either stolen or lost from the wagon—we are nearly out. The last issue has been made. In Mr. Whipple's mess they have about 2 lbs.—in our mess about 5 lbs. The Teamsters have been out for several days & are living on "Corn Coffee" which is said to be a very good substitute. We will have to try it in a few days.

January 27. Camp 107. Ther. sunrise 21.° Made today 12 m. 2160 ft. Road good tho' a few bad cañons had to be crossed. Nothing more heard from Ex'n party tho' 'tis the intention to go on tomorrow. A Teamster discharged this morning & put in charge of the guard for unnecessarily beating his mules.

January 28. Camp 108. Ther. sunrise 21.°5. Started this morning without hearing from Ex'n party & without any knowledge of the country ahead. Travelled about 4 miles & were obliged to turn back on account of cañons which 'twas impossible to cross. Will have to wait 'till further orders from Mr. Whipple. Encamped near our old camp of yesterday—which was the first Camp of Ex'n party— Whole distance travelled today 6m. 3502 ft. Very warm tonight. Ther. 9 p.m. 40°— 3 p.m. 68.°5—

January 29. Ther. sunrise 28.° 3 p.m. 67.° Lay by—but no news from Ex'n party. About 4 p.m. a couple of Mexy's came in leading two Indians whom they found skulking round camp & captured. They represented themselves as Tonto's.[11] The Mexy's

[11] Tonto was a name applied to a group of Athapascan-speaking western Apaches, who ranged from the Tonto Basin and Mogollon Rim to as far north as present-day Flagstaff; they sometimes were called Tonto-Apaches. There is considerable confusion about the Tontos (the name means "fools") to this day. But these Indians may have been Hualapais or northeastern Yavapais, bands of Yuman stock. Because of their hair style and the pouches they carried, the anthropologist Albert H. Schroeder believes that these Indians were Yavapais, though the Yavapais usually roamed much farther south. The treatment the two Indians received was unusual for this expedition and may be explained by Lieut.

crept on them unnoticed untill within a short distance of them, then rising brought their rifles to bear. The Indians threw their bows & arrows on the ground & sat down at the same time throwing their hands in the air. They were then taken prisoners & led them into camp. At the time of their Capture, two others were seen on distant ridges as "lookouts." After they were brought into Camp they appeared frightened & suspicious. A blanket & food was given them. At dark they were placed at the Mexy's fire with a Mexy & soldier over them, to keep them till morning in case they were wanted as guides for water—or to prevent any depredation from the rest of the tribe. About 8 in the evening as they were sitting in the midst of about 30 they both jumped & attempted to escape in opposite directions, but were prevented. Shortly after they made another jump & one escaped. The other being thrown down by those present & prevented. The one who escaped would have been shot had not orders been given to the contrary. In order to prevent the remaining one from going, a chain & padlock was put round each ankle, the chain being fastened to a picket, which was driven firmly in the ground. While the process of locking was going on the Indian took the locks in his hand & examined them closely. He appeared much pleased with the brass over the key-hole. After they were locked he couldn't understand why they would not come off. At short intervals he shouted something for the other but no answer excepting the distant howling of a wolf, which was thought to proceed from some of his comrades. This was kept up during the evening & is still heard in the distance (10 p.m.). A call is expected from them tonight & every one is prepared—an extra guard is put round the animals. Very few will sleep tonight without a pistol within reach.

One of the Indians had no clothing excepting a tattered blanket thrown over the shoulders & tied round the waist with a string of bark. The escaping one left behind his blanket—also bow & quiver of skin filled with arrows. Some of the arrows were pointed

---

Whipple's absence. Möllhausen sketched the pair, and Whipple wrote that though the sketch indicated the stupidity reflected in the name "Tontos," Leroux believed that they were clever thieves and remarkably shrewd. See Schroeder and Thomas, *Yavapai Indians*, Part I, p. 83; *Reports of Explorations and Surveys*, III, Part III ("Indian Tribes"), p. 32.

A lithograph of a crude field sketch by Möllhausen of two Indians captured on January 29, 1854, and identified as Tontos. Möllhausen considered these Indians repulsive. *Reports of Explorations and Surveys,* vol. III.

with sharp hard wood, some with stone and some with iron. Bet a bottle of wine with Mr. Marcou, that neither of the Indians would get away before morning, lost in about ten minutes. Made another one, that the remaining one would not & won.

Möllhausen, *Diary*, II, pp. 210–11: "More repulsive physiognomies and figures than those of our two prisoners could hardly be imagined. They were a young and an older man, somewhat below the middle size, but powerfully made; with large heads, projecting cheekbones and foreheads, very thick noses, swelled lips, and little slits of eyes with which they looked about as fierce and cunning as wolves. Their skins were darker than I had ever seen those of Indians, though the usual Indian topknot, tied round with some pieces of stuff and leather, was not wanting."

January 30. Camp 109. Ther. sunrise 30°. No call from Indians last night. The remaining Indian pulled up his picket-pin several times but did not effect his escape.

This morning 9:30—two Mexys came in stating that the Ex'n party were three days march from here in the Mountains & they came to guide us to the place. On their way to us, they were accompanied part of the way by two Indians. They left the Ex'n party yesterday about 3 p.m. They state that the party have in & near the Camp a large number of Indians. So far they appear very friendly & peaceable. They are "Yampires."[12]

When we found they had Indians, our Captive was unchained, presents made him & he was made free. When loose, he left with all possible haste, scarcely believing his own senses. As soon as the express came in, struck Camp & moved 11 m. 4304 ft. An abundance of water in Camp, also wood. Road good with exception of first 4 or 5 miles which was hilly. After our arrival at Camp saw the signal fire of the other party apparently 10 or 12 miles distant. We will in all probability reach them tomorrow, as we fear the Indians may prove Treachorous [*sic*] & take advantage of our absence. Undoubtedly they have been round our Camp in numbers & that these seen were spies, to ascertain our force & report to the main body of the [their] party. Finding us the strongest part [of the wagon train], if they intend anything will make the most of our absence.

Weather very pleasant & warm today. Ther. 3 p.m. 69°.5. Left several of the men behind this morning as they did not think of our starting and went out hunting *Indians.* They caught us before reaching camp & were unsuccessful in their search.

Stanley, Diary: "We had a message from Lieut. W. this morning advising us to move and, hearing that he had met Indians, we concluded to

[12] "Yampais" was the name Leroux gave to the Yavapais; they sometimes erroneously were called Mohave-Apaches. Though the historian Andrew Wallace writes that only Hualapai inhabited this region and the Yavapai were found farther south near the junction of the Santa Maria and the Bill Williams Fork, Albert H. Schroeder concludes that these two, like the "Tontos" in Sherburne's camp, were northeastern Yavapais on a trading expedition. See Whipple, *Report*, Dec. 7, 1853, Jan. 28–29, 1854; *Reports of Explorations and Surveys*, III, Part III ("Indian Tribes"), p. 50; Wallace, "Across Arizona to the Big Colorado," pp. 350–51; Schroeder and Thomas, *Yavapai Indians*, Part I, pp. 81–83.

let our captive go, so after amusing ourselves for some time by making him show the road, we unlocked the chains, loaded him with old clothes, blankets, etc., and sent him off. The first time, perhaps, that any one of these poor miserable people had ever received kindness at the hands of a stranger."

January 31. Camp 110. Ther. sunrise 29.° 3 p.m. 79.° Travelled 4 m. 4406 ft. Road very rough & rocky with very bad hills. Mr. Whipple's Caratella broke the axle close to the hub of the wheel so as to render it impossible to repair it. It was strapped & dragged behind a wagon untill within about a mile of camp when the team gave out & they were obliged to abandon it. Before reaching Camp three teams gave out. It was necessary to ascend a hill about 400 ft. high on the sides of which the snow had melted & made it very miry. The wagons sunk to the hubs of the wheels. The main body of the train got into Camp early & mules were sent back sufficient to put 10 in [to] each wagon. The wagons, & Caratella of which I had charge, arrived in Camp about dark. The Ex'n party are in Camp about ½ mile from us—but owing to the bad state of the mules, we were unable to reach them. Those who got in Camp early went over to them & returned. All are in good health. Campbell, A., & Dr. Bigelow are the only ones who have honored us with a visit. The whole number of Indians that have been in their Camp amounts to *two*. They have seen but *five*.[13] The Mexy's large number has decreased rapidly.

A wolf jumped into the sheep tonight & carried one off—although fired at by a sentinal, succeeded in escaping with his prey. The shot alarmed Camp & made us suppose at first that 'twas Indians.

February 1. Camp 111. Ther. sunrise 41.° 3 p.m. 73.° Made an early start this morning & in about ½ an hour reached the Camp of Ex'n party. They were encamped on the edge of a steep hill

[13]The exploring party saw seven Indians, but only two visited Whipple's camp. The wagon train has followed Whipple's route northwest but well south of the Sitgreaves trail. It has left Cañon Creek and now is traveling along White Cliff Creek, which rises in a range Whipple named Aquarius. The train is camped at the base of the Cottonwood Range and Cactus Pass, the latter named by Dr. Bigelow, who found there specimens of his favorite plant. Cactus Pass is about twenty miles southeast of present-day Truxton, Arizona. See Whipple, *Report*, Jan. 29, 31, 1854; Möllhausen, *Diary*, II, p. 214; Tidball, Diary, Jan. 28, 1854.

which we were obliged to descend [Cactus Pass]. The packs were all taken from the wagons & sent ahead, thus rendering the wagons comparitively [*sic*] light. All the mules were taken out but two which were left to guide the wagon. The wheels were then locked & the wagons let down by ropes—one spring wagon upset three times & the Caratella once. No damage done. The steep descent was in a ravine, on each side of which the mountains rose several hundred feet. The steepest descent which was almost perpendicular was for ½ mile though for two miles the road was steep & rocky. We made during the day 9 m. 1760 ft. Descent 1500 ft.

The bedding of Ex'n party was all left behind & sent after about 4 p.m. too late for the packers to get back again till morning. After waiting untill 12 for them & finding no prospect of their coming, tho't it advisable to make a family bed in my tent where five turned in & tho' rather close stowage, made out to weather it till morning.

February 2. Ther. sunrise 35°.5. 12 [noon] 71°.5. Lay by today. The packers came in about 9 a.m. The Ex'n party started again with the change of Lieut. Jones for Lieut. Tidball. We will not move untill we hear from them. Country ahead looks very mountainous. Our coffee gave out today & we took to "corn coffee" which we found a very good substitute. Several of the mess who were not aware of the fact didn't recognize the change. Only one ration of provisions issued today to the three messes in place of one & a half which has formerly been issued. We will undoubtedly be short of a great many things before reaching settlements, notwithstanding the precautions taken. Slight attack of chills tonight.

February 3. Ther. sunrise 39° 3 p.m. 69°.5. Lay by today—Express came from Ex'n party tonight, with instructions to follow the stream till we struck "Bill Williams Fork" (this proving not to be that river) about 20 m. distant—to follow that untill stopped.[14] We start tomorrow. No wood in Camp tonight.

[14] At last Whipple has found the elusive Bill Williams Fork or, more accurately, the Big Sandy River, an affluent of the Bill Williams Fork that turns south to join it. Though he called Big Sandy the Bill Williams Fork, Whipple knew, probably from Leroux, that the Big Sandy had been discovered and named by Joseph R. Walker, the celebrated trapper and guide, in 1851. The upper section of the

February 4. Camp 112. Ther. sunrise 41°. 3 p.m. 75°. Made an early start & made 11 m. 2430 ft. Encamped on the same stream as last night, between two high ridges. Had a severe attack of chills & fever today—chill lasted 4 hours. No wood at Camp—Descended 800 ft.

February 5. Camp 113. Ther. sunrise 37°. 3 p.m. 69°.5. Struck Bill Williams Fork today about 12 & found a running stream & quite large. After following it for several miles, the water suddenly disappeared in the sand. Filling all the canteens & kegs, moved on & went into Camp about 3:30 p.m. No grass at Camp. Made 13 m. 940 ft. Descended 600 ft. Slight attack of chills & fever tonight.

February 6. Camp 114. Ther. sunrise 39°. 3 p.m. 80°. Made today 9 m. 2054 ft. No grass in camp—plenty of water. For the last three days we have been travelling in the river bottom— Sand very deep, the wheels sinking nearly a foot, making it very difficult travelling. The animals have had no grass of any consequence for four nights & are in a very poor condition. Three or four gave out today. At 11 came to a spot of good grass, laid by till one & travelled again till sunset. It was the intention to lay by tomorrow but as there's no grass here, must travel till we come to a good grazing spot.

Vegetation is far advanced along the route. Grass (where there is any) is several inches in height—bushes leaved out & the Country has assumed the appearance of spring. Passed some immense Cactii today[15]—some having one straight stem others branching out with two or more. I visited one near the road. It was 14 ft. in height & about 20 inches in diameter. Others were larger. Firing a pistol ball into it, the sap run out in a steady stream & having a sweet taste.

---

river now is known as the Little Sandy. See Whipple, *Report*, Feb. 1, 1854; Barnes, ed., *Arizona Place Names*, p. 203.

[15] This is the *Cereus giganteus*, to Möllhausen "the queen of the cactus tribe." Dr. Bigelow, who first glimpsed a specimen on Feb. 4, thought it the most interesting cactus of the region and "probably the whole world." Though so familiar now, this giant cactus invariably astounded travelers like Sherburne when they saw it for the first time. On Sept. 16, 1853, Sherburne had described cacti a mere five or six feet in height as "immense." The wagon train now is moving south along the river. See Möllhausen, *Diary*, II, p. 218; *Reports of Explorations and Surveys*, IV ("Botanical Character"), p. 12; Tidball, Diary, Feb. 5, 1854.

Stanley, Diary: "Marched nine miles down the sandy bed of the creek today. Nothing but sand, deep, all the day long, the neighboring hills being of the same. Our mules suffered terribly, this being the third day they have had no grass. Encamped upon a small marsh with a few bunches of grass. Saw the cereus gigantus for the first time today. Tired, disheartened and disgusted."

February 7. Camp 115. Ther. sunrise 32°. 12 [noon] 75°.2. Obliged to move this morning on account of scarcity of grass. Got into Camp 12 m. Mules in better travelling condition than yesterday. Part of the way were obliged to travel in the river—water 1½ ft. deep & an abundance of *mud*— Passed two Beaver dams. Saw a large number of the gigantic Cactii of yesterday—some not being less than 20 ft. in height. Go on tomorrow. Lucky enough yesterday to find half a bag of dried peaches which we luxuriated on today, much to our satisfaction. They were stolen from the mess some time since, by one of the Teamsters.

February 8. Camp 116. Ther. sunrise 42°.9. 3 p.m. 81°. Made today 6 m. 1766 ft. Our March was through the Rio bottom, most of the time passing through water. As we approached a bend of the river, the mountains approached each other, forming a perpendicular wall on each side—to all appearances there was an impassible barrier on both sides & in front. The walls came closer & closer & not untill within 40 yds. of the wall in front, could we see any outlet. Then the hills opened to the right & we passed through a narrow defile—keeping in the bed of the stream. About a mile farther on came to a bed of quick-sand. The first wagon sunk to the wagon bed & the mules went down, nothing being visible of the two foremost but their heads. With some difficulty the mules were got out & the wagon pulled through by extra mules. Doubling the remaining teams, they got through very well as the road was broken by the first wagon.

Stanley, Diary: "Left camp early and . . . we entered finally the cañon of the river where it passes through the mountain. Here our passage was very difficult. The mountains arose on each side from the waters edge and we were compelled to move down the bed of the stream with our waggons. The bottom of the stream was quicksand and our poor mules floundered distressingly, sometimes down and altogether refusing to pull. We encamped, after several hours hard labor crossing a narrow strip of quicksand . . . Indians lurking about. Weary, disgusted and tired to despair."

A lithograph of Balduin Möllhausen's drawing of a "cactus forest" along Bill Williams Fork. The artist called this cactus, the *Cereus giganteus*, the "queen of the cactus tribe." The lithographer added the Indians (unseen during this stage of the journey), presumably to add exotic color and to demonstrate the height of the cacti. Courtesy David Miller.

February 9. Camp 117. Ther. sunrise 42°.5. Made today 4 m. 818 ft—as there was a bad place to cross, two of the escort wagons were left back & their mules put in the other teams. After arriving at Camp, the wagons were sent back after them & brought them in about 4½ p.m. A large number of immense Cactii round Camp tonight, one of which is estimated at 45 ft. in height. Several more have been cut down with axes, measuring 25–30 & 36 ft. in length—from 4 ft. 1 in. to 7 ft. 9 in. in circumference.

We will undoubtedly hear from the Ex'n party tomorrow, as they took ten days rations which are out tomorrow night. We have had but one express from them which was the second day—

Rather "hard up" for provisions—but 17 days full rations left—will be on half rations in a few days. 9 p.m. Looking on the hills to the right of Camp, it resembles one vast cemetery. The moon shining on the green trees—& the spiral Cactii rising into the air look like tall monuments. The evenings are delightful—like the spring evenings of the States. Ther. at 9 p.m. being as high as 45° & 50°—

February 10. Camp 118. Ther. sunrise 42.° 3 p.m. 72.° Travelled 6 m. 1052 ft. A large number of the mules gave out today. One escort wagon abandoned—the mules & load being distributed to the remaining wagons. After arriving at Camp & pitching tents, Leroux, Campbell, A., & Dr. Bigelow came in from the other party. They came for provisions as the party was nearly out & in fact quite out. They have not seen the Colorado, although had been about 15 miles ahead. They think it about 20 miles. Road through Rio bottom. Two days ration will be sent in the morning. We expect to see them at the end of that time. Half rations issued tonight as 'tis impossible to reach settlements before March. 10 days rations issued for 20 days—leaving 7 days more.

February 11. Camp 119. Ther. sunrise 52.°5. 3 p.m. 57.° Rations sent exploring party this morning for two days only— Travelled today 5 m. 3574 ft. Obliged to stop on account of two teams breaking down. Rained nearly all day.

February 12. Camp 120. Ther. sunrise 47.° 3 p.m. 72.°5. Travelled today 6 m. 3040 ft.[16] Before leaving Camp one of the escort wagons, containing soldiers tents, & mess chests, & a box of ammunition was abandoned. After arriving at Camp, Lieut. Jones

[16] The wagon train on this day passed the spot where the Santa Maria River joins the Big Sandy from the east.

& White came in. They say the Camp of Ex'n party is about 4½ miles from here. The Colorado no one knows where—*probable some where West.*

Möllhausen, *Diary*, II, pp. 221–22: "There was now always an abundance of excellent water near; but our cattle had suffered too much to be able to recover themselves in a short rest. Not a day went by without our having to shoot, or leave behind, some of them; and one waggon after another was abandoned, and its load distributed, as well as might be, on the sore backs of our poor beasts, so that we were every moment reminded to lose no time. We were threatened also with another trouble; our flocks of sheep were diminishing rapidly, for 116 men had to get from them daily rations of meat . . . and our appetites unluckily seemed to increase as our supplies diminished."

February 13. Camp 121. Ther. sunrise 32°.5. 3 p.m. 63°.5. Travelled 6 m. 3446 ft. & came to camp of Ex'n party. They were encamped on a kind of mesa in wigwams made of willow boughs & thatched with grass & bushes—which gave quite an Indian-like appearance. 'Tis decided to lay here tomorrow & make arrangements for throwing away all [but] indispensible boxes, trunks, etc & for the abandonment of several of the wagons.

February 14. Ther. sunrise 40°. 3 p.m. 63°. Lay by today— All the wagons unloaded & a general sacrifice of boxes, trunks, mess chests, & other articles "too numerous to mention." The medical stores were greatly reduced. Quite a large quantity of sago, tapioca & arrowroot were distributed to the three messes. Also a quantity of mustard & pickled onions which were found stowed away in some corner. These will greatly benefit our half rations. Three of the Survey & escort wagons are to be left tomorrow. We start from here with five wagons & one Caratella & have a change of mules. Tomorrow morning the latter [carretela] & tents are expected to be left, for 'tis necessary to reduce transportation as much as possible & push for the Settlements—& as the Dr. says "The Divil of it is, no one knows how far to the Colorado."

Tidball, Diary: "Arrangements were made today to abandon 3 more of the wagons. A very sensible idea especially since all the mules are broken down and not able in teams of 8 & 10 to drag along the wagons comparatively empty. A great sacrifice was made of trunks and large chests. Every young gentleman of the party of which there are any number as meteorologists etc. have supplies of trunks, chests and carpet bags enough to freighter a steamer."

February 15. Camp 122. Ther. sunrise 45°. 3 p.m. 75°. Started this morning, leaving behind four wagons, mess tables, boxes—& a great deal of useless trash including *medicine, wagon covers,* etc. Made 9 m. 1136 ft. Some of the teams seem pretty well tired out, although every wagon had ten mules—one of the escort wagons brought in with 14 mules, another had a change of six.[17] Travelled thro' a cañon, the walls rising perpendicularly on each side, varying from 100 to 300 ft. We were in water most of the time. Saw a large quantity of ducks on the route. Gathered flowers in bloom, a pretty good indication of coming spring.

February 16. Camp 123. Ther. sunrise 41°. 3 p.m. 70°.5. Travelled 6 m. 5126 ft. Left behind one of the escort wagons—leaving three survey wagons, one escort wagon & one Caratella, thus reducing our train from 15 to 5 & that within 30 miles of this place. Before leaving Camp, "cached" three tents, a box of candles, can of oil, & a lot of extra harness. Our mess today shot 14 ducks of which Mölhausen killed 12—About supper time Dr. Bigelow came into Camp in high glee holding in his hand a flower in full bloom, which he said was almost solely an occupant of Calafornia. We must be near the Colorado & hope to be there in two or three days at the farthest.

Tidball, Diary: "Traveled 7 mi. due west along the creek: very deep sand: teams gave out: one wagon abandoned: no grass: plenty of weeds along the creek: lots of wild ducks: warm delightful weather: flowers in bloom ———; Dr. Bigelowe in glory."

Stanley, Diary: "Made a cache this morning, which we filled with cast away property, tents, candles, oil, etc., and dropping another wagon (Lieut. Jones') we moved on. Our way still through a deep cañon with bleak, rocky peaks arising on either side, perfectly bare, black and forming a prospect gloomy beyond description. The bottom of the cañon is sandy and the whole country entirely uninteresting. Everyone is thoroughly tired and disgusted."

[17] On February 19, Whipple discovered that the "sudden failure" of the mules, which contributed to the decision to abandon wagons and supplies, occurred because the sentinels had kept the herd in the same spots each night for protection against Indians. Thus they were prevented from grazing. The wagon train now is moving west along the Bill Williams Fork. See Whipple, *Report*, Feb. 19, 1854.

February 17. Camp 124. Ther. sunrise 47°.7. 3 p.m. 63°.5. Before leaving Camp this morning a box of candles & several other articles were "cached"—as they could well be spared & were a useless incumbrance. Travelled 7 m. 1966 ft. & obliged to encamp without water or grass. Rained hard during afternoon & evening till about 10 p.m. We all got pretty well drenched before reaching Camp.

Whipple, Diary: "Night is gloomy. The remnant of our journey too looks a dark uncertainty like the close of day."

February 18. Camp 125. Ther. sunrise 45°.6. 12 [noon] 56°.4. Left several trunks behind this morning. Road during march wet & heavy. Stopped at 10 a.m. at the first grass, to graze the mules, intending to move again about one, but rec'd a message from Leroux, that there was no grass for six or eight miles & fearing we would not reach grazing before dark, concluded to remain here & make an early start in the morning. Left camp this morning about 8 & made 3 m. 5202 ft. Raining nearly all the morning & a shower about sunset. Within half an hour from that time, not a cloud could be seen.

Tidball, Diary: "Another sacrifice of big trunks was made this morning to lighten the wagons. It is with rueful countenances that the young dandies of the party look upon such destruction of their perfumery and other like atire so suitable for a trip of this kind."

Whipple, Diary: "Stars appear affording to Lieut. Ives good astronomical observations. These roughly computed place us to my surprise in Latitude 34° 14′. We therefore appear to be far south of the junction of this river with Rio Colorado, as indicated by the map of Capt. Sitgreaves. I am troubled at this and doubtful how to proceed."

February 19. Camp 126. Ther. sunrise 30°.5. 3 p.m. 64°. Very heavy frost last night & thick fog at sunrise this morning. Made an early start & travelled 8 m. 4856 ft.— Saw a large number of ducks & one flock of geese— One of the mess shot six large ducks of which he obtained four. Left the escort wagon & our survey wagon this morning before leaving camp—which reduced our train to one Caratella & two wagons. After arriving at Camp, one of the men ascended a peak near by & said he could see the water in the Colorado, but we could not reach it tomorrow, as the Rio ran some distance to the S.E. If he in fact saw it, of which I have some doubt, we will be there on the 22nd—perhaps tomorrow.

Left this morning a box of candles & several trunks, also some instruments, which were useless to us now. Saw today, tracks of Indians to all appearances made in the morning. They came up the creek & turned back, probably from seeing our Camp fires, or train. Part of the route today was through a cañon, the sides of which were estimated at 400 ft. perpendicular.

Whipple, Diary: "Astronomical observations this night place us in Lat. 34°15′. Can Capt. Sitgreaves have made a mistake in the position of the mouth of this stream?"

February 20. Camp 127. Ther. sunrise 38.° 3 p.m. 68.°5. Ducks cackling & wolves howling round camp all night, which was a change in the programme which no one called for & was far from agreeable. Made an early start this a.m. About 11 a.m. were startled by an unusual discharge of fire arms—as volley after volley rang through the air & resounded through the hills, arose the shout, "Here's the Colorado"— Sure enough we were close on the banks & the river rolled past us from 200 to 300 yds in width— Every one was in a high flow of spirits & appeared as well satisfied as though we were already in settlements. By fortune there was good grass at the junction of Bill Williams Fork with the Colorado. The teams were unhitched & animals turned out to graze. The junction was determined by observations. After laying by three hours started up the river. The distance from Camp to the Rio was about 4 miles & from the junction to this place, near the same—making in all 8 m. 2183 ft. It is the intention to travel up this Rio till reaching the Mohave Creek, about 40 or 60 miles above[18]—then follow that West— We will pass thro' the Mohave villages & hope to obtain some provisions from them—tho' 'tis said they live on corn & pumpkins—[19]

[18]The Mojave River does not flow into the Colorado, although this was not known at the time. In California, though not in Arizona, "Mohave" is spelled with a "j" rather than an "h." On the Sitgreaves map the cartographer, Richard Kern, mistook the mouth of Paiute Creek, which flows into the Colorado, for the Mojave. Earlier maps also showed the Mojave River flowing into the Colorado from California. The expedition now moves north along the river in order to find a crossing closer to the 35th parallel. See Wallace, "Across Arizona to the Big Colorado," p. 354, n. 68, Peirson, *The Mojave River*, pp. 62–63, 88–90.

[19]This information probably came from Leroux, now in familiar territory.

Möllhausen's drawing of the junction of Bill Williams Fork and the Colorado River, finally reached by the expedition on February 20, 1854. One of the few drawings Möllhausen executed in a romantic mode, it nevertheless is topographically accurate. Courtesy Oklahoma Historical Society.

After striking the Rio, saw plenty of Indian tracks & trails—some old—some fresh. We expect every hour to see some of the tribe. A signal fire was built this a.m. to draw them in, but as yet without effect. Every one in the train on half rations & sufficient for about three weeks. We must reach settlements in that time or take the consequences of mule meat.

After arriving in Camp tonight the Dr. (Bigelow) in order to *reduce transportation & by & with the advice of those assembled*—issued 8 bottles of Brandy. It was drank "clear" & in "Toddies" "*mit sugar*"—to the Colorado.

Traveling northwest beyond Bill Williams Mountain, the Sitgreaves expedition in 1851 crossed a long stretch of desert and the Cerbat and Black mountains to reach the Colorado farther north than Whipple's wagon train, at present-day Bullhead City, Arizona. It then moved south along the Colorado to Fort Yuma in California, near the Mexican border, and was attacked by Mohave and Quechan (Yuma) Indians. In passing the junction with the Bill Williams Fork, the latitude was calculated incorrectly by Sitgreaves. See Sitgreaves, "Report," Nov. 5–Nov. 30, 1851; Wallace, "Across Arizona to the Big Colorado," pp. 353–58.

The Colorado River to Los Angeles

February 21–March 23, 1854

On February 21 a sadly reduced expedition travels north along the east bank of the Colorado River, having abandoned the two remaining wagons. Six days later it crosses the Colorado into California, near what is now the town of Needles. The men then move northwest across the Providence Mountains and on March 8 reach Soda Lake near the present-day town of Crucero. There Lieutenant Whipple discovers that the Mojave River disappears into a sink instead of flowing east to the Colorado, as earlier maps had indicated. The commander divides his men into three groups to cross the desert at intervals, so that pools of water along the way can refill after use by the different parties. Traveling west along the 35th parallel, on March 13 the company reaches the road that connects the Mormon settlement of San Bernardino in California with the Great Salt Lake in Utah. Two days later the company leaves the river at present-day Oro Grande and moves southwest toward Cajon Pass, between the San Gabriel and San Bernardino mountains. At the base of the pass they take a road to the west, away from San Bernardino. Passing through a lovely valley dotted with ranchos, on March 21 they reach Los Angeles, "that long looked for place."

On this final stage of the journey the men experience their most prolonged contact with Indians. Proceeding northward along the Colorado River they meet the Mohaves. A tribe of Yuman-speaking Indians, the Mohaves were considered dangerous and unpredictable by earlier travelers along the river. For the Whipple expedition, however, the encounter is a pleasurable one except to Lieutenant Stanley, who despises all In-

dians. The men trade for food and "Indian Curiosities" and eat well for the first time in weeks. Without these friendly Indians, John Sherburne writes, "'tis impossible to tell how we could have got along." Mohaves lead them to the site chosen for the crossing of the Colorado and Mohaves help them cross the wide and treacherous river. John Sherburne, who vividly describes the event, considered it one of the most memorable days of the trip. Moreover, the Mohave chiefs provide the expedition with two excellent guides to lead them across the desert to the well-traveled Mormon Road.

On the trail west of the Colorado, with journey's end only a few weeks away, the expedition suffers its first human casualty. One of the New Mexican herders is killed by Paiute Indians near the present-day town of Daggett. A few days later some passing Mormons inform the men that the commander of another Pacific Railroad expedition, Captain John Gunnison, had been killed by Paiutes in Utah some months before, along with other members of his company.

By March 13 the men of the Whipple expedition are subsisting on unsalted mutton, but three days later a Mormon trader meets them with provisions that last until they reach the ranchos beyond Cajon Pass. One day after the expedition emerges from the pass on March 16, John Sherburne writes in his diary, with no fanfare, that he had "made an agreement" to stay in California (a word he learns to spell along the way) with William White, another meteorological assistant. When the expedition disbands in Los Angeles, Lieutenant Whipple and the remaining members of the scientific corps leave by stagecoach for the port of San Pedro. There they board a steamer for San Francisco. From that city they plan to embark on the journey back to Washington, where Lieutenant Whipple must prepare his report to Congress.

According to Balduin Möllhausen, members of the scientific corps assembled on March 23, 1854, in a Los Angeles coffeehouse to say farewell "to the companions they were leaving behind." John Sherburne tells us he does not regret his decision to stay in California, and on that day he ends his diary.

February 21. Camp 138. Ther. sunrise (not taken). 3 p.m. 71°.7. Travelled today till about 11 & coming to a good grazing spot concluded to lay by a little & graze while the country for a few miles ahead was explored—after about an hour, Mr. Whipple, Leroux, & Sevadra [Stanley] returned with tidings that the wagons could not pass ahead. Went into Camp & made arrangements for abandoning the remaining two wagons. The Caratella will be taken anyhow—as the Instruments must be carried in it & the distance must be measured. We have done what has never been done before, that is brought wagons to the Colorado by a central route. The rest of the route is not of so much importance as 'tis well known that a wagon road can be made from Mohave Creek to Los Angeles. Made today 5 m. 662 ft. Leroux brought with him two Mohaves.[1] They were entirely destitute of clothing, excepting the breech *clout*— Shortly after two more came in—one who appeared to be "Bos," said they were sent by their chief to meet us, having heard some time since of our coming. They were fine looking fellows. The finest Indians yet seen—one of them brought some beans which were purchased from him. They received many presents. They said there were plenty of pumpkins, corn, wheat & beans—& signified their desire to trade. We will in all probability obtain sufficient provisions to last us through. About dark, an Indian from another tribe came in, bringing beans for trade. They [Mohaves] said a short time since that a scouting party from Fort Yumah came this way & made peace with them. They described the Commander as being a *flat-nosed* man & the Lieut. as a man with but one arm. The latter was recognized as Lieut. ——— who lost his arm in Mexico.[2]

[1] The Mohaves, of Yuman stock, lived chiefly on the east bank of the Colorado River, in what now is called the Mohave Valley. Farmers and sometime traders, they were also great travelers and aggressive warriors to whom intertribal warfare with arrows and clubs was a semireligious activity. Whites who knew of the Mohaves regarded them as unpredictable and dangerous. They had attacked Jedediah Smith's trapping party in 1827, for example, and Leroux undoubtedly informed Whipple that they had harassed the Sitgreaves expedition, wounding its surgeon. See Forbes, *Warriors of the Colorado*, p. 42; Kroeber, *Mohave Indians*; Spicer, *Cycles of Conquest*, p. 267; Wallace, "Across Arizona to the Big Colorado," pp. 354–55.

[2] Whipple thought the "Commander" may have been Major H. L. Kendrick of the Sitgreaves expedition or Major Samuel P. Heintzelman, then commander of the southern military district of California. But he was Major E. H. Fitzgerald, commander of a detachment of dragoons based in San Diego. The lieutenant was Thomas W. Sweeny, a colorful officer stationed at "Camp Independence" near Fort Yuma, about 200 miles south at the confluence of the Colorado and

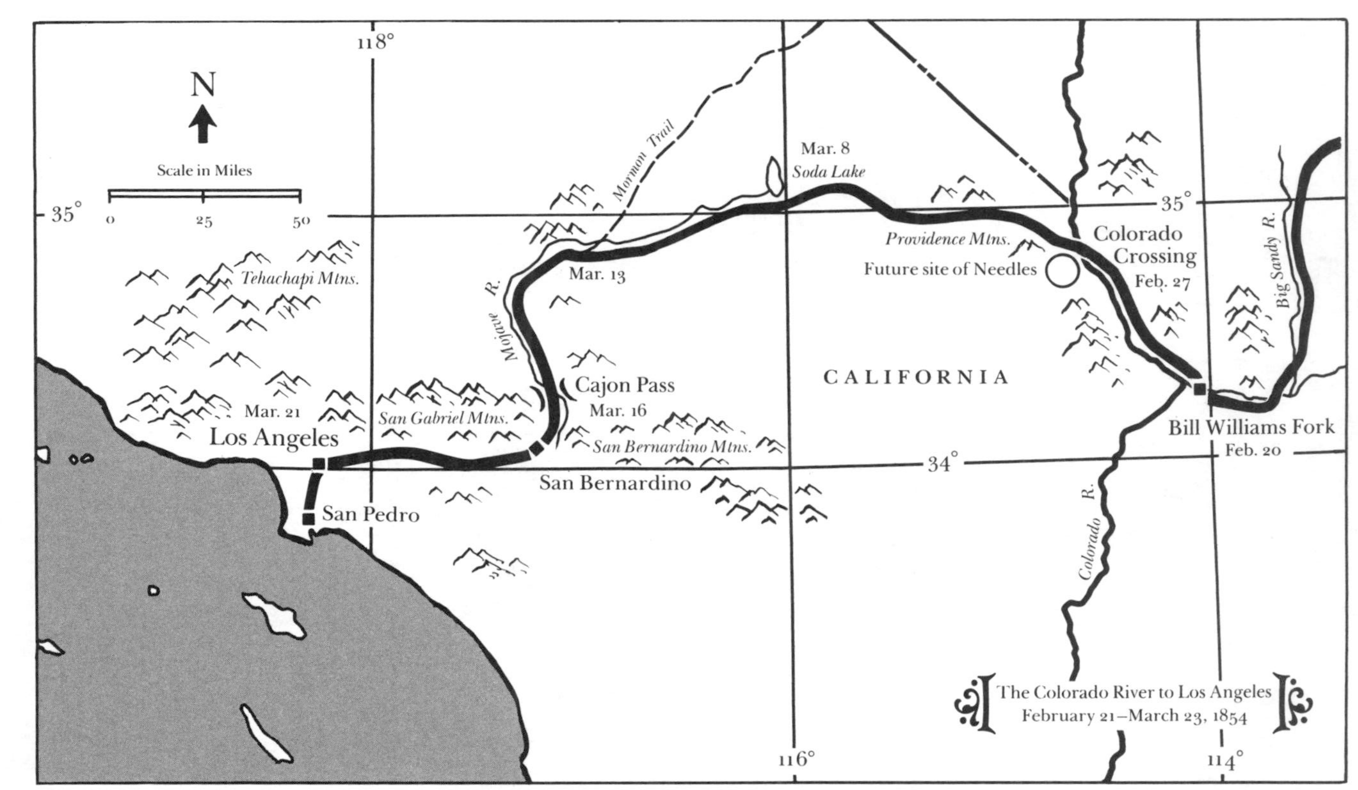

The Colorado River to Los Angeles
February 21–March 23, 1854

They gave a very amusing description of the manner in which he attempted to hide it under his coat or blanket. All professed to be great friends & appeared glad to see us. A sketch of them was taken.

Whipple, *Report*: "We saw, standing in bold relief, several Indians, apparently much excited. . . . They walked along, their muscular and well-proportioned limbs, without covering, showed to great advantage. They were tall and erect, with a step as light as a deer's. Their faces were painted black, with a red streak along the nose. . . . They stalked into camp with the dignity of princes. . . . Everybody treated them with distinguished consideration."

Möllhausen, *Diary*, II, p. 243: "Our visitors had rats, squirrels, and frogs dangling to their girdles, and wished to roast them at our fires, but as they were new specimens we exchanged them for mutton, and added them to our collection."

February 22. Camp 129. Ther. sunrise 53°.5. 12 [noon] 69°.7. Started this morning with the Caratella & a dozen men, leaving behind the last of the wagons. We started about 2 hours before the rest of the party, but were joined by Escort & mules about 6 miles from Camp. Obliged to take out the mules & carry the Caratella about ½ mile by main strength, over rocks,—perpendicular & running in every direction. A greater part of the way, 'twas necessary to prevent a capsize by ropes on the side. Let it down steep declivities by ropes & hauled it up by ropes, assisted by four mules. Met on the road between 60 & 80 Indians belonging to the Mohave, Pahutah & several other neighboring tribes. Some were magnificently formed & had fine faces. They were better clothed than those of yesterday having in addition a blanket or buckskin thrown obliquely across the shoulder. They also had beads & trinkets—few— They bro't corn, wheat & beans to trade—many traded away their bows & arrows for old clothes. They were very much interested in the motion of the Caratella & a crowd of from 20 to 30 were along side all the time. Very few understood any Spanish—one brought letters of recommenda-

---

the Gila rivers; he lost his arm during the Mexican War. On March 27, 1852, Sweeny accompanied Major Fitzgerald and a company of dragoons on an expedition up the Colorado to punish the river Indians for an earlier attack against Fitzgerald's company. See Whipple, Diary, Feb. 21, 1854, Whipple Papers; Forbes, *Warriors of the Colorado*, pp. 325, 329–38; Woodward, ed., *Journal of Lieutenant Thomas W. Sweeny*, pp. 151–53; for Sweeny see also *DAB*.

tion from some Americans—two written in English & one in Spanish recommending them to all Americans as friends. They led us through the best road & passes—& camped us on a spot of green grass close to the river. Made today 8 m. 3200 ft. Just before dark, the Indians brought corn, wheat, pumpkins & beans— Traded for a considerable quantity.[3] They prefer old clothes, even ragged, to trinkets— The pumpkins when cooked are very sweet, as though cooked with sugar. They are all prepared for *pumpkin pies.*

Möllhausen, *Diary*, II, p. 263: "Our appearance in the settlements and villages of these savages created no little sensation,—though only of a pleasant and good-humored kind. The hills and roofs were quickly covered with natives of every age and sex, who enjoyed thence a full view of the long procession of strangers; and our copious beards, which had now the benefit of nearly a year's undisturbed growth, and with most of us reached down to the breast, seemed particularly to amuse the ladies. . . . Whenever one of us bearded fellows rode past them, the women burst into a fit of laughter, and put their hands before their mouths, as if the sight of us rather tended to make them sick."

February 23. Camp 130. Ther. sunrise 41°.3. 3 p.m. 71°. Travelled today 11 m. 3828 ft. Along the first part of the route found a large quantity of Indians, most of whom left us before noon. On arriving in Camp about 250 came in & traded. Large quantity of corn, beans & pumpkins—also some excellent corn meal—were traded for. Blankets, old clothes, & beads were traded for bows, quivers, arrows, lances & Indian Curiosities. Late in the evening a Yumah came in, who crossed the Colorado with Mr. Whipple when he was in this Country before—tho' lower down than this.[4] He said the Yumahs were coming to see us. Quite a

[3]The traders are Chemehuevis (a Mohave word adopted by Whipple), who were an offshoot of the southern Paiutes and a division of Shoshonean Indians. The expedition has traveled north along the Colorado, between the east bank and the Mohave Mountains. The Chemehuevis, whose village was across the river in California, were accompanied to camp by their chief, who drew for Whipple a sketch of the locations of the different tribes living along the Colorado, and gave him a vocabulary. The vocabulary was the first ever published. Whipple wrote that these Indians were "less majestic" than the Mohaves. See Whipple, *Report*, Feb. 22, 1854; *Reports of Explorations and Surveys*, III, Part III ("Indian Tribes"), pp. 16, 32, 76; Kroeber, *Mohave Indians*, pp. 11, 13–16.

[4]Whipple had known the Yuma (Quechan) Indian, whom he called José, when he was surveying below the mouth of the Gila River for the U.S.-Mexico boundary commission in 1849; the Yumans or Quechans were kin to the Mohaves.

large number of Indians remained & slept in Camp during the night. Passed today a wheat & corn field. The wheat planted in hills was about 2 inches out of the ground, but of the corn nothing remained but the last years stalks— About 10 or 11 mules gave out today & were left.

February 24. Camp 131. Ther. sunrise 55°.6. 3 p.m. 65°.5. Took three Indians for guides this morning round a ridge of mountains which 'twas impossible to cross with the Caratella. Made rather an early start—before the pack-mules, as they were to cross by a shorter route over the mountains. Travelled all day untill sundown, without any signs of the rest of the party & there being with us nothing to eat or drink—were about thinking of going into Camp till morning when we saw flash signals about two miles distant & after heard the report of pistol signals. Kept travelling untill an hour after dark, when we came to Camp of main body—Lieut. Tidball being a mile farther on. Travelled 22 m. 4312 ft. They estimated their distance as 16 miles.

Not many Indians in camp tonight. Heard from Tidball's camp that there were about 200 with him. Had an attack of chills this a.m.

Whipple, *Report*: "Again we have experienced the advantage of having cultivated a kindly feeling with the natives. Our parties today have necessarily been scattered widely, and an attack by Indians would have proved disastrous to the expedition. But instead of impeding our operations, they have rendered good service, giving valuable information and faithful guidance."

February 25. Camp 132. Ther. sunrise 45°.5. Sunset 70°. Moved today to Tidball's camp—distance 1 m. 222 ft. & laid by for the day, as there was excellent grass. Found him in the midst of a large crowd of Indians. He had great difficulty in getting them

---

José, who had a Mexican mother, no doubt told the Mohave chiefs of Whipple's good reputation with the Quechans. The expedition has passed along the present Chemehuevi Valley (first named by Whipple), and the Chemehuevis were careful to turn back when the expedition reached the first of the Mohave villages. Allowed to live in a defined area, they nevertheless were dependent upon the goodwill of the Mohaves, who claimed all land on both banks along the middle region of the Colorado River. See Whipple, *Report*, Feb. 23, 1854; *Reports of Explorations and Surveys*, III, Part III ("Indian Tribes"), p. 16; Kroeber, *Mohave Indians*, pp. 10–12, 254; Kroeber and Kroeber, *A Mohave War Reminiscence*, pp. 82–84; Edwards, ed., *The Whipple Report*, Nov. 2, 1849.

out of camp last night & driving them out one threatened to strike him with a stick.[5] Large quantities came into Camp after our arrival—at one time they were counted & made 320 after which large squads or families came in. There must have been at least 400 to 500. A large guard was put on & they were kept out of Camp as much as possible. A great deal of trading carried on by everyone. No one can imagine the noise kept up by the squaws—being in among them was worse than Bedlam. Their dress consists of a bark *petticoat,* coming to the knees & fastened round the waist by a string of the same material. These bark unmentionables are very curious & many were traded for—to be taken to the states as a curiosity. Had another attack of chills & fever today.

Whipple, *Report*: "Soon a long procession of warriors approached headed by the chief and his interpreter. . . . These Indians are probably in as wild a state of nature as any tribe now within the limits of our possessions. They have not had sufficient intercourse with any civilized people to acquire a knowledge of their language or their vices. Leroux says that no white party has ever before passed without encountering hostility. Nevertheless, they appear to be intelligent, and to have naturally pleasant dispositions. The men are tall, erect, and finely proportioned. . . . The apron or breech-cloth for men, and a short petticoat made of strips of the inner bark of the cottonwood for women, are the only articles of dress deemed indispensable. But many of the females have long robes or cloaks of fur. The young girls wear beads. When married, their chins are tattooed with vertical blue lines, and they wear a necklace with a single sea-shell in front, curiously wrought."

Möllhausen, *Diary*, pp. 244–45, 257: "We never tired of admiring the vigorous, powerful race, amongst whom a man of less than six feet appeared to be quite a rarity. . . . The women of the Colorado were unlike the men in growth, being short, thickset, and so fat as to border on the comic. . . . They have fine black eyes, and their somewhat broad faces have a cheerful and far from unpleasing expression, though they

[5] Whipple wrote in his diary that the Mohaves in Lieut. Tidball's camp were inclined to be insolent, one stepping upon Mr. Hutton's toes. Möllhausen, who was with Tidball, observed that an Indian behaved in an "unbecoming" manner, though he believed "more for the love of fun than from any other motive." Less amused, Tidball struck the Indian across the shoulders with his cane, whereupon the Mohave women present flew into "a furious passion." All were sent from camp but next day appeared to have forgotten the incident. On this day the expedition passed three peaks on the Arizona side of the river, which Whipple named the Needles, and arrived at the Mohave Valley. See Whipple, Diary, Feb. 24, 1854, Whipple Papers; Möllhausen, *Diary*, II, pp. 255–56.

A lithograph of Balduin Möllhausen's drawing of Mohaves, whose aid was so important to the Whipple expedition. Möllhausen was the first artist to sketch these impressive Indians. *Reports of Explorations and Surveys,* vol. III.

cannot be called handsome. They go more carefully to work with their painting than the men, and tattoo themselves more."

Stanley, Diary, February 24: "A more degraded race of Indians does not, perhaps, exist. The men go naked, except the rich ones who possess a few rags . . . and the old duds they have traded us out of. The women wear a kind of petticoat made of willow, giving them a kind of ostrich-like appearance as they shuffle along. . . . Generally they are large and stalwart, the women extremely fat, and they put me much in mind of an old matron sow—only they exceed that animal in dirt and disgusting appearance."

February 26. Camp 133. Ther. sunrise 36.° 3 p.m. 72.°7. Travelled up Rio today & about 3 p.m. halted at the crossing place.[6]

[6]The camp is across the river from and just below the present town of Needles, California. Whipple's railroad profile was drawn southwest from present-day

Distance 9 m. 3440 ft. Inflated the pontoon & floated the Caratella by the way of an experiment—found it worked very well. The Indians tonight, brought in enough grass and mezquite to feed all the animals—there being no grass on the place made it quite acceptable & actually indispensible— They brought also a large quantity of fish which were excellent for frying. Without these friendly Indians, 'tis impossible to tell how we could have got along. Everything we have on the table, excepting mutton, is got from them. Corn bread, fish, beans, pumpkins, & wheat for coffee all comes from them & stores enough will be laid in to last us untill reaching settlements.

Passed today some of their lodges which are superior to those of the Pueblos of N. Mexico. They are built by driving large poles in the ground & placing cross pieces over them—then thatching side & top with bushes & grass [they] cover the whole with mud. The front of the houses run out forming a kind of roof, open at the sides & front. The only entrance to the house was by one door in front—a small window opposite the door seemed to give a "little more light on the subject." In these houses were cans or jars of corn, beans & dried pumpkins, ranging from 1 to 4 qts.—hermetically sealed with a kind of gum or wax. Round the houses were large tanks, capable of holding 8 or 10 bushels, filled with the same articles—also mezquite beans & twigs.[7] Saw several corn & wheat fields today. A number of water

Kingman, Arizona, to this spot, omitting the long southern loop taken by the expedition. The Santa Fe Railroad moved northwest from present-day Ash Fork, Arizona, south to Kingman, and crossed the river at Topock, moving north along the west bank of the Colorado to Needles in California.

Although Whipple's party did not know it, one of the survivors of the Oatman family, Olive Oatman, was then a prisoner of the Mohaves, probably kept in a village farther north along the river. The Yavapais in 1851 killed six of the family, carried off Olive and her sister (who later died), and sold them to the Mohaves. In 1856 the Mohaves returned Olive Oatman to Fort Yuma; her face had been tattooed. See Whipple, Diary, Feb. 27, 1854, Whipple Papers; Kroeber, *Mohave Indians*, pp. 1–15.

[7]The large "tanks" were granaries holding surplus food for use in times of poor harvest. The Indians ground mesquite beans into flour and made a form of pinole. They did not store twigs, but the granaries were made of willow twigs. The splendid physique of the Mohaves and other river tribes was a testimonial to their nutritious diet, chiefly of fish, vegetables, and fruit. Sadly, and in part because of the path opened across northern Arizona to the Colorado by the Whipple expedition, the Mohaves were reduced to a wretched state within five years. See Whipple, *Report*, Feb. 26, 1854.

A lithograph of a Möllhausen drawing of a Mohave dwelling. Note the "tank" in the foreground in which Mohaves stored grain and beans for the winter months. *Reports of Explorations and Surveys,* vol. III.

melons brought into Camp—last years produce dried. They were very good, tho' had lost some of their flavor. Had about 500 or 600 Indians in Camp today, trading etc.

Whipple, *Report*: "Under the directions of Lieutenant Ives, preparations were commenced for crossing the river. An old and much worn India rubber pontoon, brought from New Mexico, was inflated, and the body of the spring-wagon fastened upon it. The vessel was then launched, and sat upon the water like a swan. The Indians were greatly disappointed, for they had hoped to ferry us across themselves, and be well paid for it. They all left camp at dark. Some think this deviation from previous custom looks ominous. But being now near to their lodges, they are doubtless only seeking warmer shelter than our inhospitable camp affords them."

Möllhausen, *Diary*, II, p. 265: "Lieutenant Ives had brought with him from Texas a canvas boat . . . . The craft consisted of three long canvas bags, connected together, and lined inside with gutta percha, so as to be perfectly air-tight. By means of a bellows . . . and some ingeniously contrived screws, it was pumped full of air, the frame of the small waggon . . . placed on it, and the sacks drawn up at each end, so that the whole had very much the appearance of a Venetian gondola."

February 27. Camp 134. Ther. sunrise (omitted, other obs'ns omitted). 9 a.m. 67°. One of the most memorable days of our trip & at the same time most amusing & interesting. Commenced early to cross the River, selecting for a place one where a sand island was placed in the center, as 'twas too broad in any other place for the ropes to reach. The river itself being 1800 ft. from bank to bank in the place where we crossed it, the sand bar filling 1200 of that space leaving a channel on each side of 300 ft. in width. Crossed a rope to the Island by means of an air mattrass—planted a post on each side of stream & connected them by ropes—between these attaching the pontoon & Caratella. The first, second & third loads went very well, but the fourth, pretty heavily laden & unfortunately having our culinary department on board, turned bottom upwards, discharging its contents into the water, with the exception of a few articles which attached themselves to the sides & top of Caratella. Most of the things floated & were brought ashore by the Indians, but all our mess kit with the exception of the Camp Kettle & a broken frying pan "went under." The rest of the goods passed safely over & most of the men, until filled with a lot of soldiers who when near the shore inclined too much on one side & [it] capsized. The water was about 1½ ft. in depth & the manner in which they scrambled out, put me in mind of a picture in a comic almanac, of a "pleasure boat excursion" in which the boat had capsized & all were scrambling for dear life. The remainder landed in safety tho' once came near a capsize from the same cause. Now came the crossing of mules & sheep. The mules were driven in some distance above & came down to the Island without difficulty. The sheep could not be driven in & the Mexicans having charge of them each caught one & swam with him to the Island. The rest run some distance from the shore, but the Indians drove them back & following the example of the Mexys soon got them all over. As every thing now was on the Island, arrangements were made for crossing to the bank & into Cala-

Balduin Möllhausen's painting of the crossing of the Colorado River on February 27, 1854. Note the *carretela* perched upon the inflatable boat. Courtesy Oklahoma Historical Society.

fornia. But here the boat did not work as successfully as before. After the first several loads five or six upset in succession, losing a good many things & very near drowning several, one a little Mexican boy being under the water for several minutes. The remainder of our mess "kit" also Mr. Whipple's entire & that of most of the Teamsters sunk to rise no more. Also lost all the packing ropes & straps & many things which cannot easily be replaced. One boat load capsized, containing the note books of nearly all the party, Dr. Bigelow's Botany—Mr. Whipple's, Mr. Marcou's, Campbell, H. & A., Garner's, Parke's, White's & my own note books were all drenched through. The Indians saved us many things & done us a great deal of service. They brought on shore my note books, Journal (which I would not have lost for a great deal) & my box of instruments which were thrown out loose. I had given them up for lost & was quite agreeably surprised on crossing to find them safe on the bank. Had all these note books been lost, money could not have replaced them. The Indians were constantly bringing things from the river. 'Twas dark before everything was across. The mules swam over without any loss, but the sheep struck the rope, which was several inches under water & about 10 or 15 caught their horns & legs in it & would have all been drowned had not the Indians loosed them. As it was three were drowned which were given to the Indians, together with three live ones. We are now in Calafornia although with the loss of some things & most of the things wet. Some had both bedding & trunks doused in the water. The panier containing the greater part of my clothes & the things I valued most, [such] as papers & Daguereotypes, did not get wet— But another containing my writing desk, shaving apparatus—"notas y esquelas amatorio"[8] & one book, sunk & was obtained filled with water. It is the intention to lay here tomorrow & dry up. There were estimated to be a thousand Indians round us today, appearing anxious to assist, even the squaws caught hold of the rope to pull the boat across. It appeared to be a gala day with them, for they were laughing, shouting, racing, jumping, playing ball & as Garner said "having a h-ll of a time." There never was a party before so successful with them & finding them so friendly. The only personal loss I've experienced during the day was the loss of a Spanish Grammar & a powder flask.

February 28. Ther. sunset 61°.9 (other obs'ns omitted). Lay by to day for the purpose of drying our things. Camp flooded with Indians. They look now like different beings from a week ago. Nearly everyone has on a shirt, coat, pair of boots, drawers, hat, or some article of clothing & some of them having a complete suit, it contrasts strangely with their black skin.

The whole camp ground was laid out with books, papers, & articles of clothing drying in the sun. Not one instance was found of any Indian trying to steal. They would pick up anything they desired to see, between their two first toes & after satisfying their curiosity leave it where 'twas picked up. Offered a reward today to the Mexys & Indians if they could bring up the packing ropes & straps from the river. The Indians would not accept it as they said the water was too cold. The Mexys took up with the offer, which was $10 & several swam the river for hours, but without the desired effect. They brought up a Prismatic Compass perfect—two broken aneroid Barometers, a powder flask (unfortunately not mine), a roll of bedding, *tin cup*, rasp &

[8] The correct Spanish would be "*notas y esquelas amatorias*," roughly "notes and billets-doux" (or "love letters"). A pannier (not panier) was a wicker basket usually carried by a mule or horse.

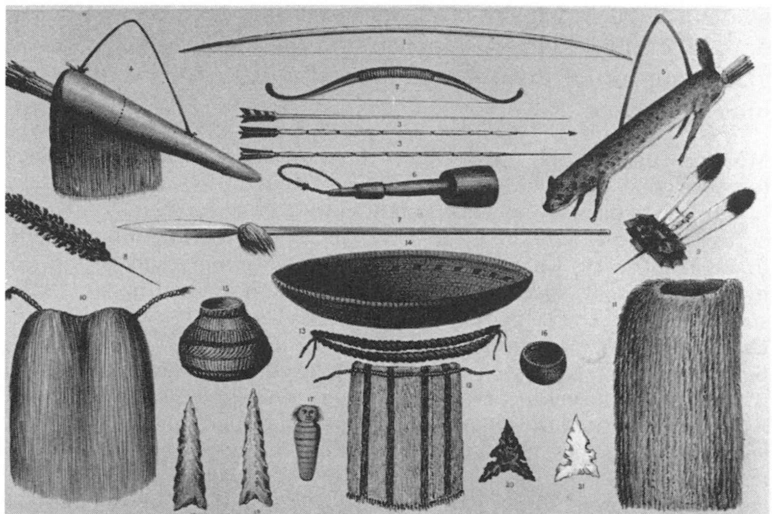

Some of the "Indian curiosities" collected by the expedition for the Smithsonian Institution, including two of the "bark unmentionables" worn by Mohave women. These exquisite drawings demonstrate Möllhausen's skill in rendering detail. *Reports of Explorations and Surveys*, vol. III.

several other small articles. The larger appeared to have floated away with the current. A great deal of trading going on during the day—corn for mules, large quantities of beans & corn meal, bows, arrows, war clubs, hair lariats, *bark petticoats*, fur robes & sundry other little "dry goods" & "domestic" articles. The last rations issued today, being 7½ days rations for 15 days—half rations. Lieut. Tidball uncorked two bottles of brandy tonight, in honor of our arrival in Calafornia. "Brandy Clear" & "toddies" flourished in abundance.

March 1. Camp 135. Ther. sunrise 37°.2. 3 p.m. 61°.2. Struck camp and made a short march of 3 m. 456 ft. up the Rio to the place from where 'tis necessary to start on our march up Mohave creek. There is a long stretch without water. The Mohave guides (of which we have two) say we cannot reach it in one day.[9] The

[9]The two guides were Cairook and his friend Irateba, both subordinate chiefs. The five principal Mohave chiefs met with Whipple on March 1 in solemn

whole tribe of Indians still followed us and kept in Camp during day and evening. They are a great nuisance and everyone will be glad to get rid of them. Quite probable we will leave them behind tomorrow.

Möllhausen, *Diary*, II, pp. 81–82: "[In the encampment] I and Lieutenant Fitzball [Tidball] both remembered some of the conjuring tricks of our boyish days, and performed them with great success. . . . But the crowning marvel was when the lieutenant, showing [the Mohaves] one of his front teeth, which happened to be a false one, and kept in by means of a spring, pretended to swallow it, and opened his mouth to show them the empty place, at which they gazed with much surprise. But when, laying one hand over his mouth, and the other on his throat, he managed to replace the tooth, and displayed once more a perfect set, their surprise at such supernatural powers almost amounted to terror. They . . . entreated the lieutenant to repeat this incredible conjuration, which he did again and again . . . until one sagacious old warrior . . . wished him to perform the feat with one of his other teeth. This of course he declined to do, and the faith of the Indians in our magical power was evidently much shaken by his refusal."

March 2. Camp 136. Ther. sunrise 40°.7. 12 [noon] 65°.7. Made an early start this morning & travelled till sundown leaving behind the Colorado and Indians (excepting guides). Road good. Made 21 m. 714 ft. & camped without water, grass, or wood (excepting Cactii stumps)— Ascended 1700 ft. which could partly have been avoided by keeping a low valley on the left. Several mules gave out & left behind.

Whipple, Diary: "Great numbers followed nearly the whole day. Although they saw that we had nothing more to give or to sell yet they

---

consultation and agreed to furnish a guide, Cairook, to accompany the expedition as far as the well-traveled Mormon Road in California, by way of a trail across the Mojave Desert that would provide some water and grass. The price of the guide's services was a blanket, a serape, a few strings of white beads, and a dragoon overcoat. The additional guide was later furnished upon Cairook's request. Whipple wrote that the guides spoke only a little Spanish but used signs, and both were intelligent and good men. Möllhausen described them as "gigantic" and "stately"; Cairook was nearly six feet, six inches in height, and he wore a nose ornament that Whipple bought for the Smithsonian. From one of the five chiefs Whipple obtained a Mohave vocabulary, the first ever published. See Whipple, Diary, Mar. 12, 13, Whipple Papers; *Report*, Mar. 1, 5, 12, 1854; *Reports of Explorations and Surveys*, III, Part III ("Indian Tribes"), pp. 51, 102; Möllhausen, *Diary*, II, p. 282; Ives, "Report," p. 69. See the Biographical Appendix for the sad fate of Cairook and Irateba.

evidently regretted our departure. They had been well treated by us[;] gifts had been made not as offerings of scorn to inferiors nor as a bribe from the weak to the powerful but as friends to friends. . . . The effect has been to make them pleased with themselves and with us. Instead of annoying us as they might during the crossing of the river, for trifling rewards they aided us greatly. . . . Although vigilence was not relaxed we slept as free from care in the midst of a thousand[10] savage warriors as we could have done in any city of the union.

"They were pleased at the idea of other Americans parties making the route through their country a thoroughfare, and hereafter should collision arise between them and whites I believe it will be through mismanagement or encroachment of the latter."

March 3. Camp 137. Ther. sunrise 43.° 12 [noon] 69.°3. Started 7½ & came about 12 to water & grass [Paiute Creek]. Camped & lay by for the day to allow the animals chance to graze. Made 9 m. 1340 ft. Road rough mostly volcanic rocks. Very cool breeze during day from N.W. No wood in Camp. Left one or two mules behind.

March 4. Camp 138. Ther. sunrise 40.°7. 12 [noon] 59.° Made 13 m. 3460 ft. Road good. After leaving Camp travelled up a bad cañon and crossed a steep hill about 800 ft. above Camp. Then descended about one hundred ft. into an almost level plain. Range of mountains ahead apparently 20 or 25 miles, the tops covered with snow. We are to pass through them [Providence Mountains] & probably will have cool weather again. Obliged to make a shorter march than was the intention as a large number of the mules gave out. No water in camp. No wood, excepting a kind of palm. Grass in abundance. Have been ascending continually since leaving the Rio are now about 4000 ft. above it.

March 5. Camp 139. Ther. sunrise 38.°2. 12 [noon] 52.°8. Started this morning at 6½. Strong wind blowing from W. About 10½ came to water. Distance 6 m. 4188 ft. Lay by for the day. Abundance of grass—no wood. About 40 mules strayed off last night but were mostly found this morning. Mules are left every day broken down for want of grass & water.

[10] In his official journal Whipple changed this number to 600. In his official report on Indian tribes, Whipple wrote that the guides estimated the number of warriors at 381, though Whipple thought the total probably was "somewhat greater." See Whipple, *Report*, Mar. 2, 1854; *Reports of Explorations and Surveys*, III, Part III ("Indian Tribes"), p. 17.

Road good today. Encamped in a valley among hills spotted with snow & in the valley are places a couple of inches in depth. Ascended today about 500 ft. The train is to be divided tomorrow into three parties as the water for some distance ahead (as well as known) is very scarce. Not sufficient for the whole train. The first water is about 20 miles & at the foot of the mountains. From there to the Spanish trail,[11] about 40 miles, very little water if any to be found. The first party, which is very small, among which are White & myself, to start tomorrow morning early with Caratella. Camp tomorrow night at foot of mountains. The next day to travel round the mountain and continue after getting round, guided by a Mohave Indian. The 2nd party, consisting of I know not whom, to start tomorrow night, travel during night to mountain & the next night or afternoon to cross. The 3rd party to start day after tomorrow & follow same route.[12] The place we are to cross during the next four or five days (the probable time of separation) is the most doubtful part of the trip & the object is, if one party be unsuccessful, the others by taking a different time & route, may be successful. The mules are now at the extent of their strength & a tight place for water or grass would be fatal to most of them & cause not only suffering, but many things to be left. The Caratella takes eight mules, four for a change at 12 [noon] every day.

March 6. Camp 140. Ther. sunrise 31°. 3 p.m. 57°.0. The first of the three parties started this a.m. in the face of a cold W. wind & slight flitting of snow. The party consists of Lieuts. Stanley & Ives, Mölhausen, Campbell H., Parke, White, & myself, Sevadra and brother, 6 Teamsters, 1 cook & 2 servants. Had 9 pack

[11] The Old Spanish Trail, part of Frémont's route in 1844, headed northwest from Santa Fe across present-day southern Colorado, Utah, and Nevada, then south into California across the Mojave Desert, reaching Los Angeles through Cajon Pass. It had been traveled since about 1829 by New Mexican traders, trappers, forty-niners, and other emigrants.

[12] On the advice of the Indian guides, Whipple divided the expedition so that pools ahead on the desert could refill after each party's use. Whipple led the second party, with the pack train carrying the precious reports and specimens. The third party consisted of herders with the animals. The expedition has moved in a curve north of west from the Colorado River crossing. The railroad profile was drawn on a more direct route west, through present-day Ludlow, Newberry, and Daggett, California, to the Mojave River; it was the later route of the Santa Fe Railroad. See Whipple, Diary, Whipple Papers, and *Report*, Mar. 6, 1854.

mules and 8 mules for Caratella, 4 running loose for change at 12. Lieut. Tidball & escort accompanied us today, but we separate in the morning, he with his comp'y going over the mountains & the rest of us passing round. We took the two Indians [Cairook and Irateba] with us, one to guide him & the other for us. Travelled 18 m. 34 ft. Road good, tho' rolling. Halted within about 2 miles of water & camped, as there was no grass on the hills ahead. No wood in Camp. During the morning descended a hill, sloping gradually, the hill being 5 miles [?] from top to bottom & the descent about 800 ft. Immediately after commenced ascending & find ourselves tonight about 400 ft. below last night's camp. About noon saw on our left fires of the Pahutahs several miles distant.

March 7. Camp 141. Ther. sunrise 38°.5. 3 p.m. 58°. Started 6½ & made water [Marl Spring] in 1½ miles & found plenty for all the animals—after watering we separated leaving Lieut. Tidball & Company without any expectation of meeting him again for four days & perhaps untill reaching San Bernadino [*sic*] as he intended if provisions held out to go on & endeavor to reach that station in a few days. Passed round the mountain & by making a short cut over some hills made the distance very short. About 11 o'clock, on looking back, saw Lieut. T. & men 2 miles in rear. They joined us about 12 & camped together. Distance 17 m. 2892 ft. No wood or water in Camp. Descended about 1900 ft. Struck a large Pahutah trail & passed some of their camps. Our Indian said "the fires were two days old and they had gone West, being also a large party." If we met them, they would be good friends but try to steal our animals.[13] The later part of our march was through a cañon.

March 8. Camp 142. Ther. sunrise 49°. 3 p.m. 83°.2. Made 13 m. 3236 ft. The road all deep sand. Arrived in Camp about 1½ p.m. Crossed the bed of a salt lake which was nearly circular

[13]The Pahutahs were southern Paiutes, part of the Uto-Aztecan linguistic family. Kin to the Chemehuevis, they were wide-ranging desert people, adept at stealing livestock for food. The Mohave guides told Whipple that the river Paiutes (Chemehuevis) were good, but these mountain Paiutes were hostile to Mohaves and Americans and it would be well for the latter to bring soldiers and wipe them out. See Sherburne, entry of Mar. 12, below; Whipple, *Report*, Mar. 8, and Diary, Mar. 12, 1854, Whipple Papers; Möllhausen, *Diary*, II, p. 307.

with a radius of about 4 miles.[14] The ground was perfectly white, the surface being encrusted with a layer of salt. Obliged to halt on the border of it & obtain water by digging. After obtained, 'twas very salt and brackish. Scarcely drinkable. The mules, tho' without water for 36 hours, first refused & when thirst obliged them to drink it did not appear to satisfy their thirst, although apparently filled.

Lieut. T. and company started tonight about 5 intending to travel till 12 & obtain good water. He was uncertain whether he would lay by for us or not, as he is very anxious to reach settlements. His men are out of meat, & have nothing but a short ration of flour, pork & beans. He took an Indian for guide & left one for us, although the latter appeared unwilling to stay, saying there were too many Pahutahs round for so small a party. Last night from Camp their fires were seen quite plainly only 3 miles from us. There being so many unmistakable signs that they were all round us, we concluded to take our turn at standing guard, there being only 15 in Camp altogether & besides ourselves but 9. Accordingly drew lots for the portion of the night we should stand. I drew the first relief & as I then thought fortunately, but which afterwards proved to the contrary. About fifteen minutes after my time was out, Mr. Whipple & all of the party with exception of Campbell, A., Dr. Kennely, Lieut. Jones & escort, came into camp. Lieut. Jones & party were one day behind. This rendered it unnecessary for the remainder of us to go on guard.

The party had travelled since morning—32 miles—they saw our Camp fires 14 miles distant & struck for them. Were tired, but had been remarkably fortunate, losing only one mule.

During the night the herders saw Lieut. Jones' fire at our last Camp & Lieut. Tidball's about 12 miles ahead.

March 9. Camp 143. Ther. sunrise 48°.2. 3 p.m. 83°.2. Started this a.m. two hours before packs & made 12 m. 2958 ft. Halted

[14] The expedition has crossed the lower tip of the playa or dry lake Whipple named Soda Lake and has reached Soda Springs. Whipple now has realized that the Mojave River does not flow into the Colorado, as he and others had believed, but disappears into the Mojave Sink. Lieut. R. S. Williamson in 1853, on a Pacific Railroad survey in California, had proved this conclusively, but Whipple had not yet read his report. The expedition now is some twenty miles north of present-day Ludlow. See Whipple, Diary, Mar. 8, 9, Whipple Papers, and *Report*, Mar. 12, 1854; Peirson, *Mojave River*, p. 89.

on Mohave Creek with running water, the first evidence of there being such a creek in existence. Found Lieut. Tidball had gone ahead. Before Mr. Whipple left camp Lieut. Jones came in, his train being many miles behind. He stated that Campbell, A., & Dr. Kennely with some pack mules & some of his men had got lost & he had not seen nor heard of them since yesterday morning. Quite probable they found grass & camped, & it being dark when Lieut. Jones came along he might have passed them. As yet 6½ p.m. neither Lieut. Jones or the others have come into our camp—but will probably be in before midnight, as there is a moon till that time.

Whipple, *Report*: "This evening our Indian guide [Cairook] repeated the object of the Mohaves and their chiefs in sending him with us. 'The road,' said he, 'is good. Water is sufficient. Mules do not die of thirst. Mojaves have a good heart, and are friends to Americans. We want you to write these things to your great chief, that his people may come and buy our corn and flour, and vegetables. Let them, in return, give us clothing and knives. If they need assistance, Mojaves will afford it, and will guide them where water and grass may be found.' It would seem as if these simple people were really pleased with the first dawning light of civilization. They feel the want of comfortable clothing, and perceive some of the advantages of trade. There is no doubt that, before many years pass away, a great change will take place in their country. The advancing tide of emigration will soon take possession of it, and unless the strong arm of government protects them, the native population will be driven to the mountains or be exterminated."

Möllhausen, *Diary*, II, p. 290: "When the Mohave guides joined us on the day of our departure from the Colorado, their fine muscular naked forms were fully displayed; but now their powerful limbs were hidden under such a heap of clothes and coverings, they were scarcely recognizable. Every one had been so eager to bestow on the guides who had served us so faithfully whatever article he could spare from his wardrobe, and they had immediately donned it with stoical composure, so that they now looked like wandering bundles of old clothes."

March 10. Camp 144. Ther. sunrise 44°.6. 12 [noon] 84°.7. Lieut. Jones & men came in last night about 10½. Dr. Kennely & Campbell were with them. The cause of their separating from the train was on account of their camping about 2 miles from the road & allowing the remainder to pass them during the night. Started before the rest this a.m. & before most of them were out of bed. Travelled up the canon of Mohave Creek & made 13 m.

256 ft. Passed an old Camp of Lieut. Tidball. The remainder of the train joined us about 10 a.m. having taken a shorter cut over the hills. They crossed the creek & took the hills on the opposite side. Their mules broke down about 11 & they were obliged to lay by till then, arriving at Camp 6 p.m., three hours after us. Quite a large number of ducks on route today, but unable to shoot any.

It was the intention to lay here tomorrow but as Lieut. Jones wishes to go on the Caratella starts at daybreak & the Pack train 3 or 4 p.m. It is supposed to be only 10 miles to the Spanish trail, or as the Indians call it, "Camino Americano." From there about four days to the nearest settlement.

March 11. Camp 145. Ther. sunrise 47°.6. 12 [noon] 68°. Turned out this a.m. at 4½ but owing to some misunderstanding or misarrangement did not get off till 6½. Made 11 m. 2162 ft. and camped on or near the Spanish trail & about 10 miles from the wagon road, connecting Salt Lake with San Bernadino & the settlements[15]—on the route met, returning, the Indian guide of Lieut. Tidball. He had a mule & any quantity of blankets, coats, etc.—also a Note from Lieut. T. giving us the distance to road & accounts of plenty of grass and water. He mentions giving things to the Indian [Irateba] as a reward for his faithfulness in showing him the road. He (Lieut. T.) started this a.m. for settlements. He will be there probably as soon as one week from today. Our flour & meal gives out tonight. Salt gone two days ago. Untill we get in, will have to live on beans, mutton without salt, & corn meal coffee without sugar. What a meal for an epicure! As a substitute for tobacco, which gave out "long long ago" we use tea leaves, corn grounds & dried willow leaves. 11 p.m.— The remainder of pack mules & several of the party came in about 7½ p.m. Lieut. Jones & escort—also Dr. Bigelow, Möllhausen, Stanley & a few others were behind.

Yesterday a Mexican belonging to the escort was left behind with three mules to bring them into camp. This morning came &

[15] The wagon road, called the Mormon Road, originated at San Bernardino, California, a settlement founded in 1851 by Mormons. It moved through Cajon Pass, crossed the Mojave River at present-day Oro Grande, turned north and northwest onto the Old Spanish Trail, and then branched off to Salt Lake City upon reaching present-day Utah.

'twas found that he had not arrived. He had no arms with him which was well known.[16]

About 8 a.m. four Mexicans, well armed, went out in search of him. Several hours after & about 8 or 10 miles distant, suddenly there arose a dense column of smoke, without doubt a hasty signal fire & in the direction taken by those going out. Immediately Lieut. Jones took ten men & accompanied by Dr. Bigelow, Mr. Mölhausen, Lieut. Stanley, Leroux, Sevadra & brother started in the direction of the fire. As yet they have not returned & nothing heard from them. Mr. Whipple & party started soon after to join us, as we were so small a party. There is very little doubt existing in Camp but the Mexican has been killed by the Indians & that the latter four sent for him are in trouble, perhaps surrounded, & some killed or wounded. We will undoubtedly hear the extent of the trouble as soon as a dispatch can be sent us.

March 12. Ther. sunrise 37°.7. 3 p.m. 63°.1. Lay by today as we did not like to move before hearing from those behind. About 11 a.m. Dr. Bigelow, Mr. Marcou, Leroux, Sevadra & brother came in. They stated that the party sent in search of the lost Mexican returned to camp about dark, last night. They found one of the mules that was left in charge of the Mexican lying on the ground dead, with an arrow directly through his heart, had been killed but a very short time & the Indians had not removed it. All search for the Mexican was in vain. They returned to Camp perfectly satisfied that he had been killed by the Indians. The large fire which started them was made by the first four Mexicans sent out in hopes of driving the Indians from the tall grass which covered the bottom of the creek. They first found the dead mule & drew out the arrow which they brought to camp. This morning another party started early, in hopes of finding the body of the Mexy, taking with them a spade to bury

[16] According to Möllhausen, the herder carried a rifle but, scoffing to other herders that the fear of Indians was all nonsense, he had thrown it across the back of one of the mules. Also according to Möllhausen, the herder, whose name was Torrivia, had a wife and five children in New Mexico. The company is near present-day Daggett, California. See Möllhausen, *Diary*, II, pp. 300, 304; Whipple, Diary, Mar. 12, 1854, Whipple Papers; Foreman, ed., *A Pathfinder*, p. 262, n. 11.

it. They found the tracks of two mules & some Indians, which they followed as well as they were able, untill they were brought to the brow of the hill. Just before arriving at the top they found the bones of one of the mules, the flesh having been removed. As they crossed the summit, they came unawares upon an Indian camp. The coals were still red & several pieces of mule flesh were roasting. The Indians had not been gone more than five or ten minutes, as they had fled in great haste, leaving behind their bows, arrows & quivers, also a large number of baskets, some traps & some cooking utensils. All search for them was in vain, although they could see the country for miles round, & looked into every niche and corner. A short distance from the fire & which had been dropped in the flight were the pants & moccasins of the poor Mexy—both saturated with blood, thus leaving them no longer in doubt as to his fate. Near the waist of the pants were seven arrow holes, any one of which would have proved fatal. All these holes gave evidence that he was shot while running as they were behind. His shirt could not be found & there is no telling how many wounds he had received, probable a large number. No trace of the body could be found. In a quiver they found lying in a small arroyo, was a bloody arrow with the point broken off. On a small isolated peak near[by] was found a watch tower, in which a fire was burning & a large quantity of meat was found, also some few Indian articles. From this place the approach of any one could be seen. All the articles found with the exception of some few brought away, were heaped up & burned.[17] Bows, arrows, quivers, baskets, etc. shared the same fate. Cooking things were destroyed.

As 'twas dark they were obliged to return to their camp & reached us about 9 p.m. It is regretted by every one that we cannot lay here a week & revenge the death of one of our party, but as many have only one or two days half rations left, it is impos-

[17] Actually members of the party collected a bow and arrow and a "prettily plaited" basket that Whipple thought was beautiful and skillfully made. These artifacts were sent to the Smithsonian Institution. Sherburne must have listened very carefully to reports from members of the party who set out in pursuit of the Indians, since his accurate description is the most detailed of all the diarists' accounts. See Möllhausen, *Diary*, II, pp. 300, 304; Stanley, Diary, Mar. 12, 1854; Whipple, Diary, Mar. 12, 1854, Whipple Papers; *Reports of Explorations and Surveys*, III, Part III ("Indian Tribes"), p. 51.

sible. My mess, which is as well off as any, have only one more meal of bread & beans and this was given us by a joint contribution—all gone but mutton— We start tomorrow.

The two Indian guides were both presented with a mule, any quantity of blankets, old clothes, trinkets, etc.[18] They gave their mules back again as they were afraid the Pahutahs would kill them for the sake of the mules & what other things they possessed. They will probably travel back in the night & lay by during the day in some secluded spot.

They say the "Americanos" should come & kill all the Pahutahs, as they are bad Indians. Just about dark the prairie caught fire from the herders' fire & with the united exertions of all in camp it was an hour & a half before we could consider the Camp as safe. Had it not been for a creek & sand bank on each side we would not have been able to stop it. A place was burned about ½ a mile in width & a mile in length. It was a beautiful sight as the flames and clouds of smoke rolled up towards the sky.

March 13. Camp 146. Ther. sunrise 39.° 3 p.m. 74.°3. Started at 7 a.m. & after about 4 miles struck the Mormon road. Travelled till 11 a.m. making a little over 12 miles. Grazed till 2, hitched up & encamped again at 5 p.m. making a march of 19 m. 4638 ft. Had another prairie fire tonight, which was extinguished in a short time.

March 14. Camp 147. Ther. sunrise 29.°8. 12 [noon] 66.°5. Made today 22 m. 4395 ft. although detained a half an hour by about a dozen mules getting mired & by grazing from 12 till 3— On the Road met two Mormons on their way from San Bernadino to Salt Lake City. They said it was about 85 miles to settlements & they met Lieut. Tidball & company yesterday about 40 miles from San Bernadino. They informed us of the melancholy death of Capt. Gunnison & 7 of party by the Indians on the 5th of Nov. They were killed by the same party through which we've just passed, the Pahutahs.[19] We also learned of the

[18] Whipple gave Cairook and Irateba warm letters of recommendation, one of which (for Irateba) he copied into his diary. Lieut. Ives met both men again when he explored the Colorado River during 1857–58. Ives wrote that Cairook, by then the head Mohave chief, inquired particularly about Lieut. Whipple, of whom he had formed an "exalted opinion." See Whipple, Diary, Whipple Papers, and *Report*, Mar. 12, 1854; Ives, "Report," pp. 69–89, 180–81.

[19] Capt. John W. Gunnison was the topographical engineer in charge of the

[Crimean] war between Turkey & Russia. Lieut. Williamson (whose trail we have seen) followed this river untill the water gave out, then sending the wagons to San Diego, returned to San Francisco.[20]

March 15. Camp 148. Ther. sunrise 44° 3 p.m. 62°5. Lts. Jones & Stanley, also Escort left us this a.m. intending to reach settlements as soon as possible. We camped about a mile from them tonight. Made an early start this a.m. & reached the point where the road leaves the Rio, about 11½—distance near 15 miles. Stopped till 3 & dined. Travelled again till 7 p.m. making 25 m. 538 ft. No water in camp.

March 16. Camp 149. Ther. sunrise 37°5. 3 p.m. 61° Turned out 4 a.m. started 6½. Made Cahone pass[21] about 10½ & entered it following down the bed, untill near 12 when we struck running water [Cajon Creek]. Lay by till 3 to graze & found on starting that Lieut. Jones was but a ½ mile from us. Met a Mormon from San Bernadino sent by Lieut. Tidball with flour, pork, coffee, sugar, tobacco, pipes & other little sundries. Obtained from him a small piece of butter, which his wife (which one?) had laid up for his own use. No one but those in the same situation as ourselves can tell how delightfully it tasted. Five months since we've had or seen anything of the kind. The prices of things were very

---

Pacific Railroad survey between the 38th and 39th parallels, from Fort Leavenworth, Missouri, to Sevier Lake in the Great Basin, near Utah Lake. Gunnison and seven others were killed in Utah by Paiutes on October 26, 1853. Antoine Leroux served for a time as guide for Gunnison but left before the massacre, returning to Taos to await Whipple's arrival in Albuquerque. See *Reports of Explorations and Surveys*, II, report by Lieut. E. G. Beckwith, Gunnison's replacement as commander.

[20] In early July 1853, Lieut. R. S. Williamson (see n. 14 above) began the Pacific Railroad survey in California to locate suitable passes in the California coast ranges that would connect with Whipple's survey and the route along the 32d parallel. He completed his much shorter survey in December 1853. See Goetzmann, *Army Exploration*, pp. 292–93; Russel, *Improvement of Communication*, p. 176.

[21] Sherburne spells Cajon Pass phonetically. Leroux was familiar with this route, having traveled previously along the Old Spanish Trail. Travel by white men through the pass dated back to at least 1806. As Sherburne noted on March 15, the expedition left the Mojave (at present-day Oro Grande) and is now moving southwest, along the future route of the Santa Fe Railroad. Secretary of War Davis had instructed Whipple to move westward from the Colorado to Walker's Pass, but Whipple knew that that pass was too far north of the 35th parallel. See Whipple, *Report*, Mar. 15, 1854; Beattie, *Heritage of the Valley*, p. 328.

high. Flour 16 c. per lb., pork 40c., sugar 25 c., coffee 35 c., Tobacco 25 c., per paper. He brought two doz. eggs which he sold one dollar a dozen, a keg of indifferent whiskey at $6 per gall. Lieut. Tidball was still at S. Bernadino, he was soon to move to the garrison [San Diego]. It is decided not to go to San B- as 'tis out of our road.[22] We will strike for Los Angeles, distance 60 m., three days march. Many of our men are sick & lame & desire to be discharged here. They have been obliged to walk & their shoes given out, besides being on half rations.

Stanley, Diary: "We came suddenly, after ascending a low elevation, upon the entrance to the Cahon Pass. Notwithstanding the constant association of wild and sublime scenery that has been with me on this tour, I have seen nothing so wild, majestic, and awful as the view down this cañon-like pass. Mountains, that seem as if nature had used her most irregular and roughest mould, are piled upon each other in sublime disorder, their naked sides and bald rocks conveying the idea of the most wretched desolation. . . . We continued rapidly to descend and it was most interesting and pleasant to notice the gradual change in the scenery. The rugged features gradually softened down, vegetation revived, and when midday arrived we stopped to graze in a scene of surpassing loveliness. . . . Mr. Leroux' remark, that at Cahon we suddenly dropped into Heaven, was almost realized, for this place you might easily imagine created for a Paradise. Pursuing our course down the cañon, it gradually becomes wider, its bubbling stream becomes larger . . . [and] our dropping upon a party of shepherds and their flocks, made Arcadia complete."

March 17. Ther. sunrise 42°.6. 3 p.m. 50°.7. Lay by today. Raining in torrents from morning till night. About 10 a.m. the sergeant of Lieut. T. came into Camp with a note from Lieut. T. stating that he had sent the sergeant from the post with a wagon load of provisions. The wagon was encamped with Lieut. Stanley about 4 miles behind.[23] As we already had a sufficiency it was sent back.

[22] The road forked at the base of the pass, one road leading to San Bernardino and the other, taken by the expedition, turning westward toward Los Angeles. Both Whipple and Lieut. Williamson decided that Cajon Pass afforded a difficult but practicable railroad route to Los Angeles if a tunnel were constructed. The Santa Fe Railroad eventually reached Los Angeles through this pass without building the tunnel. See *Reports of Explorations and Surveys*, III ("Preliminary Report"), p. 31; Whipple, *Report*, Mar. 16, 1854; Russel, *Improvement of Communication*, p. 176; Marshall, *Santa Fe*, p. 190.

[23] Lieuts. Tidball and Stanley have arrived at the small army post established

The accounts of Teamsters made out today & all the Americans, with four exceptions, were discharged. Had a little trouble with them in the evening as they took too much "rotgut" whiskey & rum, boisterous—one was tied to a tree to meditate, there being no other way of quieting him. Made an agreement with White to stay in California.

Whipple, *Report*, March 16: "A Mormon from San Bernardino [came] out to meet us with a load of provisions for sale. He professed to be one of the saints, but nevertheless charged the most exorbitant prices for his sugar, flour, and coffee. He also smuggled in a keg of whiskey; but as none of the men have money, it is likely to remain untouched."

Möllhausen, *Diary*, II, p. 314: "The trader was strictly enjoined not to sell brandy, as there were many among our men who did not know how to keep within bounds. . . . The trader promised to obey the injunction, but there were nevertheless in a short time several drunken men found in the camp, who gave us a great deal of trouble. One of them, and he, my own servant, had to be kept out of mischief, by having his hands tied to the bent-down branch of a tree, so that when it recovered its position, the culprit could only just touch the ground with the tips of his toes, and he was left there till he recovered his senses."

March 18. Camp 150. Ther. sunrise 42°.6. 3 p.m. 47°.5. Started this morning about 7 & travelled 19 m. 3140 ft, leaving San Bernadino on our left. Camped at Cocomongo Ranch—so called—a place of 8 or 10 ranchos. Herds of Cows, goats, horses & mules, also hens, pidgeons, pigs, etc. in abundance. This is the first appearance of civilization for several months. There is a large peach orchard in bloom, a vineyard & many appearances of agriculture. Got from the people living here (who were Spanish & Indians as laborers) curd-cheese, wine & goats milk.[24] One large

---

in 1852 on the Jurupa or Jarupa land grant, near present-day Riverside, California. Lieuts. Tidball, Stanley, and Jones now have left the expedition. They headed south from San Bernardino to the army garrison at San Diego. See Stanley, Diary, Mar. 17–26, 1854.

[24] The Cucamonga Ranch was on land granted to an influential Californian, Tiburcio Tapia of Los Angeles. His daughter and her husband, Leon V. Prudhomme, lived in the main house, which was built like a fortress to guard it against Indians, particularly the Cahuillas, a band in the Uto-Aztecan linguistic family that inhabited the region. The Indian laborers were domesticated Cahuillas, and both Möllhausen and Whipple commented on their malnourished appearance and lowly status as peons on the estate. Whipple collected a vocabulary from one of the Spanish-speaking Indians. In his official report, Whipple

rancho is filled with American Emigrants who arrived here the 24th of Dec. last & are recruiting their animals. They were followers of [Captain John] Gunnison's train, crossed the Grand & Green Rivers & came down the Salt Lake Road.

Rained hard all day & quite cold. Every one got drenched to the skin & having no change obliged to sleep so.

Passed three ranchos on the route. Had an attack of the chills last night & this morning, but slight, probable from eating *too much* after fasting so long. Had the weather been pleasant today, the route would have been delightful. We travelled through a beautiful valley, the ground covered with millions of flowers—

March 19. Ther. sunrise 45° Lay by today to dry up & reduce weight.

March 20. Camp 151. Travelled 24 m. 3550 ft. Passed a large number of ranchos & many herds.[25]

Whipple, Diary: "Leaving the Rancho Cucomonga we continued our course W.S.W. by a road nearly as smooth as if graded for a railway 24 miles to El Monte. . . . All are charmed by the beautiful scenery & heavenly climate. Fine spreading oaks and sycamores are sprinkled in pleasing variety with flowering shrubs through the valley. . . . The [town of] Monte, upon Rio San Gabriel, is a settlement of emigrants upon a Spanish claim supposed to be invalid. Our camp is at the house of a recent settler upon a lovely spot."

March 21. Camp 152. Travelled 14 m. 2884 ft. Halted in Los Angeles that long looked for place, *etc.*

Whipple, *Report*: "We passed to the left of the beautiful mission of San Gabriel, and were near enough to see that it was a fine old ruin, surrounded by gardens and vineyards. . . . Our road entered a ravine among ridges of hills, passed over broken ground for a short distance,

---

described them as squalid, miserable, and degraded. See Möllhausen, *Diary*, II, p. 327; Whipple, *Report*, Mar. 18, 19, 1854; Foreman, ed., *A Pathfinder*, p. 273, n. 9; *Reports of Explorations and Surveys*, III, Part III ("Indian Tribes"), p. 34.

[25] One of the large ranchos passed on this day was the well-known Rancho de Chino, or more correctly Rancho Santa Ana del Chino, the home of the heiress to a huge Mexican land grant who about 1841 married Isaac Williams, an Easterner who became a Mexican citizen. Williams aided thousands of forty-niners passing the ranch after a long trek along the Gila Trail, and he kept a register of their names, now in the Huntington Library, San Marino. The camp at El Monte was east of present-day Alhambra, California. See Whipple, *Report*, Mar. 29, 1854; Foreman, ed., *A Pathfinder*, p. 275, n. 10.

and then, from a slight eminence, we looked down upon the valley and city of Los Angeles. Descending, we crossed the river which waters the valley, and entered the city. . . . Along dismal-looking lanes were scattered piles of adobe houses, and the intervening spaces were lined with mud walls and cactus hedges. But as we proceeded towards the plaza, the sombre character of the place nearly disappeared before the march of American improvements. There were respectable indications of business and activity. We noticed hotels, cafes, barbers' signs, and a long array of flaunting shops. . . . As we were now within the limits of the operations of the 'Coast Survey,' and an almost unbroken plain is said to lead from Los Angeles to San Pedro, we determined to disband the party and proceed with all possible dispatch to Washington; there to make known the results of our explorations. As there was no officer of the government in the place to whom the United States' property could be turned over, it appeared necessary to dispose of it, and immediate notice was given that a public sale would take place at the plaza, on the morrow."

Möllhausen, *Diary*, II, pp. 335–36: "Many of our party, on looking down towards the busy city, and seeing signs of advanced civilization, began now to be troubled with the thoughts of what kind of a figure they might cut in the streets, and to contemplate rather bashfully the equipments of their outward man. Eleven [?] months of uninterrupted travelling through the wilderness had reduced most of the garments indicative of civilization to such a state of decay that they either hung in rags or had had their deficiencies supplied by patches of leather blackened by the smoke of many a camp fire. The same useful material wrapped around the feet supplied the place of boots, a distinction of which few could boast even in the most attenuated form, and our round felt hats had assumed every conceivable fantastic shape, and seemed to adhere to the tangled hair, which in many cases hung down on the shoulders. But though conscious that our costume and personal appearance might have admitted of some improvement, we were not without a certain feeling of pride in the evidence of our long and toilsome journey, afforded by the aspect of our brown and long-bearded company, and their meagre, tired cattle [mules]. Our weapons, too, were in first-rate condition, and our rifles, revolvers, and broad knives glittered as if they had just come out of the arsenal, from which an observer might have inferred that they had been of some importance to us on the journey. . . . We meant to hold an auction of our entire stock of mules and their accoutrements, as well as of various other properties . . . and we employed ourselves in the interim chiefly in arranging and packing our papers and collections, though some time was devoted to the repair and beautification of our exterior, and a little, too, to the solace of the inward man with the creature comforts of the hotel."

March 22. Sold most of the mules today.

Möllhausen, *Diary*, II, pp. 337–38: "Our mules and other effects were sent into town (our last sheep had been long since eaten up) . . . a man having been engaged to act as auctioneer, who could praise the goods in Spanish and English. . . .

"Among the bidders were, besides Leroux and some of the Mexican muleteers, two of the American members of our expedition, Messrs. Sherburne and White, on whom the sight of this beautiful verdant country had made such an impression that they had determined to settle there, and renounce their previous intention of returning with us to Washington.[26] Like true Americans, they made light of the inconveniences and difficulties they would have to struggle with in commencing as rancheros, in a country new to them, and thought only of the results to be obtained by the energetic pursuance of their plans. They not only bought mules, therefore, and articles necessarily accompanying them, but also the only tent that remained to us, and various cooking utensils with which they meant to begin their housekeeping."

March 23. Sold remainder of mules & Caratella today & all the party, excepting White and myself, started for San Francisco via San Pedro. I envied them their pleasure but did not regret my decision of staying in California.

Möllhausen, *Diary*, II, p. 339: "We assembled for the last time in the little coffee-room near the post office: the whole party was there with the exception of the officers, who had gone to San Diego, and our good Dr. Bigelow, who, being a zealous Catholic, could not prevail on himself to leave Los Angeles without paying a visit to the mission of San Gabriel, eight miles off. . . .

"With the joy of our return was mingled some feeling of melancholy, as we clinked our glasses for the last time with the companions we were leaving behind, and wished them success in their undertaking. The parting was painful to them, for when we were gone they would not have a single friend near to take an interest in their welfare; but the enterprising spirit of the Americans, and their incessant brooding over the question of how to obtain an independent position in society, allows little room for feelings of this kind, and it seems to them, as it is in fact, a mere matter of course, that when men have to follow various vocations they cannot always remain together."

As my connection with the surveying party has ceased, so ceases my Journal. May it prove interesting & amusing to those who are *fortunate* enough to have its perusal. 'Tis said to be one great

[26] Whipple wrote only that "Mr. White and Mr. Sherburne, . . . delighted with the beauty of the country, preferred to remain in Los Angeles." See *Report*, Mar. 24, 1854.

fault of a *traveller,* his magnifying & unnecessarily "branching out." The former I've endeavored to prevent—of the latter 'tis not for me to judge tho' I think I could have "expatiated" considerable more & still have been within limits. Que piensa Vsnd?[27]

Adios—

The distance travelled by us from Ft. Smith, Arks., to Albuquerque, N.M.—was between 860 & 900 miles. The distance from Albuquerque, N.M., to Los Angeles, Cal., between 1000–1100 miles—making in all between 1800 & 1900 miles.

Our warmest weather 119° Fah.—Coldest −5.°5 (below zero).[28] "Placing my hand on my heart and bowing, I bid adieu, while the curtain falls to slow music"—John P. Sherburne

Late *asst.* Pacific Railway Survey—

[27] The Spanish means "What do you think?" Sherburne apparently attempted to write a shortened form of "vsted," usually written as "Vd." or "Ud."

[28] The highest temperature (actually 114°) was recorded at 3 p.m. on Aug. 18, 1853, at Old Camp Arbuckle in present-day Oklahoma. The lowest was recorded at sunrise on Dec. 26, 1853, at Leroux's Spring. The official mileage given for the journey from Fort Smith to Los Angeles was 1822.27 miles. The expedition has traveled approximately 257 miles on this leg of the journey. See *Reports of Explorations and Surveys*, III, Appendix B, pp. 33–36; Appendix D, p. 220.

Editor's Afterword

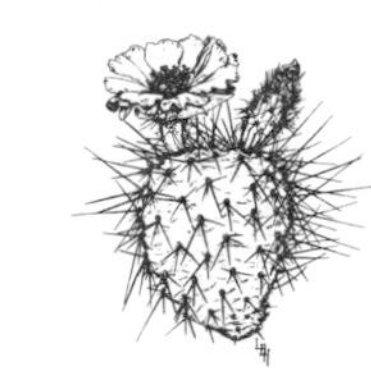

Editor's Afterword

For the Whipple expedition the arrival in Los Angeles was journey's end. To John Sherburne it heralded the beginning of another new experience. One of the purposes of this Afterword is to provide glimpses of Sherburne's life in the decades following his decision to remain in the West. Another is to elaborate upon the significance of the expedition in which Sherburne so proudly claimed membership when he wrote the coda to his diary.

Although the expedition's arrival in Los Angeles signaled the accomplishment of the exploring mission, it was by no means the termination of the duties assigned to Lieutenant Whipple and his senior staff. After reaching San Francisco by steamer from the port of San Pedro, Whipple and a number of the members of the scientific corps embarked for New York City via the Isthmus of Panama. Following a brief reunion with his family, Whipple arrived in Washington on May 6, 1854, to prepare his report for Congress. Lieutenant Ives, Dr. Bigelow, Albert Campbell, Dr. Kennerly, and Jules Marcou set to work on their reports either in the capital or at their homes. Balduin Möllhausen remained in Washington for a few months to put the finishing touches on his drawings before returning to Berlin.[1]

[1]Whipple to Lieut. Ives, Mar. 23, 31, May 2, 1854; to "Major" [Emory?], Mar. 29, 1854; to Dr. Kennerly, May 26, 1854; to Capt. A. A. Humphreys, Oct. 26, 1854; Spencer F. Baird to Whipple, Nov. 21, 1854; Baron Gerolt [Prussian ambassador] to Whipple, Nov. 21, 1854; Whipple, Diary, Apr. 11–May 6, 1854, all in Whipple Papers; Möllhausen, *Diary*, II, pp. 340–74. Some of the men, including Möllhausen and Kennerly, left San Francisco on the *Oregon* on Apr. 1 or 2, 1854; Whipple, his clerk George Garner, Bigelow, and Marcou followed about two weeks later. The Whipple party arrived in New York harbor on Apr. 26.

In 1855 Congress published Whipple's preliminary report, along with those produced by the other survey commanders. The lieutenant grumbled that he had been "obliged" to complete his report for the Secretary of War by July 31, 1854, even though some of the other commanders "took their own time." As a result, he wrote, it was "hastily, crudely and imperfectly" prepared, and the published version appeared full of the "grossest" typographical errors. Whipple's estimate of the cost of railroad construction along his route, however, was not a printer's error. He calculated that cost at nearly $162,000,000, an astronomical sum far higher than the estimates given by the other commanders.[2]

With the aid of an additional appropriation from Congress, Whipple remained in Washington to prepare the final report. When published in two volumes in 1856 it included maps, extracts from the preliminary report, Whipple's daily journal, and his reports on topography and Indian tribes, the latter written in conjunction with ethnologists at the Smithsonian Institution. Lieutenant Ives compiled the long lists of astronomical and magnetic observations, mileages, and daily temperatures that formed the appendixes. The scientists' botanical, geological, and zoological reports were augmented by descriptive essays and engravings of the specimens contributed by colleagues at the Smithsonian. The final report was lavishly illustrated with lithographs

---

Only Isaac Stevens delivered his preliminary report in time to meet the unrealistic deadline set by Congress of the first Monday in February 1854; see 33d Congress, 2d session, House Executive Document 91, pp. 4–5, for Jefferson Davis's remarks on the preliminary reports.

[2] Whipple, Diary, Aug. 14, 1854; quotations from Whipple's letter to Jules Marcou, Jan. 14, 1855, both in Whipple Papers. Lieuts. Beckwith and Williamson did not complete their preliminary reports until Jan. 1855. Part of Whipple's unhappiness during the summer of 1854 was the result of Jefferson Davis's displeasure over his budget, which he exceeded by over $10,000. Through lengthy correspondence with Davis and Col. J. J. Abert, Whipple succeeded in justifying the excess (caused by the unexpected delay in Albuquerque, the hiring of two guides and additional herders, and the cost of extra supplies). The excess was paid for by an appropriation from Congress. See, e.g., Whipple to Jefferson Davis, May 16, 18, Oct. 25, 1854; to Col. J. J. Abert, June 1, 1854, Whipple Papers. Whipple's preliminary report can be found in Humphreys' and Davis's report to Congress, published in 33d Congress, 2d session, House Executive Document 91; the exact estimate of railroad costs was $161,829,625. See also *Reports of Explorations and Surveys*, III ("Extracts from Preliminary Report"), pp. 30–31.

and woodcuts of Balduin Möllhausen's drawings, supplemented by some landscapes drawn by Albert Campbell and Lieutenant John Tidball, both competent artists. Whipple's report was far more detailed than those submitted by the other commanders, except for the one produced by Isaac Stevens, leader of the elaborate northern survey.[3]

The commanders' primary mission, of course, had been to determine the practicability of their routes for a Pacific railroad. Lieutenant Whipple professed impartiality, but he was unabashedly enthusiastic about the path along the 35th parallel. Declaring that a more favorable location for a railroad than the course from Fort Smith to Albuquerque "could scarcely be desired," he found the route as a whole "eminently advantageous." Despite widespread belief that the region was part of the "Great American Desert," Whipple had discovered (to his own surprise) valleys and river bottoms all along the route that were suitable for grazing or cultivation and therefore attractive to future white settlers. Familiar with the favored southernmost route, Whipple contrasted its "extremely arid" climate in "desert latitudes" with the more abundant rainfall, rich grasslands, and possibilities for irrigation found in the areas bordering the 35th parallel. In the final report the commander drastically revised his original estimate of railroad costs, arriving at a far more acceptable sum of approximately $94,000,000, nearly $70,000,000 below his earlier estimate.[4]

[3] See 33d Congress, 2d session, House Executive Document 91, chap. 267 (Aug. 5, 1854) for the appropriation by Congress to enable all the survey commanders to prepare the final reports. Whipple's final report is contained in volumes III and IV of the Pacific Railroad *Reports*, with vol. IV containing the illustrated botanical and zoological reports. Both Whipple's and Isaac Stevens's final reports were contained in two volumes.

[4] Whipple painted a somewhat rosy picture of the climate and productivity of the region; territory west of the 90th meridian was semiarid or arid land. See White, *The Roots of Dependency*, especially chap. 10. Whipple's new estimate of railroad costs was $93,853,605, which in November 1855 the Office of Explorations and Surveys revised slightly upward to $94,720,000. Whipple most likely was shocked to read the preliminary estimates submitted by other survey commanders, all much lower than his calculation. In his final report Whipple pointed out that he was "deficient" in practical railroad engineering and, since all the estimates varied so widely, those costs should not determine decisions about the merits of the different routes. Whipple relied upon Albert Campbell's expertise, and Campbell probably calculated the original high estimate, but Whipple ac-

In August 1854, Captain Andrew A. Humphreys of the Corps of Topographical Engineers had replaced Major Emory as chief of the Office of Pacific Railroad Explorations and Surveys. On February 5, 1855, Humphreys submitted to his superior, Jefferson Davis, a report of his "examination" of the survey commanders' preliminary reports. Humphreys found merit in all the routes and agreed with Whipple that his had many unexpected advantages. But he was disturbed by the "great length" of the course and the exorbitant cost of railroad construction projected in the original estimate. Humphreys' clear favorite was the route along the 32d parallel, and to it he devoted most of the space in his report. Within a few weeks Jefferson Davis presented his own report to Congress, unequivocally recommending that southernmost route. Davis did not change his decision after receiving the final reports from the survey commanders some months later.

To critics from other sections the decision by the Southern Secretary of War seemed all too predictable. Congress had hoped to find a solution to the political impasse by appealing to "the impartial judgment of science." But Jefferson Davis's choice of a location running through the Deep South merely intensified "the passions of the politicos and the promoters." Angry legislators focused their energies upon opposition to the southern route. In a Congress even more sectionally divided after passage of the Kansas-Nebraska Act in 1854—regarded as yet another sop to the slave South—it was clear that no Pacific Railroad bill could pass in either house.[5]

---

cepted the responsibility for it. See *Reports of Explorations and Surveys*, III ("Report on Topographical Features"), pp. 62–77.

[5] Capt. Humphreys, who wrote his report with the aid of Lieut. G. K. Warren, found no merit in Capt. Gunnison's route near the 38th parallel (nor did Gunnison), but he acknowledged that the 41st parallel route explored in 1854 by Gunnison's successor Lieut. E. G. Beckwith in an expanded survey had, like Whipple's, many advantages. Despite railroad engineers' belief that snow and ice were no deterrents to railroad construction and upkeep, Humphreys and Jefferson Davis used the climate and the harsh terrain as major arguments against the Stevens and Beckwith routes. William H. Goetzmann persuasively argues that Humphreys and Davis were clearly biased in favor of the southernmost route and that Davis perceived the surveys as "a ritual that had to be undergone" before the rest of the country could appreciate the advantages of the route along the 32d parallel. The Gadsden Purchase of 1853 demolished one major argument against the southern route—that parts of the railroad would move through

Because the costly explorations failed to influence public policy and achieved no immediate practical result, they have been judged a failure. In taking a longer view this opinion seems unduly harsh. The reports of all four of the major surveys demonstrated that each route was a feasible one for a railroad to the Pacific. After the South left the Union, a Pacific Railroad bill passed in Congress in 1862. By 1869 the first transcontinental railroad linked Omaha, Nebraska, with Sacramento in California and followed much of the route near the 41st parallel explored by Lieutenant Edward Beckwith after Captain John Gunnison's death. Eventually transcontinental railroads were built along parts of all the routes explored by the surveys. That transportation "revolution" ushered in a new age for the West.

The Whipple expedition laid the foundation for change in the southwestern region it explored scientifically for the first time. Like every commander of a railroad survey, Whipple recognized the "chain relationship" between exploraton, wagon-road construction, and railroads. He indicated repeatedly in his report that the 35th parallel route was eminently suitable for a wagon road, the necessary precursor of a railroad. Though unable to unite on a Pacific Railroad bill, the Thirty-fourth Congress did seek to placate settlers demanding improved transportation between the East and the West. In 1856 the federal government established a wagon-road program, and one of the three authorized roads was to follow Whipple's route. The War Department chose Edward F. Beale, an experienced Western explorer, to superintend the first stage of the project, the construction of a wagon road from Fort Defiance in Navajo territory to Los Angeles. Taking camels with him as beasts of burden, the colorful Beale set out from the fort on August 27, 1857, picking up Whipple's trail beyond Zuñi two days later. An artist in self-promotion, Beale reported on his expedition as if he were the first to cross the region with wagons. But he relied heavily upon Whipple's maps and journal and frequently noted in his diary that he could see the faint tracks of Whipple's wagons. Acting

---

Mexican territory. See Goetzmann, *Army Exploration*, pp. 295–304, quotation on p. 298; Russel, *Improvement of Communication*, pp. 182–86; 33d Congress, 2d session, House Executive Document 91, and *Reports of Explorations and Surveys*, I, pp. 3–111, both of which contain Humphreys's and Davis's reports.

upon Whipple's advice, Beale avoided the southern loop along Bill Williams Fork and pushed directly across what is now the Aubrey Valley to Truxton Wash, thence south by west to the gap between the Cerbat and Hualapai mountains. From the site of modern Kingman, Arizona, Beale pushed across the Black Mountains to the Colorado River. West of the Colorado he followed Whipple's path across the desert and through Cajon Pass to Los Angeles.

The Whipple expedition had struggled for over four months to find a trail for wagons from Zuñi to Los Angeles. Because of such pathfinding, Beale accomplished his journey in half that time. In October of the following year he completed the second stage of the wagon-road project. Leading another wagon train, this time from Fort Smith to Los Angeles, Beale improved some difficult sections of the route, most of them east of the Rio Grande. Although the route across present-day Arizona was practical for travel, it was little used until after the Civil War, when troops protected emigrants from Indian attacks. Between 1864 and 1883, it carried livestock and miners into northwestern Arizona and Nevada.[6]

No transcontinental railroad ever followed the 35th parallel route in its entirety, although Edward Beale, as enthusiastic a promoter as Amiel Whipple, declared that it was "better than any line between the two oceans." Only shorter railroad lines (the Chicago, Rock Island, and Pacific, the Fort Smith and Western, and the Missouri, Kansas, and Texas) moved along parts of the Marcy-Whipple route near the Canadian River. But a transcontinental railroad, the Atchison, Topeka, and Santa Fe, followed Whipple's railroad profile for much of the way from Albuquerque to Los Angeles, crossing the Rio Grande at Whipple's designated location of Isleta and continuing west along the 35th parallel. The crews took fifteen months to build a bridge, at a

[6]See Goetzmann, *Army Exploration*, p. 304, for the view that the railroad explorations were a failure; see also Goetzmann, *Exploration and Empire*, pp. 292–93; Dupree, *Science in the Federal Government*, p. 95. For the wagon-road program, see Turrentine Jackson's excellent book *Wagon Roads West*, pp. 241–55, quotation on p. 243. For Beale's expeditions, see Beale, "Report on Wagon Road from Fort Defiance to the Colorado River," and "Report on Wagon Road—Fort Smith to Colorado River"; Thompson, *Edward F. Beale*, chap. 7; Hollon, *The Southwest*, p. 252.

cost of more than $250,000, across the deep chasm that Whipple in disgust had named Cañon Diablo. Bridging the Colorado River at what is now Topock in Arizona, the line moved north for a short distance along the west bank of the river to Whipple's crossing at present-day Needles, California. Following his railroad profile, it reached the Pacific Coast through Cajon Pass. In 1883 the running time of the first train that left Albuquerque for Los Angeles was clocked at thirty-five hours and five minutes.[7]

In a roundabout way, therefore, the Whipple expedition left an enduring mark on the Southwest. It played a formative role in the development of the region. In that process the "wild" tribes were subdued, the reservation policy evolved, Indian land was appropriated for white settlement, and Anglo-American domination was secured. The railroads brought a steady stream of settlers, the new territories prepared for statehood, and the economy began its gradual procession toward modernization. In that sense the Pacific Railroad survey along the 35th parallel was a distinct success.

The government explorations, as we know, also served the broader purpose of expanding scientific knowledge about the West. One of their substantial and practical accomplishments was the production of a map of the trans-Mississippi West, published in 1859 in volume eleven of the official Pacific Railroad reports. Based upon the cumulative data of sixty years of exploration and produced by Lieutenant G. K. Warren of the Corps of Topographical Engineers, the map owed its level of sophistication to the more accurate information furnished by the railroad surveys' astronomers. Warren's map was a milestone in cartography and an essential guide for all future explorations and

[7] For Beale's enthusiasm about the route's potential, see Thompson, *Edward F. Beale*, p. 22. For railroads, see Riegel, *The Story of the Western Railroads*; Marshall, *Santa Fe*, chaps. 11, 17; Lamar, *The Far Southwest*, p. 461. In 1866 the Atlantic and Pacific Railroad received a charter to build from Albuquerque along the 35th parallel to the Pacific. It essentially was a paper railroad reorganized in 1876 as part of the St. Louis and San Francisco Railroad. In 1880 the Atchison, Topeka, and Santa Fe acquired a half interest in the Atlantic and Pacific, which was then enabled to build west from the Rio Grande to the Colorado River. By agreement with the Southern Pacific in 1884, it secured rights to continue the line through Cajon Pass to Los Angeles and on to San Diego.

settlement of the West. Because Lieutenant Whipple insisted upon a plentiful supply of instruments that included an astronomical transit, which he and Ives used with care and expertise, his observations were especially useful to Lieutenant Warren. They enabled him to correct earlier maps produced by Lieutenant Simpson, Captain Marcy, Major Emory, and Captain Sitgreaves, the last of whom had carried with him only a compass and sextant. Moreover, Whipple accurately located the Bill Williams Fork, confirmed that the Mojave River flowed into a sink west of the Colorado, and named and mapped important landmarks in the territory west of the Rio Grande. Allied with Warren's map in usefulness were the daily records of weather and mileage kept by assistants like John Sherburne. With the completion of the railroad explorations, the contours of the trans-Mississippi West clearly emerged for the first time.[8]

But to politicians and much of the population the scientific reports seemed arcane and academic. They have been criticized more recently as examples of the limitations of antebellum American science.[9] In that pre-Darwinian age botanists and zoologists listed and classified their specimens and geologists described landforms, speculating about their nature and their place in geological time. The scientific profession had matured to the point where classification and description conformed to established rules and nomenclature, and its practitioners had acquired sufficient knowledge or confidence to venture generalizations and test evidence against reigning theories. But they made many mistakes along the way and embraced hypotheses that in retrospect seem naive and even bizarre. None made Charles Darwin's leap of the imagination that forged a grand theory from the evidence of recorded detail.

Nevertheless, American scientists were building the corpus of knowledge that is essential to scientific progress and engaging in

[8] See "Memoir of Lieut. G. K. Warren," *Reports of Explorations and Surveys*, II, pp. 87–102; Goetzmann, *Army Exploration*, pp. 313–16 and Appendix C, esp. pp. 446–49, 451, 453. Lieut. Whipple, who used a complex instrument known as the "Fox" dip-circle, also made observations, as he had during his service with the Mexican boundary commission, for the measurement of terrestrial magnetism; see *Report*, Nov. 7, 1853.

[9] See, e.g., Goetzmann, *Army Exploration*, pp. 305–6, 336; *Exploration and Empire*, pp. 330–32.

the "fruitful doing" that is the cardinal principle of their profession.[10] The railroad surveys provided an unprecedented opportunity to expand available knowledge about the astonishing country west of the Mississippi. They served as "great graduate schools" for a generation of American scientists. The collections at the Smithsonian swelled as cases of specimens arrived at the institution, which was fast becoming a national museum and a center for scientific research. The new knowledge was disseminated at home and abroad with remarkable speed. Only five years elapsed between the publication of the first and final volumes of the Pacific Railroad *Reports*, and Congress ordered first printings of 10,000 for each volume. Duplicates of specimens and copies of the reports were distributed abroad, and Europeans with the expeditions (six in all) furthered their careers and helped to circulate the new information. Long interested in the North American continent, scientists like Alexander von Humboldt in Prussia, Sir William Hooker in England, and Alphonse De Candolle in Switzerland were excited by the revelations about a far western country hitherto seen largely as another *terra incognita*. The international exchange of ideas fostered by the explorations strengthened the scientific profession. Thus, even though they reflected the limitations of the age, the scientific reports are considered quite rightly as a "glorious chapter" in the history of American science.[11]

Natural scientists who worked in the field, like Dr. John Bigelow and Dr. Caleb Kennerly, rarely achieved the stature of their colleagues who remained at "headquarters" to describe and classify collections. But those "ardent recorders of nature's facts"

[10] Quotation from the brilliant review of Elliot Rudwick's *The Great Devonian Controversy* by Stephen Jay Gould in *New York Review of Books*, Feb. 27, 1986, p. 9; see also McKelvey, *Botanical Exploration*, Introduction, p. xix. Congress's dispatch in publishing the Pacific Railroad *Reports* was remarkable. The final volumes of the Wilkes expedition (1838–42) appeared in 1874. See Stanton, *The Great United States Exploring Expedition*, Chap. 22.

[11] Quotations from Dupree, *Science in the Federal Government*, p. 94, and *Asa Gray*, p. 208. See also Goetzmann, *Army Exploration*, pp. 311–82; Meisel, *A Bibliography of American Natural History*, vol. III, pp. 189–221; Merrill, *The First One Hundred Years of American Geology*, pp. 313–23; Dupree, *Asa Gray*, pp. 211–15, 414–15; McKelvey, *Botanical Exploration*, Introduction, p. xxiii, and pp. 673–74; Alexander von Humboldt to Whipple (in French), Aug. 18, 1855, Whipple Papers.

made basic contributions to the advancement of knowledge. For the Whipple expedition's report, Dr. Bigelow contributed an essay (written in direct and charming prose) on the botanical character of the region. He also drew a simple profile of the distribution of forest trees along the route, probably at the instigation of the secretary of the Smithsonian Institution. Joseph Henry encouraged such efforts as possible aids to the lumber industry and as demonstrations of the Smithsonian's dedication to "useful" as well as theoretical science. Bigelow's chart of elevations at which certain trees were found, nevertheless, was a pioneering attempt in plant ecology. Two of the leading scientists who described the botanical collection, Asa Gray and John Torrey, were delighted with Bigelow's labors. Dr. Torrey wrote that his collection was "twice as large as Beckwith's and Pope's put together," and it was brought home in perfect order. In all, several new genera and over sixty new species of plants were discovered. Decades later botanists still praised the richness of the Whipple collection. And even though botanists like Gray and Torrey have been criticized for devoting their energies to taxonomy rather than to theoretical speculation, such journeyman labor paid dividends for a botanist of Gray's ability. Through his tireless classification of plants, Gray amassed a vast knowledge of North American flora and developed an intuitive grasp of the variations in plant forms. With his prepared mind Gray immediately grasped the significance of Darwin's theory of evolution and went on to become an internationally recognized scholar and the most distinguished American botanist of his time.[12]

Like John Bigelow, Caleb Kennerly exulted in his "rich harvest" of specimens. His zoological collection, gathered with the aid of Balduin Möllhausen, was studied along with those from

[12] Quotation on field scientists from Stephen Jay Gould's review of Rudwick, *The Great Devonian Controversy*, in *New York Review of Books*, Feb. 27, 1986. For Bigelow's essay and profile see *Reports of Explorations and Surveys*, IV ("Botanical Character"), Nos. 1 and 2. For Joseph Henry see Dupree, *Asa Gray*, pp. 206–7, 387. Dupree writes extensively on the importance of Gray's taxonomic work in his development as a botanist; see, e.g., pp. 214–15, 249. Goetzmann, *Army Exploration*, pp. 323–26, 328, 331, 333, comments on the scientific reports of the Whipple expedition, but Grant Foreman, the editor of Whipple's journal, ignores the scientific aspect of the expedition. David Conrad, another scholar who has written extensively on the Whipple expedition, examines the scientific aspect only in one article, "Whipple at Zuni."

the other railroad surveys by scientists at the Smithsonian Institution working under the supervision of Spencer F. Baird. An authority on mammals and reptiles, Baird informed Lieutenant Whipple that he was overwhelmed by the number of new species of birds, mammals, fish, and reptiles, and especially pleased with specimens from the unknown territory along the Bill Williams Fork. The collection of "rodent quadrupeds" alone, he wrote, required revision of the invertebrate zoology of North America. The expanded zoological studies of all the collections, illustrated with elegant engravings, eventually filled three volumes of the published Pacific Railroad *Reports*. They were the first comprehensive scientific studies of North American zoology produced in the United States.[13]

No such excitement greeted the publication of the Whipple expedition's geological report. Since Jules Marcou was the only geologist to cross the entire country west of the Mississippi, his findings were awaited with keen anticipation. But the French geologist became the center of a controversy that caused Lieutenant Whipple no little embarrassment and severely damaged Marcou's reputation in the United States.

After completing his preliminary report and dispatching his specimens of rocks and fossils to the Smithsonian Institution, Marcou claimed poor health and obtained leave from Whipple to recuperate in France, where he planned to complete his final report. Upon learning of Marcou's intentions, Jefferson Davis ordered him to remain in the country. The volatile geologist promptly resigned from the scientific corps and embarked for France. A few months later, under threat of prosecution by the Secretary of War, Marcou relinquished his duplicate notes and specimens to an official at the American legation in Paris. Although Whipple, who admired Marcou, urged him to return and write the final report, the geologist refused, incensed by the blows to his *amour propre* administered by a Secretary of War with "overbearing manners and tyrannical power."[14]

[13] For Kennerly's brief essay, see *Reports of Explorations and Surveys*, IV ("Explanations and Field Notes"), pp. 1–9. For Spencer F. Baird's correspondence, see Baird to Whipple, Nov. 31, 1854, June 29, 1855, Whipple Papers. See also Goetzmann, *Army Exploration*, pp. 328–31.

[14] See Whipple to Capt. A. A. Humphreys, July 26, Oct. 26, Dec. 16, 1854; Whipple to Jefferson Davis, Dec. 16, 1854; to Jules Marcou, Dec. 1, 1854,

A photograph of Jules Marcou, the Whipple expedition's geologist. Marcou gave this photograph to John Sherburne, most likely when they met again in Washington, D.C., during the Civil War. Courtesy Elena Klein.

The task of writing the final geological report was assigned to W. P. Blake, a young protégé of James Hall, the New York paleontologist who agreed to examine Marcou's rocks and fossils. Irritated by Marcou's behavior and ethics and ruffled by his presumptuous publication of a geological map of the United States before they could publish their own, Blake and Hall undermined Marcou's preliminary report. Blake vigorously denied the validity of a number of Marcou's theories, and both Blake and Hall made no secret of their dissatisfaction with the preliminary report and the collection of specimens. The damage to Marcou's reputation and the general disparagement of his findings led to the widespread belief that the Whipple expedition's geological report was glaringly deficient.

Yet Marcou was an able geologist. His real achievements were ignored by a profession noted for its heated controversies, personal rivalries, and resentment of foreigners invading its territory. Marcou made a number of factual errors and indulged in sweeping generalizations based upon flimsy evidence. But his firsthand observations of territory unknown to geologists pro-

---

Jan. 14, 1855; Capt. A. A. Humphreys to Whipple, Oct. 1854, all in Whipple Papers. For Marcou's opinion of the Secretary of War see Merrill, *The First One Hundred Years of American Geology*, Appendix, p. 681.

vided valuable information, and some of his major hypotheses, most notably those respecting the age and formation of the mysterious *Llano Estacado* and of the Sierra Madre, were verified by later geologists. Marcou's report, like others submitted by the railroad surveys, most importantly revealed the huge gaps in knowledge about the fantastic topography of the West, and advertised the exciting opportunities awaiting future geological exploration. Those reports paved the way for the great Western discoveries after the Civil War that commanded the respect of geologists throughout the world.[15]

Although one of the duties of each of the railroad surveys was to provide information about Indian tribes, Lieutenant Whipple alone produced a lengthy ethnological report.[16] The necessity for rapid exploration admittedly made the task a difficult one, and the massacre of Captain Gunnison's party underscored the hazards of encounters with some of the tribes. But Whipple was unusually interested in the subject and conscientiously recorded information about the Indians met with along the route.

William W. Turner, one of the practitioners of the infant sci-

[15] Blake, for example, vehemently denied (and continued to deny in later publications) Marcou's theory that the *Llano Estacado* was basically of Triassic formation and that the uplift of the tableland followed the formation of the Sierra Madre; he insisted incorrectly that the *Llano* was formed in the later Cretaceous period and that the Sierra Madre had been formed prior to the *Llano*. Blake and Hall also complained that rocks and fossils were mislabeled, and that European rocks were included among the specimens. It is clear from the Whipple correspondence, however, that Marcou sent five cubic feet of specimens to the Smithsonian before he left the country and that they were arranged correctly; the mislabeled specimens were among the duplicates he returned to the American legation. Hall referred to Marcou as a "scientific quack," and most geologists, including James Dwight Dana, the leading American geologist, were incensed by Marcou's geological map of the United States, which, like most other geological maps of the time (including Blake's and Hall's), was filled with errors. Marcou had an equally low opinion of Blake and Hall, informing Whipple that Blake was "*parfaitment incapable de faire un rapport géologique*" and that Hall was "*le plus grand jésuite*" he had ever met. For Blake's general report, which included Marcou's preliminary daily "*résumé*" (in French and in translation) plus Hall's report on rocks and fossils, see *Reports of Explorations and Surveys*, III, Part IV, pp. 1–175. See also Merrill, *The First One Hundred Years of American Geology*, pp. 315–17, and Appendix, pp. 675–81; Goetzmann, *Army Exploration*, pp. 323–26.

[16] *Reports of Explorations and Surveys*, III, Part III ("Indian Tribes"), pp. 1–127. Capt. Pope included five pages on Indians in his report, and George Gibbs, a scientist with the Isaac Stevens expedition, incorporated some material on Indians in his report; see *Reports of Explorations and Surveys*, vols. I and XII.

ence of ethnology at the Smithsonian, listed and described the vocabularies painstakingly collected by Whipple. Some, like those of the Kiowa and Mohave, were the first ever published. Turner divided most of Whipple's vocabularies, along with others known to him, into six linguistic groups that basically remain unchanged today. Whipple's Navajo vocabulary, collected from one of his Mexican herders who had been a Navajo captive, confirmed Turner's theory that it was part of the Apache linguistic family, and reinforced his thesis that the clear linguistic ties between the southwestern Apaches and the Canadian Athapascans indicated a southward migratory path from the Bering Sea land bridge.[17]

Another Smithsonian ethnologist, Thomas Ewbank, described Whipple's artifacts. Although Ewbank failed to appreciate the sophistication of Indian design and workmanship, he was impressed by the skill and taste of an "untutored people." In all, the Whipple collection was rich and varied and included shards of pottery from the ruins of ancient pueblos along the Little Colorado River. Those fragments, so unlike any contemporary pottery made by North American Indians, were, Ewbank wrote, "fine specimens of the potter's art in past times." The Whipple collection was an important addition to the Smithsonian's resources and a priceless archive of Native American cultures.[18]

The most personal contribution was Whipple's essay of nearly forty pages on the various tribes he encountered. He briefly described such characteristics as dress, ornaments, dwellings, traditions, "superstitions," and pictographs, and he clearly was aware of the variety and complexity of Native American cultures. Because a number of encounters were fleeting and some informa-

[17] *Reports of Explorations and Surveys*, III, Part III ("Indian Tribes"), pp. 54–103. The six linguistic groups were Algonkin, Pawnee, Shoshone, Apache, Keres, and Yuma. Turner by then was familiar enough with Indian vocabularies to realize that the Choctaw, Caddo, Kiowa, and Zuñi languages did not fit into group classifications.

[18] Lieut. Whipple seemed scrupulous about buying or bartering for Indian "curiosities." Less scrupulous was Dr. Kennerly who, as we know, stole a skull from the Laguna Pueblo on Nov. 14, 1853. Though Zuñi officials warned the Whipple party that a spring near their pueblo was sacred, Kennerly stole some beautiful jars painted with frogs and butterflies from the spring. The skull and jars became part of the Smithsonian collection. See the Diary above, Nov. 14, 1853; Whipple, *Report*, Nov. 20, 1853; *Reports of Explorations and Surveys*, III, Part III ("Indian Tribes"), pp. 45–46.

tion was received secondhand, Whipple's most informative descriptions were those of little-known people like the Mohaves. His chief purpose, however, was to instruct the government in the proper conduct of Indian-white relations.

It is obvious from entries in his journal and remarks in his essay that Whipple approved of Indians like the Choctaws, who had adopted many of the ways of white society, and that he admired the Zuñians and Mohaves, who had retained their cultures and lived in "fixed residences and permanent abodes." To him nomadic Indians like the Comanches and Kiowas were, on the other hand, "perfect types of the American savage." Nevertheless, Whipple did attempt to perceive the process of Anglo-American expansion from the standpoint of the Indians themselves. He recognized that many Indian "depredations" were desperate measures to protect their territory and guard against "the menace to their liberties." He argued that the aborigines could see no reason to yield up their homes and the graves of their ancestors "to the first grasping white man who courts the spot." Believing that there was little hope for tribes "hemmed in by descendants of a foreign race," and accepting the reality of white expansion, in which he of course was an active participant, Whipple urged the government to extend "the powerful arm of the law" to protect them from aggression, secure their rights, and afford them facilities and aid in acquiring the arts of civilization. In one sense he was representative of a minority of Anglo-Americans who hoped to resolve the "Indian question" by assimilating Native Americans into white society. In another Whipple was unusual in that he respected many aspects of Indian life and revealed considerable ambivalence about the "blessings" of Anglo-American society.[19]

All the words in all the reports, however, could not convey graphic images of the exotica of Western life or the majesty of the Western landscape. That task was left to the artists who accompanied the railroad explorations. Of those who served with the major surveys—and they included such well-known artists as

[19] *Reports of Explorations and Surveys*, III, Part III ("Indian Tribes"), pp. 7–43. Because of Whipple's relative sensitivity toward Native American cultures and his ambivalence about the impact of white society, his stance does not fit neatly into the thesis presented in Slotkin, *The Fatal Environment*, that violence underlaid white attitudes toward Indians. See also Berkhofer, *The White Man's Indian*.

Richard Kern, John Mix Stanley, and F. W. von Egloffstein—the most underrated is Balduin Möllhausen. Lieutenant Whipple expressed disappointment with his artist's early landscapes of the southern plains, and in his official report he complained that the artist, in two of his drawings, had portrayed his Indian subjects inaccurately. The foremost historian of the railroad explorations, William H. Goetzmann, is more sweeping in his appraisal. Möllhausen's landscapes, he writes, were "twisted and exaggerated," and in his work as a whole the artist "never allowed facts or the demands of literalism to interfere with his romantic imagination."[20]

Actually Möllhausen's landscapes are small in scope and they specifically depict the local scenery. Though a romantic writer, he restrained his imagination in most of his renditions. None is twisted and few are exaggerated. His landscapes were not vehicles for the portrayal of the sublime, like von Egloffstein's, or vivid panoramas, like Stanley's. In fact, Möllhausen does not conform to Goetzmann's thesis that explorer-artists conveyed a common image of the West as "a romantic horizon." The artist's failure to satisfy contemporary conceptions of the Western landscape—the awe-inspiring vistas that "stunned" the imagination—may explain the comparative neglect of his work. Technically, Möllhausen was not an artist of the caliber of Kern, Stanley, or von Egloffstein. But he clearly was a competent topographical artist, faithful to the charge that he produce precise drawings of scenery along the route. Some of the drawings, however, are more than competent. Those depicting Fort Smith from the

[20] Richard Kern accompanied the Gunnison party, but this fine artist's sketches were few and incomplete because he died with Gunnison. John Mix Stanley, another excellent artist, was with the Stevens expedition, and F. W. von Egloffstein was with Lieut. Beckwith's. Egloffstein, who drew Lieut. G. K. Warren's famous map, was the embodiment of the romantic artist. For Whipple's poor opinion of Möllhausen's early landscapes, see Whipple to Spencer F. Baird (from Albuquerque), Nov. 8, 1853, Whipple Papers. Baron Leo Gerolt (the Prussian ambassador in Washington), however, saw these drawings at the Smithsonian and pronounced them "beautiful" in a letter to von Humboldt, dated Nov. 28, 1853; see Barba, *Balduin Möllhausen*, App. II, pp. 162–63. For Whipple's complaints about two of the Indian drawings, see Whipple, *Report*, Aug. 23, 1853; *Reports of Explorations and Surveys*, III, Part III ("Indian Tribes"), pp. 27, 31. For William H. Goetzmann's comments, see his *Army Exploration*, p. 233, and his *Exploration and Empire*, pp. 214, 220. For another negative critique, see Weitenkampf, "Early Pictures of North American Indians," p. 605.

Arkansas River, the Kiowa encampment, the Zuñi and Santo Domingo Pueblos, the San Francisco Mountains, and the crossing of the Colorado are striking images. Möllhausen's real skill as a draftsman—the delicate touch and the attention to detail—is particularly evident in his exquisite drawings of rock strata, Indian artifacts, and native plants like the cactus. These were much admired by Lieutenant Whipple and Smithsonian scientists.[21]

Möllhausen's most interesting work undoubtedly is seen in his drawings of Indians. Unlike Karl Bodmer, the finest artist of the American West, he had no great skill in portraiture. A number of his sketches, such as those of Black Beaver and two Tontos he thought repulsive, are crude and one-dimensional. Lieutenant Whipple correctly noted that two Navajo horsemen he sketched had the features of Pueblo Indians. Yet despite these limitations, most of the drawings are exceptionally rich in ethnographic detail, and noteworthy because the artist captured the human quality in people all too frequently portrayed in stereotypes. Möllhausen's stunning field sketches of Choctaws and Shawnees, of the Zuñi chiefs, of the Navajo horsemen (despite their Pueblo Indian features), and of the magnificent Mohave warriors and the diminutive, tattooed women with their short grass skirts, are similar to Karl Bodmer's in their detail and humanity. The Whipple expedition's published report on the Indian tribes of the Southwest caused such excitement in the East that in 1858 it

[21] All Western artists, including the great Karl Bodmer, engaged in artistic license. Möllhausen's few romanticized landscapes include topographically accurate but surrealistic "moonscapes" (painted in gray wash on white paper) of the junction of the Bill Williams and Colorado rivers, and a drawing of the Zuñi Pueblo in which he exaggerated the size of the cliffs towering over the multileveled structure in order to dramatize the setting; both are reproduced in the text. Möllhausen was chiefly self-taught but took drawing lessons in Berlin in 1853 and additional lessons after he returned to Berlin in 1854. On the Ives expedition along the Colorado in 1857, his drawings of the Grand Canyon are exceptionally fine and accurate renditions, far more realistic than von Egloffstein's. For contemporary appreciation of Möllhausen's skill as a draftsman, see geologist W. P. Blake, *Reports of Explorations and Surveys*, III, Part IV, pp. 18, 25; botanist George Engelmann, *ibid.*, Part V, p. 58; Amiel Whipple to Alexander von Humboldt, Aug. 8, 1854, reprinted in Barba, *Balduin Möllhausen*, pp. 164–65. For thoughtful critiques of Möllhausen, see Miller, "Balduin Möllhausen," Chap. 9; Miller, "The Ives Expedition Revisited"; Taft, "The Pictorial Record of the Old West: VI. Henrich Balduin Möllhausen"; and Taft, "The Pictorial Record of the Old West: XIV. Illustrators of the Pacific Railroad Reports."

was reprinted in *Harper's Magazine*. The journal included fifteen woodcuts of the artist's drawings; some tribes, such as the Mohave, had never before been sketched by an artist. Möllhausen's extensive collection of Indian drawings forms a remarkable ethnographic record of the exploration along the thirty-fifth parallel, and it captures on paper the natives of the region before white progress changed their lives.[22]

One historian of science has written that, "to the student of the flora, fauna, and geology of the West," the Pacific Railroad volumes seem "as live and important" today as when first published in the nineteenth century.[23] For historians of the Southwest the detailed, illustrated reports of the Whipple expedition remain fascinating archives, conveying as they do a rich history of a region long since changed and of a way of life forever lost.

But what of young John Sherburne, last heard of in March of 1854 when about to begin another new adventure? Though Balduin Möllhausen seemed to think Sherburne planned to farm in California, he and his companion, William White, may have intended to prospect in the gold mines to the north. Each man collected over $300 in pay, and on March 22, 1854, Sherburne and White bought a tent, five mules, saddles, a pistol for White, and provisions of pork, flour, coffee, and sugar at the auction of the expedition's goods and equipment. They were still in Los Angeles in June, however, and remained there at least until March of 1855. Lieutenant Whipple, who left the meteorological instruments in their charge, employed the men in June 1854 to

[22] For the rich ethnographic detail of Möllhausen's drawings, see Ewers, "An Anthropologist Looks at Early Pictures of North American Indians"; Miller, "Balduin Möllhausen," pp. 244–45, 260; Amsden, *Navaho Weaving*, Plate 97a; Taylor and Wallace, *Mohave Tattooing and Face Painting*, pp. 2, 7, 9. See also *Harper's New Monthly Magazine*, 17 (Sept. 1858), pp. 448–67. Whipple complained about only two of the Indian drawings. In his report on Indian tribes he claimed that the artist failed to capture the "wild look" of two Wacos, even though in his daily journal he made no comment about their fierceness (nor did others in their journals), and thought one of them looked sick. As we know, Whipple thought the two Navajo horsemen looked like Pueblo Indians and, except for the rendition of the Indian blanket, believed that the artist had failed to picture their demeanor accurately. See Whipple, *Report*, Aug. 23, 1853; *Reports of Explorations and Surveys*, III, Part III ("Indian Tribes"), pp. 27, 31.

[23] Dupree, *Science in the Federal Government*, p. 95.

make an "elaborate" series of observations until March of the following year, paying each $50 a month. In November 1854, John Sherburne wrote to his nephew Willie Whipple in Portsmouth, telling him he was sending "a real California half a dollar" for a Christmas present. At the time he was sitting in his Los Angeles "office," exulting in the warm weather, the green grass, and the flowers of a California winter.[24]

John Sherburne remained in California for another two years. There are no letters or diaries that provide glimpses of his life during that time, but apparently he returned in 1855 to El Monte, the settlement some twelve miles east of Los Angeles where on March 21, 1854, the Whipple expedition made the final camp before reaching its destination. Lieutenant Whipple noted at the time that El Monte consisted of some five hundred families who had left the gold mines and "squatted" on a large rancho after learning that there was a flaw in the Mexican title to the land. "Each spot of 160 acres, for miles in all directions," Whipple wrote, "appeared to be ditched around, hedged, and cultivated. Houses of canvas, brush, boards, or adobes, gave shelter each to a family of settlers. Improvements were rapidly progressing. There were the cheerful sounds of American voices, of the blacksmith's hammer, and the merry laugh of children trudging to school. The whole scene appeared very odd, as if a New England village had by some magic sprung up upon the Pacific." When visiting or living in El Monte in 1855, John Sherburne met Jennie Smith, daughter of one of the settlers, Dr. Isaac William Smith. He married Jennie, and in October 1856 a daughter named Evelyn was born. From a photograph of the richly dressed Jennie Smith Sherburne (possibly her wedding portrait), she appears very young with a round face and masses of long, dark curly hair topped by an elaborate flowered hat.[25]

Assuredly neither Sherburne nor White prospered in Cali-

[24] Whipple, Diary, Mar. 22, 1854; ledger, 1853–54; John P. Sherburne to Willie Whipple, Nov. 18, 1854; Whipple to William White and John P. Sherburne, June 1, 1854, all in Whipple Papers. According to Whipple's accounts, the balance of John Sherburne's salary was $301.31; White's was $384.40.

[25] Whipple, *Report*, Mar. 21, 1854; John Pitts Sherburne, Diary of trip from El Monte to Fort Lancaster, 1856–1857 (henceforth Sherburne Diary), Nov. 9, 12, 15, 1856.

A photograph of the youthful Jennie Smith Sherburne, daughter of California settlers and the wife of John Sherburne. This undated photograph, taken in San Francisco, may have been her wedding portrait. Courtesy Elena Klein.

fornia. Perhaps because of his impending fatherhood, John Sherburne joined the army in June 1856, receiving a commission as a second lieutenant in the 1st Regiment of Infantry. Living then in El Monte, he received orders on November 1 of that year to join his regiment for frontier duty at Fort Lancaster in Texas. Established in 1855, the fort guarded the Pecos River crossing on the road from San Antonio to El Paso. Sherburne had enough money to provide for emergencies and to buy a "private" wagon and mules to transport his family across the plains. Otherwise he was dependent upon his army pay and quartermasters' drafts for subsistence. He persuaded his old friend William White to accompany the family as far as El Paso, agreeing to supply the apparently impoverished White with provisions and a small wage.[26]

During the journey to Fort Lancaster, John Sherburne kept another diary, making the first entry on November 8, 1856, in the remaining pages of his original diary of the Whipple expedition. Only that portion, which records the trip until January 27, 1857, when the party reached a spot west of Fort Thorne on the Rio Grande, has been preserved in the papers passed down through his family. The diary is not a daily account. Sherburne frequently wrote "from recollection" for periods covering ten days or so. He tells us that he did not intend to keep a journal but decided to do so upon recalling the pleasure he derived from looking over the diary of his first overland journey.[27]

Beyond Fort Yuma, at the junction of the Gila and Colorado rivers, the road to Fort Lancaster was considered dangerous since it passed through Apache and Comanche territory. Sherburne planned to move from fort to fort, collecting his pay and provisions at army posts and hoping to secure armed escorts at the posts for each stage of the journey. From Fort Yuma the road led east southeast to Los Calabasas (now simply Calabasas), an army post some 50 miles south of Tucson, where four companies of dragoons were stationed. From Los Calabasas, situated in the Gadsden Purchase in what is now southern Arizona, the route followed a southern loop that crossed into Mexico and

[26] Army Commission, John B. [*sic*] Sherburne, June 27, 1856, in the possession of Elena Klein; Sherburne, Diary, Nov. 9, Dec. 7, 1856; *Soldier and Brave*, p. 175.

[27] Sherburne, Diary, Jan. 23, 1857.

moved northeast through New Mexico Territory to Fort Thorne. From Fort Thorne the road followed the Rio Grande to the south, passing El Paso and leaving the river at Fort Davis. East of the fort it crossed the Comanche war trail before reaching Fort Lancaster.

The trip began badly. Retracing the path taken by the Whipple expedition, the small party passed the Cucamonga rancheria where John Sherburne had spent the night of March 18, 1854, then traveled through San Bernardino to visit Jennie Sherburne's family, by that time settled nearby on a section of Rancho San Gorgonio in the San Gorgonio Pass. There the wagon broke down and Sherburne found that Dr. Isaac W. Smith drove a hard bargain. His father-in-law demanded the broken wagon plus $175 in exchange for another wagon in good repair. It was an "enormous price," John Sherburne wrote, "but there was no way of getting out of it." On November 18, with diminished financial resources, the travelers finally set out to join the "main road" across the desert to Fort Yuma, reaching there on December 1 after a journey of 321 miles. Unable to secure an escort because there were no mounted troops available, and afraid that if he delayed he might be stationed at Fort Yuma, considered a hellhole in the summer, Sherburne resolved to leave on December 8 when two passing travelers agreed to accompany him to Tucson. By the time he paid his unexpected expenses, Sherburne was left with only $30 to last until he reached Los Calabasas.[28]

[28] *Ibid.*, Nov. 9–Dec. 7, 1856; quotation from entry of Nov. 16. See also Sacks, "Sylvester Mowry," pp. 16–17. On Nov. 10, near San Bernardino, Sherburne met a man called Hage who, like William White, agreed to accompany the Sherburne party in return for provisions and a small wage. The hard-bargaining Dr. Isaac William Smith became a well-known figure in San Bernardino County. Though a non-Mormon, he was respected by the Mormon settlers in San Bernardino and was elected to the California legislature in 1857. He became a leading advocate for a stage-coach route from San Francisco to Yuma via San Gorgonio Pass, and in 1858 the Butterfield Stages opened that route. Apparently Dr. Smith bought a section of the San Gorgonio rancho, given to the noted guide Pauline or Powell Weaver under a Mexican land grant; Weaver settled there for a time in 1846, and his brother, Duff Weaver, was living there in 1856. See deed from John P. Sherburne to William H. Sears, Jan. 1, 1869; attorney Harold Smith to John Shurburn [*sic*] (John P. Sherburne's son), May 21, 1894, about this land apparently inherited by the Sherburnes; all in possession of Elena Klein. See also Beattie, *Heritage of the Valley*, pp. 288, 358–59, and Ingersoll, *Century Annals*, pp. 114, 669.

Passing through the hospitable Pima and Maricopa Indian villages, the company reached Tucson without incident on December 21, having covered 287 miles in twelve and one-half days. Sherburne deposited his wife and baby in a hotel and rode on alone to Los Calabasas to collect his pay and secure a military escort for the most dangerous part of the journey. Along the way he was dismayed to find many graves of settlers and the town of Tubac deserted and devastated as a result of Apache raids, with the adobe houses mostly in ruins and the church "entirely destroyed." Finding that a mail train with escort would depart for Fort Thorne on January 4, 1857, Sherburne returned to Tucson. There he found his daughter so sick that for four nights the young couple thought she would not live "from one hour to the other." The baby did recover and was well enough to travel on January 6, but by that time the mail train had left Los Calabasas. The Sherburnes and their two companions struggled on to the army post to wait for another escort. On January 18 they finally left with a train of empty wagons dispatched to Fort Thorne by the quartermaster to collect corn for the post. The train consisted of nine wagons and 54 mules, none shod and "all poor and scarcely able to take empty wagons." No extra equipment was provided for the wagons in case of accidents, and rations were issued for only 21 days. There were eighteen men in all but only three guns, one belonging to Sherburne. On January 27 John Sherburne wrote the last entry in the diary, with a note that his diary was continued on page 44 of a second book, now lost. The train was camped near Guadalupe Canyon, about one hundred miles east of Mission Santa Cruz in Sonora, Mexico. On that day it passed two "monuments" marking the boundary between the two countries.[29]

In this portion of his diary John Sherburne makes few personal remarks. In fact, he never refers to his wife and daughter by their names and we learn nothing about Jennie Sherburne's reactions to the hard travel with a baby only weeks old. Nevertheless, a different Sherburne emerges in these pages, far more

[29] Sherburne, Diary, Dec. 11–21, 1856 (one entry), Jan. 6–27, 1857; Bancroft, *History of Arizona and New Mexico*, p. 496. The army post at Los Calabasas was known as Camp Moore.

serious and careworn than the cheerful young man who lightheartedly crossed the plains in 1853. By now, at the age of twenty-five, he was absorbed with the responsibilities of caring for his family, worried about his lack of money, and dismayed by the frustrations of army life. He was disgusted that the commandant at Los Calabasas would send his family across Apache country with such poor wagons and mules, and "not only with a scarcity of provisions but without protection in case of attack." Even the sight of a fandango in Tucson had failed to cheer him or to recall fond memories of his favorite pastime in Albuquerque in 1853. To the young family man a fandango by then seemed similar to all Mexican dances, "full of greasers and Americans, dust and Tobacco smoke."[30]

Though we know nothing about their subsequent adventures along the road in 1857, the Sherburnes reached Fort Lancaster and while stationed there had another child, John Nathaniel, named for Sherburne's father, who died in Portsmouth in 1859. By the time the Civil War broke out Sherburne apparently had been transferred to the North, and on April 8, 1861, he received a promotion to first lieutenant. In October 1861 he became a captain in the 19th Infantry, and by July 1862 he was stationed in Washington as an assistant adjutant-general with the rank of major, living in the capital with his family. Sherburne evidently saw his sister Nell Whipple regularly, since she came from Portsmouth to stay with his family when her husband obtained leave from campaigning in Virginia.[31]

Amiel Whipple, promoted to captain in 1855, was posted to Detroit after completion of his duties for the Office of Pacific Railroad Explorations and Surveys. In Michigan he superintended the improvement of waterways from Lake Superior to the St. Lawrence River. Whipple returned to Washington at the outbreak of war and eventually became the chief topographical engineer on the staff of General Irvin McDowell; his wife and

[30] Sherburne, Diary, Dec. 11–21, 1856, Jan. 20, 1857.

[31] Army Commissions, John P. Sherburne, in the possession of Elena Klein; telegrams addressed to Mrs. Amiel Whipple, care of John P. Sherburne, Washington, D.C., Whipple Papers. Sherburne's sister Nell Whipple apparently returned to Portsmouth when her husband began campaigning in Virginia in 1862. Her daughter Elizabeth (Lizzie) remained at a Georgetown convent.

children joined him in Washington during that time. A major by 1861 and a brigadier general the following year, Whipple in 1862 requested field duty and in December commanded a division at Fredericksburg. On May 4, 1863, on the second day of the battle of Chancellorsville, Whipple was severely wounded. Taken from Virginia to Washington, he died at the Sherburne residence on May 7, surrounded by his family. Amiel Whipple's funeral procession, led by his riderless horse and "Mr. Lincoln in an open carriage showing such respect," began its solemn march to the Capitol from John Sherburne's house.[32]

In 1864 Major John Sherburne, apparently anxious for service in the field, transferred to the 11th New York Regiment of Cavalry, receiving the rank of colonel of volunteers, and the brevet rank of lieutenant-colonel in the regular army "for faithful and meritorious service." In July of that year he became colonel-in-chief of cavalry in the Department of the Gulf, with its headquarters in New Orleans. In 1865 he was promoted to the brevet rank of colonel in the regular army. Sherburne returned to the West with his family when posted in 1868 to the assistant adjutant-general's office in San Francisco. On December 28, 1870, he "mustered out."[33]

The remaining years of John Sherburne's life can be glimpsed only in a few official records, and those glimpses reveal a life of sad decline. Sometime after 1870 John and Jennie Sherburne separated and were later divorced. Upon his retirement from the army, John Sherburne became an "inspector" in the San

[32] Telegrams, letters, and newspaper clippings about Whipple's death are in the Whipple Papers. John Sherburne notified official circles and friends of Whipple's death and helped to arrange the impressive funeral; see, e.g., W. G. Peck to Major John P. Sherburne, May 8, 1863; Adjutant-General to Major John P. Sherburne, May 11, 1863. The Secretary of War promoted Whipple to major general on the day of his death; the commission dated from May 4, when he was wounded. For the quotation about Lincoln, see Julia Turner Lee to Mrs. R. W. Huntington (Lizzie Whipple), Oct. 24, 1916, Whipple Papers, in which Mrs. Lee, a classmate of Lizzie's at the Georgetown convent, reminisced about the funeral. For Whipple's military exploits, see *The War of the Rebellion*, vols. 1, 2, and 3.

[33] Army Commissions, John P. Sherburne, in the possession of Elena Klein; Heitman, *Historical Register*; *The War of the Rebellion*, vol. 41, pp. 799–80. A photograph of Jennie Sherburne, taken in Washington, shows that she had matured into a plump, good-looking matron with a discontented mouth. Her hair was dressed high and decorated with a Spanish comb. Photograph in the possession of Elena Klein.

The only known photograph of John Pitts Sherburne, taken most likely in the 1860's, before he mustered out of the army in 1870. Courtesy Elena Klein.

Francisco Custom House (retaining the title of colonel). Despite the fairly impressive sound of the position, however, he did not receive a regular salary. Instead, he was paid four dollars a day, which, if he worked regularly, represented an annual amount no higher than that paid to the lowliest clerk in the Custom House. The explanation for his troubles, passed down through the family, is that Sherburne became a heavy drinker, an occupational hazard for army officers. From his diary of the Whipple expedition we know of his fondness for the bottle.

On January 9, 1880, John Pitts Sherburne died in San Francisco. There was no obituary, only a brief newspaper notice announcing that his funeral would take place on Sunday, January 11, from the Great Army Hall on New Montgomery Street. He was 48 years old.[34]

[34] *Report*, Commission on the San Francisco Custom-House (U.S. Treasury Department, 1877), p. 35, and Appendixes A and B; San Francisco *City Directory*, 1868–80; San Francisco *Call*, Jan. 11, 1880; papers of Charles William (Willie) Whipple, Whipple Papers. Information on Sherburne's drinking comes from Elena Klein. Sherburne's daughter Evelyn was a schoolteacher in San Francisco in 1875 and lived with her mother in a separate residence from John P. Sherburne. His son John worked for the Southern Pacific Railroad, married, and had three daughters and a son who died as a child. One of his daughters, Elise, had a son Sherburne William Klein, who inherited the John Pitts Sherburne diaries and other records. In 1875 John Pitts Sherburne's brother Nathaniel, a master mariner, also lived in San Francisco. His sister, Nell Whipple, died in Portsmouth in 1874; his mother outlived both him and Nell.

Reference Matter

Biographical Appendix: Information on Persons Mentioned in the Diary

The names of members of the Whipple expedition are indicated by asterisks.

Armijo, Salvador. Called "don Salvador" by John Sherburne, this merchant and member of Albuquerque's Hispanic "aristocracy" gave a fandango on October 8, 1853, in honor of the Whipple expedition's officers and gentlemen. Sherburne was impressed by the carpeting and decoration of Armijo's "ballroom," and found some of the señoritas "quite beautiful." After the Civil War Armijo became one of the most prominent businessmen and landowners in Albuquerque and an enlightened citizen. His brother Ambrosio, owner of freight wagons plying the Santa Fe Trail, was very helpful to Lieut. Whipple, taking charge of sending the expedition's reports and specimens to Washington, D.C. See Simmons, *Albuquerque*, pp. 182–83, 195–96, 199, 208–9; Whipple, Diary, Nov. 1, 7, 1853, Whipple Papers.

Baird, Spruce McCoy. John Sherburne mentioned meeting with Baird and his friend and political ally Richard Weightman at Galisteo, New Mexico Territory, on October 1, 1853, as the "trotting train" traveled between Anton Chico and Albuquerque. Baird and Weightman were on their way east from Albuquerque to the county court at San Miguel. Lieutenant Whipple did not mention in his official report that they brought the first news of Lieutenant J. C. Ives's failure to arrive in Albuquerque weeks before the expedition, as planned in Washington. Sherburne called Baird "Judge," a Texas title he used throughout his life. Kentucky-born, Baird had arrived in New Mexico from Texas in 1848 and prospered in Albuquerque as a lawyer and landowner. His most celebrated case as a lawyer was his successful defense of Richard Weightman at his trial in 1854 for the murder of the well-known explorer and trader François X. Aubry. During the Civil War, Baird threw in his lot with General Henry Sibley, who in 1861 invaded New Mexico with a Confederate force from Texas. Driven from the Territory in 1862 by Federal troops, Sibley was accompanied on his retreat by Spruce Baird and his family. In 1863 Baird's large estate in Pajarito, near Albuquerque, was sold at auction. See Whipple, *Report*, Oct. 1, 1853; Simmons, *Albuquerque*, pp. 156–61, 180–81, 186–88, 191–92.

*Bigelow, John Milton. The botanist and surgeon with the Whipple expedition, Bigelow was born in Vermont in 1804. He moved to Ohio in 1815 and in 1832 graduated from medical college in Cincinnati. Settling in the Ohio town of Lancaster he engaged in medical practice, married, and began his interest in botany through the study of medicinal plants. Bigelow became known to scientists connected with the Smithsonian Institution through his friendship with W. S. Sullivant, a rich Ohio botanist considered the country's leading authority on mosses and liverworts. He made his first Western exploration with the survey of the boundary between the United States and Mexico from 1850 to 1853, and there he became friendly with Amiel Whipple. Though considered eccentric, as John Sherburne makes clear, Bigelow was a "general favorite" and "a pattern of gentleness and patience" on the Whipple expedition according to Balduin Möllhausen. He is identified incorrectly as Jacob Bigelow (a well-known elderly Harvard physician and botanist) in Conrad, "The Whipple Expedition in Arizona." After writing his botanical report for Lieutenant Whipple in 1854, Dr. John Bigelow resumed his medical practice in Ohio. Dr. John Torrey found his botanical specimens from the expedition "a pleasure to study." Probably through the influence of Amiel Whipple, to whom he remained close, he was appointed in 1860 as the meteorologist, oddly enough, with the Great Lakes survey; Whipple at the time was superintending the improvement of Great Lakes waterways from his headquarters in Detroit. When Amiel Whipple returned to Washington in 1861 at the outbreak of the Civil War, the two men corresponded regularly, and Bigelow was deeply distressed upon learning of his former commander's death in 1863. Remaining in Detroit, Bigelow became Professor of Botany and Pharmacy at the Detroit Medical College and in 1868 was appointed surgeon to the Marine Hospital in that city. He died in 1878.

See Waller, "Dr. John Milton Bigelow"; Atkinson, ed., *Physicians and Surgeons*; Dupree, *Asa Gray*, pp. 205–7; Möllhausen, *Diary*, I, p. 33; Bigelow and Whipple correspondence, especially Bigelow to Mrs. Amiel Whipple, May 8, 1863, Whipple Papers.

Black Beaver. The most noted guide and interpreter of his region, Black Beaver was the chief of about 500 Delaware Indians settled in 1853 at Old Camp Arbuckle, an abandoned army post in what is now Oklahoma. He had accompanied Captain R. B. Marcy on his 1849 expedition from Fort Smith to Santa Fe, and Lieutenant Whipple was anxious to secure his services when the railroad survey arrived on August 18, 1853, at Old Camp Arbuckle. But Black Beaver declined because of poor health. Balduin Möllhausen, who drew a hasty sketch of the chief, wrote that he had "long black hair framed in a face that was clever, but bore a melancholy expression of sickness and sorrow, though more than forty winters could not have passed over it." See Möllhausen, *Diary*, I, p. 93; Whipple, *Report*, Aug. 18, 1853; Hollon, *Beyond the Cross Timbers*, p. 126.

Bushman, John. Another well-known Delaware Indian guide, Bushman accompanied Captain R. B. Marcy on an expedition to the Red River in 1852. Marcy considered him "dignified, reserved, and taciturn, self-reliant, independent, and fearless." Lieutenant Whipple hoped that Bushman would accept the post of guide for the expedition through Comanche territory, but he, like Black Beaver and the half-Cherokee trader Jesse Chisholm, declined. Balduin Möllhausen wrote that Bushman visited the Whipple expedition at Old Camp Arbuckle on August 19, 1853, accompanied by his young son and "a beautiful squaw." See Möllhausen, *Diary*, I, p. 95; Whipple, *Report*, Aug. 18, 19, 1853; Hollon, *Beyond the Cross Timbers*, p. 127.

Cairook. This Mohave "sub-chief" was one of the guides chosen on March 1, 1854, to lead the Whipple expedition across the desert from the Colorado River to the "Mormon Road" in California. He and his companion, Irateba, were much admired by members of the expedition who, in gratitude for their services, presented them with old clothes in addition to the payment given by Lieutenant Whipple. John Sherburne did not mention him by name in his diary. Lieutenant J. C. Ives and Balduin Möllhausen met the guide again when in 1857 and 1858 Ives explored the Colorado River; by then Cairook was the leading Mohave chief. He and "Madam Cairook," one of his four wives and a "savage beauty" with "captivating features," according to Möllhausen, rode on Ives's steamboat for a day or so. Warfare broke out between the U.S. Army and the Mohaves in 1858 and 1859 because the Indians resented the encroachment of emigrants and the army into their territory. Cairook in 1859 agreed to army terms that he and other Mohave leaders serve as hostages at Fort Yuma to atone for a raid upon an emigrant wagon train in which eighteen were killed, including José Savedra (q.v.); the train had followed the path pioneered by the Whipple expedition. According to the army, Cairook was bayonetted at the fort while trying to escape. Lieutenant Whipple's forebodings, expressed in his diary on March 1, 1854, about future Anglo-American relations with the Mohaves, so admired by members of the Whipple expedition, were realized; of course, it is ironic that the Whipple expedition contributed to Mohave troubles. See Whipple, Diary, Mar. 2, 12, 13, 1854, Whipple Papers; *Report*, Mar. 1, 5, 9, 12, 1854; Ives, "Report," pp. 69–91, 180–81; Spicer, *Cycles of Conquest*, pp. 269–70; Miller, "The Ives Expedition Revisited," p. 16.

*Campbell, Albert H. The principal assistant engineer and surveyor with the Whipple expedition (Whipple himself held the titles of chief engineer and surveyor), Campbell was born in Charleston, Virginia (later West Virginia), in 1826, and in 1847 graduated from Brown University. A competent artist, he contributed three landscapes to the final official report published in 1856. Though a senior member of the scientific corps, Campbell allied himself with the "young gentlemen" and shared a tent with John Sherburne and others. Sherburne obviously found him full of fun. After assisting Lieutenant Whipple in preparing the topographical report for Congress in the summer of 1854, Campbell left in the fall to serve with Lieutenant John G. Parke's shorter railroad survey along the California coast and part of the 32d parallel route. Campbell was appointed the engineer and artist with that expedition. In 1857 he became general superintendent of the newly established Pacific Wagon Roads Office in Washington, D.C.; one of his sponsors was Jefferson Davis. In 1861 Campbell resigned to become chief of the topographical bureau of the Confederate Army, with the rank of major. After the Civil War he returned to West Virginia, where he was chief engineer for a number of railroads. Campbell died in 1899. See *Reports of Explorations and Surveys*, vol. III ("Topographical Report"); Jackson, *Wagon Roads West*, pp. 178, 182–83, 218–20; Taft, *Artists and Illustrators*, pp. 264–66.

*Campbell, Hugh. An assistant astronomer with the Whipple expedition, Campbell came from Texas and served as an assistant astronomer under Lieutenant Whipple with the United States and Mexico Boundary Survey from 1850 to 1853; Whipple thought highly of him. He was the highest-paid ($900) of all the assistants. He joined Whipple's expedition in Albuquerque on October 7, 1853, having accompanied Lieutenant J. C. Ives and Dr. C. B. R. Kennerly on an adventurous trip overland from San Antonio, Texas, to Albuquerque. John Sherburne reported that, soon after his arrival in Albuquerque, Campbell narrowly escaped death when a rifle was discharged accidentally by a U.S. dragoon stationed there. Hugh Campbell accompanied Lieutenant Whipple and other members of the scientific corps from San Pedro to San Francisco on March 23, 1854, and from there returned to Washington. Nothing is known of his whereabouts after the completion of his duties with the Whipple expedition. It is likely that he served in the Civil War, but the name "Hugh (or H.) Campbell" was a common one in army lists. See Whipple, Diary, Oct. 28, 1850, Jan. 8, 1851, Jan. 16, 17, 1853; ledger, 1853–54, all in Whipple Papers.

Chisholm, Jesse. Of part Cherokee descent, Chisholm was a noted guide, and a trader among the Indians of what is now Oklahoma. He married the half-Creek daughter of James Edwards, who owned an important trading post at Little River near Old Camp Arbuckle. His name is commemorated in the Chisholm Trail, the cattle trail that moved north from Texas and through Oklahoma to Kansas. When the Delaware Indian Black Beaver declined to act as guide for the expedition across Comanche territory, Whipple on August 17, 1853, sent a messenger to Little River, where Chisholm lived, requesting his services. Chisholm also declined, to Whipple's regret and annoyance. The lieutenant, who met Chisholm at Old Camp Arbuckle, described him as a man of considerable wealth and excellent judgment, who understood the Comanches better than anyone not belonging to their tribe. See Whipple, *Report*, Aug. 17, 19, 1853.

Douglass, Henry. On August 6, 1853, John Sherburne met Douglass, an "old acquaintance," near Shawnee Village in what is now eastern Oklahoma when Douglass was leading a wagon train from Fort Gibson in Indian Territory to Fort Smith. A West Point graduate of 1848 from New York City, Douglass then was serving as a lieutenant in the Seventh Infantry at Fort Gibson, the same regiment as Lieutenant John M. Jones, the Whipple expedition's commander of escort. His was the only wagon train encountered by the Whipple expedition during the entire course of the trip. See Stanley, Diary, Aug. 6, 1853; Cullum, *Biographical Register.*

*Gaines, Abner. An assistant surveyor with the Whipple expedition, Gaines was hired in Little Rock, Arkansas, when Lieutenant Whipple and his party stopped there on their way to Fort Smith. Whipple wrote in his diary that Gaines's family lived in Roseville, Arkansas. In his official report the lieutenant mistakenly stated that Gaines replaced Walter Jones of Washington in July at the Choctaw Agency in

Skullyville (now Oklahoma) after Jones resigned from the scientific corps. In his report Whipple also claimed incorrectly that Gaines came from Oregon. Gaines became sick at Old Camp Arbuckle on August 20, 1853, and resigned from the scientific corps. John Sherburne wrote on August 21 that some members of the corps thought Gaines was tired of the trip and perhaps did not like the idea of meeting Indians on the plains. Whipple, however, wrote that Gaines was very sick and that he was sorry to see "the excellent young man" leave, for his "gentlemanly deportment and amiability had won a stronghold on our regard." Whipple provided him with a pistol, and Gaines and a guide furnished by Black Beaver proceeded on August 22 to nearby Fort Arbuckle so that Gaines could seek medical attention. During the Civil War he served as a captain in the Arkansas infantry and was captured in Arkansas on November 5, 1863, by Union troops. See Whipple, Diary, June 26–29, Aug. 21, 1853, Whipple Papers; *Report*, Aug. 20, 22, 1853. See also *Reports of Explorations and Surveys*, III, Introduction, p. 3; *War of the Rebellion*, Series I, vol. 31, p. 35.

Garland, John. Garland became the general commanding the military department of New Mexico in July 1853, with his headquarters in Albuquerque. He refused to release his mounted troops as an escort for the Whipple expedition but provided an escort of soldiers, some mounted on mules, from Fort Defiance. He attended the lavish ball given by Lieut. Whipple in honor of Albuquerque's "aristocracy" and, according to Balduin Möllhausen, "mingled in the dance with as much frolicsome activity as the youngest lieutenant." Garland thought Albuquerque "the dirtiest hole in New Mexico" and spent most of his time campaigning or living in Santa Fe. See Möllhausen, *Diary*, II, p. 20; Simmons, *Albuquerque*, pp. 152, 165, 168.

*Garner, George G. Born in Maryland and an assistant astronomer with the Whipple expedition, Garner served with Lieutenant Whipple on the United States and Mexico Boundary Survey from 1850 to 1853; Whipple thought highly of him. On February 7, 1853, Whipple wrote in a diary while winding up his duties with the survey in Texas that Garner had proposed marriage to the daughter of the Mexican Collector of Customs at El Paso (now Ciudad Juarez, Mexico); the outcome of his suit is unknown. Garner became Whipple's clerk on the railroad expedition and was one of the "young gentlemen," sharing a tent with Thomas Parke, another assistant astronomer. He continued to act as Whipple's clerk during the journey home from California by ship in 1854 and later in Washington until he left the payroll on June 30, 1854. During the Civil War, Garner served on General

Braxton Bragg's personal staff in the Confederate Army, with the rank of major. In 1863 he became chief of staff of the Department of the Gulf in Mobile, Alabama, and was promoted to colonel. See Whipple, Diary, Feb. 7, 9, Apr. 30, June 27, 1853; ledger, 1853–54, all in Whipple Papers; Möllhausen, *Diary*, I, p. 270; *War of the Rebellion*, Series I, vol. 53, *passim*, Series IV, vol. 2, p. 710.

Gunnison, John W. Leader of the Pacific Railroad survey between the 38th and 39th parallels, Captain Gunnison was a graduate of West Point, a member of the Corps of Topographical Engineers, and an experienced Western explorer. He set out from Fort Leavenworth, Kansas, on June 23, 1853. On October 26 Gunnison and seven of his party were killed by Paiute Indians near Sevier Lake in Utah. John Sherburne learned of his death on March 14, 1854, when he met two Mormons on their way from the Mormon settlement of San Bernardino in California to Salt Lake City. Their reported date of his death, November 5, 1853, was incorrect. See Cullum, *Biographical Register*; Whipple, *Report*, Mar. 14, 1854; Goetzmann, *Army Exploration*, pp. 219–20, 222–23, 283–86.

*Hicks, [Newton?]. The wagon master for the Whipple expedition, he was Whipple's second choice for the post. Whipple discharged his original wagon master on the first day out from Fort Smith when he disobeyed orders to camp at the first house on the route beyond the Poteau River. As a consequence Whipple had to wade through mud and water for two and one-half miles farther along the route. Hicks, the replacement, remained the wagon master (though without wagons except for one carretella after the expedition's arrival at the Colorado River) until he was paid off in March 1854. There were two men named Hicks with the wagon train, Newton and Thomas. Since Thomas was a herder, the wagon master's name almost certainly was Newton. See Whipple, Diary, June 18, July 15, 1853; ledger, 1853–54, both in Whipple Papers.

Hubbell, James Lawrence. Called "Mr. Hubbel" by John Sherburne, he was a former soldier from Connecticut who reached New Mexico during the Mexican War. He married the Hispanic heiress to a huge land grant in Pajarito, south of Albuquerque, and became known as "don Santiago." John Sherburne and company "took dinner" at his rancho in Pajarito on November 9, 1853, and Hubbell traveled with the expedition until November 17. He later branched out into the freighting business. Two of his sons became successful traders to the Navajos, and another, Frank Hubbell, became a political power in turn-of-the-century Albuquerque. See Stanley, Diary, Nov. 17, 1853; Simmons, *Albuquerque*, p. 161.

*Hutton, N. Henry. From Washington, D.C., Hutton was an assistant surveyor with the Whipple expedition and one of the "young gentlemen." He shared a mess with John Sherburne. Hutton inadvertently almost caused an "incident" when on February 23, 1854, a Mohave warrior stepped on his toes at an encampment on the Colorado River. Lieutenant Tidball, one of the commanders of escort, lashed the warrior with his stick. The large company of Mohaves, particularly the women, became so angry that they were ordered from camp, but the storm blew over next day. Hutton returned to Washington in 1854 with other members of the scientific corps and in the fall of that year accompanied Albert Campbell on Lieutenant John Parke's railroad survey along the California coast and part of the 32d parallel route. In 1856 Hutton served with Lieutenant G. K. Warren's exploration of the Yellowstone River. Upon his return, undoubtedly through the influence of Albert Campbell, then general superintendent of the Pacific Wagon Roads Office, he became in 1857 the chief engineer for the Wagon Roads Office. Hutton continued working in the field, improving wagon roads in the West such as the road from Fort Yuma in California to El Paso, Texas. He was considered a very able engineer. See Whipple, Diary, Feb. 23, 1854, Whipple Papers; Möllhausen, *Diary*, I, pp. 255–56; Bancroft, *History of Arizona and New Mexico*, p. 496; Jackson, *Wagon Roads West*, pp. 176–77, 220, 225–27.

Irateba. A Mohave Indian, Irateba acted as one of the guides for the Whipple expedition between March 1 and 13, 1854, on the route from the Colorado River to the "Mormon Road" in California. There are a number of variations in the spelling of his name, which was not given by John Sherburne in his diary. He and his companion, Cairook, were much admired by members of the expedition. Lieutenant Ives met Irateba (called Irataba) again in 1857 and 1858 when he explored the Colorado River, and Irateba acted as his guide. Ives considered him "the best Indian" he had ever met, and *Harper's Weekly* in 1864 characterized him as "the finest specimen of unadulterated aboriginal on this continent." When his friend Cairook was killed in 1859, Irateba replaced him as the Mohave "head chief." In 1865 the Indian agent for Arizona Territory sent Irateba to Washington to present to the government the needs of the Mohaves (by then "subdued" by the army) for a reservation. He was lionized in the capital and received by President Lincoln, and he reputedly returned with the uniform of a general. In 1870 Irateba persuaded many Mohaves, by then enduring a period of ever greater demoralization and poverty, to move to farmland in the northern part of the Colorado River reservation. Fighting ensued there among the Mohaves and Chemehuevis and other Paiutes. In a battle with Paiutes, Irateba was captured and disgraced by being disrobed. From then until his death in 1874 his prestige among the Mohaves declined. See Ives, "Report," p. 92; Spicer, *Cycles of Conquest*, pp. 270–71; Miller, "The Ives Expedition Revisited," pp. 178–83, with quotation from *Harper's Weekly*, Feb. 13, 1864; Woodward, "Irataba," pp. 53–68.

*Ives, Joseph Christmas. Lieutenant Whipple's chief aide and assistant astronomer on the Pacific Railroad survey, Ives was born in New York City in 1828. After attending Yale College for one year, he entered West Point, graduating in 1852 near the top of his class. At the time of his appointment to the Whipple expedition he was serving in the headquarters of the Corps of Topographical Engineers in Washington. Along with Hugh Campbell and Dr. Kennerly he joined the expedition in Albuquerque, arriving on October 6, 1853, a day or two ahead of his companions. Lieutenant Whipple planned originally that the Ives party would reach Albuquerque weeks ahead of the expedition so that Ives could make preparations for the most difficult part of the journey across present-day Arizona. But Ives, who left for Texas in June 1853, was delayed at Fort Inge by sickness and the inability to obtain a military escort across Comanche territory to the Rio Grande. That delay caused Lieutenant Whipple additional expense, since the expedition was forced to stay in Albuquerque far longer than anticipated. Ives returned with Whipple to Washington in 1854 and assisted in preparing the astronomical and meteorological observations for the official report. He published a military map of Florida in 1856, and in 1857, promoted with uncommon speed to first lieutenant, was appointed commander of an expedition to explore the Colorado River. On that expedition Ives chose Balduin Möllhausen as his artist and saw again the two Mohave guides, Cairook and Irateba, who had proved so useful to the Whipple expedition. Ives, who greatly admired Amiel Whipple, named one of the peaks along the Colorado "Mt. Whipple." Upon his return he wrote a masterly report for Congress. From 1859 to 1860 Ives served as chief engineer for the construction of the Washington Monument, and in 1860 he saw a good deal of Amiel Whipple in the capital. In 1855 Ives had married a Southern belle, the niece of John B. Floyd, who succeeded Jefferson Davis as Secretary of War, and that connection may have contributed to Ives's swift promotion and choice assignments. Late in 1861 Ives, though born in the North, joined the Confederate Army as a captain of engineers, and from 1863 to 1865 he served as Jefferson Davis's aide-de-camp. He and his wife were social ornaments in the Confederate capital of Richmond. Though he survived the war, Ives died in New York City in 1868 at the early age of forty. See Whipple, Diary, Jan. 20–28, 1860, Whipple Papers; Ives, "Report," especially pp. 60, 69–89; Wallace, *The Great Reconnaissance*, chaps. 14–15; Woodward, ed., *Mary Chesnut's Civil War*, pp. 553–55 and *passim.*

Johnson, John. Johnson, a Shawnee Indian, was mentioned by John Sherburne on August 15, 1853, as the guide obtained at Shawnee Village near Old Camp Arbuckle in what is now Oklahoma. Lieutenant Whipple secured his services (at $3 a day) because the trail mapped by Captain Marcy in 1849 was difficult for wagons and he sought an easier route. Whipple wrote that Johnson possessed a small shop adjoining an orchard with boughs breaking under the burden of fruit, and that his servant was a young Mexican captive whom he treated badly. Möllhausen described Johnson as "a little stunted-looking Indian" who was very taciturn and a "crafty" hunter. See Whipple, Diary, Aug. 13, 15, 1853, Whipple Papers; *Report*, Aug. 14, 1853; Möllhausen, *Diary*, I, p. 76.

*Jones, John Marshall. The commander of the military escort for the Whipple expedition, the Virginia-born Jones had been a classmate of Amiel Whipple at West Point. His ranking at graduation in 1841 was a lowly 39 out of a class of 41 cadets; Whipple's was 5. In 1853 Jones was serving as a first lieutenant in the Seventh Infantry at Fort Gibson in Indian Territory. He joined the Whipple expedition, with 30 soldiers, on July 2, 1853, at Fort Smith. Jones left the expedition with his troops on March 15, 1854, proceeding through Cajon Pass in California to the army post at San Diego. From there he set out to rejoin his regiment. He was promoted to captain in 1855, but in 1861 he resigned to join the Confederate Army. Promoted swiftly to brigadier general, he was killed on May 10, 1864, at the battle of Spottsylvania in Virginia. See Cullum, *Biographical Register*; Whipple, Diary, June 2, 1853, and U.S.M.A. class rankings, 1841, both in Whipple Papers.

*Jones, Walter. An assistant surveyor with the Whipple expedition, Jones came from Washington, D.C. Suffering from a fever when the expedition left Fort Smith, he resigned from the scientific corps on July 29, 1853, because of poor health, shortly after the wagon train left Skullyville in what is now eastern Oklahoma. John Sherburne, who had shared a mess with Jones, took over his duties when he left on July 30, "completely disheartened." Placed in the care of Choctaw farm women, Jones planned to return to Fort Smith when he recovered. In 1855 he joined the U.S. Army as a second lieutenant in the infantry, but he resigned in 1861 to become a captain in the Confederate Army. In 1863 he was a major commanding a post in Mobile, Alabama, serving under Colonel George G. Garner. See Whipple, *Report*, July 29, 30, 1853; Heitman, *Historical Register*; *War of the Rebellion*, Series IV, vol. 2, p. 710.

*José. Lieutenant Whipple's servant, José was addressed only by his first name. Though Lieutenant Whipple's ledger lists a "José Mestes," there were a number of "José's" among the herders and teamsters. José had been Whipple's servant during the lieutenant's term of duty with the United States and Mexico boundary survey from 1849 to 1853. In March of 1853 he agreed to continue in Whipple's employ. He traveled with the lieutenant as far as Cincinnati that month, when Whipple was returning to Washington to receive his new orders. From there he made his way to Fort Smith and left with the Pacific Railroad expedition in July 1853. Whipple obviously thought highly of him. José's whereabouts after the expedition arrived in Los Angeles are unknown. See Whipple, Diary, Mar. 17, 19, 29, Apr. 11, Sept. 2, 1853, and ledger, 1853–54, Whipple Papers.

*Kennerly, Caleb Burwell Rowan. The physician and naturalist or zoologist with the Whipple expedition, Kennerly studied zoology at Dickinson College in Pennsylvania under Spencer F. Baird, later the assistant secretary to the Smithsonian Institution. He practiced medicine at White Post, Virginia, and received his appointment with the Whipple expedition through the influence of Baird. He joined the expedition in Albuquerque, New Mexico Territory, about October 8, 1853, having traveled overland from San Antonio, Texas, with Lieutenant J. C. Ives and Hugh Campbell. He became a "constant companion" of Balduin Möllhausen because of their mutual interest in animal life, and the two indefatigably hunted and fished for specimens to add to their collection. Möllhausen admired Kennerly for his "frank, upright character," but Kennerly stole an Indian skull from the Laguna Pueblo on November 13, 1853, "for the cause of science," knowing full well it was a crime in Indian eyes. He may have been responsible, too, for the looting of some exquisite pots from the sacred springs of Zuñi. After preparing his zoological report for Whipple in the summer of 1854, Kennerly joined the final phase of the United States and Mexico Boundary Survey under Major William H. Emory in 1854 and 1855. In 1857 he received an appointment as surgeon and naturalist for the United States and Great Britain survey of the northwest boundary. Kennerly died on board ship while returning to the United States in 1861 from Canada. See Whipple, *Report*, Nov. 13, 1853; *Reports of Explorations and Surveys*, III, Part III ("Indian

Tribes"), pp. 40, 45–46; Möllhausen, *Diary*, II, pp. 36, 57; Smithsonian Institution, *Annual Report, 1861*; Baker, *Survey of the Northwestern Boundary*, pp. 13–15.

*Leroux, Antoine. A guide for the Whipple expedition from Albuquerque to Los Angeles, Leroux was born around 1801 in St. Louis of a French-Canadian father and a mother of Hispanic descent. He arrived in New Mexico around 1822, married an heiress to a huge Mexican land grant, and settled in Taos. Leroux was a noted trapper and guide who had accompanied Captain Lorenzo Sitgreaves on his expedition in 1851 from Zuñi to Fort Yuma, and therefore he was regarded as the essential guide for the Whipple expedition. Leroux was severely wounded by Indians in present-day Arizona on the Sitgreaves trip. Although Lieutenant Whipple became increasingly irritated with Leroux because he persisted in advocating the Sitgreaves route north of the 35th parallel, Whipple treated the guide with great respect and formality. Leroux was rich, literate, and traveled always with his personal servant, a Crow Indian. He returned to Taos after his arrival in Los Angeles with the Whipple expedition, traveling overland along the Virgin River and retracing the Whipple route from the Little Colorado to Albuquerque. He continued to act as guide for a number of government explorations in the West before his death in Taos in 1861. See Whipple, Diary, May 30, 31, 1852, Oct. 14, 22, Dec. 27, 1853, Jan. 11–14, 1854, Whipple Papers; Parkhill, "Antoine Leroux"; Wallace, "Across Arizona to the Big Colorado."

*Marcou, Jules. The geologist with the Whipple expedition, Marcou was born in France in 1824 and first arrived in the United States in 1847. Through the influence of his mentor, Harvard Professor Louis Agassiz, Marcou received his appointment with the expedition. He returned to Washington with Lieutenant Whipple after the completion of the mission in 1854. Despite the embarrassment Marcou caused Whipple by failing to complete his geological report, the two men remained close friends and corresponded regularly. In his diary in 1853, Whipple described the geologist as "tall, of finely chiselled features and of elegant manners." Although Marcou's geological findings were severely criticized in the United States, his reputation in Europe was high. Returning to France in September 1854, he became professor of paleontology at the University of Zurich the following year and published prolifically, including a number of editions of a geological map of the United States. The map, which was an ambitious endeavor for a man who had made one trip across the West, contained a number of errors (as did most geological maps of the time) and was reviewed harshly by American colleagues. Marcou returned to the United States in 1860 and from 1862 to 1864 was the geologist for Harvard's Museum of Comparative Zoology. Marcou continued his close friendship with Amiel Whipple and apparently saw John Sherburne again, probably in Washington when Sherburne served there in the army in 1862. He gave Sherburne a photograph of himself (reproduced in this volume) that remains in the memorabilia preserved by Sherburne's family. Upon Amiel Whipple's death in 1863, Marcou wrote to his widow that the general was his closest and dearest friend in America. He remained in touch with Whipple's family throughout his life. Marcou served as the geologist with one other Western exploration, a survey of southwestern Nevada in 1875 under Lieutenant George M. Wheeler. He continued his battles with American colleagues, believing that he was deprived unjustly of recognition for achievements in his field. Late in life he wrote a two-volume biography of his mentor Louis Agassiz. Despite the controversies surrounding him during his lifetime, Marcou today is regarded as a distinguished geologist. He died in Cambridge, Massachusetts, in 1898 at the age of 74. See *DAB*; Merrill, *The First One Hundred Years of American Geology*, pp. 276, 303, 308, 315–16, 519, 540, 678–81; *Concise Dictionary of Scientific Biography*; Goetzmann, *New Lands, New Men*, p. 182; correspondence between Marcou and Amiel Whipple, Nell Whipple, and Charles W. Whipple; Whipple, Diary, Aug. 28, 1853, all in Whipple Papers.

Marcy, Randolph B. Born in Massachusetts in 1812 and an 1832 graduate of West Point, Captain Marcy in 1849 led a military escort from Fort Smith, Arkansas, to Santa Fe, New Mexico Territory. His duties were to survey in rough fashion a suitable route for wagons and to protect goldseekers crossing the plains on their way to California. In 1853 the Whipple expedition followed the Marcy route much of the way from Fort Smith to Anton Chico, the first New Mexican settlement. A "trotting train" under Lieutenant Whipple, of which John Sherburne was a member, continued along Marcy's route northwest to the Pueblo of Santo Domingo, then branched off to follow the Rio Grande south to Albuquerque. Lieutenant Whipple and John Sherburne both carried with them Marcy's report of his expedition. Marcy spent many years on the frontier as an infantry officer and between 1859 and 1871 published a number of highly regarded books, including *The Prairie Traveler* (1859) and *Thirty Years of Army Life on the Border* (1865). He retired as a general and died in 1887. See Cullum, *Biographical Register*; Hollon, *Beyond the Cross Timbers*; Whipple, *Report*, Sept. 21, 1853.

*Möllhausen, H. Balduin. Born in Prussia in 1825, Möllhausen was the artist for the Whipple expedition; he also assisted in collecting zoological specimens for the Smithsonian Institution. Möllhausen wrote his first book, based upon his experiences with the Whipple expedition, upon his return to Prussia; it was published in 1857. His second book, published in 1861, was based upon his experiences as an artist with Lieutenant J. C. Ives's exploration of the Colorado River in 1857–58. After that trip (his third) he never again visited the United States. In 1855 he married the daughter of the personal secretary to Alexander von Humboldt, his mentor, and obtained a sinecure as keeper of the royal libraries at Potsdam. That position provided him with the leisure to write during his lifetime 178 volumes of novels and short stories, many about the American West. Möllhausen died in Berlin in 1904. Most of his original drawings of the West, including a number produced while with the Whipple expedition, were lost in April 1945 when the State Museum for Folklore (*Staatliches Museum für Völkerkunde*) in Berlin was destroyed during the closing days of the Second World War. The largest collection of his drawings extant can be found in the Oklahoma Historical Society. These watercolors, drawings, lithographs, and woodcuts, most relating to the Whipple expedition, were presented to the Society in 1950 by the descendants of Amiel Weeks Whipple. See Barba, *Balduin Möllhausen*; *DAB*; Taft, *Artists and Illustrators*, chap. 2; Wallace, *The Great Reconnaissance*, chaps. 11–15; Evans, "Itemized List of the Whipple Collection," pp. 231–34; Miller, "A Prussian on the Plains," and "Balduin Möllhausen."

Montgomery, Alexander. Captain Montgomery, originally from Pennsylvania, was the quartermaster at Fort Smith who, John Sherburne tells us, dispatched messengers from the fort with mail for the Whipple expedition on three occasions until the expedition moved west of the trading post at Little River, near Old Camp Arbuckle in present-day Oklahoma. A West Point graduate of 1830, Montgomery had been at Fort Smith since 1849 and was considered a very able quartermaster. He helped to outfit the Whipple expedition. When the U.S. Army evacuated Fort Smith in 1861 after the outbreak of the Civil War, Montgomery remained behind to close the fort and was captured by Confederate forces. See Whipple, Diary, July 15, 19, Aug. 10, 25, 1853, Whipple Papers; Bearss and Gibson, *Fort Smith*, pp. 197–98, 212–13, 242–43.

*Parke, Thomas J. From Pennsylvania, Parke was an assistant astronomer with the Whipple expedition and one of the "young gentlemen." He shared a tent with Whipple's clerk, George Garner, another junior astronomer, and quarters in Albuquerque with John Sherburne.

During the rugged trek across the mountains of what is now Arizona, Parke suffered from painful rheumatism of the knee. He returned to the East with members of the expedition in 1854, but nothing is known of his whereabouts after that time. See Whipple, Diary, June 26–29, 1853; ledger, 1853–54, both in Whipple Papers.

Ring, George. Ring was the owner of the farmhouse where John Sherburne spent his first night out from Fort Smith on July 15, 1853, sleeping on the floor in wet clothes because of a bad storm that had soaked the travelers. Sherburne spelled his name as "Ringg." Ring was a white man from Kentucky, but because of his marriage to a Choctaw woman he was allowed to own property in Indian Territory. He owned black slaves, who kept his farm "well cultivated." The farmhouse was six miles from the Choctaw Agency in Skullyville, in what is now eastern Oklahoma. See Whipple, Diary, July 15, 1853, Whipple Papers; *Report*, July 15, 19, 1853; Wright and Shirk, eds., "The Journal of A. W. Whipple," p. 247, n. 19.

Rogers, Bill. One of the young friends John Sherburne made in Fort Smith before setting out for the West on July 15, 1853, Bill Rogers probably was related to Captain John Rogers who owned the Fort Smith hotel where members of the scientific corps stayed before moving into "Camp Wilson." On July 17, 1853, Rogers and his cousin rode out to the expedition's encampment and brought Sherburne a "very acceptable" present of bottles of liquor. On August 10 he appeared again at a camp near Shawnee Village, west of Skullyville in what is now Oklahoma, with the mail carrier from Fort Smith. He begged to accompany the expedition, and professed willingness to travel without pay. Whipple refused to take him because his party was complete. See Whipple, *Report*, Aug. 10, 1853.

*Savedra, José Manuel. Of Mexican descent, Savedra was hired in Albuquerque as a guide for the Whipple expedition from the Rio Grande to Los Angeles. Antoine Leroux, Whipple's original choice as a guide, informed Whipple on October 14, 1853, that he was too sick to travel. In desperation Whipple hired Savedra at a salary of $1200 (half the amount offered to Leroux) and put him to work hiring additional herders in Albuquerque. One of those he hired was his brother. Leroux eventually became well enough to travel, but Savedra, who claimed to have crossed what is now Arizona when he accompanied Moqui (Hopi) Indians on an expedition against the Mohaves in 1842, was taken along as a second guide. In his diary Lieutenant Stanley referred to Savedra on a number of occasions in respectful tones, calling him "don Manuel." In his memoirs he recalled Savedra as "an old humbug of a Mexican." Lieutenant Whipple made no criticism of

Savedra in his diary or official journal and found all kinds of jobs for him on the expedition. Because of his service with Whipple, Savedra was hired as a guide in 1857 by Edward F. Beale when he superintended the improvement of the wagon road along the Whipple route. Beale described Savedra as "a wretch" and "the most ignorant and irresolute old ass extant." In 1858 Savedra (or more correctly Saavedra) was killed at the Colorado River by Mohave and Chemehuevi Indians while guiding an emigrant wagon train along the 35th parallel route. See Whipple, Diary, Oct. 14, 22, 24, 27, 1853, Whipple Papers; Stanley, *Personal Memoirs*, p. 30; Thompson, *Edward F. Beale*, p. 108; Kroeber and Kroeber, *A Mohave War Reminiscence*, p. 12.

Simpson, James H. A lieutenant in the Corps of Topographical Engineers, Simpson served as a topographer and assistant to Captain R. B. Marcy on the 1849 expedition from Fort Smith, Arkansas, to Santa Fe, New Mexico Territory. His report of the journey, like Captain Marcy's, was published by Congress, and Simpson provided an excellent map. Both Lieutenant Whipple and John Sherburne carried with them Simpson's report and map, since the expedition followed the 1849 route for most of the way from Fort Smith to Albuquerque. After his arrival in Santa Fe in 1849, Simpson explored the Navajo country west of the Rio Grande, writing a noteworthy report on country unknown to most North Americans. Lieutenant Whipple used that report while traveling with the expedition from Albuquerque to Zuñi in November 1853. Simpson went on to a brilliant career as an explorer and surveyor of Western regions such as the Great Basin and the Wasatch Mountains. He regarded the Southwest as an "unmitigated" desert. See Whipple, *Report*, Sept. 3, 6, Nov. 16, 18, 1853; Hollon, *Beyond the Cross Timbers*, pp. 60, 66, 68, 74; Goetzmann, *Army Exploration*, pp. 213–17, 240–41, 350–53, 396–99, 400–404.

*Stanley, David Sloane. The quartermaster and commissary for the Whipple expedition, Stanley was born in Ohio in 1828 and graduated from West Point in 1852, the same year as Lieutenant J. C. Ives. Stanley emerges in the diary he kept of the expedition as a disgruntled young cavalry officer who hated his role as quartermaster, disliked all Indians, and rarely participated in the camaraderie of camp life. Stanley left the expedition when it reached Cajon Pass in California on March 17, 1854, and proceeded to the army post at San Diego. From there he took ship to San Francisco and sailed east to rejoin his regiment of dragoons in St. Louis. Promoted to first lieutenant in 1855, Stanley was stationed at Fort Smith at the outbreak of the Civil War. He escaped to the North and by 1862 was a major general of volunteers in the Union Army. Stanley won many medals for bravery, including the Medal of Honor, although General Sherman severely criticized his military tactics during the march through Georgia. At the end of the war, Stanley reverted to the rank of colonel in the regular army and transferred to the infantry. He campaigned on the "Indian frontier," chiefly in Colorado and Texas. One historian (in the *DAB*) writes that he was considered "a master in handling Indians." Stanley reportedly made many enemies during his life because of his "deep prejudices." He retired as a major general in 1892 and died in 1902. His memoirs appeared posthumously. See Stanley, Diary, Mar. 17–26, 1854; Stanley, *Personal Memoirs*; *DAB*; Cullum, *Biographical Register*; Lidell Hart, *Sherman*, p. 301.

Sturgis, Samuel Davis. An 1848 graduate of West Point, he was the only officer stationed at Albuquerque mentioned by name in John Sherburne's diary. A lieutenant (not a captain as reported by Sherburne) in the dragoons, Sturgis campaigned against the Mescalero Indians during 1854 and 1855 and earned the thanks of the New Mexico territorial legislature. At the outbreak of the Civil War, Sturgis was Lieutenant David Stanley's commanding officer at Fort Smith, with the rank of captain. He, like Stanley, escaped to the North. See Cullum, *Biographical Register*; Bancroft, *History of Arizona and New Mexico*, p. 670; Bearss and Gibson, *Fort Smith*, p. 242.

*Tidball, John Coldwell. Born in Virginia in 1825 and a graduate of West Point in 1844, Tidball was commander of the military escort from Fort Defiance in Navajo territory. He and his troops joined the Whipple expedition on December 12, 1853, at the Little Colorado River in present-day Arizona, and left the party on March 11, 1854, for the army post at San Diego, California. From his diary we know that he had a low opinion of the dandified "young gentlemen." A competent artist, Tidball contributed three landscapes to the official report of the expedition. Apparently he was quite a character, for Möllhausen reported that Tidball entertained the Mohaves on the banks of the Colorado River by playing a "magic" trick—removing and replacing his false tooth. When Lieutenant J. C. Ives explored the Colorado in 1857 and 1858, he wrote that some Mohaves gleefully remembered Tidball's entertainment, which failed to fool some of them. Tidball rejoined his regiment at Fort Defiance following his duties with the Whipple expedition, but by 1859 he was serving in the East, for he accompanied Robert E. Lee that year on the expedition against John Brown and his followers at Harper's Ferry. Unlike his fellow Virginians on the expedition, Albert H. Campbell and Lieutenant John M. Jones, Tidball remained in the Union Army. He served with great distinction in the Army of the Potomac and fought against his old comrade Jones at the battle of Spottsylvania, where Jones was killed. Promoted to the wartime rank of major general, Tidball now is remembered in military circles as the officer who initiated the custom of playing "Taps" at military burials during the war. At the end of the war Tidball reverted to the rank of captain in the regular army, but his subsequent career was not spectacular, like David Stanley's. He retired as a colonel in 1899 and died in 1908. See Cullum, *Biographical Register*; *DAB*; Taft, *Artists and Illustrators*, pp. 256–57; Wallace, *The Great Reconnaissance*, p. 187; Tidball, Diary, Jan. 3–Feb. 20, 1854.

*Vincente. A young Mexican, Vincente joined the Whipple expedition on August 21, 1853, at Old Camp Arbuckle in what is now Oklahoma, as interpreter for the journey across Comanche territory. His full name was not recorded. The son of "Demensio" of Parras, Mexico, he had been captured by Comanches as a small boy and bought by the noted guide and trader Jesse Chisholm for goods valued at $200. In 1853 Vincente and other captive children lived with Chisholm and his wife at the Little River trading post owned by James Edwards, Chisholm's father-in-law. When Chisholm refused to act as guide for the expedition, he offered Vincente's services as interpreter; the boy spoke fluent Comanche. Whipple agreed to ensure that Vincente returned to Little River from Albuquerque. Balduin Möllhausen wrote that the youth was fourteen years old. Lieutenant Whipple estimated his age at sixteen or seventeen but wrote that he was "no larger than a well-developed lad of eleven." Vincente presumably returned safely to Little River from Albuquerque, since in later years he was known as Jesse Chisholm's adopted son. See Möllhausen, *Diary*, I, p. 95; Whipple, Diary, Aug. 19, 1853, Whipple Papers; Whipple, *Report*, Aug. 23, 1853; Shawver, ed., "Artist Möllhausen in Oklahoma," p. 413.

Warren, Abel. A well-known trader in Fort Smith and on the Red River, Warren accompanied the Whipple expedition from Skullyville to Old Camp Arbuckle. He sold corn and livestock to Lieutenant Whipple. Warren returned to Fort Smith on August 19, 1853, carrying the expedition's mail and specimens collected by Dr. Bigelow and Balduin Möllhausen for the Smithsonian Institution. See Whipple, Diary, July 26, Aug. 3, 19, 1853, Whipple Papers; Foreman, ed., *Marcy and the Goldseekers*, p. 166; Bearss and Gibson, *Fort Smith*, p. 172.

Weightman, Richard. Accompanied by his friend Spruce Baird, Weightman met the Whipple "trotting train" at Galisteo in New Mexico Territory on October 1, 1853. John Sherburne in his diary spelled his name phonetically as "Waitman." Born in Maryland, Weightman was expelled from West Point in 1837 for cutting another cadet's face with a knife. Arriving in New Mexico in 1846 as an officer in the U.S. Army, he settled in Albuquerque, practicing law and engaging in politics. He served for a time as an Indian agent and as a territorial delegate in Congress. In 1854 he stabbed the well-known explorer and trader François X. Aubry, reportedly with the same knife used in the incident at West Point. Tried for murder and represented by Spruce Baird, Weightman was acquitted. Promoted rapidly to the rank of colonel when he joined the Confederate Army, he died while commanding a brigade in 1861 in Missouri. See Keleher, *Turmoil in New Mexico*, pp. 124–25; Simmons, *Albuquerque*, pp. 144–45, 148, 158–59, 164; *War of the Rebellion*, Series I, vol. 3, pp. 23–25.

*Whipple, Amiel Weeks. The commander of the Pacific Railroad survey along the 35th parallel during 1853 and 1854, Whipple was the brother-in-law of John Sherburne. He was recognized as the commander of the most efficient and harmonious of all the railroad expeditions. His relations with his scientific corps were particularly amiable, and his enthusiasm and interest were appreciated by the senior members. Dr. Bigelow, Jules Marcou, and Lieutenant J. C. Ives all recorded their admiration and respect for Whipple. Balduin Möllhausen, who read Whipple's occasional critical comments about his drawings in the official report, nevertheless wrote in his book (published in 1857) that, in addition to "special professional qualifications," Whipple possessed "particularly pleasing manners and inspired confidence in all who approached him." After completing his duties in Washington in 1854 and 1855, Whipple received a promotion to captain and served in Detroit until 1861 with the Topographical Engineers. He returned to Washington at the outbreak of the Civil War, serving in the force defending the capital and as an important mapmaker for the Army of the Potomac. While in Washington Whipple met Abraham Lincoln, who was openly interested in his career and warm in his friendship. When Whipple, by then a brigadier general, died of wounds on May 7, 1863, after the battle of Chancellorsville, the Secretary of War at President Lincoln's request promoted him to major general, the commission dating from May 4, when Whipple received his terrible wound in the abdomen. Lincoln attended Whipple's funeral, presented his widow with his autographed picture, and awarded a presidential appointment to West Point to his eldest child, Charles W. (Willie) Whipple. The younger son, David, later entered Annapolis. His only daughter, Elizabeth (Lizzie), married a man who became a marine colonel. Whipple's name was commemorated in Mt. Whipple, a peak along the Colorado

River named by Lieutenant J. C. Ives, the Fort Whipple that later became Fort Meyer, and Fort Whipple, established in the general's memory in 1864 near what is now Prescott, Arizona. In addition, Dr. John Bigelow named dozens of exotic plants collected on the Whipple expedition in his honor. See Möllhausen, *Diary*, I, p. 15; Ives, "Report," p. 60; Cullum, *Biographical Register*; *DAB*; *War of the Rebellion*, Series I, vol. 50, pp. 653–54; Stoddard, "Amiel Weeks Whipple" and "Charles W. Whipple"; clippings and records of Whipple's death and funeral, Whipple Papers.

*White, William. From Pennsylvania, White was a meteorological assistant with the Whipple expedition. He had served with Lieutenant Whipple on the United States and Mexico Boundary Survey, joining as an assistant on August 24, 1850. Whipple knew White's parents in Philadelphia and dined with them more than once when he passed through the city. Whipple thought highly of the young man, who was senior to John Sherburne in the meteorological department. White shared a mess with John Sherburne and the two became friendly on the journey. When the expedition arrived in Los Angeles, White and Sherburne remained, determined to seek their fortunes in California. Apparently White, like Sherburne, failed to prosper, and by 1856 he was far worse off than his friend, who had joined the army. He accompanied John Sherburne and his family on the journey east from El Monte, California, in 1856. Sherburne planned to join his regiment at Fort Lancaster, Texas, and White proposed to travel as far as El Paso in return for provisions and a small wage. Sherburne remarked in his diary that White was known "on the road" as a "bag of sand," indicating that White was very heavy. His whereabouts after his arrival in El Paso in 1857 are unknown. He may have been the Colonel W. W. White who served in the Civil War with the 7th Pennsylvania Volunteers. See Whipple, Diary, Aug. 24, 27, 1852, Jan. 16, 17, Feb. 5, 7, 1853; Whipple to White and Sherburne, June 1, 1854, all in Whipple Papers; Sherburne, Diary, Nov. 8, 1856, to Jan. 27, 1857, *passim*, with quotation in entry of Jan. 10, 1857; *War of the Rebellion*, Series II, vol. 4, p. 441.

Bibliography

MANUSCRIPTS

Sherburne, John Pitts. Diary of a Trip from Fort Smith, Arkansas, to Los Angeles, California, 1853–1854. Notebooks in the possession of Elena Klein. The original diary, written in pencil, was contained in two notebooks, but only one, beginning with the entry of September 7, 1853, and ending with the final entry of March 23, 1854, has been preserved. This notebook also contains part of a diary kept by John Sherburne on a trip from El Monte, California, to Fort Lancaster, Texas, in 1856 and 1857. Sherburne, however, copied the entire diary of his trip from Fort Smith to Los Angeles in 1853 and 1854 into one large notebook, in ink. The copy, also preserved, is the diary used in this volume.

———. Papers and Memorabilia. In the possession of Elena Klein.

Stanley, David S. Diary of a March from Fort Smith, Arkansas, to San Diego, California, July 24, 1853, to April 18, 1854. Typescript in the Bancroft Library, University of California, Berkeley.

Tidball, John C. Diary, Jan. 3 to Feb. 20, 1854. Typescript in Special Collections, University of Arizona Library, Tucson.

U.S. Military Academy. Letters of Appointment, 1849. National Archives, Washington, D.C.

———. Merit and Conduct Rolls, 1849–1853. Archives, U.S.M.A., West Point, N.Y.

———. Staff Records, vol. 5, 1849–53. Archives, U.S.M.A., West Point, N.Y.

Whipple, Amiel Weeks. Papers. Originals and microfilm: Oklahoma Historical Society. These papers include Amiel Whipple's diary of the expedition from Fort Smith, Arkansas, to Los Angeles, California, 1853–54. This diary formed the basis for Whipple's official itinerary or journal, published in *Reports of Explorations and Surveys*, vol. 3, cited below under United States. The official journal has been edited and published as *A Pathfinder in the Southwest*, by Grant Foreman. The Whipple Papers also contain diaries intermittently kept by Whipple from 1849 to 1863; correspondence; maps and drawings; government pamphlets and documents; genealogical notes on the Sherburne and Whipple families; some papers kept by Whipple's son, Charles W. Whipple; and original drawings and lithographs by H. B. Möllhausen.

PUBLISHED WORKS

Albright, George L. *Official Explorations for Pacific Railroads, 1853–1855*. Berkeley, Calif., 1921.

Amsden, Charles Avery. *Navaho Weaving, Its Technique and History*. Santa Ana, Calif., 1934.

Archambeau, Ernest R. "Lieutenant A. W. Whipple's Railroad Reconnaissance Across the Panhandle of Texas in 1853." *Panhandle–Plains Historical Review*, 44(1971): 1–128.

Atkinson, William Biddle, ed. *The Physicians and Surgeons of the United States*. Philadelphia, 1878.

Aubin, Agnes Austin. *A Warner House Biography*. Boston, 1935.

Axtell, James. *The European and the Indian: Essays in the Ethnohistory of Colonial North America*. New York, 1981.

Baird, W. David. *The Choctaw People*. Phoenix, Ariz., 1973.

Baker, Marcus. "Survey of the Northwestern Boundary of the United States, 1857–1861." *Bulletin of the United States Geological Survey*, 174. Washington, D.C., 1900.

Bancroft, Hubert Howe. *History of Arizona and New Mexico, 1530–1888*. Albuquerque, N.M., 1962.

Barba, Preston. *Balduin Möllhausen, the German Cooper*. Philadelphia, 1914.

Barnes, Will C., ed. *Arizona Place Names*. Revised and enlarged by Byrd H. Granger. Tucson, Ariz., 1960.

Bartlett, John Russell. *Personal Narrative of Explorations and Incidents in Texas, New Mexico, California, Sonora, and Chihuahua, During the Years 1850, '51, '52, and '53*. 2 vols. New York, 1854.

Beale, Edward F. See under *United States Government Publications*.

Bearss, Ed, and Arrell M. Gibson. *Fort Smith: Little Gibraltar on the Arkansas*. Norman, Okla., 1969.

Beattie, George William, and Helen Pruitt Beattie. *Heritage of the Valley: San Bernardino's First Century*. Pasadena, Calif., 1939.

Bender, Averam B. *The March of Empire: Frontier Defense in the Southwest, 1848–1860.* Lawrence, Kan., 1952.

Berkhofer, Robert F., Jr. *The White Man's Indian: Images of the American Indian from Columbus to the Present.* New York, 1978.

Bieber, Ralph P., ed. *Exploring Southwestern Trails, 1846–1854.* Glendale, Calif., 1938.

———. *Southern Trails to California in 1849.* Glendale, Calif., 1937.

Briggs, Carl, and Clyde F. Trudell. *Quarterdeck & Saddlehorn: The Story of Edward F. Beale, 1822–1893.* Glendale, Calif., 1983.

Concise Dictionary of Scientific Biography. New York, 1981.

Conrad, David E. "Explorations and Railway Survey of the Whipple Expedition, 1853–1854." M.A. thesis, Univ. of Oklahoma, 1955.

———. "The Whipple Expedition on the Great Plains." *Great Plains Journal* 2 (1963): 42–66.

———. "The Whipple Expedition in Arizona, 1853–1854." *Arizona and the West* 11 (1969): 147–78.

———. "Whipple at Zuni." In Ronald Lora, ed., *The American West: Essays in Honor of W. Eugene Hollon.* Toledo, Ohio, 1980.

Cullum, George W. *Biographical Register of the Officers and Graduates of the U.S. Military Academy at West Point.* 2 vols. New York, 1868.

Daniels, George H. *American Science in the Age of Jackson.* New York, 1968.

DAB. Dictionary of American Biography. Allen Johnson and Dumas Malone, eds. 22 vols. New York, 1928–58.

Davidson, James West, and Mark Hamilton Lytle. *After the Fact: The Art of Historical Detection.* 2 vols. New York, 1986.

Dippie, Brian W. *The Vanishing American: White Attitudes and U.S. Indian Policy.* Middletown, Conn., 1982.

Dozier, Edward P. "Rio Grande Pueblos." In Edward H. Spicer, ed., *Perspectives in American Indian Culture Change.* Chicago, 1961.

Driver, Harold. *Indians of North America.* Chicago, 1969.

Dupree, A. Hunter. *Science in the Federal Government.* Cambridge, Mass., 1957.

———. *Asa Gray, 1810–1888.* New York, 1968.

Dutton, Bertha P. *American Indians of the Southwest.* Albuquerque, N.M., 1983.

Edwards, E. I., ed. *The Whipple Report: Journal of an Expedition from San Diego, California, to the Rio Colorado, from Sept. 11 to Dec. 11, 1849. By A. W. Whipple.* Los Angeles, 1961.

Evans, Charles. "Itemized List of the Whipple Collection." *Chronicles of Oklahoma* 28 (1950): 231–34.

Ewers, John C. "An Anthropologist Looks at Early Pictures of North

American Indians," *New York Historical Society Quarterly*, 33 (1949): 223–34.

Fewkes, J. Walter. "Casa Grande, Arizona." In Bureau of American Ethnology, *Twenty-eighth Annual Report*, Washington, 1912.

Forbes, Jack D. "The Indian in the West: A Challenge for Historians." *Arizona and the West* 1 (1959): 206–15.

———. *Warriors of the Colorado: The Yumas of the Quechan Nation and Their Neighbors*. Norman, Okla., 1965.

Foreman, Grant, ed. *Adventure on Red River: Report of the Exploration of the Headwaters of the Red River by Captain Randolph B. Marcy and Captain G. B. McClellan*. Norman, Okla., 1937.

———. *Marcy and the Goldseekers: The Journal of Captain R. B. Marcy*. Norman, Okla., 1939.

———. *A Pathfinder in the Southwest: The Itinerary of Lieutenant A. W. Whipple During His Explorations for a Railway Route from Fort Smith to Los Angeles in the Years 1853 and 1854*. Norman, Okla., 1941. An edition of Whipple's daily journal, published in *Reports of Explorations and Surveys*, vol. III.

Forman, Sidney. *West Point: A History of the United States Military Academy*. New York, 1950.

Gilbert, Bil. *Westering Man: The Life of Joseph Walker*. New York, 1983.

Goetzmann, William H. *Army Exploration in the American West, 1803–1863*. New Haven, Conn., 1959.

———. *Exploration and Empire: The Explorer and the Scientist in the Winning of the American West*. New York, 1966.

———. *New Lands, New Men: America and the Second Great Age of Discovery*. New York, 1986.

Gregg, Josiah. *Commerce of the Prairies*. Ed. Max. L. Moorhead. Norman, Okla., 1954.

Gudde, Erwin G., ed. *California Place Names: A Geographical Dictionary*. Berkeley, Calif., 1949.

Hagan, William T. *United States–Comanche Relations: The Reservation Years*. New Haven, Conn., 1976.

Harper's New Monthly Magazine, 17 (Sept. 1858): 448–67.

Heitman, Francis B. *Historical Register and Dictionary of the United States Army, 1789–1925*. 2 vols. Washington, D.C., 1903.

Hollon, W. Eugene. *Beyond the Cross Timbers: The Travels of Randolph B. Marcy, 1812–1887*. Norman, Okla., 1955.

———. *The Southwest: Old and New*. New York, 1961.

Horgan, Paul. *Lamy of Santa Fe*. New York, 1980.

Ingersoll, L. A. *Century Annals of San Bernardino County, 1769 to 1904*. Los Angeles, 1904.

Ives, Joseph C. See under *United States Government Publications.*

Jackson, W. Turrentine. *Wagon Roads West: A Study of Federal Road Surveys and Construction in the Trans-Mississippi West, 1846–1869.* Berkeley, Calif., 1952.

Jacobs, Wilbur R. "The Indian and the Frontier in American History—A Need for Revision." *Western Historical Quarterly* 4 (1973): 43–56.

Josephy, Alvin M. Jr., ed. *The American Heritage Book of Indians.* New York, 1961.

Keleher, William A. *Turmoil in New Mexico, 1846–1868.* Santa Fe, N.M., 1952.

Kenner, Charles L. *History of New Mexican–Plains Indian Relations.* Norman, Okla., 1969.

Kroeber, A. L. *Mohave Indians.* New York, 1974.

———, and C. B. Kroeber. *A Mohave War Reminiscence, 1854–1880.* Berkeley, Calif., 1973.

Lamar, Howard Roberts. *The Far Southwest, 1846–1912: A Territorial History.* New Haven, Conn., 1966.

———, ed. *The Reader's Encyclopedia of the American West.* New York, 1977.

Lamar, Howard Roberts, and Leonard Thomas, eds. *The Frontier in History: North America and Southern Africa Compared.* New Haven, Conn., 1981.

Lecompte, Janet. "The Independent Women of Hispanic New Mexico, 1821–1846." *Western Historical Quarterly* 22 (1981): 17–35.

Lidell Hart, B. H. *Sherman: Soldier, Realist, American.* New York, 1958.

Mallon, Thomas. *A Book of One's Own: People and Their Diaries.* New York, 1984.

Marcy, Randolph B. See under *United States Government Publications.*

Marshall, James. *Santa Fe: The Railroad That Built an Empire.* New York, 1945.

Mathews, Mitford M., ed. *A Dictionary of Americanisms: On Historical Principles.* Chicago, 1951.

McKelvey, Susan Delano. *Botanical Exploration of the Trans-Mississippi West, 1790–1850.* Jamaica Plain, Mass., 1955.

Meisel, Max. *A Bibliography of American Natural History: The Pioneer Century, 1769–1865.* 3 vols. Brooklyn, N.Y., 1924–29.

Merrill, George P. *The First One Hundred Years of American Geology.* New York, 1969.

Miller, David H. "Balduin Möllhausen: A Prussian's Image of the American West." Ph.D. dissertation, Univ. of New Mexico, 1970.

———. "A Prussian on the Plains: Balduin Möllhausen's Impressions." *Great Plains Journal* 12 (1973): 175–93.

———. "The Ives Expedition Revisited: A Prussian's Impressions." *The Journal of Arizona History,* 13 (1972): 1–25.

———. "The Ives Expedition Revisited: Overland into the Grand Canyon." *The Journal of Arizona History,* 13 (1972): 177–204.

Möllhausen, H. Baldwin. *Diary of a Journey from Mississippi to the Coasts of the Pacific.* 2 vols. Translated from the German by Mrs. Percy Sinnett. Introduction by Peter A. Fritzell. Reprinted; New York, 1969.

Noggle, Burl. "Anglo Observers of the Southwest Borderlands, 1825–1890: The Rise of a Concept." *Arizona and the West* 1 (1959): 105–31.

Ortiz, Alfonso, ed. *Handbook of North American Indians.* Vols. 9, 10. Washington, D.C., 1983.

Parkhill, Forbes. "Antoine Leroux." In Leroy R. Hafen, ed., *The Mountain Men and the Fur Trade of the Far West.* Vol. 4. Glendale, Calif., 1966.

Pearse, Thomas Mathews, ed. *New Mexico Place Names: A Geographical Dictionary.* Albuquerque, N.M., 1965.

Peirson, Erma. *The Mojave River and Its Valley.* Glendale, Calif., 1970.

Phillips, George Harwood. *Chiefs and Challengers: Indian Resistance and Cooperation in Southern California.* Berkeley, Calif., 1975.

Phoenix, John [Lieut. G. H. Derby]. *Phoenixiana or Sketches and Burlesques.* New York, 1903.

Reports of Explorations and Surveys. See under *United States Government Publications.*

Richardson, Rupert Norval. *The Comanche Barrier to South Plains Settlement.* Glendale, Calif., 1933.

Riegel, Robert Edgar. *The Story of the Western Railroads.* New York, 1926.

Robinson, Cecil. *Mexico and the Hispanic Southwest in American Literature.* Tucson, Ariz., 1977.

Ronda, James P. *Lewis and Clark Among the Indians.* Lincoln, Neb., 1984.

Russel, Robert R. *Improvement of Communication with the Pacific Coast as an Issue in American Politics, 1783–1864.* Cedar Rapids, Iowa, 1948.

Sacks, B. "Sylvester Mowry, Artilleryman, Libertine, Entrepreneur." *The American West,* 1 (1964): 14–24.

Scharf, Thomas C. "Amiel Whipple and the Boundary Survey in Southern California [1849]." *Journal of San Diego History* 19 (1973): 18–31.

Schroeder, Albert H., and Alfred B. Thomas. *Yavapai Indians.* New York, 1974.

Schubert, Frank N. *Vanguard of Expansion: Army Engineers in the Trans-Mississippi West, 1819–1879.* Washington, D.C., 1980.

Shawver, Lona. "Stanley [Lieut. David S.] Explores Oklahoma." *Chronicles of Oklahoma* 22 (1944): 259–70.

Simmons, Marc. *Albuquerque: A Narrative History*. Albuquerque, N.M., 1982.
Simpson, James H. See under *United States Government Publications.*
Sitgreaves, Lorenzo. See under *United States Government Publications.*
Slotkin, Richard. *The Fatal Environment: The Myth of the Frontier in the Age of Industrialization, 1800–1890*. New York, 1985.
Smithsonian Institution. *Annual Report, 1861*. Washington, D.C., 1862.
Soldier and Brave: Indian and Military Affairs in the Trans-Mississippi West. New York, 1963.
Spicer, Edward H. *Cycles of Conquest: The Impact of Spain, New Mexico, and the United States on the Indians of the Southwest, 1533–1960*. Tucson, Ariz., 1962.
Stanley, David S. *Personal Memoirs of Major-General D. S. Stanley, U.S.A.* Cambridge, Mass., 1917.
Stanton, William. *The Great United States Exploring Expedition of 1838–1842*. Berkeley, Calif., 1975.
Stewart, George R. *John Phoenix, Esq., the Veritable Squibob: A Life of George H. Derby, U.S.A.* New York, 1937.
Stoddard, Francis Russell. "Amiel Weeks Whipple." *Chronicles of Oklahoma* 27 (1950): 226–30.
———. "Charles William Whipple." *New York Genealogical and Biographical Record* 48 (1917): 11–15.
Taft, Robert F. *Artists and Illustrators of the Old West, 1850–1900*. New York, 1953.
———. "The Pictorial Record of the Old West: VI. Heinrich Balduin Möllhausen." *Kansas Historical Quarterly* 16 (1948): 225–44.
———. "The Pictorial Record of the Old West: XIV. Illustrators of the Pacific Railroad Reports." *Kansas Historical Quarterly* 19 (1951): 354–80.
Taylor, Edith S., and William J. Wallace. *Mohave Tattooing and Face-Painting*. Los Angeles, 1947.
Thompson, Gerald. *Edward F. Beale and the American West*. Albuquerque, N.M., 1983.
"The Tribes of the Thirty-Fifth Parallel." *Harper's New Monthly Magazine* 17 (Sept. 1858): 448–67.
Unger, Irwin. *These United States: The Questions of Our Past*. 2 vols. Boston, 1978.

UNITED STATES GOVERNMENT PUBLICATIONS

Beale, Edward F. "Report on Wagon Road from Fort Defiance to the Colorado River," 1857. House Executive Document 124. 35th Congress, 1st Session, 1857–58.

———. "Report on Wagon Road—Fort Smith to Colorado River," 1858. House Executive Document 42. 36th Congress., 1st Session, 1859–60.

Bureau of the Census. *Population Schedule*. 6th Census, 1840.

Congressional Globe. *Debates on the Pacific Railroad Bill*. 32d Congress, 2d Session, 1853.

Humphreys, Andrew A., and Jefferson Davis. "Conclusion of the Official Overview of the Reports upon the Explorations and Surveys for Railroad Routes from the Mississippi River to the Pacific Ocean." House Executive Document 91. 33d Congress, 2d Session, 1854–55. This report included the preliminary reports of the commanders of the railroad surveys.

Ives, Joseph C. "Report upon the Colorado River of the West, Explored in 1857 and 1858." House Executive Document 90. 36th Congress, 1st Session, 1860–61.

Marcy, Randolph B. "Report of the Route from Fort Smith, Arkansas, to Santa Fe, New Mexico," 1849. Senate Executive Document 64. 31st Congress, 1st Session, 1849–50.

Reports of Explorations and Surveys, to Ascertain the Most Practicable and Economical Route for a Railroad from the Mississippi River to the Pacific Ocean, 1853–54. 12 vols. in 13. Washington, D.C., 1855–60.

Simpson, James H. "Report and Map of the Route from Fort Smith, Arkansas to Santa Fe, New Mexico," 1849. Senate Executive Document 12. 31st Congress, 1st Session, 1849–50.

———. "Report of an Expedition into Navajo Country in 1849." Senate Executive Document 64. 31st Congress, 1st Session, 1849–50.

Sitgreaves, Lorenzo. "Report of an Expedition Down the Zuni and Colorado Rivers," 1851. Senate Executive Document 59. 32d Congress, 2d Session, 1852–53.

Unruh, John. *The Plains Across: The Overland Emigrants and the Trans-Mississippi West, 1840–60*. Urbana, Ill., 1979.

Utley, Robert M. *Frontiersmen in Blue: The United States Army and the Indian, 1848–1865*. New York, 1967.

———. *The Indian Frontier of the American West, 1846–1890*. Albuquerque, N.M., 1984.

Wallace, Andrew. "Across Arizona to the Big Colorado: The Sitgreaves Expedition of 1851." *Arizona and the West* 26 (1984): 325–64.

Wallace, Edward S. *The Great Reconnaissance: Soldiers, Artists, and Scientists on the Frontier, 1848–1861*. Boston, 1955.

Wallace, Ernest, and E. A. Hoebel. *The Comanches: Lords of the South Plains*. Norman, Okla., 1952.

Waller, A. E. "Dr. John Milton Bigelow, 1804–1878: An Early Ohio Physician-Botanist." *Ohio Archaeological and Historical Quarterly* 51 (1942): 313–31.

The War of the Rebellion: A Compilation of the Official Records of the Union and the Confederate Armies. 55 vols. Washington, D.C., 1881–1901.

Weber, David J. *The Mexican Frontier, 1821–1846: The American Southwest Under Mexico.* Albuquerque, N.M., 1982.

Weitenkampf, Frank. "Early Pictures of North American Indians: A Question of Ethnology." *Bulletin of the New York Public Library* 53 (1949): 591–614.

Wendell, William G. "History in Houses: The McPheadris-Warner House in Portsmouth, New Hampshire." *Antiques,* June 1935.

White, Richard. *The Roots of Dependency: Subsistence, Environment and Social Change Among the Choctaws, Pawnees and Navajos.* Lincoln, Neb., 1983.

Woodward, Arthur, ed. *Journal of Lieutenant Thomas W. Sweeny.* Los Angeles, 1956.

———. "Irataba—'Chief of the Mohave.'" *Plateau* 25 (1953): 53–68.

Woodward, C. Vann, ed. *Mary Chesnut's Civil War.* New Haven, Conn., 1981.

Wright, Muriel H., and George H. Shirk, eds. "The Journal of Lieutenant A. W. Whipple." *Chronicles of Oklahoma* 28 (1950): 235–83.

———. "Artist Möllhausen in Oklahoma, 1853." *Chronicles of Oklahoma* 31 (1953): 392–441.

Index

In this index an "f" after a number indicates a separate reference on the next page, and an "ff" indicates separate references on the next two pages. A continuous discussion over two or more pages is indicated by a span of page numbers, e.g., "pp. 57–58." *Passim* is used for a cluster of references in close but not consecutive sequence.

Abert, John J., 3f, 6, 7n, 22, 218n
Abert, J. W., 17n
Agassiz, Louis, 16, 258f
Agassiz, Mount, 153, 154n
Albuquerque, N.M. Terr., 17, 19, 31, 92–152 *passim*, 214, 222, 223n
Alhambra, Calif., 211n
Antelope, 73–79 *passim*, 95–103 *passim*, 135, 137, 149, 152
Antelope Hills, 60, 76, 79
Anton Chico, N.M. Terr., 92, 102–5, 259
Apache Indians, 113, 115n, 139n, 168n, 230, 239
Aquarius Range, 172n
Arapaho, Okla., 73
Arkansas River, 21, 36n, 56n
Armijo, Ambrosio, 247
Armijo, Salvador, 116, 247
Artifacts, Indian, 19, 93n, 97, 126, 140, 150, 165n, 166n, 206, 230
Ash Fork, Ariz., 161n, 163n, 167n, 192n
Ash Fork Draw, 161n
Astronomy, 218. *See also* Comets; Meteors
Atchison, Topeka, and Santa Fe Railroad, *see* Santa Fe Railroad
Athapascan Indians, 230
Atlantic and Pacific Railroad, *see* Santa Fe Railroad
Atsinna (pueblo), 128n
Aubrey Valley, 222
Aubry, François X., 118n, 132n, 248, 265
Axtell, James, 31
Aztec Pass, 166
Aztecs, religion of, 112

Bache, Alexander, 6f
Baird, Spencer F., 6, 15, 227, 257
Baird, Spruce M., 111, 247–48, 264f
Barometers, 36, 48
Beale, Edward F., 262; expedition of, 221–22
Bears, 75, 77, 160
Beaverstown/Beaversville, *see* Old Camp Arbuckle
Beckwith, E. G., 218n, 220n, 221, 232n
Belknap family, 16
Bernadillo, N.M. Terr., 114n
Bigelow, Jacob, 248
Bigelow, John M., 15f, 22f, 41, 43, 49, 51, 65n, 73, 79–87 *passim*, 95n, 99, 102, 106, 116, 143, 151, 154, 162–82 *passim*, 195, 204f, 213, 248; and purloined knapsack,

Bigelow, John M. (*continued*) 54–55; report of, 217; contribution of, 225–26; respect for Whipple of, 265; names plants in Whipple's honor, 266
Big Sandy River, 153n, 156, 173n, 177
Bill Williams Fork, 152n–82n *passim*, 222, 224; and junction with Colorado R., 157, 181; fauna of, 227
Bill Williams Mountain, 149n, 153n, 156, 159n, 160, 182n
Black Beaver, 52n–59 *passim*, 64, 175, 233, 249, 251
Black Mountains, 182n, 222
Black River, 139n
Blacks, 39, 70
Blake, W. P., 97n, 228, 229n
Blunt, John, 11
Bodmer, Karl, 233n
Bond, William, 10
Book of One's Own, A (Mallon), 32
Botany, 19, 226. *See also* Bigelow, John M.
Bragg, Braxton, 253
Brazos River, 68n
Brewster, William, 13
Brown, John, 263
Buffalo, 57n, 61n, 73, 76–83n *passim*
Bullhead City, Ariz., 182n
Bushman, John, 55, 56n, 249
Butterfield Stages, 238n
Byars, Okla., 52n
Byington, Cyrus, 40n

Caciques, 129n
Cactus, 72, 95, 99, 114, 172n, 174–77
Cactus Pass, 156, 172n, 173
Cahuilla Indians, 210–11n
Cairook (Mohave guide), 197–98n, 201, 203, 207n, 249–50, 254
Cajon Creek, 208
Cajon Pass, 183f, 200n, 204n, 208f, 222f
Calabasas, 237
California, 4, 183, 194–96
Camels, on Beale expedition, 221
Camino Americano, *see* Old Spanish Trail
Campbell, Albert H., 15f, 21ff, 41, 71, 99, 123, 131, 143, 154, 162–77 *passim*, 195, 202f, 250, 254, 263; leads main party from Anton Chico, 92, 106n; report of, 217; cost estimates of, 219n; drawings of, 219, 250; with Confederate Army, 250
Campbell, Hugh, 16f, 19, 115, 119, 123, 127f, 152f, 195, 200, 250–51, 257
Campbell's Pass, 132n
Camp Independence, 185n
"Camp Wilson," 22
Canadian, Tex., 81
Canadian River, 17, 35, 50n, 60, 71, 80–92 *passim*, 222
Cañon Bonito, 127
Cañon Creek, 167f, 172
Cañon de Chelly, 136n
Cañon Diablo, 144n, 146n, 147, 223
Carretellas, 36n, 53n
Carson, Kit, 19n
Cataract Creek, 161n
Catholicism, 112; of Albuquerque, 120–21; of Zuñi Pueblo, 129. *See also* Franciscans
Cattle, with expedition, 178
Cedars, 101, 134, 149, 161, 164, 166
Cerbat Mountains, 182n, 222
Chancellorsville, battle of, 241, 265
Chemehuevi Indians, 188–89n, 201n; at war with Mohaves, 255
Chemehuevi Valley, 189n
Cherokee Indians, 43
Cherokee Nation, 56n
Chicago, Rock Island, and Pacific Railroad, 222
Chickasaw Indians, 35, 47n, 48, 56, 57n
Chino Valley, 156, 160n
Chisholm, Jesse, 50n, 53n, 55f, 57n, 58f, 249, 251, 264
Chisholm Trail, 251
Choctaw Agency, 251
Choctaw Indians, 31, 35–47n *passim*, 52n, 56f
Cienaga, N.M. Terr., 111
Cienguilla, N.M. Terr., 111n
Cincinnati, Ohio, 21
Ciudad Juarez (El Paso del Norte), Mex., 19n
Clark, George Rogers, 6
Cliff drawings, 97, 140
Coconino, *see* Havasupai Indians

Colorado Chiquito, *see* Little Colorado River
Colorado River, 18, 147f, 152f, 156, 168, 178, 180–82, 222f; and junction with Bill Williams Fork, 157, 181; expedition along, 181–98; expedition's crossing of, 184, 193–96; Ives's exploration of, 255, 260, 263. *See also* Little Colorado River
Columbia River, 5n
Comanche Indians, 17, 50–61 *passim*, 73, 80–84, 90–91, 93n, 99, 107, 109, 113, 115, 231, 238
Comancheros, 31, 84n, 92, 98n, 99
Comet Creek, 75
Comets, 64, 68, 73n, 76
Commerce of the Prairies (Gregg), 17, 84n
Connelly, Henry, 119n
Conrad, David, 89n, 226n
Continental Divide, 128
Conway, Mary, 72n
Cooper, Douglas H., 37n
Coronado, Francisco de, 60
Cosnino Caves, 123, 150
Cottonwood Range, 156, 172
Cottonwoods, 36, 45, 65
Couts, Cave, 29
Coyote Butte, 163n
Coyoteros, 139
Coyotes, *see* Prairie wolves
Creek Indians, 31, 35, 50n, 57n
Cross Timbers, 57n, 67–68n, 72n
Crow Indians, 151
Crucero, Calif., 183
Cucamonga Ranch, 210f, 238

Daggett, Calif., 184, 200n, 205n
Dana, James Dwight, 229
Darwin, Charles, 224, 226
Davis, Jefferson, 3ff, 15, 18, 22n, 208n, 218n, 220, 227, 250, 255
Davis, Okla., 54n
De Candolle, Alphonse, 225
Deer, 43, 54, 61–79 *passim*, 89f, 95, 145, 150, 162
Delaware Indians, 35, 52n, 57, 249
Derby, George Horatio, 25
Diary of a Journey from Mississippi to the Coasts of the Pacific (Mollhausen), 23, 26–27
Douglass, Henry, 47, 251
Dry lakes, *see* Playas
Ducks, 75, 165, 179ff, 204
Dudley, Thomas, 11

Eaton, Theophilus, 11
Edwards, James, 50n, 251, 264
Egloffstein, F. W. von, 232, 233n
Elk, 95
El Monte, Calif., 211, 235, 266
El Morro, see Inscription Rock
El Paso, Tex., 19n, 238
El Paso del Norte, *see* Ciudad Juarez, Mex.
Emigrant Trail, 71
Emory, William H., 4, 7f, 22, 220, 224, 257
Espejo, Antonio de, 18n
Ethnology, 10, 218, 229
Ewbank, Thomas, 230
Experiences of a Forty-Niner (Johnston), 30n
Explorations and Surveys, Office of, 219n

Fandangos, 92, 103–6, 108, 115–20, 126, 240
Fatal Environment, The (Slotkin), 231n
Fires, prairie, 44f, 50, 52, 60–70 *passim*, 76, 78, 89, 207
"Fitzball, Lieutenant," *see* Tidball, John C.
Fitzgerald, E. H., 185–86n
Fitzpatrick, Thomas, 89n
Flagstaff, Ariz., 123, 152n, 168n
Floyd, John B., 255
Foreman, Grant, 20n, 23, 226n
Fort Arbuckle, 54
Fort Atkinson, 89n
Fort Bridger, 5n
Fort Davis, 238
Fort Defiance, 118n, 122, 127, 128n, 131, 138n, 221
Fort Gibson, 20, 56, 251
Fort Inge, 115, 255
Fort Lancaster, 237, 240
Fort Leavenworth, 5n, 208n
Fort Smith, 3, 17, 20–23, 36, 214, 222
Fort Smith and Western Railroad, 222
Fort Thorne, 237ff
Fort Union, 115n
Fort Valley, 152

Fort Whipple, 266
Forty-niners, 30, 211n
Fort Yuma, 18f, 182, 185, 237f, 254
Franciscans, 122, 153n
Franklin, *see* El Paso, Tex.
Franklin, Benjamin, 7, 12
Frémont, John C., 25, 160n, 200n

Gadsden Purchase, 220n, 237
Gaines, Abner, 21, 39, 251–52; resignation of, 58–59, 64, 252
Gaines Creek, 47n
Galisteo, N.M. Terr., 92, 110–11
Gallinas River, 102
Gallup, N.M., 128n
Garcés, Francisco, 18n
Garland, John, 118, 119n, 127n, 132, 252
Garner, George G., 16f, 39, 41, 65n, 117, 145, 195f, 217n, 252–53, 257, 260
Gerolt, Leo, 15, 232n
Gila River, 5, 10, 18, 29, 153, 187n, 188n
Gila Trail, 17, 211n
Goetzmann, William H., 7, 20n, 220n, 232
Gold, 4, 10, 17, 30
Grand Canyon, 233n
Grand River, 56n, 211
Grape Creek, 82
Grapes, 80, 82, 114
Gray, Asa, 6, 226
Great Basin, 208n, 262
Great Salt Lake, 183
Green River, 211
Gregg, Josiah, 17, 79n, 84n, 93n
Guadalupe-Hidalgo, Treaty of, 59n
Guides, Indian, 35, 44, 56–57, 60, 133, 184, 188–93, 197. *See also individual guides by name*
Gunnison, John W., 5, 20, 211, 220n, 221, 232n, 253; murder of, 184, 207, 208n, 229
Gypsum, 60, 73–74, 77

Hall, James, 6, 228, 229n
Harper's Ferry, Va., 263
Harper's Magazine, 234
Hassler, Ferdinand, 6
Havasupai Indians, 150n
Heintzelman, Samuel P., 185n
Henry, Joseph, 6, 226
Hicks, Newton, 56, 253
Hicks, Thomas, 253
Holbrook, Ariz., 138n
Hooker, William, 225
Hopi, *see* Moqui Indians
Hualapai Indians, 168n, 171n
Hualapai Mountains, 222
Hubbell, Frank, 253
Hubbell, James Lawrence, 125, 253
Humboldt, Alexander von, 15, 64n, 225, 232, 260
Humphreys, Andrew A., 220
Humphries, Mount, 153n
Hurrah Creek, 101
Hutton, N. Henry, 16–17, 54, 141, 143, 190, 254
Hydro, Okla., 72n

Indian Affairs, Office of, 10
Indian Creek, 83n, 87
Indians, 10, 17, 30ff, 50, 70, 74, 159, 205–7; gifts for, 10, 20; as guides, 35, 44, 56–57, 60, 133, 184, 188–93, 197; graves of, 89, 94–95; effect of European diseases on, 128–29n; as expedition captives, 168–72; as California peons, 210n; languages of, 230. *See also individual tribes by name*
Indian Territory, 17, 20, 35, 40n
Information . . . of the Indian Tribes of the United States (Schoolcraft), 11n
Inscription Rock, 127
Instruments, scientific, 19f, 36n, 48, 78–79, 115n, 181, 195f, 224n
Irateba (Mohave guide), 197n, 201, 204, 207n, 249, 254–55
Isleta (pueblo), 122f, 125, 222
Ives, Joseph Christmas, 15, 19, 20n, 93, 111, 114, 119n, 122f, 144–52 *passim*, 161, 163n, 180, 193, 200, 207n, 249f, 254–57, 262, 266; joins expedition, 115; report of, 217f, 255; and Colorado R. expedition, 233n, 255, 260, 263; in Confederate Army, 255–56; as Washington Monument engineer, 255; and respect for Whipple, 265

Jacob's Well, 134, 135n
Johnson (Shawnee guide), 51f
Johnson, John, 256
Johnston, William G., 30n
Jones, John Marshall, 19–21, 37n, 56–57, 80, 83, 88, 118, 127f, 131, 140, 142f, 150n, 153, 164, 173, 178, 202–5, 208, 251, 256, 263
Jones, Walter, 16f, 41, 251–52, 256–57; resignation of, 43–44, 210n
José (expedition servant), 22, 39, 51, 80, 102, 106–15 *passim*, 257
José (Quechan Indian), 188–89n
José Hacha (Zuñi guide), 133n, 138n
José Maria (Zuñi guide), 133n, 138n
Juan Séptimo (Zuñi guide), 133n
Juniper Mountains, 156, 166n

Kansas-Nebraska Act, 220
Kansas Territory, 5n
Kearny, Pat, 75
Kendrick, H. L., 153n, 185n
Kendrick Peak, 153n
Kennerly, C. B. R., 15, 19, 115, 123, 126, 149, 152f, 161, 202f, 250, 257; report of, 217; contribution of, 225ff; unorthodox collecting techniques of, 230n
Ker, Croghan, 128
Kern, Edward, 160n
Kern, Richard, 117n, 160n, 163n, 181n, 232
Kichai Indians, 60, 61f, 65
Kickapoo Indians, 57n
Kingman, Ariz., 192n, 222
Kiowa Indians, 17, 31, 57n, 61, 83–88, 230f
Klein, Elena, vii, viii, 12n, 14n, 236, 237n, 238n, 241n, 242n, 243n
Klein, Sherburne W., 243n
Knight, John A., 147

La Cuesta, N.M. Terr., 106–10
Laguna (pueblo), 122f, 126, 230n
Laguna lake, 110
Las Vegas, N.M. Terr., 115n
Lava, 112, 127, 149, 161
Lava Spring, 161n
Lee, Robert E., 14, 263
Leroux, Antoine, 19, 119n, 122, 127, 131, 138–47 *passim*, 150–56 *passim*, 160n–90 *passim*, 205, 208n, 213, 258, 261
Leroux's Spring, 123, 148, 152, 214n
Lewis, Meriwether, 6
Lincoln, Abraham, 254; at Whipple funeral, 241, 265
Lithodendron Creek, 137
Little Colorado River, 122, 133, 138–47, 230
Little River, 50n, 59n, 251
Little Rock, Ark., 21
Little Sandy River, 174n
Llano Estacado, 60, 92, 96–97, 101, 229
Los Angeles, Calif., 3, 17, 183, 209, 211–14, 222f
Los Calabasas, 237ff, 240
Ludlow, Calif., 200n, 202n

McAlester, Okla., 47n
McCurtain, Cornelius, 42n
McDowell, Irvin, 240
Magoffinsville, Tex., 19
Mallon, Thomas, 32
Manypenny, George, 10–11
Marcou, Jules, 15–16, 22, 41, 88, 99, 102, 106, 116, 167, 170, 195, 205, 258–59; report of, 217; controversy involving, 227–29, 258; as Whipple admirer, 265
Marcy, Randolph B., 54n, 69, 102, 259; expeditions of, 17, 28, 52n, 56n, 64, 72, 75, 76n, 96–97n, 249, 262; trail of, 35, 60, 68, 74, 79n, 256; maps of, 71, 224
Maricopa Indians, 239
Marl Spring, 201
Melons, 48, 56, 112, 114, 192–93
Mescalero Indians, 263
Mesquite beans, 192n
Meteors, 50–51, 64, 74
Mexicans: with expedition, 57ff, 88, 119n, 142, 146, 150–51, 168–69, 194, 196, 204–5, 213; of Anton Chico, 103–5; as superior horsemen, 146; and Indian murder, 205–7. *See also* Comancheros
Minnesota Territory, 5n
Mirages, 64, 97
Mississippi River, 21
Missouri, Kansas, and Texas Railroad, 222

Missouri River, 5n
Mogollon Rim, 139n, 149n, 168n
Mohave-Apaches, *see* Yavapai Indians
Mohave Creek, *see* Mojave River
Mohave Indians, 31, 182n–99 *passim*, 203, 230, 249–50, 254–55, 263
Mohave Mountains, 188n
Mohave River, *see* Mojave River
Mohave Valley, 185n, 190n
Mojave Desert, 198n, 200n
Mojave River, 152, 181n, 185, 200n–204n *passim*, 208n, 224
Mojave Sink, 202n
Möllhausen, H. Balduin, 15f, 22–28 *passim*, 41–42, 49, 64n, 67n, 69n, 88n, 97n, 99, 106, 113, 117n, 123, 131, 132n, 145, 152n, 162, 169n, 174n, 179, 184, 190, 200, 204f, 212–19 *passim*, 226, 232–34, 249, 255–65 *passim*
Montezuma, 112
Montgomery, Alexander, 260
Moqui Indians, 18, 19n, 118n, 119n, 138–39
Mormon Road, 184, 198n, 204n, 207
Mormons, 183f, 204n, 207–10
Mosquitoes, 69
Mules, expedition, 36, 39, 42, 44, 48, 51, 57, 194–95, 199f, 212–13
Mustangs, wild, 71

Napoleon, Ark., 22n, 36
National Institution for the Promotion of Science, 7n
Natural Mounds, 69, 72n. *See also* Rock Mary
Navajo, Ariz., 135n
Navajo Indians, 17n, 123, 127, 134, 136, 230, 253
Navajo Springs, 135
Needles, Calif., 183, 191n, 223
Needles, the, 190
Newberry, Calif., 200n
New Mexico Territory, 5n, 17; expedition enters, 92, 98n
New Year's Spring, 159n, 161, 166n
Nuñares, Andres, 84n

Oaks, 36, 166, 211
Oatman, Olive, 192n
Odometers, 53n
Ohio River, 21
Old Camp Arbuckle, 35, 52, 54n, 214n, 249, 251
Old Spanish Trail, 17, 200n, 204, 208n
Omaha, Neb., 221
Oñate, Juan de, 18n
Oregon, USS, 217
Oregon Trail, 5n
Oro Grande, Calif., 183, 204n, 208n
Overman, Charles, 128
Owls, 138

Pacific Railroad Explorations and Surveys, Office of, 4, 7, 15, 18f, 220
Pacific Railroad *Reports* (U.S. Congress), 225, 227
Pacific Wagon Roads Office, 250, 254
Pahutah Indians, 187, 201f, 207
Paiute Creek, 181n, 199
Paiute Indians, 184, 188n, 201n, 208n, 253, 255
Pajarito, N.M. Terr., 125
Panhandle, Texas, 17, 60; expedition enters, 79n
Parke, John G., 5, 250, 254
Parke, Thomas J., 16f, 41, 43, 117, 123, 145, 147, 149, 161, 195, 200, 252, 260–61
Partridges, 43, 75, 161n
Partridge Stream, 161n
Pathfinder in the Southwest, A (Whipple), 20n, 23
Paul Wilhelm, Duke of Württemberg, 16, 27
Peace-pipe, 48–49, 81–82
Peaches, 48, 113, 210
Pecos River, 17, 92, 102, 237
Personal Memoirs (Stanley), 24, 27
Personal Narrative (Bartlett), 25n
Petrified Forest, 137n
Phoenix, John, *see* Derby, George Horatio
Phoenixiana (Derby), 25n
Picacho Peak, 163n
Picacho Spring, 163, 166n
Pierce, Franklin, 65n
Pima Indians, 5n, 239
Pines, 101, 109, 127, 149f, 154, 157, 166
Pino, Pedro, 129n
Pioneer (journal), 25n

Plains Across, The (Unruh), 30
Plains Indians, *see* Comanche Indians; Kiowa Indians
Playas (dry lakes), 202n
Plaza Larga, 92
Pope, John, 5
Porcupines, 138, 142
Portsmouth, N.H., 11–12
Poteau River, 21, 23, 35, 36n
Prairie chickens, 61, 64, 68, 71
Prairie dogs, 79, 81f, 99, 101
Prairie wolves, 61, 64, 75
Prescott, Ariz., 160n, 166n, 266
Preston, Tex., 5n
Providence Mountains, 183, 199
Prudhomme, Leon V., 210n
Pueblo Creek, 165n, 166n
Pueblo Indians, 31, 89–98 *passim*, 112–13
Pueblos, 17, 18n, 112–14, 122, 127, 128n, 140, 230. *See also* Zuñi
Pumpkins, 188

Quechan Indians, 10, 182n, 188–89n
Quicksand, 87, 175
Quinine, 39

Rabbits, 71, 145, 149
Railroads, transcontinental, 4, 219–23 *passim*, 253
Rancho de Chino, 211n
Rancho San Gorgonio, 238
Rancho Santa Ana del Chino, 211n
Rattlesnakes, 36, 45, 75, 80
Red River, 5n, 56n, 249
Reports of Explorations and Surveys (U.S. Congress), 23
Ring, George, 36n, 39, 261
Rio Colorado, *see* Colorado River
Rio Grande (Rio del Norte), 5n, 17, 19, 30, 92, 113, 119–25 *passim*, 222
Rio Puerco, 138n
Rio Puerco of the West, 132n, 137n
Rio San Gabriel, 211
Rio Yampay, 167n
Riverside, Calif., 210n
Rock Mary, 60, 72–73
Rocky Mountains, 5n, 100, 110
Rogers, Bill, 37, 261
Rogers, John, 37n, 261
Rush Springs, Okla., 67n

Sacramento, Calif., 221
Saint Louis and San Francisco Railroad, 223n
Saint Paul, Minn. Terr., 5n
Salt Lake City, 204n
Salt River, 139n
San Bernardino, Calif., 183, 204n, 208f, 210n
San Bernardino Mountains, 183
Sandia, N.M. Terr., 114n
San Diego, Calif., 17, 210n
San Domingo, N.M. Terr., 111–13
Sandstone, 69n, 72, 137, 147
Sandy Creek, 53
San Francisco, Calif., 184
San Francisco Mountain, 122, 140, 147n–54 *passim*
San Francisco Peaks, 153n
San Francisco Volcanic Field, 149n
San Gabriel (mission), 211, 213
San Gabriel Mountains, 183
San Gorgonio Pass, 238
San Jose River, 122
San Juan Mountains, 160n
San Pedro, Calif., 18, 184
Santa Fe, N.M. Terr., 17, 52n, 111
Santa Fe Railroad, 123n, 132n, 135n, 138n, 152n, 166n, 167n, 192n, 200n, 208n, 209n, 222–23
Santa Fe Trail, 83n, 115n, 247
Santa Maria Mountains, 166n
Santa Maria River, 171n, 177
Santiago, don, *see* Hubbell, James Lawrence
Santo Domingo Pueblo, 92
Savedra, José Manuel, 119n, 122, 132, 140, 143, 147, 152–62 *passim*, 168, 185, 200, 205, 250, 261–62
Schoolcraft, Henry Rowe, 10, 11n
Schroeder, Albert H., 171n
Scott, Winfield, 65n
Seminole Indians, 52, 53n, 56f
Senoritas, 103, 106, 116, 123, 126
Sevier Lake, 208n, 253
Shady Creek, 90
Shawnee Indians, 35, 48–57n *passim*
Shawnee Village, 251
Sheep, with expedition, 142, 144, 172, 178, 194–96
Sherburne, Charles, 12n
Sherburne, Elise, 243n
Sherburne, Eveline Blunt, 11

Sherburne, Evelyn, 243n
Sherburne, Jennie Smith, 235, 239, 241, 243n
Sherburne, John Nathaniel (father of John Pitts Sherburne), 11
Sherburne, John Nathaniel (son of John Pitts Sherburne), 240, 243n
Sherburne, John Pitts, 3–20, 23, 27–32; personality of, 28–29; post-expedition life of, 234–43
Sherburne, Nathaniel, 243n
Sherman, William Tecumseh, 263
Shoshonean Indians, 188n
Sibley, Henry, 248
Sickness, 39, 54, 56. *See also* Smallpox
Sierra Madre, 18, 122, 132n, 229
Sierra San Francisco, 149n
Simpson, James, 17, 28, 30, 60, 69n, 72n, 83n, 96n, 97n, 101n, 127, 262; maps of, 224
Sitgreaves, Lorenzo, 18f, 132n, 144n, 149n, 258; trail of, 30, 117n, 122, 156, 161n, 172n; expedition of, 127, 133n, 137n, 138n, 147n, 149n, 152n, 153n, 182n, 185n; unreliable maps of, 156f, 160n, 163n, 167n, 180f, 181n, 224
Skullyville, Indian Terr., 35, 37n, 39, 252
Slaves, Comanche, 58–59
Slotkin, Richard, 231n
Smallpox, 122f, 128–32, 138–39, 144, 146f, 149, 152, 161
Smith, Isaac William, 235, 238
Smith, Jedediah, 185n
Smithsonian Institution, 6f, 10f, 57, 218, 225ff, 230
Soda Lake, 183, 202n
Soda Springs, 202n
South Canadian River, *see* Canadian River
Southern Pacific Railroad, 223n
South Pass, 30f
Spaniards, New World, 18, 112
Spicer, Edward H., 112n
Spiro, Okla., 37n
Spottsylvania, battle of, 256, 264
Squibob, *see* Derby, George Horatio
Staked Plain, see *Llano Estacado*
Stampedes, 123, 138, 140–41, 146, 167
Stanley, David S., 19–28 *passim*, 37, 39f, 45f, 80, 88, 128, 143, 147, 151, 153, 200, 204f, 208f, 261ff; aversion to Indians of, 128, 183–84, 191, 262f; leaves expedition, 210n
Stanley, John Mix, 232
Stevens, Isaac I., 5, 20; report of, 218n, 219
Sturgis, Samuel Davis, 118, 263
Sullivant, W. S., 248
Sweeny, Thomas W., 185–86n

Taos, N.M. Terr., 160n
Tapia, Tiburcio, 210n
Texas, 5n; expedition leaves, 92, 98n
Tidball, John C., 24, 27, 122, 137, 142ff, 154, 167, 173, 189–90, 197f, 201–10 *passim*, 219, 254, 263–64
Tobacco, 20, 48, 204
Tonto-Apaches, *see* Tonto Indians
Tonto Basin, 168n
Tonto Indians, 168, 169n
Topock, Ariz., 192n, 223
Topographical Engineers, Corps of, 3–8
Torrey, John, 6, 226, 248
Torrivia (Mexican herder), 205n
Truxton, Ariz., 172n
Truxton Wash, 167n, 222
Tucson, Ariz., 5n, 238f
Tucumcari Mountains, 98
Tukpafka Creek, 53
Turkey Creek, 165
Turkeys, 54, 68, 71, 73, 75, 79, 81, 165
Turner, William W., 229–30
Twain, Mark, 25

United States and Mexico Boundary Commission, 8, 22n, 25n, 115n
Unruh, John, 30
Utah, Mormon Road to, 204n
Utah Lake, 208n
Ute Indians, 160n

Val de China, *see* Chino Valley
Valley River, 83n
Verde River, 153n
Vincente (Mexican guide), 57–66 *passim*, 73, 76, 81, 83, 102, 106, 264

Vocabularies, Indian, 19, 40n, 50n, 57n, 67n, 84n, 98n, 129n, 136n, 188n, 198n, 210n, 230
Von Egloffstein, F. W., 232, 233n
Von Humboldt, Alexander, 15, 64n, 225, 232, 260

Waco Indians, 60, 66–67, 70–71, 234n
Walker, Joseph R., 117n, 132n, 147n, 173n
Walker's Pass, 208n
Wallace, Andrew, 19n, 154n, 171n
Walnut Creek, 68
Walnut Creek (Pueblo Creek), 165, 166n
Warner House, 12–13
Warren, Abel, 52, 53n, 57n, 264
Warren, G. K., 220n, 223–24, 232n, 254
Wasatch Mountains, 262
Washington, George, 11
Washita River, 54n, 60; valley of, 75n, 76n
Water: crucial importance of, 56, 58, 74–80 *passim*, 99–100, 127, 134–38 *passim*, 156–78 *passim*; polluted by smallpox, 139; in Mojave Desert, 202
Weaver, Duff, 238n
Weaver, Pauline, 19n
Weightman, Richard H., 111, 247f, 264–65
Wentworth, Benning, 11
Wheat, 188f, 192
Wheeler, George M., 259
Whipple, Amiel Weeks, 3, 5, 8–11, 17–24, 37n, 61–88 *passim*, 93n, 97n, 98n, 107, 117n, 265–66; and report to Congress, 217–19, 221; fruits of expedition led by, 221–34; ethnological contributions of, 229–31; Civil War service of, 240–41; and friendship with Lincoln, 265
Whipple, Charles W. ("Willie"), 235, 265
Whipple, David, 265
Whipple, Eleanor Sherburne, 13
Whipple, Elizabeth, 240n, 265
Whipple, Nell Sherburne, 240, 243n
Whipple, Mount, 255; named by Ives, 265
"Whipple at Zuni" (Conrad), 226n
Whiskey, 209f
White, William, 16f, 21, 23, 37n–43 *passim*, 56, 65n, 78f, 123, 127f, 141–54 *passim*, 162, 167, 178, 195, 200, 213, 234f, 237, 238n, 266; decides to remain in California, 184, 210
White Cliff Creek, 172n
Whitney, Asa, 3
Wilkes expedition, 225n
Williams, Isaac, 211n
Williams, "Old Bill," 160n
Williams, Ariz., 159n
Williams Fork, *see* Bill Williams Fork
Williamson, Robert S., 5, 202n, 208, 209n, 218n
Wing Mountain, 153n
Winslow, Ariz., 138n, 152n
Wolves, 47–56 *passim*, 63, 77, 80, 89, 115, 139f, 167–68, 172, 181; prairie, 61, 64, 75

Yampais, *see* Yavapai Indians
Yampais Creek, 167
Yavapai Indians, 168n, 171n, 192n
Yellowstone River, 254
Yuma Indians, *see* Quechan Indians
Yumans, *see* Quechan Indians

Zuñi (pueblo), 17f, 122, 128–33, 221f
Zuñi Indians, 18, 231; smallpox among, 122, 128–32; with expedition, 133, 138–39; sacred spring of, 230n
Zuñi Mountains, 128
Zuñi River, 128

Library of Congress Cataloging-in-Publication Data

Sherburne, John P. (John Pitts).
Through Indian country to California.

Bibliography: p.
Includes index.
1. Southwest, New—Description and travel.
2. Whipple, Amiel Weeks, 1818–1863.
3. Sherburne, John Pitts—Diaries. 4. Overland journeys to the Pacific. 5. United States—Exploring expeditions. 6. Explorers—United States—Diaries. I. Gordon, Mary McDougall. II. Title.
III. Title: Whipple Expedition, 1853–1854.
F786.S55 1988 917.8'042 88-2152
ISBN 0-8047-1447-9 (alk. paper)

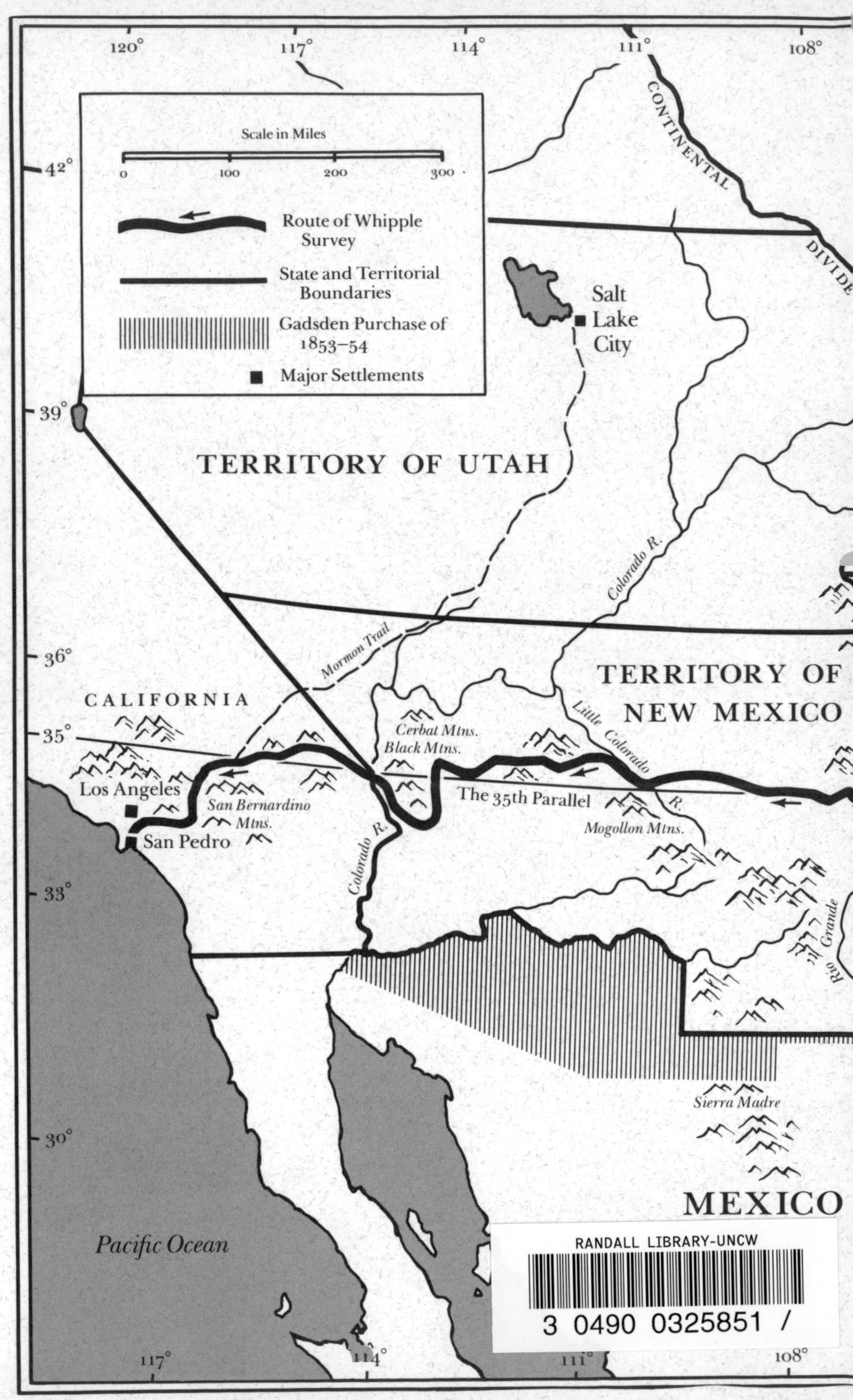

120°
117°
114°
111°
108°
42°
39°
36°
35°
33°
30°
Scale in Miles
0
100
200
300
Route of Whipple Survey
State and Territorial Boundaries
Gadsden Purchase of 1853–54
Major Settlements
CONTINENTAL DIVIDE
Salt Lake City
TERRITORY OF UTAH
Colorado R.
Mormon Trail
TERRITORY OF NEW MEXICO
CALIFORNIA
Cerbat Mtns.
Black Mtns.
Little Colorado R.
Los Angeles
San Bernardino Mtns.
San Pedro
The 35th Parallel
Mogollon Mtns.
Colorado R.
Rio Grande
Sierra Madre
MEXICO
Pacific Ocean
117°
114°
111°
108°